INVADING AMERICA

The replica of the Roanoke-based *Elizabeth* under sail.

Invading America

THE ENGLISH ASSAULT ON THE NEW WORLD, 1497–1630

David Childs

Seaforth
PUBLISHING

Copyright © David Childs 2012

First published in Great Britain in 2012 by
Seaforth Publishing
An imprint of Pen & Sword Books Ltd
47 Church Street, Barnsley
S Yorkshire S70 2AS

www.seaforthpublishing.com
Email info@seaforthpublishing.com

British Library Cataloguing in Publication Data
A CIP data record for this book is available from the British Library

ISBN 978 1 84832 145 8

Typeset and designed by JCS Publishing Services Ltd, www.jcs-publishing.co.uk
Printed and bound by CPI Group (UK) Ltd, Croydon CR0 4YY

To Jane
A Joy on the Journey

Contents

Maps

Preface

The title of this book is, I hope, challenging but not emotive. From the moment, in 1496, Henry VII conferred upon John Cabot the right to 'conquer, occupy and possess' all lands 'unknown to Christians', the English committed themselves, albeit slowly, to the conquest of America. The conquest was intended to be both permanent and absolute, involving the acquisition of 'all the land, mineral rights and commodities whatsoever' that might be developed or discovered, as long as it 'was not actually possessed by any Christian Prince or People'. Not being Christian, those in prior possession would have no right of retention. Not that the faith of foreigners was that important to the English, who were at the same time carrying out a similar occupation of Catholic Ireland that also aimed to drive the natives from their land.

Before they could occupy, the English needed to invade. So, in the long century that stretched from 1497 to 1630, they concerned themselves, once ashore, with establishing secure beachheads along the lengthy American littoral. Thus the first permanent structure to be erected in Virginia in 1585 was a fort, while, as late as 1624, the Virginia Assembly ordered 'that every dwelling house shall be pallisaded', a degree of defence that was equally necessary in New England. Not until that secure hold was achieved could the invasion transform itself into a conquest, a process that began with the arrival of Winthrop's Massachusetts Bay colonists in 1630, and continued with the mass immigration caused by Archbishop Laud's policy of persecuting Puritans and their fellow-travellers.

A great number of studies have been made of the several arrivals of North America's first European settlers. Most have examined these beginnings as independent events separated by the long latitudes that lay between each landing. Yet the encouragement for them came from the same country, even the same three cities (London, Bristol and Plymouth), while the right of occupation was awarded by just one authority: the English sovereign.

Treating the invasions as a collection of separate stories rather than as episodes in a single serial ignores the commonalities which form the main characters of this saga. Thus problems such as reinforcement and resupply, evacuation and abandonment, defence and leadership can be seen to be present throughout the period. Two other topics that are so often ignored are seamanship and navigation, as if writers, like most of the settlers, are so keen to step ashore that they forget the craft and art that brought them safe to land. Looked at collectively it can be seen that the invaders' very survival depended on control of the waterways and support from the sea, which is not surprising because they were engaged in the longest amphibious operation in English history. By dealing thematically with the topics listed above, I hope the importance of each will be clearly shown.

The arrival of the English did not lead to a clash between 'civilization' and 'savagery', whatever the contemporary propagandists tried to suggest. The term 'civilization' implies a certain level of development and infers a degree of humane behaviour. During their conflict throughout the long century, it is not easy to decide which, if either, side earned that admirable epithet, for the much-heralded civilizing mission of the English was never dispatched. From our most distant and greener-biased age it is very easy to discern that it was the Amerindians who had a more environmentally friendly and sustainable way of life than the English, whose planting of nutrient-hungry tobacco, and demand for more and more fur, destroyed both fauna and flora. Yet, in their social interaction, the 'savages' also showed signs of belonging to a superior civilization. In their treatment of and attitude to, women, sex, including homosexuality, crime and punishment, rules of war, religious toleration and care of the elderly, the 'savage' Amerindians were much more in tune with the liberal and 'civilized' views of the enlightened twenty-first century than were the more 'barbarian' invaders. So this clash along the coast was a struggle between two competing cultures, one of which was a more specialized society with more technologically advanced support, especially in the arms that they possessed. In the end it was the arms that counted, along with the alien epidemics – that first and most fatal invader which so depleted the population that it left too few to absorb the onslaught of the English. In America as a whole, as Francis Jennings wrote: 'On a thousand frontiers Europeans used the technology of superior ships and guns to gain beachheads; they then imposed on top of indigenous societies the devices best understood by the conquerors.'

What, along with their better weaponry, the English also had in their favour was a fitter, larger and more fecund population. Over time, they beat their opposition by their activities in the bedroom, not their prowess on the battlefield. Their long decades sheltering behind palisades on riverbanks or bays until more babies born in Britain could be exported as manpower is proof enough of that.

Finding themselves, because of their seaside sojourn, forced to recognize their foe, the English propagandists turned to irrefutable fact to stiffen their diatribe against the handful of people that were preventing their breakout from the beachheads. Even then, such derogatives as 'illiterate' had little meaning in a society that had no need for the written word. Indeed, such 'backwardness' benefited the invaders, for the distraught villagers of Virginia, unlike the downtrodden Irish or the overridden peasants of Europe, were not able to lay down their woes on paper for future generations to read about and comprehend their grief. And 'ignorance', another pejorative, could be turned on its head when comparing the likely chances of survival of an Englishman and an Amerindian, both lost within the new world's woods. Even when huddled among their own, the invaders proved to be incapable of survival without the help of those whose ways they most readily spurned, so that they were forced to live in a snarling symbiosis with those they regarded as savages. It was then that the inability of the English to deal with that recalcitrant 'other' became manifest. While the invasion was taking place, many opportunities arose for innovative ways of establishing friendly relations between two disparate peoples. None of these, including intermarriage, was seen as a path to success. The Bible, newly translated into English, had instilled in its readership both a biblically induced terror of miscegenation and a belief in their own racial superiority as new Israelites entering their own promised land. Thus did an alien myth infect and damage a new world.

In the preparation of this book I have had much recourse to original documentation, some of which is quoted at length. After much thought I have made changes to modernize some of the spelling and punctuation, a decision that sacrifices much pleasure for greater clarity. I have also referred to the native peoples of America as Amerindians: this may not be the term that they themselves use, but to define them as Indians, as did the confused and careless invaders of that land, does not, I think, acknowledge their essential geographic and ethnic difference from those whom the English believed they were at first meeting and, finding themselves in error, were too idle to correct.

The work as presented is not a narrative history, rather it examines individual aspects of the invasion of America and suggests how these influenced the people and events of this confused, conflicting and challenging time. Those who would wish to read episodically are referred to the most excellent volumes of the Hakluyt Society and any work by that peerless recorder of the early English colonization of America, David Quinn.

Unless otherwise specified, all the pictures are from my collection.

I would like to express my thanks: to my publisher, Rob Gardiner, for commissioning this work and accepting my many changes to the original concept with equanimity; to Jessica Cuthbert-Smith for her incisive editing and helpful suggestions, all of which led to an improvement; and to Dominic Fontana of the University of Portsmouth for the great deal of time he spent turning my rough scribbles into presentable maps, which were then completed for publication by Peter Wilkinson. Finally, this book would not have been written were it not for the support of my long-time travelling companion and wife, Jane.

CHAPTER I

Five-Finger Exercise

Be it known and made manifest that we have given . . . to our well-beloved servant
John Cabot . . . licence . . . to conquer, occupy, possess whatsoever towns, castles, cities
and islands by them thus discovered . . . acquiring for us the dominion, title, and
jurisdiction of the same . . .

Letter Patent granted to John Cabot by Henry VII, 5 March 1496

In an invasion that occupied much of the sixteenth and the early part of the seventeenth
century the English thrust five widespread, thin, stubby and acquisitive fingers into the
lengthy flank of the North American continent, where they were bitten off, chewed
up or spat out, until at last their persistence allowed them to grasp their prize which
was, from Baffin Island in the north to the Carolina Outer Banks in the south, the
possession of lands, the rights to which they had been granted by a sovereign who did
not own them.

This largesse in grants of land was a feature of the royal charters, whether they were
issued to individuals or to companies. Thus, in 1584, Walter Ralegh (the spelling of his
name was amended by later generations to Raleigh, a version which was never used
by the man nor his peers) was given overlordship of an area extending to six hundred
miles either side of his first settlement, which he sycophantically and sensibly named
Virginia in honour of the holy state of Elizabeth his Queen, whose favourite he was.
Her successor, James I, in the first Virginia Company Charter of 1606, licensed the
colonization of a tract of land from 34° North to 45° North, a distance of 660 miles,
while the later Virginia Charters extended the land grant from sea to shining sea, that
is from the Atlantic to the Pacific oceans. The letters patent of the Newfoundland
Company awarded them the whole of that island for their venture.

Royal generosity not only permitted the prime movers 'to have, hold, occupy and
enjoy' any 'remote, heathen and barbarous lands' not held by any Christian people but
also allowed them the right to sell on vast areas of them. Thus John Dee stated that
'Sir Humphrey Gilbert granted me my request to him made by letter, for the royalties
of discovery all to the north above the parallel of fifty degrees of latitude' – that is
present-day Canada, stretching upward from a line drawn between the mouth of the St
Lawrence River and Vancouver Island. Further south Gilbert assigned some 8.5 million
acres of his potential holdings on the mainland of America to Sir George Peckham and
a further 3 million acres to Philip Sidney, who promptly offloaded 30,000 of them onto
Sir George. Nor were poorer potential planters to be left disappointed. The Virginia
Company, for example, ensured reasonable tracts of land would be made available to
those who purchased shares in their enterprise or who were prepared to sail to the new
world to work for themselves or to serve a period, usually seven years, as indentured

labour. Even convicted criminals and the indigent were to be offered the chance to start afresh in pastures new. A new world and a new life beckoned and yet the gap between the size of the area granted in the Charters and the land which was actually grabbed was enormous for, by 1630, at the end of all this gracious royal distribution, the English occupied the banks of one river, the James, and a number of bays. So, with only effort or ambition providing a boundary for their acres, the questions that have to be asked are: why did the newcomers take so long to establish their domains, and why did they so frequently fail in their endeavours so to do?

Spain, the other nation with major American interests, moved with far greater rapidity than did England. In September 1498 Christopher Columbus, on his third voyage, became the first European to set foot on the mainland of South America when he stepped ashore on what is now the coast of Venezuela. A year previously, on 24 June 1497, John Cabot, a Venetian in the service of Henry VII of England, became the first European since the Vikings five centuries earlier to set foot in North America, when he was rowed ashore, probably somewhere in Newfoundland.

Although those dates are so very close to each other, what happened in Spanish and English colonies in the next ninety years differed greatly. In that time Spain conquered three American empires and each year ferried back a fortune that easily exceeded the total annual income of the English Crown. The English did not return to the land until the very end of the period, for just two years, merely as sojourners who failed to make any private profit for the small group of investors who had placed their funds and their faith in the venture. Thus, while New Spain became the financial salvation of Old Spain, the English settlements on the western Atlantic littoral were never more than an eccentric sideshow for the Tudor and Stuart court.

The phrase 'British Empire', coined in 1577 by John Dee, gives the impression that Britannia wished to set her bounds wider still and wider for the glory of Queen, country and the Protestant creed. The actuality is far removed from the vision. The early argument for overseas settlement was based around: finding a passage to Cathay; discomforting Spain; settling indigent or criminal elements; monopolizing the distant fishing grounds; searching for precious metals and resettling loyal but non-Protestant groups. All of these could claim to be endeavours in the national interest, but the overweening desire of those masterminding the venture to Virginia was self-aggrandizement. This was the age of avarice, when lesser gentry, who were loath to besmirch themselves with trade, sought other ways to enrich themselves, preferably through the hard work of others. Henry VIII had answered this craving for some, through the dissolution of the monasteries, which freed great estates for his courtiers to grab. By Elizabeth's reign this source had dried up but, fortunately, three new founts of both wealth and land arose to fill the gap. The first was being carried in the holds of Spanish and Portuguese ships returning deep-laden from the Indies. The second was the great estates of Ireland, which were being made available to 'planters' once the rebellious previous owners had been evicted. Thus, those who wished to encourage the third – the settlement of America – had to compete with the more rapid and richer returns from piracy and the closer proximity of Irish estates. Added to this was the fact that the distant unknown land area available for the English to experiment with settlement in America had been selected for them by the Pope and the Spanish.

In 1494, to settle a dispute between Spain and Portugal over global hegemony, Pope Alexander VI brokered the Treaty of Tordesillas, which drew an imaginary line through the Atlantic Ocean 370 leagues west of the Cape Verde Islands, granting lands discovered to the west of this line to Spain and those to the east to Portugal. This separation of interests between two potentially conflicting nations rendered both of them an added service, for it encouraged them to develop only their own hemispherical rights: Portugal, trading in the east and Spain exploiting and extracting in the west. The English, with no legal area to call their own, tried to spread themselves thinly over both regions, incorporating both an East India and a Virginia Company, with not enough funds available to ensure that both could thrive.

No sooner was the papal curtain drawn than the English began to consider ways of getting around it to reach the markets of Cathay, but it was not until eighty years later that Francis Drake, passing through the Straits of Magellan in the far south of America, showed how it was possible both to prey on the Spaniards and to reach the eastern markets. Others considered similar outcomes could be achieved by a much shorter journey through a northwest passage over the 'top' of America. This mythical passage would occupy many English minds and cost the lives of several English mariners while those who thought of America as an obstruction and not an opportunity refused to be convinced by the evidence of the survivors. In this the English differed from the Spanish for, although Columbus had sailed west to discover a new route to the Indies, when he failed, the Spanish were, understandably, content to concentrate on the serendipity of wealth their new discoveries could bring them and which they were determined to protect from any intruders, which was their second contribution to the English choice of settlement site.

Both the English and the French knew that for any of their plantations in North America to survive they needed to be both distant and hidden from Spanish forces. The French ignored this and paid the price when, in 1565, the Spanish exterminated their colonists at Fort Caroline in Florida. News of this massacre created a quandary for those planning the first English settlement which, while needing to be accessible to the sea for succour, would also need to be secure from assault from that quarter as well. Yet, when it happened, that assault would be launched by the native people whose objections to the arrival of the English none took into account.

It is a strange paradox that the Spanish wiped out three developed civilizations – Inca, Maya and Aztec – with brutal ease, whereas the English, confronting a native population which they regarded as 'savage', took far longer to overthrow their opposition. The obvious answer is a simple one: the nations with a developed infrastructure collapsed when their social fabric was ripped apart and their buildings razed; those who could live off the land as hunters and gatherers could abandon their settlements and move on with greater ease, while still being able to assault the fixed dwellings of the interlopers who had no such native skills. In America this led to a war in the woods, a type of warfare which the English, throughout their long sojourn on American soil, were neither comfortable with nor prepared for. By not acknowledging that they were invading a foreign land and planning accordingly, the English guaranteed failure for five major reasons: lack of original numbers; unreliable reinforcement and resupply; failure of local self-sufficiency; the inability to overawe the enemy and a lack

Frobisher at Bloody Point. From the beginning native opposition to English landings was strong enough to dismay but never powerful enough to deter. (British Museum)

of leadership. In the end they overcame these, but it would take a long while before they were confident enough to move on from the beachhead and wrestle control of a continent from a group who were less numerous, less united and less industrialized than were the invaders. The final conquest would take several hundred years to achieve, with victory coming, not through conversion, persuasion, integration or inter-marriage, nor from any form of superiority, apart from the gun, weight of numbers and grim and implacable hate. When the numbers and weaponry were better matched, the outcome was often far different. The war was finally won because the English tribe outbred its opponents. For, whereas disease, one of the invaders' allies, was capable of devastating an Amerindian village or confederacy beyond the stage where it was capable of recovery, when it decimated English colonies they survived because reinforcements were ferried out to them from the unlimited English pool of labour, although these seldom included sufficient soldiery for the immediate task in hand.

Spain was a military nation with a professional, ruthless army that had been at war for generations. This brutal tradition its conquistadors took to New Spain where, it has been estimated, between 1519 and 1600, they reduced the population of that region from 25 million to 1.5 million. Even allowing for the fact that they were operating in a far less densely populated area, the English did not cause such commensurate devastation. They were different. For one thing, they did not possess a professional army and it showed. It was not so much that few English troops could be spared to spearhead an invasion of America but that so few such practitioners of the profession of arms existed in England that none was available for what was, essentially, a sideshow. Only Ralph Lane, who was summoned from Ireland, was a professional soldier: John Smith and Miles Standish had been schooled as mercenaries. Neither would any experienced or senior soldiers have felt honoured by being offered the command of such petty numbers as were deployed.

Spain also possessed, in the Jesuits, a priesthood that was as much an arm of the state as the army. Together this holy alliance slaughtered and subdued all of that part of southern America with which they came into contact. The English did not possess a proselytizing organized priesthood. Whereas Spain held to one true and exportable faith, the English struggled to know what to believe and on whom to impose that belief. One result of this was a reduction in the number of people in holy orders who could be spared to accompany settlers heading for America. Those that did were, for the most part, fully occupied with the bodily and spiritual survival of their own flock.

It is not only in comparison with Spain that England's slow advance across America seems sluggardly. The nation had had its own experience of invasion recorded in the shadowy tattered texts of its distant historic past, each with its own significant impact on the indigenous inhabitants. Yet, whereas the Romans, Saxons and Normans had flowed tidally across England in successive and successful waves, the English assault on Virginia was splattered across the shoreline like spray breaking on impermeable and impregnable cliffs which, for all its initial force, is dissipated well before it trickles inland.

The Claudian invasion of England took place in AD 43: Hadrian's Wall, which marked the final frontier between Roman England and Pictish Scotland, was built between AD 122 and 133. The Germanic tribal chiefs Hengist and Horsa landed in Kent in AD 429; the Battle of Catterick, which confirmed Saxon suzerainty over England, was fought in AD 590. William the Conqueror arrived at Pevensey in 1066 and could claim he controlled all of England by 1070. By contrast, although Cabot arrived off America on his mission of conquest in 1497, it was not until the Crown took control of southern Virginia in 1625 and Winthrop's Massachusetts Bay settlers arrived in 1630 that it could be said with any certainty that the English occupation of a small part of America was even reasonably secure.

Although different in many ways, those three ancient invasions shared an ingredient of success – numbers. The Romans had landed in Britain with four legions, about 25,000 men; the Saxons brought a whole people over in successive tides, most of whom were strong enough to overcome local resistance; William took a gamble with numbers but still brought 3,000 followers with him to Pevensey to conquer an island kingdom. Yet, although Sir Humphrey Gilbert suggested a figure of 5,000 troops would be needed to challenge Spanish domination of the new world, Sir Walter Ralegh dispatched a company of 107 men, to conquer a continent, and a village to settle Virginia. It is not surprising, therefore, that failure rather than success was the reward for these efforts and that few inroads were made away from the shore.

This lack of penetration has meant that, while historians talk readily enough about the Age of Invasion that followed on from the Roman withdrawal from Britain, few apply the same term to the period of English settlement in America following the grant of a Charter to John Cabot. Yet both involved landings from the sea, the seizing of land and the subjugation of the native population who were driven eventually either to extinction or into wilder unwanted lands.

The only difference, apart from the fact that one invasion took place in the dark abysm of time, is that whereas the Saxons arrived as kindred groups wishing to farm and achieve self-sufficiency, the English initially arrived in America to provide profit for absentee landlords, who were almost disastrously incompetent in the planning, execution and support of their operations. Only when the *Mayflower* settlers arrived in 1620, with a similar mindset to their Anglo-Saxon forebears, determined to establish a close-knit domestic community and not return home, did a successful, permanent and self-sufficient settlement in America seem likely. Up until then the English had established beachheads which they always struggled to hold and were often forced to evacuate.

Thus, from the start the English planned an approach to settlement that differed hugely from that being pursued by Spain in South and Central America. There the strategic plan was to exploit, extract and export, for the benefit of the Crown whose servants the settlers were. This had the great advantage that neither soldiery nor money were to in short supply, and that an identifiable and understood political and military hierarchy ordered and governed each settlement, town, city, mine and enterprise that Spain undertook. It also meant that the native population, who had little to offer the enterprise once their wealth had been seized, could be treated with ruthlessness, their extermination being compensated for by the importing of slaves from Africa. Most of all, New Spain succeeded because it was rich in highly sought-after commodities, especially gold and silver. This was far from the case in North America.

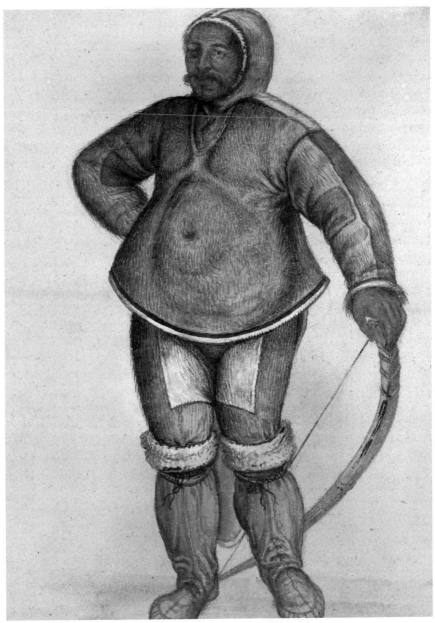

The kidnap of the Inuk Kalicho by Frobisher in 1576 established a pattern whereby natives were taken, often by force, with the aim of 'educating' them so they could return to serve as liaison officers and interpreters. Most of them died. (British Museum)

The ores that the English did export were found to be valueless and, without riches beyond the dreams of avarice being landed at Plymouth, Bristol or London, the investors lost interest and virtually abandoned their project and the desperate souls that they had dumped over the ocean to work for them. Besides, piracy, supported by the Queen, encouraged any English sailor to crew a ship and sail to intercept the wealth of Spain that was being shipped across the Atlantic in conveniently slow-moving containers. Why do the hard work when another nation – and a papist foe at that – was prepared to do it for you? The English thus found themselves in a similar position to the Somali pirates of today who have found a way of preying on deep-laden oil-tankers with impunity. Elizabeth's sea-dogs, either as pirates or state-sponsored privateers, did not need to dream up expensive and risky settlement schemes to fill their own or the Queen's coffers. Ideally, for the likes of Ralegh, but not to the benefit of those they had settled on the shores of American, the best use of resources was for the ships to go a-plundering on both the outward and inbound voyages, and to establish a settlement in North America which could act as a haven for privateers, allowing them to replenish, refit, rest and recuperate from their Indies raids without having to return across the Atlantic. When the accession of James I led to the outbreak of peace with Spain the distraction of privateering was, for the most part removed, but that did little to concentrate the minds of American entrepreneurs on the existing American real estate, which they still saw as a very large bulwark separating them from Cathay.

Only one thing could have enticed the investors to abandon their dream of reaching their oriental goal, and that would have been the presence of gold; its absence turned them into lying apothecaries blinded to the potential offered by the land that surrounded them. Of course there were visionaries, and the history of colonial America is evidence that they won through, representing the triumph of practical determination over proofless dreaming. Until sufficient of those masses arrived, the few early settlers travelled to this awkward new world and clung to its shores like shipwrecked mariners, watching weakly as comrades succumbed to the misfortune of disease and the arrows of Amerindians until, finally, a day dawned when they realized that sufficient reinforcements had arrived for them to stand up and advance inland.

FIVE-FINGER FONDLING

The five fingers with which England cautiously caressed the great body of America were dislocated one from the other. They had neither the overarching aim nor control on activity that the Spanish head of state was able to provide for his colonists. This meant, however, that although they lacked the force of a fist, each finger could survive the painful withdrawal of another.

Newfoundland: Cabot's Index Finger

The letters patent which Henry VII presented to John Cabot had not specified that he was to search out a new route to Cathay, although this was evidently what he desired to establish. Indeed, his landfall on the coast of Newfoundland owed much to the advice and direction he had received during his research in Bristol, whose merchants had been cautiously finding their way towards America from as early as 1480, encouraged by the more prosaic search for cod rather than Cathay. They also knew that the coast that their fishermen reported as lying over the misty horizon was not Cathay, but they were prepared to tell Cabot that it lay on the route to the Orient and its wealth. The impatient Cabot first sailed in 1496. Overhasty in its preparation, the voyage ended with a mutinous crew, a shortage of food, and energy-sapping gales. The better-planned voyage of *Matthew* in 1597 had a better outcome – just. Cabot did step ashore in America but lacked the courage to 'advance inland beyond the shooting distance of a crossbow'. This by a man to whom Henry VII had donated a continent! Cabot had little option but to conduct a follow-up voyage to prove that Cathay lay along the route he had pioneered. The King provided him with one ship, London merchants, strangely, rather than Bristol ones, the other four that formed his fleet. They sailed in May 1498; one ship, storm battered, returned to Bristol. The remainder vanished.

Henry, however, felt that his seamen had a viable idea and in March 1501 letters patent similar to those issued to Cabot were granted to Richard Ward, Thomas Asshenhurst, John Thomas, João Fernandez, Francis Fernandes and João Gonzalez:

> to find, recover, discover and search out whatsoever islands, countries, regions and provinces of heathens and infidels in whatever part of the world they lie . . . to set up our banners and ensigns in any town, castle, island and mainland by them thus newly found and to enter and seize these same towns and as our vassals and governors, lieutenants and deputies to occupy, possess and subdue these, the property, title, dignity and suzerainty of these same being always reserved for us.

Nothing came of the voyage and, when Henry VIII married Katherine of Aragon, the King of Spain's daughter, government sponsorship of plans to settle in lands claimed by Spain by virtue of Tordesillas were not considered diplomatic, besides which, Henry VIII's main interest lay in fighting the French on European soil. Atlantic crossings did take place during his reign but their horizons lay beyond his vision.

The first was undertaken by the King' ships, the 160-ton *Mary Guildford*, commanded by John Rut, and her consort *Samson* and was sponsored by the Bristol merchant Robert Thorne, who had interested Cardinal Wolsey in the idea of the existence of a northwest passage to Cathay. The ships sailed from Plymouth on 10 June 1527 but lost contact during some fierce Atlantic gales, meaning that Rut reached Newfoundland by himself. Here he found fishing vessels a-plenty and penned the first known letter written in the new world, in which he informed the King that he had:

> entered into a good harbour called St John and there we found Eleven Sail of Normans and one Britain and two Portugal barks all a fishing and so we are ready to depart towards Cap de Bras that is 25 leagues as shortly as we have fished and so along the Coast until we may meet with our fellow and so with all diligence that lies in me toward parts to that Islands that we are command at our departing and thus Jesu save and keep your Honourable Grace and all your Honourable Retinue. In the Haven of St John the third day of August written in haste 1527, by your servant John Rut to his uttermost of his power.

Squirrel would have been ideal for inshore exploration but proved too frail to withstand the great gales of the mid-Atlantic, foundering with the loss of Humphrey Gilbert and all her crew. (National Trust)

However, having encountered icebergs on the outward voyage, Rut chose to head south rather than continue into Labrador's icy maw and returned home after sailing past the Carolina Outer Banks.

Rut's failure to find a northwest passage satisfied the King's curiosity and he no more showed an interest in American adventures. Public curiosity and private initiative was not, however, stifled. In 1536 a London merchant, Richard Hore, invited 'divers gentlemen' to sail across the sea 'on a voyage of discovery upon the Northwest parts of America . . . to see strange things of the world'. He was not short of volunteers and thirty such gentlemen embarked in *Trinity* and *Minion* which, sailing from London at the end of April, travelled to Newfoundland, by way of the West Indies, before, finding themselves short of victuals, they resorted to cannibalism, first by stealth but then by lots, until they seized a well-victualled French ship and sailed home in it. This murderous farce ended happily for all those left alive, for:

Certain months after, those Frenchmen came into England, and made complaint to King Henry VII: the king causing the matter to be examined, and finding the great

Stretching for hundreds of miles along the American coast, the Carolina Outer Banks offered so little shelter for ships heading north from Florida that the smallest inlet was seen as advantageous.

distress of his subjects, and the causes of the dealing so with the French, was so moved with pity, that he punished not his subjects, but of his own purse made full and royal recompense unto the French.

The challenge both to discover a route to Cathay and to persecute the Spanish was revived during Elizabeth's reign by a number of propagandists and visionaries. Among these was Sir Humphrey Gilbert, whose appetite for each was shown in his two publications, *Discourse of a Discovery for a New Passage to Cathay* and *A Discourse How Her Majesty May Annoy the King of Spain*. Desirous to do both, Gilbert failed to do either, heading too far south to achieve the former and too far north to effect the latter. The result was almost an exact copy of Cabot's ventures: a hasty first voyage that failed and a second journey, in which, having claimed Newfoundland for the Queen, much to the bemusement of the fishermen from several nations gathered as witnesses at St John's, Gilbert sailed on to lose one ship on the rocks and then to die himself when the diminutive *Squirrel* foundered in the waters north of the Azores.

With northern conquest thus discouraged, the focus returned to the fish, and in 1610 a company was formed to establish a permanent presence ashore in Newfoundland which, despite the many vicissitudes of climate and dearth of arable land, they succeeded in doing. With few ambitions, none of them unrealistic, the small groups of hardy settlers who moved ashore and clung limpet-like to the coast helped to contribute to the only positive return that the English were to receive from their American ventures for many years.

Baffin Island: Frobisher's Thumb

In 1576, 1577 and 1578 Martin Frobisher led three voyages to the supposed entrance of the (mythical) Straits of Anian, which cosmographers – with no evidence – stated led from the Atlantic to the Pacific, disemboguing close to and opposite modern-day Japan. On his first voyage Frobisher tapped cautiously at these icy portals and withdrew, but returned with some samples of rock he had picked up near Baffin Island. These were declared to be gold-bearing and this false analysis changed the whole aim of the expeditions. In 1578 Frobisher returned to his supposed gold quarries, with a prefabricated hut which was to serve as the home for a team of 100 miners, who were also provided with rations sufficient for eighteen months. Their ordeal was not aided by the fact that the few Inuit in the region had been involved in violent exchanges with Frobisher during his two previous visits. Luckily for the settlers, the main frame of their accommodation sank and they were allowed home, along with some thousand tons of worthless ore. Frobisher had stuck in his thumb and pulled out no plum. Unperturbed, the investors in America continued to demand gold, be it from Virginia or Guiana, to whose maze of jungle rivers the gold-besotted Walter Ralegh was to lead two disastrous voyages, the last of which led directly to his execution by James I.

Roanoke: Ralegh's Ring Finger

Although Walter Ralegh took over Gilbert's Charter, almost word for word, he had his own ideas as how best an interest in America might reward his investment. Having been granted a domain beyond even his dreams of acreage, he decided that the land alone would not return the reward he wanted. The owner of his own pirate fleet, Ralegh decided that his Charter gave him the opportunity to create a corsair's lair in the new world from where he could annoy the King of Spain. A potential site was identified in the summer of 1584 by Captains Barlowe and Amadas, who returned with the suggestion that a settlement be established on Roanoke Island, behind the Carolina Outer Banks, in the land they reported was called Wingandacoa – which seems to have been the native phrase for 'what smart clothes you are wearing'. The sartorially elegant Ralegh, seeing great advantages in a name change, proposed to call the land Virginia after his Queen and patron and, having by this flattery secured for himself a knighthood and the governorship, dispatched a fleet of seven ships under Sir Richard Grenville, with just 107 soldiers and observers on board. They sailed in April 1585 and established their settlement at Roanoke towards the end of July. So far, Ralegh's grand project, which is discussed later, was going to plan, but a year later Ralph Lane withdrew this southernmost finger of interest, when he embarked with his men onboard the ships of Francis Drake's fleet. The next expedition, which landed in 1587, completely disappeared, its vital resupply fatally delayed by the threat of the Spanish Armada, which kept all

English vessels embargoed from sailing overseas. Ralegh, nervous not only about the fate of his settlers but also about the time expiry of his Virginian Charter, dispatched several further voyages, but the colonists remained lost and no further settlement was attempted that century.

A V for Virginia

Ralegh's interest in Virginia waned but would have ended anyway with his trial for treason, which began shortly after James I came to the English throne in 1603. A peace treaty with Spain also removed the opportunity for privateering raids into the Caribbean, but the new King was not averse to using the arm's length advantage that the Charter system provided to permit a new attempt at invading Virginia to get underway.

This time a two-fingered approach was made, with the Virginia Company Charter of 1606 having both a southern digit, based around the Chesapeake, and a northern one which started in Maine before, accidentally, slipping into the region around Cape Cod.

Rejecting the navigational difficulties of the Carolina Outer Banks for the more protected waters of the Chesapeake was a logical move and, as they lie just ninety miles north of the Roanoke, the passage thither was known. So, on 20 December 1606, the 120-ton *Susan Constant*, the forty-ton *Godspeed* and the twenty-ton *Discovery* sailed from London with 71 crew and 105 colonists for the long voyage to Virginia. Arriving on 26 April 1608 they moved up the James River, well away from the coast, before deciding to disembark on an island site they named Jamestown on 13 May. Here they clung on through a dismal winter until Captain Newport returned with some supplies. They were then required to seek out both a northwest passage and to mine for gold, two fruitless occupations that contributed adversely to their chance of survival. The winter of 1609/1610, aptly named the 'Starving Time', encouraged them to evacuate onboard a fleet of four resupply vessels, which included two remarkable ships, *Deliverance* and *Patience*, both more or less constructed from local timber and the wreck of *Sea Venture*, the 'admiral' of an earlier resupply fleet that had been run aground and wrecked in the Bermudas. They did not make it to the open ocean, for the incoming tide brought with it news of the arrival of a new Governor, Lord De La Warr, and he was not going to allow his office to end in ignominy before it began. The ships went about and sailed back with 150 new arrivals carried in the ship *De La Warr*, modestly named after the Governor.

From then on Jamestown grew, weakly, but with sufficient vitality and fresh arrivals to compensate for a mortality rate so high that the Amerindian massacre of 1622, in which 357 settlers died, shows up merely as a blip on a graph of lives lost. Yet, before that incident, the economic future of the settlement was secured, not by the growing of European crops or the establishment of English industries, but through the production of a native plant, unknown and not previously desired in England: tobacco.

In 1624, exasperated by the mismanagement by its Board, the royal hand twitched when King James decided to dissolve the Virginia Company and to make the settlement a royal colony. It was a move which, although of little impact on the banks of the James, probably guaranteed the survival of the settlement.

Unlike the build-up to the Roanoke venture, it is unclear what catalyst fomented the urge to sail to North Virginia in 1602 but, once begun, a series of such voyages established a new colonial current that would carry the most famous of all the early settlers, the Pilgrim Fathers, to the shores of Cape Cod in 1620. Before that, between 1602 and 1619 some thirty-five transatlantic crossings took place steadily and unspectacularly to this land, which lay between 40° and 45° North. While still part of greater Virginia, the area also had a name change of genius, when John Smith proposed, in 1616, to refer to it as New England rather than the native name of Norumbega. This gave the country a feeling of homeliness, a begin-again sort of place, that was not going to be too outlandish or dangerous. Indeed, the goods that were evident upon arrival were those that England needed, not because they were either valuable or exotic but because they were commonplace but in danger of exhaustion back home. In short, they were timber for masts and planks and, for a while, sassafras, a sweet-smelling shrub which was erroneously thought to cure syphilis. For their own support the colonists could rely on raising crops that they were used to growing in English soil. This new familiarity would attract sturdy, steady, level-headed folk, not the flamboyant risk-takers that might wish to seek their fortune further south. Right from the start, then, the two groups, established as parts of the same Charter by James I, would see themselves as differing from each other. It would take a war to unite them.

The series of voyages began when Bartholomew Gosnold in *Concord* sailed from Falmouth on 26 March 1602 bound for 'North Virginia' to establish a trading post at which twenty of his complement of thirty-two would overwinter. They arrived off modern-day Maine on 14 May and sailed south around Cape Cod, which thus they named, through the shoal waters of the aptly named 'Tucker's Terror', to Martha's Vineyard, a tribute to the captain's daughter. On nearby Elizabeth's Isle, they built their trading fort on an islet in a lake but then decided to abandon it and to return home, leaving no men behind. An initial attempt to build on this work by establishing a colony of loyal Catholics came to grief with the uncovering of the Gunpowder Plot, but further exploratory voyages followed, so the northern group were prepared and ready to go as soon as they knew that the King was going to present them with their Charter for settlement. From that moment all turned sour. Sir Ralph Bingley, employed to take the 160-ton *Triall* to Maine, turned pirate while, on the next voyage, *Richard*, under the command of Captain Henry Challons, having sailed in August 1606, was captured by the Spanish in November in the Florida Channel. Well before this disaster was reported, a second mission had been dispatched to support Challons's settlement. This was commanded by Thomas Hanham with Martin Pring as master but, having arrived successfully, they scoured the coast and, finding no sign of Challons, returned home.

The following year a more determined effort was made to establish a presence in the region when, at the end of May, Captain George Popham, accepting the presidency of the North Virginia Colony, sailed from Plymouth on 31 May in *Gifte of God* in company with *Mary and John*, commanded by Raleigh Gilbert. A quiet voyage saw them arrive off Maine by late July, where they navigated their way through offshore islands and encounters with Amerindians, eventually to establish a fort at the mouth of the Sagadahoc (now Kennebec) River in mid-August, where they intended their 100 potential settlers to live. They called it Fort St George, a neat tribute to both their

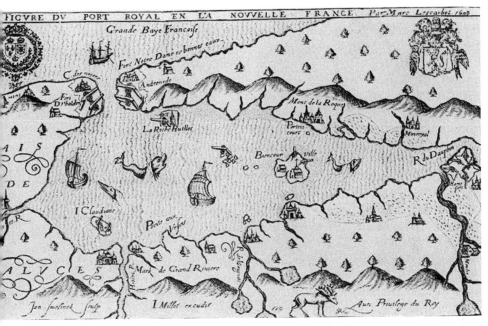

Annapolis Royal, 1604. Lying on the sheltered side of Nova Scotia, the deep inlet on which Annapolis Royal now lies proved an attractive settlement site for both the French and the English. Champlain's jolly map shows both the wonderful natural harbour of Port Royal and the young whale that amused the French with its daily performances in the bay.

president and their patron saint, but they were not to live beneath their flag for long. Shortage of supplies led to half the colony sailing home in *Gifte of God* in December. Then, in February 1608 George Popham died, while the March relief vessels brought with them news of the death of his relative and their sponsor, Sir John Popham. Worse news for the settlers came in September when they learned that Raleigh Gilbert, who had taken up the presidency, had succeeded to the Compton Castle estate. The new heir did not hesitate, choosing to return home to a far more certain and comfortable fortune. Deprived of both sponsorship and leadership, the remaining colonists decided to return with him, embarking in *Mary and John* and *Virginia*, a pinnace that they had built themselves and which has the lasting glory of being the first English ship to be constructed in the new world.

And there the whole endeavour might have ended had it not been for the decision of a small group of English Puritans, exiled in Leiden, Holland, to seek a life for their community free from persecution in the new world. The first attempt to achieve this failed in 1619, when 180 separatists were crammed into a small ship for a winter voyage to Virginia. By the time they reached America 130 of them, including their leader, had died. Yet, soon afterwards, much perturbed, and after much discussion and some dissembling, the 102 passengers of *Mayflower* watched the frame of their first house being raised at their Plymouth plantation on the far side of Cape Cod Bay. It was Christmas Day 1620 and, appropriately, it was Christian families seeking a self-sufficient life and freedom to practise a simple faith to whom the success of the English settlement in this part of America was now entrusted. Yet, despite the background and the aims of these Pilgrim Fathers, the fact that they also had arrived intent on seizing land that was not theirs and holding on to it by force made them just another group of invaders launching an amphibious assault on North America.

Plymouth had not been long established when another group of settlers, linked to the Pilgrims through the entrepreneur Thomas Weston, but dissimilar in most other ways, set out for the region. Their arrival was announced when a shallop belonging to the fishing vessel *Sparrow* sailed into Plymouth harbour in May 1622 to collect supplies before sailing up the coast to explore a new site for settlement. Finding one at Wessagusset (modern Weymouth), they sent a message back to summon a further sixty rough and ready men who had sailed from England in April 1622 onboard *Charity* and *Swan* and who, after a brief stop at Plymouth, reached Wessagusset in July 1622. Their background, demeanour, temperament and behaviour augured not well for success, and by 1624 they were no more.

However, Plymouth was not going to be a lonely outpost for long. Charters to settle both Maine and Massachusetts were soon followed up by the dispatch of hopeful settlers, and in 1629 the governors of the Massachusetts Bay Company made the bold decision to travel out with their fellow investors. At last lessons on governance and numbers had been learned. In 1630, first *Mary and John* with 140 passengers onboard and then, shortly afterwards, Governor Winthrop's main fleet of eleven vessels sailed into the bay on whose shores would rise their 'City upon a Hill'. At long last the cavalry had arrived.

Nova Scotia: Alexander's Pinkie

The smallest finger of all five was inserted at Port Royal, Nova Scotia, on the initiative of the Scottish patriot, Sir William Alexander, who, annoyed that America had a New England, New Spain, New France, New Holland and New Sweden, persuaded his countryman, King James VI, now James I of England, to grant him, in 1621, a Charter to the land now known because of the original Latin text as Nova Scotia. However, it was not until 1629 that Sir William's son, another William, sailed for this new world in four ships with a party of seventy men and two women. They selected the most beautiful of all the original sites on which to settle, a headland lying between two rivers, where they built the small Fort Charles. Pleasant it may have been but the conditions they experienced in their first winter left thirty of them dead by the spring, with the survivors weak from scurvy and malnutrition. Another Scottish fort had been established at Baleine, named after two whale-like rocks that lie offshore, near present-day Louisburg, but this was surrendered to the French in April 1629, the very same month that England agreed, under the Treaty of Susa, to return lands captured in America to France. The argument that this did not include Nova Scotia lasted until dowry negotiations for his marriage of Queen Henrietta of France persuaded the bankrupt Charles I that he had more to gain from its release than its retention.

On 24 May 1624 the Virginia Company's Charter was revoked and responsibility for the colony was placed under the direct control of the Crown. Coincident with that decision, the age of coastal conflict ended and the age of continental conquest began. The English would now move out from their beachheads to horizon-challenging frontiers, from their forts to villages and townships, and from sea to shining sea.

Thus, in their early years, none of the five fingers delivered what was expected of it. Their failure to make an impression was due mostly to the fact that expectations were based on mythical views of world geography, geology and botany, and the importance of greed as a motive for investment. Without the strong guiding will of the sovereign to control and coordinate the movement of the fingers, even at arm's length, the English in America would lack the strength or coordination to grasp the land which their lord had granted to them.

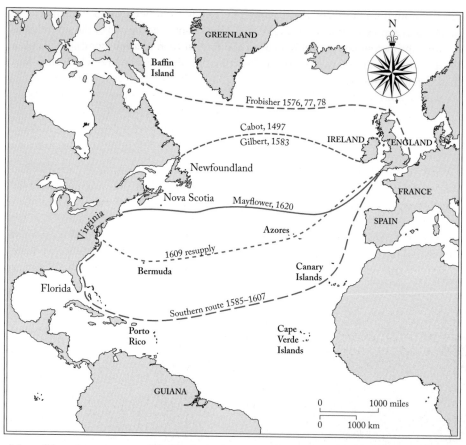

Map 1: The primary routes of the English invasion of North America, 1497–1630.

CHAPTER 2

Dreamers and Schemers

The sending forth of Colonies (seeming a novelty) is esteemed now to be a strange thing, as not only being above the courage of common men, but altogether alienated from their knowledge, which is no wonder, since that course, though both ancient and usual, hath been by the intermission of so many ages discontinued, yea was impossible to be practised so long as there was no vast ground, howsoever men had been willing, whereupon Plantations might have been made, yet there is none who will doubt but that the world in her infancy, and innocency, was first peopled after this manner.

Sir William Alexander, An Encouragement of Colonies, 1630

When, in 1597, John of Gaunt's famous soliloquy eulogizing England's 'scepter'd isle' first appeared in print, Ralegh's Roanoke experiment had finished in failure and his Guiana expedition had ended in ignominy. However, thanks to Howard of Effingham's navy, the 'moat defensive' had kept an envious Spanish army from landing on 'this blessed plot'. Shakespeare, his Queen, and his fellow countrymen thus had every right to feel proudly and defiantly insular, and John of Gaunt's word choice seemed to throw down a challenge to those who would seek an 'other Eden' across the seas. However,

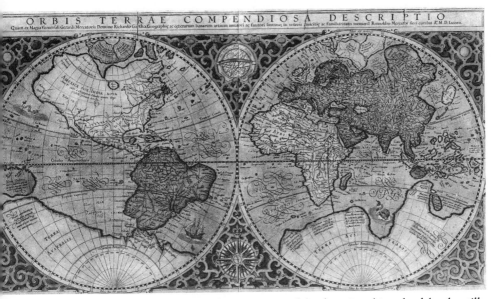

By 1587 Mercator was able to show the true extent of the American hinterland, but he still showed a narrow navigable passage passing over the North and leading to the Pacific.

by November 1611, when Shakespeare's company, the King's Men, staged *The Tempest* in front of Elizabeth's successor, their patron James I, the Jamestown settlement had been in existence for four years and this play drew its opening imagery from William Strachey's vivid account of the wreck of *Sea Venture* on the Bermudas while transporting settlers to Virginia in 1609. Yet, given the material, currency and opportunity to write a play about a newfound land, the nation's greatest playwright remained European in outlook. *The Tempest* is set on a desert island lying between Tunis and Naples, and its principal human characters are Italian noblemen and their relations. Indeed, the often-quoted lines from the play, which some suggest hark forward to a triumphant colonial future, Miranda's joyful

> How beautiful mankind is! O brave new world
> That has such people in't!

refers, not to the comely and almost-naked 'savages' that welcomed Ralegh's men, but to her first sighting of sea-soiled courtiers in whose company she will return to their ancient kingdom leaving the native, the 'aborred slave' Caliban, alone with two marooned drunks, the same number of people that Thomas Gates left in Bermuda in the original voyage. No hint of discovery and distant voyages there. Mentions of cannibals and anthropophagi and a few hints in *Twelfth Night* that Shakespeare had seen 'the new map with the augmentation of the Indies' that had appeared in Hakluyt's second edition of his *Voyages and Discoveries* is but dust in a great folio that is indifferent to the wonders of a newly discovered world.

Indeed the most popular play to be inspired by the nascent colony in Virginia was *Eastward Ho*, a satirical farce written in 1605 by Ben Jonson, George Chapman and John Marston, that so mocked the endeavours of those working towards the American plantations that the King had Chapman and Jonson imprisoned in the Tower until they saw the unfunny side of their jokes. Perhaps the dour King had a point: what was about to be undertaken under his Charters was to have more elements of tragedy than comedy.

It was the same in the world of poetry. The major English work of the time, Edward Spenser's *Faerie Queen*, was a lengthy historical allegory, the first instalment of which was published in 1590. Throughout the epic, Gloriana, the Faerie Queen, an obvious reference to Elizabeth, is served by faithful knights who undertake quests on her behalf around England, Ireland and the Netherlands; although they wander on an allegorical sea it does not take them to the newfound land that Spenser's friend, fellow poet and neighbour in Ireland, Walter Ralegh, was trying to settle. England's great Tudor epic verse is most insular in outlook, as was the remainder of English poesy. A voyage through the poems anthologized in the *Oxford Book of Sixteenth-Century Verse* and the *Oxford Book of Seventeenth-Century Verse* reveals two centuries of poets obsessed with the legends of Greece and Rome and the works of Virgil, Homer and Ovid. Just one indifferent poem on the subject of the new world, Michael Drayton's 1619 ode, 'To the Virginian Voyage', is thought worthy of inclusion. That is, apart from the most erotic poem in the English language, John Donne's 'To his Mistress Going to Bed', which was written in 1593 but was not published until 1633, denying a generation of young men the seductive aid of:

Licence my roving hands, and let them go
Before, behind, between, above, below.
O my America, my new found land,
My kingdom, safeliest when with one man manned,
My mine of precious stones, my empery,
How blessed am I in this discovering thee!

It is doubtful if Donne would have been inspired to use his principal metaphor had not Ralegh bestowed upon the newfound land the potentially erotic name of Virginia. But that was it: English popular entertainment looked to the classics for its subject matter; the newfound lands were not considered suitable or popular material.

More surprisingly, the same indifference holds true with the plastic arts. Surprisingly, because Ralegh sent a most accomplished artist, John White, with the first Roanoke party to work with his protégé, the astronomer, anthropologist, cartographer, mathematician, linguist and polymathical genius Thomas Harriot, to record what they saw. Although much of his work may have been dumped overboard in the haste to depart with Drake's fleet, White produced an accomplished portfolio depicting a brave new world with wonderful people in it. The works' significance became immediately apparent to the Flemish engraver Theodore de Bry, who left England after a three-year stay in 1588 to establish a press in Frankfurt, where White's work was copied and embellished. English artists remained wedded to the court and classical literature.

The contrast with Portugal could not be more obvious; the Portuguese national epic poem, *The Lusiads*, tells the story of how Portuguese mariners created a trading empire around the world. Published in 1572, it was written by Luis Vaz de Camoëns, and was based not only on the accounts of foreign ventures, but on his own service and adventures, in Ceuta, Goa and Macau. No English poet or playwright was similarly inspired by overseas adventures, nor did English bards wish to sail to new worlds. If England was to establish a commonwealth, as a small cabal of thinkers wished, then a great deal of persuasion and propaganda was going to be necessary. And it needed to start at the very top.

The lack of a presence in popular poetry and plays may imply but not confirm that colonial enterprises did not engage the public imagination. Yet it is quite possible to read a scholarly and detailed history of the Tudor and Stuart regimes, or even individual biographies of the monarchs and their leading counsellors, and not come across a reference to America. This would not be possible in works about the Spanish and Portuguese courts of the same period, for their monarchs were very much occupied with overseas enterprises.

CONVINCING THE COURT

In 1387 Philippa of Lancaster, the daughter of John of Gaunt, married João I of Portugal, and left her countrymen's insular views behind her as she encouraged, even to her deathbed, her adopted country's overseas expansion. Her third son, known to the world as Prince Henry the Navigator, dedicated his life to the foundation and support of

A somewhat sylvan early representation of Cupid's Cove, more beckoning than the windswept reality of a harsh Newfoundland winter, which would have attracted few immigrants.

a school of navigation and exploration at Sagres on the south coast. From here, the Portuguese island-hopped their way to India and, along the way, cornered the market in gold, ivory, spices and slaves. Impressed by what he had heard, Ferdinand of Aragon created at Seville in 1503 the Casa de la Contratación (House of Trade), with similar aims to Prince Henry, to support global expansion and trade. Ten years later Henry VIII of England founded Trinity House to chart and mark the mudflats and sandbanks of the Thames.

England did have princes who shared their distant Portuguese cousin's global outlook but both died young. The first was Edward VI, who famously dragged himself from his final sickbed to watch Willoughby and Chancellor slip down the Thames in 1553 on their voyage to search for a northeast passage to Cathay. The second was another Henry, James I's son and heir, the Prince of Wales who, on arrival in England at the age of nine, had been urged by Ben Jonson to, 'Look over the strict Ocean . . . and think where, you may lead us forth'. Defying his father, Henry even visited the imprisoned Ralegh to learn from the dreamer's own lips of the glories that awaited the bold voyager either to Virginia or Guiana. For Henry this was no passing teenage passion. In 1609 he visited the ships of the third supply as they gathered at Woolwich, and he championed the cause of the planters so strongly that the Spanish ambassador, Velasco, felt that the enterprise was surviving 'just because the Prince of Wales lends them very warmly his support'. Henry's enthusiasm for the Virginia venture was opposed by Sir Robert Cecil, the King's most trusted advisor, who may have had a hand in trying to arrange a marriage with a Spanish princess for the Prince, who would thus have been forced to accept a new virgin love and abandon the old one, Virginia. In this aim both the King and the new Spanish ambassador, Zuñiga, were reported to be in concord following their friendly meetings in July 1612. Henry, however, took matters into his own hands by dying on 2 November. The impact of his death was summed up by Sir Thomas Dale, the deputy governor of Virginia, when he wrote: 'He was the great captain of our Israel, the hope to have builded up this heavenly New Jerusalem. He interred the whole frame of this business [when he] fell into his grave.'

Apart from Edward, none of the nation's Tudor monarchs nailed their colours firmly to the colonists' masts. Catholic Mary would not encourage acts contrary to the wishes of her papal father and Spanish husband, while Elizabeth seemed to view such American expeditions as a way of indulging the fantasies of her favourites. This detached position changed with James who, although not wishing to be drawn into an argument with Spain, was nonetheless prepared to issue Charters to his petitioners as long as this did not involve any monetary commitment by the Crown.

This caution was in accord with the views of the Privy Council, who were often openly hostile to the proposed plans for settlement. Both Francis Walsingham and Robert Cecil discouraged, and even may have tried to sabotage, settlement plans, which

NOVA BRITANNIA.

OFFRING MOST

Excellent fruites by Planting in
VIRGINIA.

Exciting all such as be well affected
to further the same.

LONDON
Printed for SAMVEL MACHAM, and are to be sold at
his Shop in Pauls Church-yard, at the
Signe of the Bul-head.
1 6 0 9.

Throughout King James I's reign no opportunity was missed to publish tracts to encourage the restless to improve their lot through emigrating to a new and bountiful world.

led to a lack of unity at the highest level, preventing the creation of a coherent and enthusiastically supported plan of occupation.

With no overt encouragement from the Crown, those interested in organizing overseas voyages needed to prepare well their proposition before putting it forward for a royal patent. Cabot had the least difficulty but Henry VII had far fewer problems with his European neighbours than did Henry VIII, Elizabeth or James I, who needed more persuading. An early revivalist of the western vision was Humphrey Gilbert, who, in 1576, proposed assembling a fleet in the Bermudas that would fall upon the Spanish treasure fleets and seize Cuba and Santo Domingo. Gilbert's tracts clearly indicate that the writer had some difficulty in separating the practical from the impossible and fact from fictive hope. It is therefore somewhat surprising that Elizabeth granted him a Charter to venture westward a year after Frobisher's expeditions had failed; perhaps she did not read Gilbert's works. She would have found the pamphlet produced by Richard Hakluyt in 1584, *Particular Discourse on the Western Planting*, more digestible. In this work Hakluyt emphasized how an English colony in America would help in the struggle against Spain by providing a base from which raids could be launched on the annual Plate Fleet as well as Spanish settlements in the Indies. Once the colonists had settled peacefully and converted the natives to Christianity, boundless trading opportunities would arise that would, Hakluyt suggested, make England self-sufficient in essential commodities such as furs and timber. In other words, Hakluyt laid out the very arguments for colonization that would appeal to a hard-up and threatened monarchy.

The Crown and Council, however, needed not only to be convinced that the ideas of settlement were sound but also that they would be recognized internationally as legitimate when held up against the powerful papal authority of the Treaty of Tordesillas. The campaign to convince the sceptics was waged with flattery and the force of law.

The flattery was applied by Richard Hakluyt the younger (to distinguish him from his older cousin, also Richard, who enthused and inspired him), who in 1582 published *Divers Voyages Touching the Discovery of America*, following this up in 1589 with the book that would make him famous, *The Principal Navigations, Voyages and Discoveries of the English Nation*. The second, much larger edition, published in three volumes between 1598 and 1600, included the additional significant word, *Traffiques*, in the title after *Voyages*, for Hakluyt had appreciated that trade was going to be the mainsail that would power discovery forward, as without the hope of gain there would be no viable voyages. The first edition of this work was dedicated to Sir Francis Walsingham, 'Principal Secretary to Her Majesty, and one of Her Majesty's most honourable Privy Council'. The second volume of the second edition, published in 1599, was dedicated to Sir Robert Cecil, 'Principal Secretary to Her Majesty'. The dates of publication are important. Ralegh's Virginia adventure had ended ignominiously, giving the Queen's advisors ample opportunity to deflect her from supporting further such ventures. Hakluyt counterblasted this potential threat by stating, 'There is under our noses the great and ample country of Virginia; the inland whereof is found of late to be so sweet and wholesome a climate, so rich and abundant in silver mines, so apt and capable of all commodities . . . [and] acknowledged inland to be a better and richer country than Mexico.' With such an enthusiastic description of Virginia, Hakluyt's nose stretched,

Pinocchio-like, across the Atlantic. When the later editions of his book were being printed, England was at war with Spain, so Hakluyt, in addition to emphasizing the desire to establish a woollen trade with Cathay, made it very clear that he had included within the volumes detailed descriptions of every Spanish port in the West Indies to ease the task of would-be raiders. However, to encourage the peacemakers as well as the warmongers at Court, Hakluyt wrote:

> If upon a good and godly peace obtained, it shall please the almighty to stir up Her Majesty's heart to continue with transporting one or two thousand of her people, and such others as upon mine own knowledge will most willingly at their own charges become adventurers in good numbers with their bodies and goods; she shall by God's assistance, in short space, work many great and unlooked for effects, increase her dominions, enrich her coffers, and reduce many pagans to the faith of Christ.

LEGITIMIZING CONQUEST

The legal issues were handled by the polymath John Dee, who set out to challenge the belief that the unknown world had been divided up between Spain and Portugal, using a mixture of historical myth, geographic guesswork and incisive, incontestable, well-reasoned legalistic opinion.

To provide the proof to support the historical right of England to the lands between Florida and the Arctic, Dee turned to the work of Geoffrey of Monmouth, who had woven into his *History of the Kings of Britain*, finished in 1136, sufficient myth to demonstrate the pre-existence of a sizeable British Empire which, through King Arthur's conquests, included Ireland and the island chain that stretched to the Americas via the Shetlands, the Faroes, Iceland, Greenland and Labrador, establishing a prior claim that was reinforced by the Welshman Madoc in 1170 as far south as Florida. This ancient right of ownership over these lands was later strengthened, so Dee suggested, by the voyages of the Cabots and Frobisher, which were made while most of North America was still *terra incognita* to the Spanish.

Dee based his argument for the legitimacy of English settlement in America on Roman law, which proclaimed that rights of sovereignty over any land depended on both a demonstrable historical intent to occupy and a corporate presence being established in the territory. In other words, a ruler, or their representative, needed to be present both in body and in soul, which the Spanish evidently, were not. Furthermore, the Emperor Justinian, in the sixth century AD, had stated that, 'what presently belongs to no one becomes by natural reason the property of the first taker'. Dee expanded on this decree by demonstrating that it was insufficient to claim ownership merely by discovery; that legal title to territory depended on taking physical possession as well as putting the land to productive use. Cleverly, by the use of legal and scriptural argument drawn from irrefutable sources acceptable to both Catholic and Protestant alike, Dee ensured that his rationale could not be dismissed as heretical. Even more cannily, Dee used the same argument to support the Spanish colonization of the lands to the south of Virginia, including Florida, despite his suggestion of a prior English interest in this region.

John Dee, an influential polymath with interests in exploration, cartography, mathematics, astrology and the dark arts, occasionally mixed his enthusiasms to prove that a navigable northwest route to Cathay existed.

He then moved from mere clever discourse to genius in the way he managed to support the implications of the Treaty of Tordesillas, and the linked papal bull, *Inter Caetera*, while dismissing its application. The trouble lay, said Dee, not with the intention of the bull, but in the way the Spanish and Portuguese had implemented and interpreted it in their favour. The two states had not, for example, drawn an eastern longitudinal line to complement that in the Atlantic Ocean and thus had singularly failed to divide the world into equal spheres of influence. Even the Atlantic line, drawn 370 leagues west of the Cape Verde Islands, only stretched between 45° North and 54° South, proving, so Dee evinced, that they knew nothing of the lands that lay beyond those latitudes. What is more, the bull only granted to the Iberians those lands that had not either been 'discovered earlier by others' and those seas 'which have not hitherto been navigated'. For both these reasons they could not lay claim to those northern lands to which the British Crown had ancient title. Indeed, far from being a generous donative global gift of all hitherto unoccupied lands, Dee explained that the Pope's main purpose was to establish limits to the competitive Iberian states and thus reduce the causes of tension.

Emboldened by his own logic, Dee ventured to play with fire by claiming that the English would be breaking the law themselves if they failed to convert the heathen in the lands to which they laid claim, just as the Catholics claimed to be doing in their newfound lands. The justification for this obligation was seen by his equating Elizabeth's position as an emperor entitled to issue charters, to that of the similarly endowed Pope.

Dee's detailed, forensic, legalistic arguments were never going to command a wide readership, so the popular proselytizing was left to Hakluyt, who demonstrated his more robust and populist view by declaring, in *Discourse of Western Planting*, that the Treaty of Tordesillas was invalid because 'no Pope had any lawful authority to give any such donation'. That was a language that the English could understand.

Public Support

The ambivalence of the Privy Council was mirrored by the public at large, who were subjected to conflicting reports as to the virtues of the American enterprise. The battle for the hearts and minds of both investors and settlers began early and created a rhythmic rise and fall in popular support. Buoyed up on a tide of paper propaganda, settlers sailed westwards only for evidence of the wreckage of their hopes to return as scraps of scribbled flotsam scrawled by those whose optimism had not survived the reality of life abroad. Naturally, the death of both Cabot and Gilbert while they were deployed, with nothing achieved, won no converts, neither did the farce of Frobisher's worthless aggregate. To counter this condemnatory current, something good had to come out of America.

The good news was provided by Ralegh, who, falling prey to his own propaganda, 'sexed up' both Arthur Barlowe's report on his reconnaissance, and Thomas Harriot's account of his stay at Roanoke to better suit his purpose and to discredit the doubters. Indeed, the first few pages of Harriot's *A Brief and True Report of the New Found Land of Virginia*, as printed by Hakluyt in 1589, are a defence of the author's optimistic opinions and a refutation of those who would report otherwise. Harriot excelled as a caustic critic, stating that:

> Of our company that returned some for their misdemeanour and ill dealing in the country, have been there worthily punished, who by reason of their bad natures, have maliciously not only spoken ill of their Governors, but for their sakes slandered the country itself. The like also have those done which were their consort.
>
> Some being ignorant of the state thereof, notwithstanding since their return amongst their friends and acquaintances, and also others, especially if they were in company where they might not be gainsaid, would seem to know so much as no men more, and make no men so great travellers as themselves. They stood so much, as it may seem, upon their credit and reputation, that having been a twelve month in the country, it would have been a great disgrace unto them as they thought, if they could not have said much whether it were true or false. Of which some have spoken of more than ever they saw, or otherwise knew to be there: other some have not been ashamed to make absolute denial of that, which although not by them, yet by others is most certainly and there plentifully known, and some make difficulties of those things they have no skill of.

Harriot was writing of what had been a successful, although foreshortened, sojourn. Indeed, if loss of life, or rather the lack of it, is the major criterion, the year of Lane's occupancy, 1585/1586, was the most successful of any of the ventures in the period under discussion. In the years that followed, others would write or return home with harrowing accounts of events that the sponsors and investors would dearly liked to have kept from the public gaze. It was the dissemination of such works, balancing out those written for the purposes of propaganda, which meant that the Virginian voyages were never viewed with uncritical approval and thus wholehearted national support.

In 1609 the Virginia Company felt it had been traduced by the publication of John Smith's acerbic *A True Relation of Such Occurrences and Accidents of Note as Hath Happened in Virginia since the First Planting of that Colony.* The counterblast to what had in fact been a work forecasting an optimistic outlook once the errors of leadership had been sorted out was led by Prince Henry through his chaplain, Daniel Price, who, in an open air sermon outside St Paul's Cathedral, dismissed the sceptics and pointed out the many opportunities for both social, financial and moral advance that awaited those who ventured to the plantation of Virginia, well away from the sinful city of London. A flood of books with Virginia as their theme poured forth but, like many such floods, soon ebbed.

A similar maelstrom came out of the 1622 massacre, with the Virginia Company rapidly refuting the eyewitness accounts of the state of the colony published by such authorities as Captain Nathaniel Butler, whose *The Unmasked Face of our Colony in Virginia as it Was in the Winter of the Year 1622*, which was made available to the nation and the Privy Council, was, together with the heartbreaking letters dispatched by the survivors, responsible for a Crown Commission being established to investigate the affairs of the Virginia Company. Its unfavourable report led to the winding up of the Company in 1624. No positive propaganda had such a telling effect.

Promotional tracts did, however, continue to be published and widely read. One of the most significant was John Smith's *Description of New England*, which was issued in 1616, to be followed in 1620 by *New England Trials*, both written to encourage emigration. Smith wrote well and spoke honestly; there is little exaggeration in his statement that 'you shall scarce find any bay, shallow shore or cove of sand, where you may not take many clams or lobsters . . . or isles where you find not fruits, birds, crabs and mussels'. But he added a homely warning for the over-enthusiastic: 'all which are to be had in abundance observing but their seasons: but if a man will go at Christmas to gather cherries in Kent, though there be plenty in summer, he may be deceived; so here these plenties have each their season . . .' With such unglossed descriptions, along with his 1624 work, *The Generall Historie of Virginia, New England, and the Summer Isles*, Smith should done have much to put wind in the sails of those contemplating emigration.

TRADE

For a long time, the English were reluctant blue water adventurers. Their homeland itself gave forth an increase which was generally sufficient to feed its population, while shoals of fish still offered a net-filling sea harvest. The wealthy, mostly the aristocracy, could afford to pay for both wines from France and the expensive spices brought by

Venetian galleys annually to London and Southampton. The rising number of affluent merchants, trading mainly in wool and woollen products across the narrow seas, were also aware of their station and the problems that would confront those uppity enough to try and outshine the established hierarchy. There was, however, one trading difficulty which the English struggled to overcome. Their northerly island, warmed by the ocean current, produced woollens – too warm to be worn by their neighbours in the populous lands to the south – while the colder lands on their own latitude, or further north, were too sparsely populated and had too few goods to exchange to make trade with them worthwhile. England needed new outlets and northwest seemed best. This dilemma Richard Hakluyt spelt out in the opening paragraphs of his account of the Willoughby and Chancellor voyage, which set out in 1553 to seek out a northeast passage 'to new and unknown kingdoms' in which he stated:

> At what time our merchants perceived the commodities and wares of England to be in small request with the countries and people about us, and near to us, and that those merchandises were now neglected, and the price thereof abated, certain grave citizens of London, and men careful for the good of their country, began to think with themselves, how this mischief might be remedied.
>
> Seeing that the wealth of the Spaniards and Portuguese, by the discovery and search of new trades and countries was marvellously increased, supposing the same to be a course and mean for them also to obtain the like, they thereupon resolved upon a new and strange navigation. After much speech and conference together, it was at last concluded that three ships should be prepared and furnished out, for the search and discovery of the northern part of the world . . .

Yet trade, as it was promoted by Hakluyt, meant dealing directly with Cathay, so finding a route to this eastern market became an imperative, to the detriment of focusing on new world settlement. Or did it? There were some propagandists such as the Reverend Daniel Price, quoted earlier, who preached that America was its own cornucopia, equalling:

> Tyrus for colours, Basan for wood, Persia for oils, Arabia for spices, Spain for silks, Narcis for shipping, Netherlands for fish, Pomona for fruit, and by tillage, Babylon for corn, besides the abundance of mulberries, minerals, rubies, pearls, gems, grapes, deer, fowls, drugs for physic, herbs for food, roots for colours, ashes for soap, timber for building, pastures for feeding, rivers for fishing, and whatsoever commodity England wanted.

Why venture further? The propagandists, dreamers and schemers listened, believed and continued to invest to send others out to lose their ships and their lives trying to bypass America through the adamantine barrier of ice.

LAND RIGHTS

If the merchants and investors could be won over by suggestions of increased trade, potential settlers needed to be persuaded that a land lay waiting for them to work, a land to which they could stake a better claim than in nearby Ireland. In this respect, the legal justification the English used to legitimize their claim to America was also used to excuse the removal of the indigenous people from the land on which they lived. The argument advanced was that these people were merely sojourners in a land over which they roamed but could claim no title by right of settlement. The usurpation began with the very naming of the land and its inhabitants: the continent was called North America, after an Italian who never visited there; the English lands, Virginia, after a queen who did not invest in them, and the people, Indians, after a race who lived half a world away. Of these it was the name, Virginia, that was to do the most damage, for it hinted broadly that the land was unoccupied, untamed, unowned and ripe for possession, when, in fact, the inhabitants themselves referred to the eastern littoral as Tsenacommacah, which means 'densely inhabited land'. So it was until, in the north, European diseases, the harbingers of settlement, widowed the world on which the Puritans would step ashore.

By using the term Virginia, Ralegh implied that the land was still 'as God made it' but not that, unlike his Queen, it should not be penetrated. If this sounds too coarse then we have his views on his other new world, Guiana, to support this interpretation; for of that land, he wrote:

> Guiana is a country that hath yet her maidenhead, never sacked, turned, nor wrought; the face of the earth hath not been torn, nor the virtue and salt of the soil spent by manurance, the graves have not been opened for gold, the mines not broken with sledges nor the images pulled down out of their temples. It hath never been entered by any army of strength, and never conquered by any Christian prince.

One impression that did hold sway, for a while, was the view that the 'naturals' would warmly welcome the settlers. Arthur Barlowe, having had his feet and clothes washed by attentive Amerindian maidens, considered his reconnaissance party to have been 'entertained with all love and kindness' by a people who were 'most gentle, loving and faithful, void of all guile, and treason, and such as lived after the manner of the golden age'. Fatefully for them this included the, incorrect, observation that, like the lilies of the field, they toiled not, for 'the earth bringeth forth all things in abundance, as in the first creation, without toil or labour'. Such a naive comment, based on inadequate research, was to support the idea that the land was indeed 'virgin' and thus *vacuum domicilium*, that is, it was legally waste because the Amerindians had not 'subdued' it in a way that was recognized by European law. In fact, all along the coast the population fed itself mainly through the clever symbiotic husbandry of Indian corn (maize), beans and squashes, to which hunting provided merely a supplement. Far from being savage they were, in fact, incredibly well adapted to their *sauvage*, the country.

For most of those who intended to settle in America, arguments over the morality of land ownership were irrelevant; what they wanted was sufficient land granted to them on which they could raise both a family and a profit. If this was not going to be given, then the terms of tenure needed also to be tempting. This was the great argument that the *Mayflower* voyagers waged with their sponsors and which they would, through the advantage of distance, eventually win.

Each potential colony had its band of propagandists. Thus William Vaughan, a Welsh landowner from Carmarthenshire, wrote a rambling work, *The Golden Grove*, which encouraged the colonization of Newfoundland as a cure for overcrowding and which, combined with fishing 'Neptune's sheep', would restore the nation to economic prosperity. Newfoundland, for the occupation of which letters patent were signed on 2 May 1610, marked the first real attempt to excite interest in a land, as it was, as opposed to how it was envisioned. John Guy, the first Governor, less open to self-deception than either Ralegh or the Virginia Company, reported on what he saw; ten years later so did John Mason in his *A Brief Discourse of the New-Found-Land . . . Inciting our Nation to Go Forward in that Hope-Full Plantation Begunne*, in which, after admitting that the country had neither the fertility nor the pleasing climate of Virginia, he proposed the following reasons why Newfoundland might be preferred to Virginia:

1. The nearness to Britain, 'being but half of the way to Virginia, having a convenient passage', which made for both a short outward and a shorter return journey.
2. The great and valuable fishing trade that existed and supported thousands of English families.
3. The availability and thus the cheapness of passage for both settlers and stores.
4. The 'security from foreign and domestic enemies' because of the scarcity of 'savages' by whom 'the planters as yet never suffered damage'.

In 1620, Richard Whitbourne, a seasoned and pioneer traveller to Newfoundland who had been present when Humphrey Gilbert laid claim to the islands, published, to popular acclaim, his *Discourse and Discovery of Newfoundland with Many Reasons to Prove How Worthy and Beneficial a Plantation May There Be Made . . .*, which ran to three editions between 1620 and 1623. His key suggestion was the need to establish a beneficial link between fishing and settlement which would provide, unlike the more southern settlements, a quick profitable return. What is more, settlements would create a demand for goods which the fishing fleet could deliver, thus giving them an income on their outward voyage as well as facilitating their drying and loading of fish for the return journey, which might be to southern Europe, to exchange fish, much in demand, for goods for sale in England. Moreover, Whitbourne saw Newfoundland as being a link to a line of settlements that would stretch down the coast of the continent.

Whitbourne's work was designed to influence Lord Falkland's decision to establish a colony in Newfoundland. It is lengthy, detailed, discursive and, for the most part, full of the sort of practical advice for would-be settlers that is conspicuously and devastatingly absent from other such works, particularly those linked to the southern settlements.

Compared with both Roanoke/Jamestown and Newfoundland, very little propaganda was produced for the encouragement of settlement in New England.

Indeed, it is difficult to establish how and why the spotlight first fell on the cliffs of Maine and creeks of Cape Cod. That it did was due, not to armchair enthusiasts picking up their pens, but to the firsthand accounts by those who had sailed into these seas and landed on those shores.

The proposal to settle in Norumbega, or northern Virginia, was predicated on two main concepts. The first was the idea that its waters might provide a source of seafood as rich as that already being heavily exploited off Newfoundland; the second, inspired by the Catholic Lord Arundel of Wardour, in Wiltshire, was to establish a Catholic colony. The idea of a religious settlement had been first mooted in 1582 but was dropped through too much Spanish hostility and too little English support. Both ideas induced exploratory voyages, designed not only to report back but also to make initial trading contacts with the local population. The reports were all lucid, descriptive and positive. They began with Gabriel Archer and John Brereton's separate narratives of the voyage of Bartholomew Gosnold in 1602. These were followed by Martin Pring's account of his 1603 voyage from Bristol, which had been directly inspired by the city's cathedral prebendary, one Richard Hakluyt. George Waymouth, another seasoned voyager, produced in *The Jewell of Artes* a detailed account of the skills needed by those commanding a voyage of discovery, including how best to fortify a settlement in the new world. Yet, although the work of Hakluyt, Smith, Whitbourne, Waymouth and others was read by hundreds, there was one work of prose that would be read by thousands and have far more of an influence on the decisions of potential emigrants and their behaviour once they had stepped ashore in America – the Bible.

The Word of God

In a voyage almost as long in time and far more dangerous than many of those that Hakluyt described, a noble few had fought bravely to make an English translation of the Bible widely available since the 1520s. The first fruits were delivered by William Tyndale between 1525 and 1534, any further work being brutally cut short by his being burnt at the stake in Brussels in 1536. Coverdale continued what Tyndale and begun and presented his work to King Henry VIII in 1535. Henry then approved the production of the so-called Matthew Bible, which was placed in every parish church between 1539 and 1541, only to be burnt during Mary's reign, forcing the work of translation abroad, so that one edition of the early bibles took its name from the city where it was printed, Geneva. James I, finding the Geneva Bible and its linked works objectionable, called for a new translation, the result of which was one of the greatest works in the English language, the Authorized Version, which was published in 1611.

For many English people the Bible was the only printed word that was read to them. They thus got to know its stories and moral teachings extremely well, so that, although the Pilgrims and their coeval Protestant planters in New England generally come to mind when the influence of biblical teaching on the settlement of America is considered, it is very apparent that both the Bible story and its moral teaching infused every aspect of colonial life from the beginning. Richard Hakluyt, in the first paragraph of the epistle dedicatory of the first edition of his *Navigations and Voyages*, tells of his

These comely figures, drawn by John White, reflect the positive opinion of the natives during most of the months that Ralph Lane's expedition was ashore on Roanoke. Later, disillusionment would transform them into the Caliban-like creatures of Shakespeare's imagination. (National Maritime Museum)

being inspired by the words in Psalm 107, 'They that go down to the sea in ships, that do business in great waters; These see the works of the Lord, and his wonders in the deep.' In similar vein Sir William Alexander, the sponsor of Nova Scotia, continued his introduction to his *In Praise of Colonies*, quoted at the head of this chapter, with the words:

> The next generations succeeding Shem planted in Asia, Ham in Africa and Japheth in Europe : Abraham and Lot were Captains of Colonies, the Land then being as free as the Seas are now, since they parted them in every part where they passed, not taking notice of natives without impediment. That memorable troop of Jews which Moses led from Egypt to Canaan was a kind of Colony though miraculously conducted by God, who intended thereby to advance his Church and *to destroy the rejected Ethnics*. [author's italics]

Alexander's view was much in keeping with the earlier opinion of the priest Richard Hakluyt, and most other Protestant Englishmen: that the business that they were going about was that of their heavenly Father. Thus, as the true inheritors of God's word, they were called upon to enter the new, promised land, where they were, paradoxically, to spread the gospel of truth while being able to treat the native population as did the ancient Israelites. Thus they preached conversion and practised cant, with the result that many of the people who walked in darkness would see, not a great light but the shades of the valley of the shadow of death.

Before this ambiguity took hold, Thomas Harriot, in his account of the 1585 Roanoke settlement, seemed genuinely to believe that the Amerindians were thirsty for living water when he wrote:

> Many times and in every town where I came, according as I was able, I made declaration of the contents of the Bible, that therein was set forth the true and only God, and his mighty works, that therein was contained the true doctrine of salvation through Christ, with many particularities of miracles and chief points of religion, as I was able then to utter, and thought fit at the time. And although I told them the book materially and of itself was not of any such virtue, as I thought they did conceive, but only the doctrine therein contained: yet would many be glad to touch it . . . to show their hungry desire of that knowledge which was spoken of.

They also, according to Harriot, liked to take part in psalmody and asked for the English to pray to their God for a good harvest and for the cure of their sick.

The Harriot school of thought, with its belief that the natives, 'by means of good government . . . may in short time be brought to civility and the embracing of true religion', persisted throughout the period, with many preachers and even the Virginia Company emphasizing the need to treat the natives with converting kindness. Set against this were the pragmatic views of Catholics such as Sir George Peckham, who used his grounding in the same faith as Harriot to sanction the taking of the Amerindians' lands, 'to plant, possess and subdue' the inhabitants by force. This contradictory view reflected the difference between the Old and New Testaments.

The conquer-by-force school based their argument on texts such as Deuteronomy 7: 'When the Lord thy God shall bring thee into the land whither thou goest to possess it and hath cast out many nations before thee . . . the Lord thy God shall deliver them before thee: thou shalt smite them and utterly destroy them; thou shalt make no covenant with them nor shew mercy unto them.' Pragmatically, the English delayed applying this stern directive until the Amerindian nations had succoured the English strangers that they had found outside their gates. It was only once the possession was advanced far enough to create a feeling of self-sufficiency that the native peoples would be subject to the wrath of the English God.

The convert-through-kindness school quoted Christ who, in sending out the twelve apostles to preach, told them that, although they would be as sheep in the midst of wolves, yet they had to be as wise as serpents and as gentle as doves, treating all with respect. Sadly, many of the adherents to this kinder course of action were better preachers than practitioners, while missionaries, as such, were not sent to help convert the people.

However, conversion from pagan rituals was a useful propaganda aim for the Virginia Company, and many a text could be appropriated to support this cause. Thus the opening lines of Genesis 12: 'Now the Lord said unto Abraham, Get thee out of thy country, and from thy kindred, and from thy father's house, unto a land that I will shew thee. And I will make of thee a great nation, and I will bless thee, and make thy name great; and thou shalt be a blessing' were used to support a moral as well as commercial crusade to Virginia, where the English were being called to minister to 'a nation that never heard of Christ'. In time the Church would move from seeing these people, in 1584, as the most 'kind and loving people' in the world, to the view held in 1609 by the Reverend Richard Crakanthorpe, that they were 'heathen barbarians and brutish people' in desperate need of conversion. John Smith shared the sentiment but not the vitriol, writing in his 1608 *A True Relation*, that the aim remained: 'to the high Glory of God, to the erecting of true religion among infidels, to the overthrow of superstition and idolatry, to the winning of many thousands of wandering sheep unto Christ's fold, who now, and until now, have strayed in the unknown paths of Paganism, Idolatry and superstition'.

In response to this call, lip-service missionary work was employed to the advantage of investors. In 1616, following the arrival of Pocahontas in England, travelling under her converted name of Rebecca, the alien wife of Abraham, King James ordered the archbishops of Canterbury and York to organize a collection throughout the kingdom to raise money for an initiative to educate 'the children of the barbarians'. This aim was manifest through the setting aside of 10,000 acres of 'College Lands' near Henricus, on the upper James River, where a school for instruction in English and Christianity would be built. A priest, the Reverend George Thorpe, a highly connected Company investor, was sent out to take charge of this project, for which, by 1620, over £3,000 had been raised. Progress was slow, in part due to the fact that Amerindian mums did not want to send their children to boarding school, but mainly because the by now almost bankrupt Virginia Company was reluctant to part with its windfall delivered from the collection plates of English congregations. The list of Amerindians converted by 1630 would not take long to recite. As well as Princess Rebecca Rolfe they included Manteo, who had been persuaded to go to England with Amadas in 1584 and had returned, twice, as an interpreter and go-between, earning an elevated status which was confirmed by his baptism at Croatoan in August 1586, at which time he was invested as Lord of Roanoke. No such conversion or award was made of Squanto, who played a similar role to that of Manteo, with the Pilgrims at Plymouth. Indeed, so distrustful of Christianity was the local *sachem*, (tribal leader) Massasoit, that he stipulated that future land sales would only be agreed if the English ceased attempting to convert his people.

Scripture was not only available to justify belligerence and to Bible-bash the natives; it could also be used to punish one's own people. The most notable example of this, during the period of invasion, was when John Smith, having been released from captivity by the Powhatans, because of Pocahontas's dramatic intervention to prevent his execution, returned to Jamestown on 2 January 1608, but without his companions, Thomas Emery and Jehu Robinson, whom the Amerindians had killed. He was immediately seized by his enemies on the council, tried, and sentenced to death for allowing their slaughter, with the words from Leviticus 24:17, 'he that killeth any man shall surely be put to death', providing a justification for this crass illegal act that was not possible under English law. Smith, who seemed to have made a lifetime habit of being timely ripped from the jaws of death was, on this occasion, saved by the arrival of Captain Newport, who saw through the folly and vindictiveness of the council's behaviour.

Smith himself, who does not give the appearance of being a biblical scholar, was well able to resort to scripture when it was apposite so to do. Thus his most famous adage, 'He that will not work shall not eat', was a direct transposition from 2 Thessalonians 3:10, with the added advantage that it conferred upon Smith the enormous and unquestionable authority of Saint Paul: 'For even when we were with you, this we commanded you, that if any would not work, neither should he eat.'

Biblical teaching had a major influence on what was a most important aspect of colonial life: the settlers' relationship with the native women. Naturally, for the sake of good neighbourliness casual liaisons with these ladies was forbidden, while rape was punishable by death. However, on occasions the English, such as Amadas and Smith, were entertained lovingly, and in the case of the latter most suggestively, by ladies whose physical attributes were neither unpleasant nor well hidden. Yet, no sexual link seems to have been made across the racial divide, although the settlers were, for the most part, young unattached males many miles and months from home. Virginia was thus no Tahiti, where Captain Cook's sex-starved sailors could be well satiated in exchange for a six-inch nail. The only explanation for this enforced abstinence must be biblical teaching. Ezra 9, for example, taught that it was an abomination for the people of Israel dwelling among other nationals to 'have taken of their daughters for themselves and for their sons: so that the holy seed have mingled themselves with the people of those lands'. So bad was this transgression that Ezra had to call the people together so that they could admit that they had 'trespassed against our God' in this matter and separate themselves from these 'strange wives'. That was mild compared with the orders given by Moses in Numbers 31, in which he castigated the Israeli host for making captives – that is taking into slavery – the Midianite women and children, having slain their men folk. Moses demanded that they 'kill every male among the little ones, and kill every woman that hath known man by lying with him'. This is a direct contrast to the Amerindian tradition by which captured women and children were integrated into the tribe to compensate for those lost through warfare and disease.

More justification for separate development of the new world was found in the continuation of Deuteronomy 7 quoted above: 'Neither shalt thou make marriages with them; thy daughter thou shalt not give unto his son, nor his daughter shalt thou take unto thy son.'

In 1969 the English band Blue Mink released the song 'Melting Pot', which included the lyrics:

> What we need is a great big melting pot,
> Big enough to hold the world and all it's got,
> Keep it stirring for a hundred years or more,
> Turn out coffee-coloured children by the score.

It was a song which affirmed the oneness of mankind in the face of the enduring doctrine of racial discrimination and separation and the fear of miscegenation, the sexual relationship of people of mixed races. In the twentieth century this was seen as a black-and-white affair, but in sixteenth- and seventeenth-century greater Virginia the same condemnation, biblically supported, was very much in evidence to prevent close relationships between, mainly, white men and Amerindian women. For these settlers no dusky Ruth would snuggle down beside a white Boaz among the alien corn. Until John Rolfe, that is. His marriage to Pocahontas is as memorable for its uniqueness as for its romance. If any evidence is needed on how a biblical conscience could make hypocritical cowards of those who would court 'strange women', then Rolfe's letter to Governor Dale requesting permission to marry the princess provides, in paragraph after paragraph of sickening sycophancy, proof enough, as when he wrote:

> To you therefore (most noble Sir) the patron and Father of us in this country do I utter the effects of this settled and long continued affection (which hath made a mighty war in my meditations) and here I do truly relate, to what issue this dangerous combat is come unto, wherein I have not only examined, but thoroughly tried and pared my thoughts even to the quick, before I could fit wholesome and apt applications to cure so dangerous an ulcer. I never failed to offer my daily and faithful prayers to God, for his sacred and holy assistance. I forgot not to set before mine eyes the frailty of mankind, his proneness to evil, his indulgence of wicked thoughts, with many other imperfections wherein man is daily ensnared, and oftentimes overthrown, and then compared to my present estate. Nor was I ignorant of the heavy displeasure which almighty God conceived against the sons of Levi and Israel for marrying strange wives, nor of the inconveniences which may thereby arise, with other the like good motions which made me look about warily and with good circumspection, into the grounds and principal agitations, which thus should provoke me to be in love with one whose education hath been rude, her manners barbarous, her generation accursed, and so discrepant in all nurture from myself, that oftentimes with fear and trembling, I have ended my private controversy with this: surely these are wicked instigations, hatched by him who seeketh and delighteth in man's destruction; and so with fervent prayers to be ever preserved from such diabolical assaults (as I took those to be) I have taken some rest.

When the twice-widowed Rolfe penned his letter to Dale he must have worded it in a way that he knew his stern boss would both appreciate and understand. The whole purpose of the plea was to ask for special exemption from the strict moral biblical code that both men must have known well.

Even more sickening was the attempt, a little later, by the married Dale to procure Pocahontas's younger sister, a child of eleven, for his own bed. So upright was Dale himself that he dispatched Ralph Hamor to Powhatan, her father, to act as his pimp. Centuries later it is difficult to find any part of the following extract in the procuring bid that does not stick in the throat. Hamor told Chief Powhatan that Dale had sent him there as his suitor for the girl:

> for this purpose . . . to entreat you by that brotherly friendship you make profession of to permit her to return with me unto him, partly for the desire which himself hath, and partly for the desire her sister [Pocahontas] hath to see her, of whom, if fame hath

The most famous of the kidnapped natives, Pocahontas suffered the fate of many of her countrymen, dying in England without seeing her native land again. (National Maritime Museum)

Waterfalls cut short every expedition up the rivers of the Chesapeake aimed at seeking a passage from sea to sea. Only Henry Hudson, in reaching Albany high up the river that bears his name, made a significant voyage into the interior.

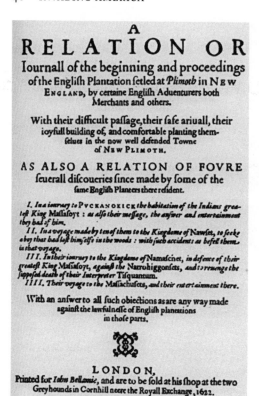

Mourts Relation, 1622. Even the separatists, convinced of the rightness of their actions in moving to their New Jerusalem, felt it necessary to include in their account a defence of the lawfulness of their actions.

not been prodigal, as likely enough it hath not, your brother by your favour would gladly make his nearest companion, wife, and bedfellow . . .

That Powhatan did not drive Hamor away, or worse, says much for his composure. What he did do was report that his daughter was already engaged, that no additional dowry would affect that arrangement and that he loved his daughter too much to let her go, saying, 'I hold it not a brotherly part of your King to desire to bereave me of two of my children at once.' Thus was the possibility of marriage alliances between two people, who could have intermingled and lived together, prevented by biblical law and one man's lust.

The propagandists have long been regarded as successful encouragers of western planting, yet these dreamers and schemers never convinced sufficient of their countrymen to ensure that the invasion gained the support essential for its success. In neither the plays, prose, poetry, parliamentary, nor Privy Council reports that have survived from the period is there sufficient reference to the new world to indicate that England, as a nation, was ready to embark on what would one day be its voyage to a global empire.

After more than a century of propaganda the outcome was close to failure. Following the 1622 massacre on the James River, Nathaniel Butler, homeward bound, via Jamestown, from his three-year governorship of Bermuda, berated the maladministration of the

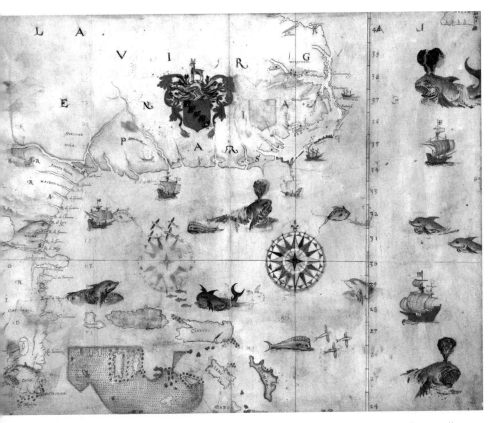

John White's all-round technical skill as a draftsman is clearly indicated in this excellent 1585 map of the Carribean and Carolinas, which he had little time to record in detail. The sketches of flying fish, dolphins and whales shows his love of recording flora and fauna, for which he had an excellent eye. (British Museum)

Virginia Company and the appalling casualty rate sustained during the invasion. Butler was of the opinion that, of the 'not fewer than ten thousand souls transported thither, there are not, through aforementioned abuses and neglects, above two thousand of them at present to be found alive . . . instead of a Plantation, it will shortly get the name of a slaughter house.' Against this loss of life Butler thought that the 347 killed in the massacre represented an insignificant number. The Company issued a refutation that damned itself in its defence, and it was left to writers such as Smith and Purchas to continue the ultimately correct propaganda, 'shewing the benefits which may grow to this Kingdom from American English Plantations and especially those of Virginia and Summer Islands'.

The propagandists were far more successful in wooing the Court than the rest of the country. Royal letters patent did get issued to the supplicants, giving them very much what their petitions requested. However, finding sufficient volunteers to travel to these gifted domains was not so easy. Frobisher's first settlement group was selected from convicted criminals; Ralegh was licensed to impress seamen for the Roanoke voyage and dispatched with White fewer settlers than he intended; in 1618 it was planned to send 100 'superfluous . . . young boys and girls that lay starving in the streets' of London to Virginia; in 1623 a memorandum suggested that encouraging emigration to New England would 'offer employment to the starving unemployed and so rid England of the expense of maintaining them', as well as giving bankrupt gentlemen an opportunity to recover their fortune. Thus, although individual ships might have been crowded, voyages were not oversubscribed. Even the Pilgrims were reduced in numbers by last-minute withdrawals.

The comparison with Spain is informative: in the sixteenth century that nation sent 240,000 of its citizens to America, with a further 450,000 joining them in the next century. To replace the lost handful that the English dispatched in the 1580s, just 150,000 souls emigrated from England in the seventeenth century, and all but a few thousand of them departed after 1630. The enthusiastic efforts of the Scot, Sir William Alexander to encourage his fellow countrymen to sail to Nova Scotia were eclipsed by the numbers of them who were prepared to be ferried over to Ireland. This would be a continuing imbalance. Between 1650 and 1700 just 7,000 Scots crossed the Atlantic to the new world, while 70,000 emigrated to Ulster. The trickle of emigrants is all the more surprising because the land from which they came was subject to dearth: the real earnings of a labourer between 1585 and 1630 never matched those of his great-grandfather during his short working life (his life expectancy was under thirty-five years). To such as these the new world should have exerted an irresistible pull; it did not.

The propaganda failed. What did succeed in the years to come and turned the invasion into a conquest was religious persecution. The Bible, or conflicting interpretations of the same, recruited far more families than did the promotional tracts. The word of the Lord, or its limited exclusive interpretation by Archbishop Laud, persuaded tens of thousands to sail west, far more than all the propagandists combined.

CHAPTER 3

The Charters: Come Over and Help Yourselves

There stood a man of Macedonia, and prayed him, saying, Come over into Macedonia, and help us.

Acts 16: 9, King James Bible, 1611

Come over and help us.

Motto of Massachusetts Bay Company, 1629

In an age of centralized authority, few Englishmen dared venture abroad without royal approval. This meant that each of the fingers thrust towards America wore upon them a signet ring in the form of a royal letters patent, or Charter (listed in Appendix 2). The exception to this was Frobisher's thumb, to whose 'Company of Cathay' the canny Queen Elizabeth, refused to give her seal of approval having lost her original investment of £1,000 in Frobisher's gold prospecting voyages. She was not to repeat that mistake. Henceforward she would always choose the cheapest option, passing off her parsimony as prudence. The publication of royal Charters would ensure that she, and succeeding monarchs, could claim a copyright without investing cash.

So, for a Crown that wished to control but not command, to create but not contribute, a concessionary awarding Charter leading to the creation of a colonial commonwealth was a very clever concept. Through the issue of such documents the monarch could claim rights and rewards without responsibilities, and authority without administration: an arrangement that demanded influence without commensurate investment. So England instilled at the start of its American adventure a system and a relationship whose final logical outcome would be a revolution proclaiming 'no taxation without representation'. There was another advantage that the Charter system had for its investors – it created a closed market. This was the age of monopolies, the purchase of which guaranteed both the seller, the sovereign, and the selected purchaser a rich return for no investment. It was not until 1624 that Parliament, manned by men of property, felt able to challenge the Crown by declaring monopolies were contrary to the fundamental laws of the land. King Charles ignored their strictures. Thus the produce of America was perceived as being beneficial to existing monopolies, such as glass, soap and silk, as well as creating new ones such as tobacco, sassafras and beaver fur.

As the century developed, and as the concept of a commonwealth matured, successive rulers introduced their own ideas as to how best to manage their overseas infants. Thus Henry VII was content to let a foreign national work speculatively for England's cause. Elizabeth, an admirer and user of favourites, felt her newfound lands were best when, in Donne's words, they were 'by one man manned', which meant Walter Ralegh. James I, who liked not Ralegh and whose own intimate 'sweethearts', Somerset and Buckingham, were not interested in overseas, began by appointing committees over whom, as his confidence waxed and their capabilities waned, he exercised gradually more management until, in 1624, the Crown took direct control of Virginia while still awarding blocks of land to a coterie.

Whoever the beneficiary, the Charter process can be summed up along the lines proposed by Francis Jennings:

1. The Crown was petitioned to lay claim to territories previously outside its jurisdiction and over which it had no true legal claim.
2. The Crown authorized a person or organized group by charter to conquer the claimed territory and to exercise a monopoly over its trade.
3. The successful conqueror became the possessor and governor of the territory, subject to the terms of the charter and the continuing acknowledgement of the sovereign's overlordship.
4. The charter holder was authorized to encourage settlement through the issues of land, mineral and fishing rights and to raise capital through the issue of shares, estates or lottery tickets to sponsors.
5. The Crown would be a beneficiary but not an investor.

If the state was going to risk little then it had, paradoxically, an interest in offering the grantee much for two very valid reasons. The first was that, having laid claim to these lands, the Crown wished to exclude any other state from either counter-claiming or muscling in on these new domains. The Charters were thus being used like balloons inserted flaccid through a small hole into a large vacuum and then blown up to fill all the space available, providing a thin but taut membrane which, if penetrated, would cause a loud explosion. No matter that the empty space was filled largely with air, it was the boundary rather than what it contained that was important. The second reason was that, by offering much, the Crown hoped that its gift would contain enough, albeit thinly spread, to produce a reasonable return. What the state never comprehended was just how vast America was and how great would be the resources necessary to tame it.

In 1496 Henry VII's Charter implied that Cabot and his crew were capable of seizing and occupying a land which, by its very description, as having towns and cities, was settled by a civilized people. In response to the King's horizon-stretching largesse, John Day reported to Spain that Cabot, after he landed in America, 'Since he was with just a few people . . . did not dare advance inland beyond the shooting distance of a cross-bow', which was hardly the action of a potential *conquistador* or even major explorer.

By the time Elizabeth was persuaded to award her first colonial Charters, the government concept of what such grants involved had matured. Thus the letters patent granted to Sir Humphrey Gilbert, his heirs and assignees in 1578 gave him very similar benefits to those awarded to Cabot, but added permission 'to build and fortify' and additional rights for those who came after 'in a second voyage of conquest'. This document also introduced: a geographical boundary and a timeframe, stating that Sir Humphrey's jurisdiction would cover those who 'abide within two hundred leagues of any said place where the said Sir Humphrey . . . shall inhabit within six years next ensuing the date hereof', and a legal control in requiring that the Secretary, Lord Treasurer and Privy Council be involved in the licensing of the resupply of any settlements. There is also a mention of the paying of duty and other taxes on any gold or silver ore that might be discovered, an acknowledgement of the success the Spanish had had in discovering such wealth, ignoring Frobisher's constant failure to do likewise.

The geographical boundaries and timeframe for establishing a settlement were obviously felt to be sound, for they remained in the Charter that Elizabeth granted to Sir Walter Ralegh in 1584, which was a redrafting of the Gilbert original, so that it could be rescued from the watery grave that was the unlucky Gilbert's lot and presented to a man who was both a relative of Gilbert and the Queen's current favourite. So beloved was he that, unlike either Cabot or Gilbert, his half-brother, Ralegh was not allowed to travel across the ocean in person. This seemingly capricious decision by the enamoured Queen established yet another pattern in the Charters, whereby the investors stayed in England and encouraged others to risk their all on their behalf. This would necessitate the appointment of a leader or governor, who might hold neither the rank nor the relationship with the sponsor to demand undisputed authority over those over whom they had been placed in command in these isolated, strange and dangerous lands. The fatal flaw thus soon emerged; where harmony was essential discord would develop.

Ralegh's demesne was created to include the shoreline settlements stretching six hundred miles both north and south from the first township he intended to build called, modestly, the City of Ralegh. To encourage wealthy sponsors he offered, the second time around, county-size estates to all who backed his scheme, selling some 8.5 million acres of these in Virginia. Sir Philip Sidney acquired 3 million acres, giving him title to an estate that was as large as the combined area of Devon and Cornwall and half of Somerset. To give just two more comparisons: the National Trust in England and Wales, owns some 550,000 acres, while the Crown estates measure just 384,000 acres. Ralegh and his friends were rewarding themselves with empires hewn from other men's lands by other men's efforts. Neither were monopolies on the extractive industries neglected: Sir Thomas Gerard was promised two-fifths of the profit from all the gold, silver, pearl and precious stones extracted from the settlement, which gave him, as it turned out, two-fifths of nothing to increase his fortune. This proposed greedy land grab again illustrates that the English were planning, badly, an invasion of Virginia. Estates of the size being offered covered lands already occupied by native peoples; the English could only claim them as their own by seizing these peoples' land and imposing their own land grant laws above that of the traditional authority.

For Ralegh, the requirement to have established settlements within six years of his Charter being granted must have seemed at the time just a legal technicality until, after Lane's colony withdrew in 1586 and White's was finally reported missing in 1590, it looked as if its term was ending. Desperate to retain his generous award, Ralegh needed to prove both that he had settlers alive in America and that he would confront any who tried to flout his authority. Thus, in 1602, he not only had Samuel Mace seek to make contact with the lost colonists but also wrote a note to Sir Robert Cecil, demanding that the cargo of sassafras landed from the returning *Concord*, following the voyage to North Virginia by Bartholomew Gilbert and Bartholomew Gosnold that same year, be impounded as infringing his monopoly. Then, realizing that he might be on shaky ground, he used his justly famous silver-tongued flattery to persuade John Brereton, who wrote the account of the Gosnold voyage, to dedicate his book to him and to include a note which stated, erroneously, that the voyage had been made 'by the permission of the honourable knight, Sir Walter Ralegh' – a tacit reminder of Ralegh's suzerainty.

This was Ralegh's last effort to retain his Charter rights. In March 1603 his Queen was dead. In July he was placed in the Tower to answer charges of treason. In November he was tried and sentenced to death. Only King James's cunning clemency granted him a stay of execution long enough to have him embroiled in a voyage to Guiana in 1617, the failure of which would finally lead him to the block. Among those who passed judgment at his first trial were Sir Robert Cecil, Sir John Popham, the Lord Chief Justice, and Sir Edward Coke, the Attorney General. A cynic might see some link in the fact that it is their names which are associated with the drafting of the first Charter for Virginia in April 1606, at a time when Ralegh had been in the Tower long enough to be either no longer a disruptive force or a man with any public following. Nevertheless, his shadow fell on the deliberations, for, among the eight suitors to be named in the Charter were Raleigh Gilbert and William Parker, respectively a relative and a servant of Sir Walter, who it can be presumed were included to avoid any outbreak of unpleasantness.

The continuing issue of Charters so early in James's reign is a cause for some surprise since the King's major foreign policy was to secure peace with Spain and not to go to war again. Yet he was content not only to sign a potentially contentious document but also to remain resolute in the face of Spanish objections. One reason for his support of this new venture was that, in the years since Ralegh's failure at Roanoke, many English merchants and speculators had learned more about the potential opportunities that America might offer. In the north, fishing, furs and forestry seemed available for exploitation, while in the south the climate could encourage the planting of crops traditionally imported from the Mediterranean, as well as offering a chance to increase the acreage the nation had devoted to industrial crops such as flax and hemp and silk, a special favourite of the King. Thus began a fault line between an extractive north and an agricultural south, which would be emphasized in the Charter of 1606 and finally shear into the earthquake of 1861. Back in 1606, however, what investors hoped to find within this landscape was mineral wealth and a navigable route to 'nearby' Cathay.

In England, the north–south divide of Virginia was reflected in an east–west divide of investors in the first Charter for Virginia, with West Country merchants of Bristol, Plymouth and Exeter being granted the right to settle and exploit the land lying between 38° and 45° North, that is from Chesapeake Bay to present-day Bangor, Maine, while London businessmen were offered the bloc between 34° and 41° North, from Cape Fear to Manhattan Island. The obvious overlap seems to have been inserted to encourage competition and expansion, but even within their exclusive boundaries the two companies established to manage the colonies were only given control of a square of territory stretching fifty miles either side of any settlement and a hundred miles inland, as well as the adjoining seas out to the same distance.

The two colonies thus created were to be organized by two separate companies that would be overseen by a royal council of thirteen members appointed by the King and named the Council for Virginia, which would include four representatives of both sub-groups.

The Charter named eight individual suitors; four West Countrymen for the northern plantation and four Londoners for the southern one. Their names and backgrounds are indicative of the purpose and development of the nascent colonies. The link with the jailed Ralegh remains even here, and there can be little doubt that the noxious Wade was present to act as a spy on the 'shepherd of the sea' now locked up ashore.

Suitors for Licence to Establish a Colony in Virginia, 1606

	Name	Background	Remarks
Northern Colony	Raleigh Gilbert		Son of Sir Humphrey Gilbert
	William Parker	Privateer	Ex-servant of Walter Ralegh
	George Popham	Privateer	Nephew of Sir John Popham
	Thomas Hanham	Lawyer	Grandson of Sir John Popham
Southern Colony	Richard Hakluyt	Writer and publicist	
	Sir Thomas Gates	Soldier	
	Edward Wingfield	Soldier	Related to Gosnold
	Sir George Somers, MP	Privateer	

Excluded by name are the 'divers others of our loving subjects', which probably encompassed Sir Robert Cecil, by now Lord Salisbury.

Members of the Council for Virginia

	Name	Background	Remarks
Londoners	Sir Thomas Smythe	Merchant	
	Sir William Romney	Merchant	
	John Eldred	Merchant	Ex-privateer
	Sir Walter Cope		Close associate of Lord Salisbury
	Sir George More		
	Sir William Wade	Lieutenant of the Tower	Ralegh's jailer
	Sir Henry Montagu	Lawyer	
West Country group	James Bagg	Ex-privateer	
	Thomas James	Ex-privateer	
	John Doddridge	Ex-privateer	Solicitor General
	Sir Ferdinando Gorges		Ralegh's cousin but supporter of his rival, Essex
	Sir Francis Popham		Son of Sir John Popham
	Thomas Warre		Grandson of Sir John Popham
	Sir John Trevor		

Unlike Ralegh before them, many of these investors did risk their own lives to gain their reward. Of the eight grantees named in the 1606 Charter of Virginia, Sir Thomas Gates, Sir George Somers and Edward-Maria Wingfield sailed to Jamestown, while Raleigh Gilbert and George Popham established the short-lived northern colony. Later, in 1628, George Calvert tried to settle in Newfoundland, where he had been granted extensive charter lands. Thus there was an attempt to lead by example and endure with equanimity the hardships that those they had almost conned into taking passage had to face with uncertain support from their backers. Their misfortune was that they were, for the most part, not able to command that which they had created.

The Jacobean Charters continued the tradition of awarding a generous grant of resources, which, of course, were not the king's to give, allowing the settlers to 'have all the lands, woods, soil, grounds, havens, ports, rivers, mines, minerals, woods, waters, marshes, fishings, commodities, and hereditaments, whatsoever, from the said place of their first plantation . . .'

Among the minerals expressly mentioned, copper, after it was reported as being much used by the native Amerindians, joined gold and silver as being one of the minerals for whose extraction the Crown required a percentage payment. The overwhelming desire for gold was nowhere more evident than in the change of plan for Frobisher's northern voyages, for no sooner had he returned from his first expedition in 1576 with a lump of black rock, than the search for a route to Cathay was abandoned in favour of gathering vast quantities of this worthless stone. The resulting attempt to establish a settlement near Baffin Island in 1578 might have been doomed, but the 100 people who were selected to form this early English colony in the new world were wisely chosen as far as their trade was concerned. They included forty seamen, thirty miners and thirty soldiers, all under the command of Edward Fenton. Luckily circumstances enabled them to avoid trying to endure the unendurable – an Arctic winter – but the mix of skills is hard to fault. This was not so in Virginia.

The 1606 first Charter for Virginia had within its framework the seeds for success, which were encouragingly watered by the issue, the following November, of *Instructions for Government*, which were enforced in December by *Orders for the Council for Virginia*, which assigned ships and their captains, to whom were issued sealed orders. However, at the same time, the London Council for Virginia issued *Instructions Given by way of Advice . . . for the Intended Voyage to Virginia to Be Observed by those Captains and Company which Are Sent at This Present to Plant*. This proved to be the inhibitor for the southern group, for it moved away from the simple aim of establishing a successful colony that would export what it was able to glean, to one which was to have, amongst several aims, the requirement for further exploration, specifically to find a way to the 'Other Sea', the Pacific Ocean, and to search for gold. It was in choosing to follow rivers that might lead to this mythical route that the colonists lost their way. The error they imported is obvious from the text which, assuming they numbered 120 and not the 104 that disembarked, required forty of them to build the fort and protect the settlement, thirty to clear and plant, ten to man a watchtower at the river entrance and forty to spend two months in exploring the route to the Pacific. In commanding this division the Council failed to appreciate several things: the challenges that the settlers would meet; the priorities that would be imposed by their circumstance; the nature and size of the terrain on which they would disembark and, probably most significant of all, the composition of the force that they would require to secure their beachhead. Records of the known occupation of some 240 of the 295 individuals who arrived in Virginia before October 1608 show that they included, *inter alia*: 119 gentlemen, forty-seven labourers, fifteen artisans, seven tailors, four carpenters and four surgeons, some 'boys', and a cooper, a couple of blacksmiths, brickies and refiners, two apothecaries, a gunsmith, a fishmonger and a fisherman, and several other individual specialists among whom was the most remarkable defensive inadequacy of an army captain, a sergeant, a soldier and a drummer.

Reading the above list of occupations one might interpret it as representing those present at a gentlemen's club picnic outing to an area where it had been rumoured some unruly behaviour had been reported but where it was still intended to construct a barbecue and spend some time choosing a selection of local valuables to take home as trinkets to pacify absent wives. In fact, as far as Jamestown was concerned, the majority of the gentlemen were a burden in several ways; firstly, they would not labour; secondly, they needed to be fed, and thirdly, they spent time in fractious intrigues that made a mockery of governance.

The contrast with the establishment proposed by the anonymous wellwisher of 1584 for Ralegh's Roanoke voyage, which laid down the trades necessary to be deployed, is all the more remarkable not only because it was again ignored but also because no lessons had been learned from the failures of 1577, 1578, 1585 and 1587. No one, it seems, drew up a profile of the ideal group necessary for establishing a colony and then sought to recruit the skills indicated. Instead, a disparate collection of motley, unhardened, untested and disunited individuals were dispatched to their doom. Had the Charter, or even the *Advice*, laid down the trades required and told the leaders to concentrate on establishing a settlement before any other activity, the result might have been less tragic and more successful.

When it became obvious, after a short while, that the northern Virginian enterprise had failed and that the southern one was not going to reward its investors in accordance with their expectations, a second Charter was drawn up, in 1609, by the King 'at the humble suit and request of sundry of our loving and well-disposed subjects'. If the first Charter failed to deliver mainly through its application rather than its text, the same could not be said of the second, which is one of the most over-optimistic pieces of paper ever penned in that, although it established a far better form of government for the settlers themselves, it created a vast joint-stock company, eager to benefit from the output of the plantation. Although not as stark as a death warrant, it was one of the longest assisted suicide notes in history, killing with kindness and an indigestible surfeit.

The kindness came with the land grant. Whereas the first Charter had granted land within fifty miles either side of the initial settlement and stretching up to a hundred miles inland, the second Charter was far less restrictive, offering the settlers dominion from sea to sea, stating:

we do also of our special Grace . . . give, grant and confirm, unto the said Treasurer and Company, and their Successors . . . all those Lands, Countries, and Territories, situate, lying, and being in that Part of America, called Virginia, from the Point of Land, called Cape or Pointe Comfort all along the sea coast to the northward two hundred miles and from the said Point or Cape Comfort all along the sea coast to the southward two hundred miles; and all that space and circuit of land lying from the sea coast of the precinct aforesaid up unto the land, throughout, from sea to sea, west and northwest; and also all the islands being within one hundred miles along the coast of both seas of the precinct aforesaid.

These boundaries encompassed the lands explored and mapped by John Smith but also kept alive the idea that somewhere in their inner regions lay the much-sought route to the Pacific.

The surfeit was created by the number of individuals and organizations who were encouraged to invest in the enterprise – pages of them. This multitude consisted of 659 individuals and 56 London livery companies as well as a number of the settlers themselves, all of whom invested in a share, or shares, worth £12 10s, or multiples thereof, a not insignificant sum, the attraction of which was partly based on the erroneous report by the returning Captain Newport that gold had been discovered in Virginia. Among those recruited to purchase stock were eight earls, one viscount, one bishop, five lords, seventy-two knights and thirty-nine naval captains, as well as the usual crowd of gentlemen and esquires. Among the guilds were the Grocers, Brewers, Fishmongers, Tallow-Chandlers, Masons, Plumbers, Brownbakers, Carpenters, Haberdashers, Gardeners, Ironmongers and Barber-Surgeons, many of whose members, if they travelled, would have had practical skills to offer the settlers; while some, such as the Company of Goldsmiths, had skills desired but unwarranted. The take-up was oversubscribed for what was on offer and included both the stay-at-homes and adventurers willing to travel towards a better life. Those who chose to venture across to Virginia were offered, for their one share, after seven years' labour, a grant of land and a share of the profit from 'such mines and minerals of gold, silver, and other metal or treasure . . . or profits whatsoever which shall be obtained'.

A clear indication that the investors realized, too late, that they were not on to a good thing, can be read in the third Charter of 1611, which stated that the Company had:

power and authority to expulse, disfranchise, and put out from their said Company and Society for ever, all and every such person and persons, as having been promised or subscribed their names to becoming adventurers to the said Plantation, of the said first Colony of Virginia, or having been nominated for Adventures in these or any other of our Letters Patent, or having been otherwise admitted and nominated to be of the said company, have nevertheless either not put in any adventure at all for and towards the said Plantation, or else have refused or neglected, or shall refuse and neglect to bring his or their Adventure, by word or writing, promised within six months after the same shall be so payable and due. And, whereas the failing and nonpayment of such monies as have been promised in Adventure, for the advancement of the said Plantation, hath been often by experience found to be dangerous and prejudicial to the same, and much hindered the progress and proceeding of the said Plantation, and for that it seemeth to us a thing most reasonable, that such persons, as by their hand writing have engaged themselves for the payment of their adventures and after have neglected their faith and promise, should be compelled to make good and keep the same; therefore, our will and pleasure is, that any suit or suits commenced, or to be commenced in any of our Courts of Westminster, or elsewhere, by the said Treasurer and Company, or otherwise against any such persons, that our judges for the time being . . . do favour and further the said suits so far as law and equity will in any wise further and permit.

This was a longwinded way of advertising the fact that the Company was in trouble: it would certainly not have been able to argue its case should a seventeenth-century credit agency have removed its AAA rating, if it had ever warranted one. Michael Lok, the Treasurer of the Cathay Company in 1578, had found himself in a similar position as far as non-payment of promised investment was concerned but, lacking the robust endorsement of his sovereign, it was he and not they who went to prison. The long quotation above serves to illustrate that the Charters were not just a means whereby the Crown gave and granted rights to a 'suit of divers and sundry loving subjects' but that they also served as a business prospectus to attract adventurers. For the most part their lengthy verbiage did not lead to long lines of emigrants queuing at the docks or investors' carriages rolling into the City. Those people that did not go did not ignore a golden opportunity for, by staying away, the probability is that they either, in the case of voyagers, saved their lives, or, in the case of investors, kept their savings. It was, in the modern jargon, a no-brainer.

The first settler groups that had landed at Jamestown had been about the size of a small English village, such as Scrooby in Lincolnshire, from where William Brewster and many of the Pilgrim Father separatists hailed. From the sweat of their brow the households of such villages had to support themselves and, probably, the lord of the manor and his family, and the local priest, while a few artisans, millers, blacksmiths and thatchers provided support either of a fixed or seasonal nature. Thus, in such communities, the majority worked the land and produced a sufficient surplus to feed a few more mouths than were hungrily opened by their own family, for it was an age of both feast and famine. Most of these communities were not entirely self-sufficient. Markets had to be visited to buy some items, while itinerants offered both extra labour when required, and additional skills when desired. Surplus? There was little or none and yet, from Virginia, such a village was meant to reward thousands!

THE CONVERSION OF SOULS

Queen Elizabeth famously stated that, as far as religion was concerned, she did not wish to have a window into men's souls. She may have well included the 'heathen' in this rubric because, despite the emphasis that both Richard Hakluyts placed on the idea that 'this western discovery will be greatly for the enlargement of the gospel', such an aim did not feature in her Charters. It was present in those awarded by King James but the emphasis varied over time. Thus in the first Charter of Virginia of 1606, paragraph three stated:

We, greatly commending and graciously accepting of, their desire for the furtherance of such noble work, which may through the providence of Almighty God, glorify his Divine Majesty, in propagating the Christian Religion to such people that live in darkness and miserable ignorance of the knowledge and worship of God, and may in time civilize, the infidels and savages, living in those parts, to live in settled and quiet government . . .

In the lengthy and businesslike Charter of 1609, this requirement was moved to the very end, where it set down: 'Lastly, because the principal effect which we always desire or expect of this action is the conversion and reduction of the native people to the worship of God and the Christianity . . . we should be loathe that any person should be permitted to pass that we suspected to affect the superstitions of the Church of Rome . . .'

Of the two aims it was probably the latter to which the King held most dear. Having managed to wind two threads together, James did likewise in the 1620 Charter of New England, in which he linked the abandonment of the land by the native population (in fact due to the ravages of imported disease) to the need for their conversion:

those large and bountiful regions, deserted by their natural inhabitants, should be possessed and enjoyed by such of our subjects and people who . . . are directed hither . . . that we may boldly go to the settling of so hopeful a work which will lead to the reduction and conversion of such savages as remain wandering in desolation and distress, to civilization.

By the time that Charles I awarded a royal patent to the Massachusetts Bay Company, in 1629, the proselytizing mission had been amended. No longer was there to be a mission of conversion but the guiding text, at least within the Charter, seems to have been Matthew 5:16. 'Let your light so shine before men that they may see your good works and glorify your Father which is in heaven.' This was transliterated into the Charter in the form: 'whereby our people inhabiting there, may be so religiously, peaceably, and civilly governed, as their good life and orderly conversation, may win and encourage the natives to the knowledge and obedience of the one true God and saviour of Mankind and the Christian faith . . .'

This was the Company whose very seal depicted a naked savage imploring, in the words of Saint Paul's Macedonian, 'Come over and Help us.' The Christians who answered that call came over and helped themselves, aided by the grants graciously bestowed upon them by their sovereign. What the 'natives of the country' received were bullets rather than Bibles.

The Virginia Company made sure that, as far as its public face was concerned, it behaved in a way appropriate to the royal wishes and so it was careful to issue with its propaganda an argument to persuade the morally squeamish that the settlements could only improve the lot of the natives from whom no land would be taken unfairly. To this end it commissioned the Reverend Robert Gray to write a book entitled *A Good Speed to Virginia*, which was published on 28 April 1609, just a month before the Charter was issued, and which assured its readers that, although:

Massachusetts Bay Company seal. The apotheosis of hypocrisy: the Indian's plaintive call for help was a travesty of the treatment that they were to receive.

The report goeth, that in Virginia the people are savage and incredibly rude, they worship the devil, offer their young children in sacrifice unto him, wander up and down like beasts, and in manners and conditions, differ very little from beasts, having no Art, nor science, nor trade, to employ themselves, or give themselves unto, yet by nature loving and, gentle, and desirous to embrace a better condition. Oh how happy were that man which could reduce this people from brutishness, to civility, to religion, to Christianity, to the saving of their souls: happy is that man and blest of God, whom God hath endued, either with means or will to attempt this business, but far be it from the nature of the English, to exercise any bloody cruelty amongst these people: far be it from the hearts of the English, to give them occasion, that the holy name of God, should be dishonoured among the Infidels, or that in the plantation of that continent,

Serendipitous geology led the Spanish to find gold where the landed in the new world. The English refused to believe that they too would not discover similar wealth and chose to ignore the evidence of its absence in the ores with which their ships' holds were filled. (National Maritime Museum)

they should give any cause to the world, to say that they sought the wealth of that country above or before the glory of God, and the propagation of his kingdom.

Yet, hidden from the public view, the Virginia Company, in 1609, informed the temporary Governor, Sir Thomas Gates, that his four priorities were:

1. To discover either a route to the Pacific or gold mines.
2. To establish trade with distant ports.
3. To exact tribute [i.e. forced payment in goods by the natives].
4. To establish local exporting industries such as glass-making.

The first of these remained the enervating chimera that John Smith railed against Christopher Newport for investing so much impractical energy. Newport had not only

Examples of the ores brought back by Frobisher erroneously thought to contain gold.
(National Maritime Museum)

tried to portage a great boat over the James Falls at modern Richmond but had ordered
the settlers to stop work on building houses and planting crops so that everyone might
fossick for gold. 'There was no talk, no hope, no work but dig gold, wash gold, refine
gold, load gold,' wrote Anas Todkill, while Smith himself in a memorable phrase spoke
of 'Freighting a drunken ship with gilded dirt'. As with Frobisher's efforts before, the
investors chose to ignore Newport's assayed failure and continued to press for the
ground to be opened up to yield its non-existent riches. Acting as an entrepôt was also
an impractical aim as long as Spain retained its adamantine opposition to any English
settlement in the Americas.

The third priority represented a major geopolitical move. When he had returned
to Virginia in 1608, Christopher Newport carried out the Company's instructions by
forcing a crown upon Powhatan's head and presenting him with a double bed by way
of acknowledging his regal status, while Powhatan confirmed his view of his position
by stating that, 'If your king has sent me presents, I also am a king, and this is my
land,' although his return gift of a second-hand pair of worn-out moccasins and a cloak
might have just implied what the local ruler thought of this imposed relationship. Now
the Company wanted to dispense with and dispel such hypocritical niceties: Powhatan
was to be taken captive and forced to pay tribute while lesser chiefs would be forced to
acknowledge King James's overlordship. This was conquest in the Norman style, with
each tribe being required to provide corn at every harvest and to labour weekly for the
English. Feudalism, dying out in England, was to be re-established in America. It did

not take hold, but from its failing sprang up a greater evil – slavery. At the time of the 1609 Charter, however, the secret orders guaranteed war where peace was the most important policy.

Outside the excavated remains of Jamestown the modern visitor can see a line of low-lying grassy banks which mark the houses and workshops of the artisans who were brought to Virginia to establish the settlement's export industry. A short distance away down an old track is the remains of the glass works. A large mulberry tree also hints at early hopes of a silk-weaving industry: the fact that it was the wrong sort of mulberry for silk worms is an arboreal indication of the lack of planning that went into meeting Gates's fourth target, which Smith also condemned by pointing out that the Baltic lands were far better able to export that which the investors demanded. Thus each instruction carried with it the seeds of failure and it was not until the settlers themselves decided to grow tobacco, or in the case of New England export furs, that commercial success ensued.

When the initial enthusiasm for shares diminished in the light of no quick return the Virginia Company hit upon another wheeze, which the King backed by the issue of the third Charter of Virginia in March 1611. This authorized a lottery to be held. With a first prize of £1,000, it proved to be an instant success and once more the coffers of the Company, but not the pockets of the investors, were filled.

The continuing failure of Virginia to deliver a sizeable and reliable return rekindled interest in the northern plantation, now renamed New England. Although this had been abandoned in 1608, interest in the area had remained because of both the great catches of fish netted from the waters off Maine and the proselytizing work of John Smith, who had published his work *A Description of New England* to encourage re-colonization, a venture in which he wished to play a key role. In March 1619 the King was presented with a somewhat grovelling and self-justifying, but short, petition for a new Charter of New England. By 3 November of that year the lengthy, fairly indigestible, Charter had been written and promulgated. Its main point was that it remained a West Country initiative, uncoupled from the arrangement with its London twin.

Those who still viewed the expanding world as one in which privateering had a part to play could also see value in retaining a settlement in Newfoundland, especially if the Government were charged 'to maintain a couple of good ships and two pinnaces in warlike manner upon the coast', for the sites selected lay not too far off the route home from the West Indies and were also a convenient halfway port of call for vessels bound for Virginia. St John's had, of course, been claimed for the Crown by Humphrey Gilbert, but the Charter of 1610, which awarded the whole island to the London and Bristol Company, did not mention this fact. Instead it attempted to link London capital with Bristol experience to create a going concern based on managing the fisheries and, that inevitable chimera, mining for gold and other precious metals. However, the company had learned from the obvious errors committed by its Virginia forerunner. In particular the first settlers sent out to Newfoundland were mainly labourers, fishermen and people with practical skills who were instructed to settle away from swampy ground, to keep busy and to establish good relations with the few native people that they encountered in this land 'so desolate of inhabitance'. The governor selected was also not an untested 'gentleman' but an experienced merchant who knew this new world well enough. The flaw in the Newfoundland Charter was the belief held by both propagandists and investors that settlement could create added value to the already efficient offshore fishing industry. It could not, nor could a land where survival alone was challenging enough provide a return to shareholders. Gradually, the latter, along with the gentlemen adventurers, moved away, but the labourers stayed. They needed no Charter to continue to eke out a living for they had sufficient land that they could call their own to support a family in freedom. Harsh as it undoubtedly was, many of them had more to lose by leaving than they would gain by remaining. More limpet than tree root, they clung on and survived.

The Charter for Nova Scotia, issued in September 1621, granted almost sovereign powers to Sir William Alexander over a tract of land stretching between Newfoundland and Maine which had previously been known by the French name of Acadia. In a supplementary document the King gave his reasons for making the grant as:

> Having ever been ready to embrace any good occasion whereby the honour or profit of our Kingdom may be advanced, and considering that no kind of conquest can be more easy and innocent than that which proceeds from plantations specially in a country commodious for men to live in, yet remaining altogether desert or at least only inhabited by infidels the conversion of whom to the Christian faith (intended by this means) might tend much to the glory of God considering how populous our Kingdom (Scotland) is at this present and the necessity that idle people should be employed, preventing worse courses there are many that might be spared, of minds as resolute and of bodies as able to overcome the difficulties that such adventures must at first encounter the enterprise doth crave the transportation of nothing but only men, women, cattle, and victuals, and not of money, and may give a good return of a new trade at this time when traffic is so much decayed. Therefore we have the more willingly hearkened to Sir William Alexander who has made choice of lands lying between New England and Newfoundland, both the Governors whereof have encouraged him thereunto . . .

It is a succinct summary of all the reasons for plantation that had appeared in earlier Charters.

When, as had happened in earlier Charters, Alexander found that he could not persuade sufficient 'idle people' to head out to the commodious lands, and, finding that the enterprise was in need of money, he hit upon the ingenious idea of offering land for honours, centuries before Lloyd George, and later politicians, saw that titles were saleable assets. He persuaded the King to create a new order of twenty-two barons, each of whom would hold titles in Nova Scotia. The estates that accompanied the titles covered up to 12,000 acres each and were available for the down payment of 1,000 marks and the dispatch of six settlers.

But sextets wishing to sail for what was in reality a scheme to restore Sir William's fortunes were not readily available and, apart from a military expedition to hold the land against prior French claims, little was achieved between the issue of the Charter and 1631 when, by treaty, the land was returned to France.

Ironically the Christian religion, or the zealously guarded Anglican version of it, delayed the departure of many who might have been expected to apply the

high-minded desire of spreading the gospel which had been expressed in the
Charters. Stuart England had a growing number of minority creeds, ranging from
the sizeable old Catholic families to the newer Puritans and other dissenters. Many
of these welcomed the opportunity to emigrate to the new world, where they were
quite prepared to work as communities to establish viable settlements, provided that
they were guaranteed freedom to worship. This King James was not prepared to allow,
being influenced most understandably by the Catholic Gunpowder Plot of 1605. Both
the 1609 and 1620 Charters included a paragraph that stated:

> because the principal effect which we can desire or expect from this action, is the
> conversion and reduction of the people in those parts, to the true worship of God
> and the Christian religion, we should be loath that any person should be permitted
> to take passage that we suspect to affect the superstitions of the Church of Rome, we
> therefore declare that it is our will and pleasure that none be permitted to pass in any
> voyage which from time to time be made to that Country, but such as have taken the
> Oath of Supremacy . . .

The paragraph went on to state that the Company and appointed officials could
demand of any settler that they swear the oath of allegiance and acknowledge the Act
of Supremacy. Not even the most illustrious could ignore this ruling.

In 1629, Sir George Calvert, Baron Baltimore and an out-of-the-closet Catholic,
cruising the American coast with his wife and family in search of a site for a settlement
more in keeping with his requirements than he had discovered Newfoundland to be, put
in to Jamestown. Here he was asked to take the oath, in accordance with the Charter,
but refused to do so, after which he departed in haste for England, leaving his family
behind. Once back at Court he did what the Virginians suspected that he would do,
and persuaded King Charles I to grant him a Charter for the future Maryland, carved
out of territory that the Virginians believed to be their own. When Charles published
the Charter it proclaimed Cecilius Calvert, Baltimore's son and heir, to be a person who
possessed 'laudable and pious zeal for the propagation of the Christian faith'.

The trials and tribulations of dissenters proposing to settle in New England were
to be famously overcome and in a way that demonstrated that the days of the royal
Charter were numbered. America had not yet sent out a cry to be given England's
huddled masses, and dissenting illegal and penniless exiles were not obvious shoo-
ins for one of the parcels of land, called hundreds, which the Virginia Company was
trying to sell. Yet, few other pre-formed communities showed willing to travel across
the Atlantic to an uncertain future, and even King James indicated that, although he
would not approve, neither would he obstruct the passage of Puritans to the new world.

Thus, after much turmoil, misunderstanding and/or double-crossing, the *Mayflower*
passengers pioneered the passage of people of faith. They did so as part of a new
London-based joint-stock company, the indenturing terms of which they were still
arguing over as they sailed. Yet, having managed to depart from Plymouth, charterless,
on the day of the first disembarkation at Provincetown, Cape Cod, they produced a
document, far shorter and much more useful than any Charter, which would reform
not only the whole manner under which such ventures would be undertaken in future,

but the way that incoming communities would regard themselves – less servility more self-worth. The *Mayflower* Compact must surely rate as the shortest revolutionary document ever scribed. Not that it appears, at first reading, to deserve that accolade, but what it introduced into the settlements for the first time was the concept of 'mutuality' and local democracy. Gone is the governing structure imposed from abroad, relying on the presence of 'gentlemen'; gone is the desire to grub up the earth for gold or to seek for ways to Cathay; gone is the overarching requirement to create wealth for absentee investors; gone, in a word, is greed.

> In the name of God, Amen. We whose names are under-written, the loyal subjects of our dread sovereign Lord, King James, by the grace of God, of Great Britain, France, and Ireland King, Defender of the Faith, etc.
>
> Having undertaken, for the glory of God, and advancement of the Christian faith, and honour of our King and Country, a voyage to plant the first colony in the northern parts of Virginia, do by these presents solemnly and mutually, in the presence of God, and one of another, covenant and combine ourselves together into a civil body politic, for our better ordering and preservation and furtherance of the ends aforesaid; and by virtue hereof to enact, constitute, and frame such just and equal laws, ordinances, acts, constitutions and offices, from time to time, as shall be thought most meet and convenient for the general good of the Colony, unto which we promise all due submission and obedience. In witness whereof we have hereunder subscribed our names at Cape Cod, the eleventh of November in the year of the reign of our sovereign lord, King James, of England, France, and Ireland, the eighteenth, and of Scotland the fifty-fourth. Anno Dom. 1620.

The very brevity and simplicity of the Compact make it a truly American text. The English Court was just not capable of such incisiveness: its Charters rolled on for page after page, often repeating the same lists and phrases. The Compact, in its entirety, was shorter than the part-paragraph of the third Virginia Charter quoted above, covering just the one topic of defaulting payments. On 11 November 1620, off Cape Cod, American public prose spoke its first words and what this infant Hercules chose to say was short, precise and clearly understandable. It was to remain so. The Bill of Rights, the Declaration of Independence, the Gettysburg Address and many more seminal documents are, in their clarity and pithiness, descendants of the style adopted in the Compact. And, like the Charters it superseded, the Compact had a dual role, for the fact that all the settlers signed it ensured it would be nailed to the door of democracy through which, eventually, all who entered the new world would pass.

Down in Virginia change was also afoot. In April 1619 Sir George Yeardley, the new Governor arrived under instruction to reform its dysfunctional governance. He started by abolishing the ghastly 'Laws Divine, Moral and Martial' and in their place established democracy, or almost. London retained control by appointing the six members of the Council of Estate but below this was established an Assembly whose twenty-two members were to be elected, two from each of the eleven settlements that lay along the James River. 'Two from each' – a form of representative government which exists in America to this day.

A mixture of fantasy (the mermaids) and reality (the Amerindian dwellings) are shown in this depiction of Walter Ralegh's mythical welcome to the new world. Both fact and fiction needed to be employed to convince would-be settlers to emigrate; neither was a powerful enough persuasion on its own. (National Maritime Museum)

Thus in the space of one year a youthful, but differing, form of democracy was introduced into both halves of English America. However, like twins separated at birth by their original Charter into 'two several Colonies and Companies', Virginia and New England were to adopt different and divergent outlooks on life so that, like characters from the Bible, which they both held in high regard, they would commit matricide and fratricide until, war weary, they came together 'one nation under God, indivisible, with liberty, and justice for all'.

There was one more step needed before the weight of the Charters could be lifted off the colonists' backs, and this came about when it was agreed that the Massachusetts Bay settlement should be self-administered, which removed the need to meet the unrealistic expectations for a return on capital held by English-based shareholders.

The great difference between the founding Charters and their new world successors was not the belief in God, the ideal of liberty and the concept of justice, not even the pursuit of happiness, but that settlers could choose what enterprise to pursue and that, taxes to one side, the wealth which they gleaned from their labours would be theirs to retain within the boundaries of the land which they now considered to be their own. However, after over a century of deployment, those arriving in the new world would still have to conquer before they enjoyed their land in comfort.

In England, King James had lived up to his sobriquet of being 'the wisest fool in Christendom'. Sandwiched between the fame of his predecessor, Elizabeth, and the fate of his successor, Charles I, this monarch, with his unhygienic personal habits and strange vices, has not been accorded the accolades deserved by the man who established the British Empire and had commanded the Authorized Version of the Bible to be translated and distributed. His wisdom is very apparent, even within the extremely verbose American Charters, for most of the near-fatal errors that affected the colonies were introduced by the Companies and not the King. The peculiar method of appointing and electing the original Council of Virginia, the emphasis on seeking for gold, the time spent in looking for a passage to the Pacific, the coronation of Powhatan, the demand for goods – all stemmed from the investors' greed and not the King's grant. In one thing only was James unhelpful, and that was in his objection to the 'noxious weed', tobacco, the production of which saved Virginia. Yet, even here, history might uphold the wisdom of the King: tobacco was to kill more of his successors' subjects than ever did the Amerindians.

For as long as he felt able so to do, James indulged the Virginia Company and its investors, even altering their Charter: to impose better government; to provide more opportunities for settlers; to pursue bad debts; to include Bermuda, and, through its lottery, provide additional ways of raising money. In return he had seen nothing but bad management, bankruptcy and great loss of life. When the latter made headline news with the report of the massacre of 1622, the King was minded no longer to reform but to revoke. Following his reading of Nathaniel Butler's exposé of Virginia at the time of the massacre, the critical views of which were independently supported by advisors whom he trusted, the King ordered, in May 1623, a Crown Commission to be established to investigate the Company's affairs. There could only be one result, and on 24 May 1624 the Virginia Company's Charter was revoked.

One year later, on 13 May 1625, the new King, Charles I, declared that:

> to the end there may be one uniform course of Government in and through our Whole Monarchy, that the Government of the Colony of Virginia shall immediately depend upon Our Self, and not be committed to any Company or Corporation, to whom it may be proper to trust matters of Trade and Commerce, but cannot be fit or safe to communicate the ordering of State-Affairs, be they of never so mean consequence.

The age of the private Company had ended; the age of the royal colony had begun.

There are two Charters that are seldom mentioned among those that affected the development of English America. The first was the one which, on 31 December 1600, incorporated the British East India Company. Although many of the voyages that took place under its auspices ended tragically, the ships that returned safe home swamped the market with cloves, peppers, silks and saltpetre. When, in 1609, the books were closed on the combined results from this Company's first two voyages, a profit of 95 per cent was declared. Nothing exported from Virginia could match that until tobacco became a major crop and furs a valuable catch. Certainly ship masts, staves, clapboard and sassafras could not compete. Those with money to invest – and many people, like Sir Thomas Smythe, were active in both the Virginia and the East India Companies – were far more likely to consider that, despite the shipwrecks and the seizures, trading voyages to the East Indies offered a better return on capital than did settler ships sailing to America. Nothing came of the other Charter, issued to Sir Robert Heath in 1629, but it is of note because it granted to this friend of King Charles the land lying between 31° and 36° North, the Carolinas, stretching well towards the region previously jealously and murderously protected by Spain (St Augustine was only sixty miles further south). As a statement of confidence in colonialism it would be hard to beat but, as it was never acted upon, it was never contended.

The Charters had been the unique way by which the English sovereign apportioned the new world to his or her subjects. It was a formulaic patent with little difference between that awarded to John Cabot in 1496 and that granted to Sir Robert Heath in 1629. All emphasized conquest, occupation and conversion. At the end of that long century a few square miles were occupied but not fully controlled, let alone conquered, and a few 'barbarous men' had been converted. The Charters presented to Cabot, Gilbert, Ralegh, Alexander, Heath and the northern Virginia Colony had come to nought; the three issued to the Virginia Company of London had proved unworkable; that for Maine, issued to Gorges and Mason, had led to a few huts being erected; Newfoundland would have struggled on without a Charter, as would have the settlement at Plymouth, while Massachusetts Bay guaranteed its success by taking the paperwork with it. Neither did the Charters of themselves address the needs of the invasion period about which its language was so up-beat. They were documents designed to ensure a quick return for the petitioners, not operational orders for invading and occupation forces. They should have been.

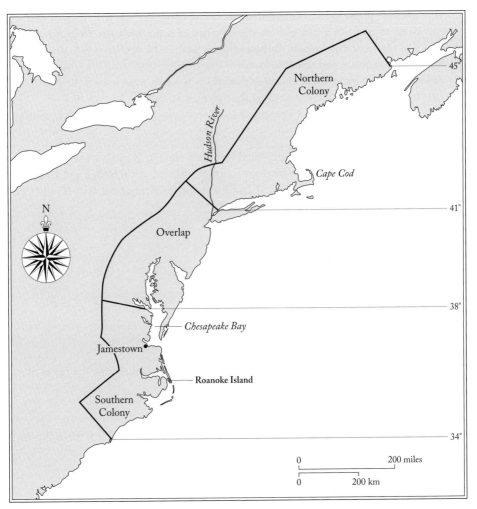

N

45°

Northern
Colony

Hudson River

Cape Cod

41°

Overlap

38°

Chesapeake Bay

Jamestown

Roanoke Island

Southern
Colony

34°

| 0 | 200 miles |
| 0 | 200 km |

Map 2: The division of Virginia under the First Charter, 1606

CHAPTER 4

Planning and Site Selection

When it shall please God to send you on the coast of Virginia, you shall do your best endeavour to find out a safe port in the entrance of some navigable river, making choice of such a one as runneth farthest into the land, and if you happen to discover divers portable rivers, and amongst them any one that hath two main branches, if the difference be not great, make choice of that which bendeth most toward the North-west for that way you shall soonest find the other sea.

Virginia Company of London, *Instructions by Way of Advice*, 1606

The English could plan competently, succinctly and clearly. They also had many who were prepared to offer detailed advice such as that directed at Frobisher and Lok, and all who wished to make *A Discovery of Lands Beyond the Equinoctial*, which indicated that any such should know:

1. The task before him.
2. That it was feasible.
3. Know what means he has available to achieve his aim (the ships, skilled navigators, trading opportunities).
4. The benefits arising from the project.
5. Answers to any objections that might be raised.
6. That there would be no confliction with any friendly nations.
7. That there was no cost to the Crown.
8. The likelihood of bringing great treasure into the realm and abating the prices of other commodities (i.e. spices).
9. The threat from other nations.

A supplementary list produced for Martin Frobisher's voyages added the following suggestions:

1. Provision of shipping, victuals, munitions and choice of manpower.
2. How to deal with strange people be they 'never so barbarous, cruel and fierce', either by leniency or otherwise.
3. How to trade without money.
4. Managing seasonal variations.
5. Navigating in ice.
6. Dangers from the length of voyage, ignorance of language, new elements, strange food, dangerous seas, robbery, wild beasts, dread of tempests, fear of rocks, fogs, exhaustion.

7. Profitability.
8. Leadership *in extremis*.
9. Provision of trusty soldiery.
10. Keeping a true record.
11. Good governance and the instruments for cosmography, geography and navigation.

Every one of the elements listed above was to play a significant part in the invasion, making them a shining example of a risk-assessment form. What is less evident is that any of the voyaging groups sat down and worked their way down the list. Simply, 'what if?' was never addressed.

The Grand Plan of 1584–87

Ironically, the best plan for the invasion of America was the one originated by Ralegh and which ended in failure. Had it been properly executed, it would have established control over Virginia much earlier and made of its begetter the noteworthy plutocrat he always wished to be.

Ralegh's main interest lay in personal wealth creation, for which he acquired an impressive portfolio. He held the monopoly on the sale of wine and spirits, controlled the West Country stannaries (tin mines) and held great estates in Ireland. At sea, he owned a number of well-armed modern privateering vessels capable of reaping rewards well beyond even his own avaricious dreams. Many of these endeavours could be combined if the lordship over vast acres of the new world that he perceived as a just reward for his interest and investment was utilized, not only to return as yet unassessed land-based riches, but also to serve to increase the opportunities for immediately realizable sea-borne wealth. Indeed, he may not have been prepared to pour money into this new venture without a default position, and that was to be plunder.

Although the evidence is conjectural, circumstantial and coincidental, the coterie involved – which included the three pirates, Drake, Ralegh and Grenville as well as their pirate queen, Elizabeth – justifies the assumption that, for one of the few occasions that it happened in Elizabeth's reign, in 1584 a joined-up plan was hatched to establish an English colony in the new world from which piratical operations could be launched.

The project should have been well planned: at his London headquarters of Durham House, Ralegh assembled the best brains available to advise and think through what was, sadly for too short a time, his pet project. These included: the cosmographer John Dee; the geographer, writer and publicist Richard Hakluyt; the scientist and mathematician Thomas Harriot and the artist John White. With such a planning team, success should have been assured. It was not, but an examination of its shortfalls serves as a template for all the other expeditions that failed to deliver their planners' expectations.

The Plan

Although no Elizabethan fly on the wall left a record of the conversations that took place in Durham House, the group of academics that Ralegh drew inside suggests strongly that in planning matters he intended to address the issues indicated in the two documents above. In this he avoided the characteristic impetuosity that had contributed to the loss of Gilbert. Instead a logical and, unusual for the time, sequential series of activities were planned for, which involved:

1. Firstly a reconnaissance to select a base, a safe distance from Spanish Florida, which could be both well-defended and easily resupplied and from which privateering raids could be launched.
2. Secondly the dispatch of a force capable of building fortifications and strong enough to hold them against all-comers.
3. Thirdly the resupply of the site and the support of the raiding fleet.
4. Fourthly the reinforcement of the site with settlers who would be able to create an adequate self-sufficiency and an exportable surplus.

If these objectives had been realized consecutively, Ralegh would be lauded and idolized as the founder of the British Empire. Unfortunately, when the first of them ran aground, the three astern, as if unable to take the speed off in time, and ill informed through the fog of distance, continued ploughing ahead until they ran into the wreckage on that dangerous western shore.

Selecting a Site

The agreed plan progressed swiftly and smoothly to its opening moves. In 1584 captains Barlowe and Amadas sailed to the new world and identified a site which they deemed suitable for establishing the English presence in America. Ralegh, having flatteringly named it Virginia, secured his very favourable Charter and in 1585 dispatched Sir Richard Grenville to land a company of soldiers under the command of the military engineer, Ralph Lane, to build a fort. Shortly after Grenville's departure, two more fleets were programmed to depart from England. The first, commanded by Bernard Drake, was to take supplies out to the expeditionary force while the second, led by Francis Drake, would lead a raid on the West Indies, where he could either seize a local town or, failing that, head north to the new outpost.

However, the plan was already going awry. Barlowe and Amadas, probably suffering from sea-voyagers' fatigue, came ashore too early, some hundred miles short of the great and sheltered haven of Chesapeake Bay. Instead, they anchored off the interminable strand of the Carolina Outer Banks, one of the least friendly shorelines off which sailing vessels could linger, which was pierced only occasionally with narrow gaps too shallow for seagoing vessels to navigate in safety. Through one of these channels they passed to Roanoke Island, which they recommended as the site for the settlement. In doing this they seem to have read but not fully comprehended Hakluyt's suggestion that they should find a defensible haven for a friendly fleet while offering no shelter for the unwelcomed, 'so as the enemy shall be forced to lie in open road without, to be dispersed with all winds and tempests that shall arise'. With Roanoke there was no compensatory shelter for friendly ships, which would be doomed to ride in an offshore anchorage more exposed than even the notorious fleet anchorage of The Downs off Kent. This problem could have been extrapolated from Barlowe's account, in which he wrote, 'we arrived upon the coast, which we supposed to be a continent, and firm land, and we sailed along the same, a hundred and twenty English miles, before we could find any entrance, or river, issuing into the sea. The first that appeared we entered, though not without some difficulty, and cast anchor . . .'

Ralph Lane's initial views of the offshore anchorage arrangements are not recorded but he was most critical of the shortcomings after the arrival of Drake's squadron in June 1586, when he wrote that much merchandise could be shipped from the colony, 'provided . . . that there also be found a better harbour than yet there is, which must be to the Northward, if any there be, which was mine intention to have spent the summer in search of'.

It was through narrow breaches in the Carolina Outer Banks that the English had to pass to reach Roanoke. Difficult in calm seas, such passage proved lethal in rough weather. (Michael Halminski)

So, the selection of Roanoke, while posing problems to a punitive Spanish force, did not provide the English with a suitable base from which to mount raiding operations themselves. They had landed and established themselves on a coast which provided neither deep and sheltered anchorages nor truly defensive harbours. Lane hints as much earlier in the letter quoted above, when he wrote:

> So all the entries into the same are so by nature fortified to seaward, by reason of a shoaly and most dangerous coast about 150 leagues lying all along this her majesty's domain already discovered, that it is not with great ships at any hand to be dealt with all. There be only three entries and ports; the one we have named Trinity Harbour, the other Ococan, in the entry whereof all our fleet struck aground, and *Tyger* lying beating upon the shore for the space of two hours . . . we were all in extreme hazard of being castaway.

The fate of the first landing force could have been decided in a far more drastic way than just the grounding of ships. Given the delicacy of its position, the settlement should have been established with the maximum secrecy. Instead, Grenville swashbuckled over to the West Indies, where he built two temporary forts, captured two Spanish ships and invited himself to dinner with the Governor. Then, after disembarking Lane, he seized a most valuable cargo from a Spanish ship on the return journey. This was irresponsible arrogance where subtle insinuation was essential. The Spanish should have acted with as swift and draconian response as that which they delivered upon the French settlement at Fort Caroline in Florida in 1565; luck and lethargy, not competent planning, saved the English settlement.

Yet, the inevitability of an exit became real when the four strands of the resupply plans began to unravel, leaving Lane holding on at the bitter end. Two convoys were scheduled to leave England in 1585. The first, commanded by Bernard Drake, was diverted shortly before its departure by the Crown, to sail for Newfoundland to warn English fishermen not to discharge their cargo in Spain, which had placed an embargo on English shipping. Drake 'made' his voyage by returning with booty worth some £60,000. However, it was made clear in subsequent High Court of Admiralty proceedings that the original purpose of his voyage had been to resupply those 'foreign parts, commonly called Wingoa de Coy, and not to the new found land, for taking Spanish ships and those of the subjects of the King of Spain'. Bernard Drake's non-arrival was a blow to Lane, whose force, after all, consisted not of farmers and fishermen, essential to the survival of any colony, but soldiers. Nevertheless, he kept his men fed and succeeded in planting sufficient for a summer harvest the following year. However, the ship dispatched by Ralegh to bring early relief did not sail until after Easter, meaning that it would also arrive far later than Lane anticipated. The third and much larger resupply commanded by Grenville did not leave England until even later, early May. In Roanoke, an empty sea and an almost empty grain store did nothing to boost morale and forced Lane not only to dispatch groups of his men to outstations to fend for themselves but also added to his demands on the reluctant natives for support, thereby increasing their animosity while reducing his effective fighting force in the fort.

Another strand, that involving naval support, was also about to fray. The anonymous wellwisher had suggested, 'The fort should be where a landing of reinforcements would always be possible,' and that the officers present should include 'an admiral', thus implying the presence of a standing naval force. As it was, no seagoing ship was left behind to ride insecurely off the Outer Banks. Such a vessel could have scouted with ease for a safer haven in the Chesapeake and have sailed back to England in an attempt to hasten the resupply, returning with both nurture and news. Indeed, in response to *Tyger's* grounding, and the ruination of her stores, John Arundell had sailed swiftly for England on 5 August, but the knighthood the admiration of his swift voyage won him at Court was not matched by the hasty dispatch of fresh supplies.

So it was that the first friendly ships that arrived off Roanoke were those of Francis Drake, heading home after a financially unsuccessful raid on the West Indies. Drake

John White's map seems to act as a warning to trespassers, judging by the number of shipwrecks shown on the Outer Banks. This was prescient: a modern chart is bar-coded with wreck sites from north to south along America's most dangerous shoreline. Close inspection of White's map also indicates a number of fortified native settlements. (British Museum)

Although this engraving depicts Columbus's voyagers being struck by a hurricane, the fate of vessels caught off the coast and the fear of those being battered ashore applied equally to the English on the Carolina Outer Banks. (National Maritime Museum)

had sailed with a large force. These included two of the Queen's ships, *Elizabeth Bonaventure* and *Ayde*, and twenty other vessels, among them *Primrose*, a well-armed London merchantman in which Martin Frobisher sailed as vice-admiral. Along with the ships went some eight sailing pinnaces, while even more were taken carried onboard to be reassembled when required. Twelve companies of soldiers, under the command of Christopher Carleill, were embarked to overwhelm any likely opposition ashore while the fleet itself was powerful enough to seize any booty on the high seas. The delayed force sailed on 14 September, arriving off northern Spain by the end of the month to demand with menaces and a show of force the release of every English ship embargoed by Spain. This done the force sailed for the Indies too late to intercept the treasure-laden Mexican *flota*. A diversion to Santiago in the Cape Verde Islands led to the men becoming infected with a fever which killed hundreds and debilitated many of those who survived. Assaults in the West Indies on Santo Domingo and Cartagena achieved military success but financial failure, which meant that, by 27 February, Drake was in command of a dispirited, disillusioned and diminished force whose commanders, when asked, preferred the option of returning home to any other plan. Yet, this was not what Drake did. Instead he delayed his departure from Cartagena until he had recruited, or seized, some 200 freed galley slaves and a further 300 Amerindians to sail with him and his ration-depleted force. After a stop at Havana, he still did not turn for England but sailed north to destroy the Spanish settlement of St Augustine in Florida (a diversion which he would not have been attempted without good cause), before continuing along the Carolina Outer Banks until he found Lane's settlement. Given the state of his ships and men there was no reason for Drake to have either burdened his pursers with providing rations for several hundred more crew or chosen to make a delaying detour on his way home. He would have known, and not suspected otherwise, that Ralegh was intending to send resupply ships to the fort. His sole justification for venturing this way must have been because he believed Lane would have established a viable corsairs' lair for his future use.

As for the galley slaves and Amerindians, Drake might have felt the former could replace the men that he had lost, although many of his dead would have been soldiers, and galley oarsmen are not readily converted into watch keepers on a sailing vessel, or, reverting to his earlier career, he might just have felt he could sell the slaves to boost the poor return on the voyage so far. Neither explanation betters the idea that the new recruits were destined for the new colony. As to their fate, they are generally awarded just a footnote in histories, but, if they were landed at Roanoke, they represent the third settlement lost on the island, ranking with Grenville's fifteen and White's 107. Popular research has brought forth the idea that the survivors merged with the Amerindians and from that union developed the Melungeons, or tri-racial groups domiciled mainly in Virginia. There is no firm evidence to support this idea, or even that Drake landed any of his recently acquired group on the Outer Banks. Their fate remains even more mysterious than that of White's settlers but has received far less attention.

Drake must have been disappointed from the moment he realized that his ships could not pass through the shallows into the shelter of Pamlico Sound but would have to anchor in 'a wild road at sea, about two miles from shore'. He would have realized straightaway that this was not the site at which to establish the desired pirate port. Even then, having listened to Lane's plan to move towards the Chesapeake, where secure anchorages could be had, he tried to salvage the plan by offering to lend the colony some appropriate boats with which to make the move. Then a hurricane with 'thunder, lightning and rain with hailstones as big as hens' eggs' scattered the fleet and, by the time it had passed on, any desire that the now-shipless Lane had to remain had dissipated. He ordered a complete evacuation, and with his departure ended the idea of an English pirate port on the coast of Virginia. It had failed because captains Amadas and Barlowe, at the end of their lengthy voyage in 1584, had stopped sixty miles short of success, not knowing that the great estuaries of the Chesapeake lay one day's sail from the shallow and unsuitable waters of Pamlico Sound.

In 1586, Ralegh's grand plan was thus dealt a double blow by two men in whom he had placed great trust. On 28 July Lane and his force disembarked at Portsmouth; a month or so later, the date is not recorded, Grenville reported back that he had left a

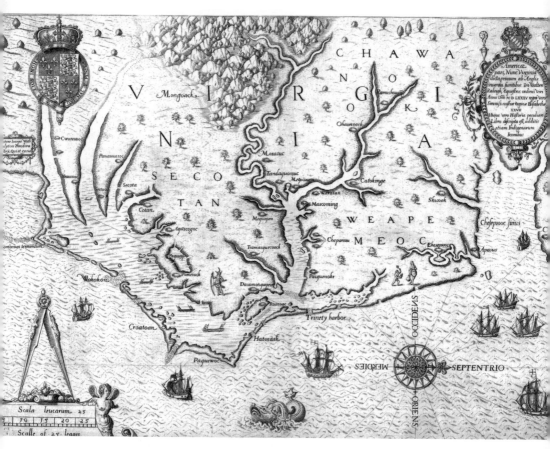

This map of the Carolina Outer Banks, which accompanied Harriot's *Briefe and True Reporte* of 1590, is far more friendly: an encouragement to settle in a land which, judging from the number of ships, is already a hub of commerce. (British Museum)

mere fifteen men behind at Roanoke. For a while, Ralegh must have considered the option of inviting (even bribing) Lane to sally forth once more or, failing that, to recruit another body of infantry to provide the cover so strongly recommended by his advisors. He did not, but neither, fatally, did he amend his overall plan. When White's colonists were dispatched to build the next stage of the 'City of Ralegh' after the firm foundations had been removed, collapse was inevitable. When White returned to Virginia in 1586, with his 117 undefended settlers, it was not their brusque, unsympathetic disembarking by the ship's master, Ferdinando, at Roanoke rather than in the Chesapeake, as agreed, that doomed them to death but Ralegh's inability to redraw his plan in the light of Lane's withdrawal. Perhaps his mind was elsewhere. On 10 June 1586, two of his pirating pinnaces, *Mary Spark* and *Serpent*, sailed from Plymouth, returning well laden with much plunder. Then, on 27 June, royal letters patent named Ralegh as the leader of a group of men who were granted the right to colonize Munster in Ireland, giving him more great estates to develop.

Even with today's sea defences hurricane strength winds can wreak havoc in the exposed Carolinas.

JAMESTOWN

Aware of the past problems of Roanoke and the still present danger of Spain, the Virginia Company gave clear *Instructions by Way of Advice* to those who were to lead its first invasion in 1607 as to where to establish their beachhead. These invited the settlers to establish their 'seat of habitation' in a healthy, defendable site, some 100 miles inland and as far up a river 'as a bark of fifty tuns will float', and so much the better if the river showed signs of providing a passage to 'the *East India* Sea'. Most of the advice was sound but the document was besmirched by the pressure to produce both a route to Cathay and a cargo of gold.

Defending the Operation

In support of Ralegh's masterplan, his anonymous advisor produced an excellent proposal for how best to manage the invasion in which, although dismissing the native threat, he proposed that:

John White's Map of Virginia, showing Roanoke Island and a hinterland almost empty of native habitation – a key justification for the occupation of this land by the English. (British Museum)

In to that country I would have men go armoured of this sort for they are to deal with naked men, yet I will have furniture to prevent the invasion of the Spaniard.

The number being 800 I would have them thus divided:

First 400 harquebusiers

Then 100 swords and light moddena targets [shield]

Then 150 long bows

Then 100 armed men with Milan corsets light [presumably with pikes]

Then 50 armed men with light corsets with short weapons

Of this number I would daily have in the fort 100 in guard, and so nightly for the sentinels, all the rest should labour until the fort be ended.

Lane's landing. Before they could fell trees to build houses, the soldiers had to live under canvas, much of it provided by adapting the spare sails of the attendant ships.

The need for a strong military show had also been appreciated by Hakluyt, who, while disparaging the 'savages', wrote, in his epistle dedicatory to Sir Walter Ralegh for his translation of René de Laudonnière's history of four French voyages to Florida:

> Now if the greatness of the main of Virginia, and the large extension thereof, especially to the West, should make you think that the subduing of it, were a matter of more difficulty than the conquest of Ireland . . . it is not to be denied, but that one hundred men will do more now among the naked and unarmed people in Virginia, than one thousand were able to do in Ireland against that armed and warlike nation.

In contradiction of his own argument, Hakluyt went on to propose that a spare 10,000 able men could not be better employed than to be sent to Virginia, 'trained up thus long in service, then in the inward parts of the firm of Virginia against such stubborn Savages as shall refuse obedience to her Majesty'. Hakluyt, of course, always justified his dream of empire by the positive good that would come from introducing the savages to God, good governance and civilization. This would have been a goodly number well outside the nation's capability to reinforce and resupply, but it was probably the sort of force that would have been required to drive inland from the beachhead. Ralegh, knowing the limit of the Queen's investment, managed to provide just 107 men to serve under Colonel Lane in the first wave. With this barely adequate force, Lane built his fort and managed the landing place so well that none died from disease or wounds during his tenure, a truly remarkable – probably unique – achievement in that period, and the only element of Ralegh's scheme that delivered according to plan, until the moment of its premature departure.

Roanoke, well-planned but poorly executed, ended in failure. Without a trained militia, succeeding settlements could have done likewise. Both Smith at Jamestown and Standish at Plymouth had urgently to organize and drill their civilian companions so that they would be able to put up some sort of fight should the natives attack the beachhead. However, so demanding of instant gain was the Virginia Company that it turned the Elizabethan suggestions on the employment of manpower on their head by advising their Governor, with his much more limited manpower, that he should appoint just forty to fortify and forty to plant crops, while the third group spent two months exploring for the route to Cathay and digging for gold.

Captain Newport followed this advice almost to the letter and also took the one skilled military man, John Smith, with him on the discovery. The result was that they returned only just in time to relieve the simply structured fort that too few men had been left behind to build and defend against the unanticipated onslaught by Amerindians. This had not been anticipated; what the Company advised awareness of while selecting the site for the fort was the Spanish. To repulse their unhealthy visitation, a warning sconce needed to be built near the coast, and the site of the settlement chosen so that fire could be brought to bear on Spanish boats from both banks of the river. In addition, the settlers were advised not to suffer 'any of the native people of the country to inhabit between you and the sea coast', in case, through discontent, they acted as guides for the Spanish. Thus the local population itself was considered to pose a major threat only if they, by reason of mishandling, allied themselves with the Spanish. Other than that they had a nuisance potential such as not trading for food, stealing firearms or leading explorers astray.

PLYMOUTH PLANTATION

With much planning, instruction and advice, both Roanoke and Jamestown headed towards disaster. It is not possible to apply such strictures to the *Mayflower* voyagers, whose very background as both refugees and invaders, with all the deprivation that that former status imposed upon them, prevented them from travelling with armed support. Thus it seems likely that they would have welcomed the shared security that would have been available had they settled alongside the Dutch whom they knew to be established in Manhattan. The turbulent waters south of Cape Cod put paid to that idea but decades of disease had also cleared the land sufficiently for them to be able, just, to defend their small holding.

The lack of a coherent plan seems to have little affected the fortunes of the Plymouth band. Neither did reams of paper help or hinder the peripheral expeditions to Baffin Island, Newfoundland and Nova Scotia. What could have ensured success was the landing of adequate supplies and a faith in timely resupply, an understanding with any local population, an enthusiastic and optimistic leader, and a bloody determination to hang on. Without these, the best-laid plans could have been cast overboard as the ships left their English harbours.

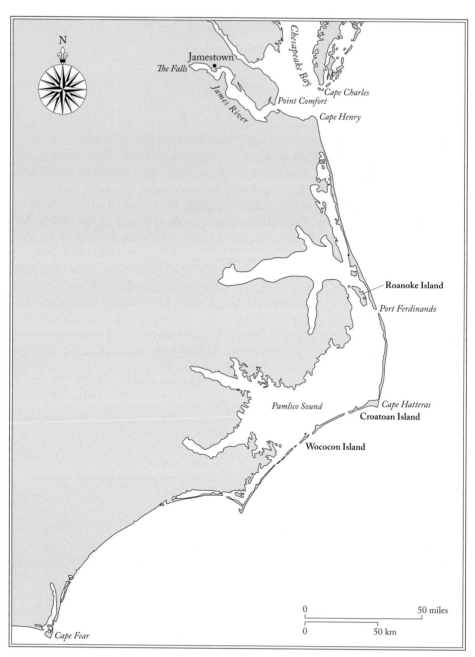

N

Jamestown
The Falls
James River
Point Comfort
Chesapeake Bay
Cape Charles
Cape Henry

Roanoke Island
Port Ferdinando

Pamlico Sound
Cape Hatteras
Croatoan Island

Wococon Island

Cape Fear

| 0 | 50 miles |
| 0 | 50 km |

Map 3: Roanoke and Jamestown

CHAPTER 5

Ships and Sailing

She was forty foot by the keel, and nineteen foot broad at the beam, six foot floor, her rake forward was fourteen foot, her rake aft from the top of her post (which was twelve foot long) was three foot, she was eight foot deep under her beam, between her decks was she four feet and a half, with a rising of half a foot more under her forecastle, of purpose to scour the decks with small shot, if at anytime we should be boarded by the enemy . She had a fall of eighteen inches aft, to make her steerage and her great cabin the more large: her steerage was five foot long and six foot high, with a closed gallery right aft, with a window on each side and two right aft . . . she might be some eighty tons burthen.

William Strachey, description of Bermuda-built *Deliverance*, 1610

Halfway across the James River, heading towards the Jamestown jetty onboard the excellent free ferry service that is provided, southern Englanders might feel that they are viewing a familiar landscape, and so they are, for the resemblance to the Solent and the ferry service between Ryde and the mainland is most striking. It must have been as obvious to the early settlers, which might account for the fact that the cities of Portsmouth and Hampton lie just downstream and that a nearby county is called Isle of Wight. But, in the wonderfully mixed-up gazetteer that sprinkles place names across America, the ferry departs from the township of Scotland in the county of Surry [sic]. As the ferry passes the halfway mark, through the mists of dawn the palisade of the rebuilt Jamestown fort on its original site can be seen silvered like an old man's toenail sticking out of a hole in a long green sock. Some moments later, bare against the same water fringing woodland, the masts of *Susan Constant*, *Godspeed* and *Discovery* can be picked out, their hulls becoming evident only as the ferry noses into its adjacent berth. From mid-river the three reconstructed settler ships look like bath toys; even close up they appear to be scaled-down models, for the idea that ships of this size would be sailed anywhere other than on the protected waters of the Chesapeake and its great rivers seems incredible. That they, and similar and smaller vessels, should have crossed the Atlantic amazes.

The sixteenth century saw an expansion in the range of ship types that were being built in Europe. On the one hand this arose to meet the demands of the Indies fleets of Spain and Portugal, which necessitated the creation of large, ocean-capable, bulk storage vessels, while England, whose merchant marine relied mainly upon coastal craft plying traditional short routes, developed several classes of warship that could be used to plunder that trade as well as defend itself against the more numerous but less effective warships of Spain. The vessels sailed under a plethora of types and classes: ships, carvels, hoys, pinnaces, crayers, ketches, lighters, boats, barges, hulks, flyboats,

The queen's ships at the siege of Smerwick in 1580. Shown here are *Ayde* (second from top), which sailed with Frobisher to Baffin's Island, and *Tyger* (bottom), which sailed with Grenville to Roanoke, two of the very few royal ships that crossed the Atlantic in support of the settlements. (National Archives, Kew)

barks, frigates, galleons and brigantines, to name just a few, but what does not appear on any list of seagoing ships is the term 'ferry' or 'liner'. With the English monarchy not prepared to release the one type of vessel that had room for passengers – their warships – transatlantic emigrants had to make do with whatever their sponsors could afford, or were prepared to pay for. Most of these would be small merchant ships designed to carry bulk items of cargo in their holds.

The main cargo carried by English merchants was wool, outbound, and wine inbound. Although ferries did ply to France and Ireland, the only passengers that were carried on longer voyages were either troops or slaves, neither of which was granted much in the way of creature comforts. Thus, when the need arose to transport settlers across the Atlantic, the ships' masters had experience of neither ocean navigation nor caring for paying passengers. In many cases those payments seemed to offer a small return and the ships slewed off course to indulge in a little piracy to ensure an adequate profit.

The choice of small ships for the exploratory and settlement voyages was thus forced upon the travellers for lack of financial and courtly support. Cabot's *Matthew* was a minuscule fifty tons; in 1576, Frobisher tried to force a northwest passage to Cathay in the thirty-ton barks *Gabriel* and *Michael*, much the size of the Viking longboats that had made the journey centuries earlier and half the size of the smallest of Columbus's

Berthed at Roanoke Island, the replica *Elizabeth* has, unlike her oceangoing predecessors, a shallow enough draft to pass into Pamlico Sound.

ships. Sir Humphrey Gilbert's fleet of 1586 comprised *Delight* at 120 tons, *Golden Hind* and *Swallow*, both of forty tons, and *Squirrel*, in which he lost his life, a mere ten tons. *Susan Constant* was 120 tons; *Godspeed* forty tons and *Discovery* twenty tons. *Mayflower*, at 180 tons, was large when compared with her predecessors, but still one-fifth of the tonnage of the great Spanish and Portuguese galleons that brought the riches of east and west to Seville and Lisbon.

The small size of the colonial transports had one long-term unforeseen and fortunate consequence – these historic vessels were far cheaper to reconstruct and man than would have been the larger warships of the Royal Navy. Thus it has been possible for many replicas to be built which, widely and appropriately dispersed, have given the present-day public a fascinating and exciting historical resource to study and enjoy, and, in turn, has given to these vessels a deserved fame and status well beyond that which was imagined at the time of their original voyages.

With few extant and detailed accounts of life onboard available to them, the builders of the reconstructed ships had very little information on which to base their designs, apart from some contemporary paintings and prints, most of which concentrate on warships rather than their smaller merchant brethren. The most certain descriptor was the tonnage, but with that measurement alone the task would have been much the same as trying to reconstruct an historic house while only knowing the number of rooms. The use of the term 'tonnage' or 'tunne' to denote either weight or volume indicates the dominance of the Gascony wine trade in English shipping, for it gave rise to the unit of measurement by which a ship's size, or burden, was measured: the ton. This was based on the amount of space required in the hold to transport 1,000 kilograms of wine in tuns, or barrels. The simplest reckoning was that this was sixty cubic feet of hull space; a ton burden is thus considered the equivalent to either a weight of around 1,000 kilograms or the volume required to hold that weight of wine in barrels.

Given a tonnage, and a few contemporary views as to the best ratio between a ship's length and her beam, it was possible, using the written record, to get some indication of the proportions and measurements of a merchant vessel. One of these sources is the writings of the early Roanoke explorer Thomas Harriot, while John Smith, in his *Accidence* and *Sea Grammar*, and the Newfoundland pirate Henry Mainwaring, both wrote glossaries describing shipbuilding and explaining construction terms. The main guidance is, however, that written by Matthew Baker, the royal master shipwright, in his *Fragments of Early Shipwrighty*, published in 1582. In this he laid down a very simple formula for estimating tonnage which, for vessels built after 1570 was:

$$\frac{K \times B \times D}{100} = \text{Tons Burden or Builder's measurement (BM)}$$

Where;

K = Keel length between start of the stem curve and the edge of the stern post

B = Beam, taken as the length of the main frame deck beam plus the thickness of the side planking

D = Depth from the underside of the main deck to the lower part of the keel

As far as other ratios were concerned, Thomas Harriot suggested that the length/breadth/depth ratio should be 1 to 0.4 to 0.2, while William Borough, the comptroller of Elizabeth's navy, had a simpler relationship, stating that: 'The shortest, broadest and deepest order is this – to have the length by the keel double the breadth amidships and the depth in hold half the breadth. This order is used in some merchant ships for most profit.'

The vessel to whom most reference is made for purposes of reconstruction is *Adventure of Ipswich*, whose dimensions, recorded in 1627, were:

Length of keel,	63ft 6in
Breadth	26ft 2in
Depth in hold	11 ft
Giving her a tonnage of 182.8	

Given such ratios, it was relatively easy to draw the first lines for a reconstructed vessel, and for many years there was little other information available. Then, in 1982, after years of painstaking and groundbreaking underwater archaeology, Henry VIII's flagship *Mary Rose* was raised from the seabed of the Solent, where she had settled after capsizing in 1545. This was a magnificent resurrection and one of perpetual significance, for now, for the first time, a whole side of an original sixteenth-century ship was bared to researchers.

At 500 tons *Mary Rose* was massive in comparison with the settlers' ships, but she was designed, constructed, equipped and fitted out in a very similar way to those more modest and later vessels. Neither did the skills used to sail her vary greatly. A sailor who went to sea in *Mary Rose* would have had no difficulty learning the ropes in *Mayflower* and would have recognized instantly the way of life, including the crammed accommodation, the limited and restricted victuals, the watch keeping routine and the instruments of coastal pilotage.

The English-built ships were constructed along traditional lines. A contract was placed, an outline drawing was made, an expedition was mounted to identify and purchase the necessary standing timber; the shipwright's practised eye was able to tell almost to the plank what each tree would yield in sawn timber. The trees were then felled, cut and dragged or floated to the saw-pits close to where the ship would be built. This would generally have been a slipway either lying on a gentle slope just above the high-water mark or, if time and tide allowed, one built between high and low water and made watertight by a U-shaped cofferdam made from rock and mud.

Here, on supporting blocks, the long keel – a bulky length of oak or, preferably, rot-proof elm – would be laid and have, abutted on to the ends by long bolted scarf joints, both the stem and the stern posts. On the union and strength of these united timbers the strength of the whole ship depended. Larger, more valuable vessels even had a false keel laid beneath the main keel to add further protection should the vessel ground; it is unlikely that the contract for smaller ships included such an additional expense. Harriot suggested that a ship of 100 tons should have a keel ten inches broad by one foot deep. The keel of the rebuilt *Susan Constant* has similar, slightly larger, dimensions, but the builders of the new *Matthew* selected a fifty-foot length of oak measuring two

Replica of *Godspeed*. Bartholomew Gosnold, the experienced captain of *Godspeed* on her outward voyage, remained behind in Jamestown when the ship returned to England in 1607, only to lose his life in the outbreak of the 'bloody flux' that struck the settlers in the early autumn.

A typical small English merchant ship, *Susan Constant* was chartered by the Virginia Company for just one transatlantic voyage, the outward leg of which took more than four months. The crowded conditions onboard led to several deaths and much argument amongst the gentlemen travellers.

The aptly named pinnace *Discovery* remained behind in the Chesapeake when Newport returned to England, carrying out many exploring and foraging expeditions for which its shallow draft was ideal.

(facing page) Mayflower II. Although crowded and uncomfortable, under Captain Jones's command the original *Mayflower* suffered few casualties during her sixty-five-day crossing of the Atlantic. (Plimouth Plantation)

foot square for her keel, some eight inches broader and deeper than that of the much larger *Mary Rose*.

On top of the keel a groove – the rabbet – was cut to accept the ends of the frames, which were also bolted down and then locked into position by another long bulky timber travelling the length of the keel, the keelson. Right aft, the keelson moved upward and away from the keel, meeting the angle stern post several feet above its junction with the keel. The space between was filled with timber scarfed together and collectively known as the deadwood.

For most ships the curved frame timbers were too long for a single cut of oak to do the job so several pieces, futtocks, were cut to shape, and butted onto each other to complete the work. It was in the shaping and fitting of the frames that the shipwright's eye was of vital experience, for these would give to the ship both her symmetry and her lines, ensuring that she would slide with grace through the water and rise with ease on the approaching wave. Any discussion as to why a ship is referred to as 'she' could be ended by a glance at the feminine curves of the ship's frame, at first convex and then concave as they rise upward from the keel. To maintain the symmetry of the port and starboard side, opposite frames were fitted in pairs with the midships and widest pair being attached first, followed by those at the bow and stern so that the curve of the sides would become readily apparent and subsequent timbers be adjusted for sinuosity.

This Newfoundland stamp pays tribute to *Endeavour*, a bark built to explore the island's coast by John Guy in 1612 and thus one of the first ships to be constructed by the English in the new world. Artistic licence and national pride have united to produce a grander version of the craft than the original.

To enable the shipwright to sense the form taking shape and to prevent the frames from shifting, they were joined together by long strips of wood known as ribbands, whose purpose would become redundant as the oak planking was fitted and secured with long, pitch-coated wooden pins known as treenails or trenails, which were hammered home through augered holes. Occasionally a wedge was driven into the outboard end of the treenail to tighten its hold still further. On all vessels care was taken that no two consecutive joints of timber lay above each other, for this would cause a weakness that could cause a major leak should a timber spring loose. A gap was also left between each row of horizontal timbers into which tarred rope would be caulked to produce a watertight seal which would be further compressed by the expansion of the timbers once they were wet. The first planking to be secured were the wales; thicker than the other planking they not only provided rigidity from the start but, lying proud of the other planks, provided a fender to receive any blows from contact with jetties or other vessels. The wales also ran both above and below the gunports, reinforcing this potential line of weakness in the structure.

With the outer shell complete, the carpenters would clamber inboard to fit the hull's internal planking. Once again care was taken to fit slightly thicker planks over the joints in the frame. Athwartships, deck beams were fitted, with allowances made both for hatchways to be built to allow access to each lower deck and the masts passed through to the keelson, where a curved 'step' was built with a central tenon to receive the base of the fore- and main mast, while a similar structure on the upper deck housed the mizzen. Where the masts passed through a deck the space was reinforced with additional bulky timbers, or partners, and the space between wedged to prevent both the ingress of water and excessive movement of the mast, thus transmitting the strain it was under to the hull itself. At the mast base holes were drilled in the steps to allow water to drain out, and it was to this point that the main pump was led.

At either end of the deck beams a large L-shaped lodging, rising or hanging knees, placed vertically or horizontally and both above and below the beam, served to bracket them to the frame. At this stage the ship was still a dead hulk incapable of either movement or direction of travel. The latter was provided by the hanging of a rudder, supported by four to six pintles onto gudgeons on the stern post to make iron hinges which allowed the rudder to be moved from side to side through its limited arc of travel. This was an area of potential weakness, iron and salt water not having a lasting relationship, so frequent examination was necessary – and not always provided – to ensure that a rudder did not break off in a stormy sea when it was most needed, as happened to Frobisher's *Ayde* in 1577, on her return journey from Baffin Island. When the rudder failed, the crew endeavoured to steer by using a spare mast, but this was battered to bits, so they had little option but to build a new rudder and then clamber over the stern to mount it – a heroic feat that almost caused death through hypothermia.

It is one of the strange facts of shipwrightery that the ship's wheel, by which the ship was steered, was a comparatively late introduction. The vessels that took the settlers to America were steered by a whipstaff, an awkward inflexible arrangement whereby a staff was passed down through a pivot ball, or rowle, and linked by a gooseneck to a ringbolt at the inboard end of the tiller, one deck below the helmsman, who thus, by moving the whipstaff in a vertical arc managed to shift the tiller, and thus the rudder,

(above) In this picture the whipstaff is clearly shown rising to pass through the deck above. Note the game of chequers laid out on the barrel placed between the bunks. Even playing such simple pastimes was subject to the vagaries of the ocean.

The whipstaff allowed the helmsman to be positioned one deck higher than the tiller itself, affording him at least some view of the set of the sails.

a few degrees in either direction. The limited alteration to the ship's course that this caused was increased by adjusting the set of the spritsail and mizzen. In rough weather the whipstaff would kick like an unbridled colt, necessitating the use of a block and tackle and many more hands to control it: Strachey, writing of the storm that wrecked *Sea Venture*, stated:

> Our sails wound up, lay without their use, and if at any time we bore but a hullock or half forecourse to guide her before the sea, six and sometimes eight men were not enough to hold the whipstaff in the steerage and the tiller below in the gunner room; by which may be imagined the strength of the storm, in which the sea swelled above the clouds and gave battle unto Heaven.

Mainwaring suggested that the whipstaff should be removed,

> When the sea is so rough that men cannot govern the helm [tiller] with their hands, they seize two blocks to the helm on either side at the end, and, reeving two falls through them, like gunners' tackles, bring them to the ship's sides; so having some at one tackle, and some at the other, they govern the helm, as directed.

It was important that Mainwaring's advice was taken prior to experiencing violent weather, not later, for, as Strachey again disclosed:

> Once so huge a sea broke upon the poop and quarter upon us as it covered our ship from stern to stem like a garment or a vast cloud; it filled her brim full for a while within, from the hatches up to the spar deck. The source or confluence of water was so violent as it rushed it carried the helmsman from the helm and wrested the whipstaff out of his hand, which so flew from side to side that when he would have seized the same again it so tossed him from starboard to larboard as it was God's mercy it had not split him. It so beat him from his hold and so bruised him, as a fresh man hazarding in by chance fell fair with it, and by main strength, bearing somewhat up, made good his place, and with much clamour encouraged and called upon others, who gave her now up, rent in pieces and absolutely lost.

Once launched, good practice would suggest that the ship was left buoyed up for a while in the water both to allow her timbers to swell and to check, especially in the soon to be inaccessible places like the hold, for leaks. Rapidly sourcing a leak while at sea and taking appropriate damage-control measures could mean the difference between sinking and survival, as Strachey once again graphically illustrated in his *Sea Venture* account:

> Howbeit this was not all. It pleased God to bring a greater affliction yet upon us; for in the beginning of the storm we had received likewise a mighty leak. And the ship, in every joint almost, having spewed out her oakum before we were aware (a casualty more desperate than any other that a voyage by sea draweth with it), was grown five foot suddenly deep with water above her ballast, and we almost drowned within whilst

The shallow draft of ship's tenders or shallops proved ideal for sailing in the waters of Pamlico Sound and the upper reaches of the Chesapeake rivers. On military expeditions boards were added to provide additional protection for the soldiers onboard.

we sat looking when to perish from above. This, imparting no less terror than danger, ran through the whole ship with much fright and amazement, startled and turned the blood, and took down the braves of the most hardy mariner of them all, insomuch as he that before happily felt not the sorrow of others, now began to sorrow for himself when he saw such a pond of water so suddenly broken in and which he knew could not (without present avoiding) but instantly sink him.

So as joining (only for his own sake, not yet worth the saving) in the public safety there might be seen master, master's mate, boatswain, quartermaster, coopers, carpenters, and who not, with candles in their hands, creeping along the ribs viewing the sides, searching every corner and listening in every place if they could hear the water run. Many a weeping leak was this way found and hastily stopped, and at length one in the gunner room made up with I know not how many pieces of beef. But all was to no purpose; the leak (if it were but one) which drank in our greatest seas and took in our destruction fastest could not then be found, nor ever was, by any labour, counsel, or search. The waters still increasing and the pumps going, which at length choked with bringing up whole and continual biscuit (and indeed all we had, ten thousand weight), it was conceived as most likely that the leak might be sprung in the bread room, whereupon the carpenter went down and ripped up all the room, but could not find it so.

Once content that the launched ship was dry, ballast would be shovelled inboard and spread down below, the actual amount based both on a formula and the practised eye of the shipwright watching the vessel settle to his planned waterline. Getting this right was important: the mighty *Vasa* sank in 1628, a few hours into her maiden voyage, precisely because she carried too little ballast. On the other hand too much ballast made a ship lie heavy and sluggish, as well as taking up space that could be allocated for cargo.

Motive power began with the fitting of the masts, which could have taken place after the ship had been launched with sheer-legs being used to lift these mighty tree trunks into place. Most of the merchant ships would have had three masts: a main, a fore and a mizzen, plus a bowsprit. For larger vessels such as English warships and Portuguese East Indiamen, to extend the length of each of these masts they were formed from a combination of several timbers to create, for example, a lower mast, topmast and top gallant. For smaller ships a single length of straight timber generally sufficed. Yet again there was a formula to be applied to establish both the length and thickness of each mast and the ratio between them and to the dimensions of the ship itself. These are summarized below, based on the measurements worked out for the reconstructions, using contemporary formulae provided by men such as Mainwaring and John Smith.

Dimensions of Ships, Using Contemporary Formulae

Ship	Matthew	Susan Constant	Mayflower
Tonnage	80	120	180
Length of keel	50'	55'2"	58'
Beam	19'	22'9"	25'
Depth in hold	6'6"	9'6"	12'5"
Mainmast			
height	70'	63"3"	71'3"
diameter	3' diameter	21"	21"
Main topmast		33'10"	30'9"
			9" dia.
Foremast	50'	53'11"	57'10"
	3'		18" dia.
Fore topmast		30'8"	26'3"
			7" dia.
Mizzen	45'	40'5"	30'
			10" dia.
Bowsprit		51'	57'9"

Such ratios were not just a matter of tradition or aesthetics: an over-masted ship could pull itself apart, an under-masted one would be a sluggish sailer.

In August 1620 *Mayflower* left Southampton in company with the inaptly named *Speedwell*. Three days out it was realized that the latter was in no fit state to cross the Atlantic. From Dartmouth, Cushman wrote to say that, 'although she was twice trimmed . . . yet now she is as open and leaky as a siever'. Plugging and other repairs led to her being declared seaworthy by 23 August, only for the leaks to return, forcing the two ships to go about and seek the shelter of Plymouth Sound. Once safely anchored, the leaks seemed to lessen, leaving the master, Captain Reynolds, to conclude that the ship was over-masted and thus shaking herself to pieces once under sail. She was abandoned and her passengers either landed or transferred to *Mayflower*, leaving that ship to continue her journey alone and thus achieve the greater share of glory.

The masts were secured by standing rigging: fore and aft by stays and athwartships by shrouds, which consisted of thick well-tarred rope tensioned by dead-eyes and regularly tightened to take up the inevitable slack; however taut the shrouds and stays, as the ship heeled the mast would move, tensioning the shrouds on one side, slackening them on the other – an effect made more prevalent by the natural elasticity wound into the fibres of the rope. The masts, of course, were present to provide support to the great spars on which the sails were hung. For most ships the sail suite would comprise: a spritsail on the bowsprit; a fore course below a foretopsail on the foremast; a main course and a main topsail and a mizzen course. In good sailing conditions the lower sails would have additional bonnets attached to them to increase the sail area. In stormy seas the sail area would be furled to reduce the force of the wind on the ship until perhaps just one topsail was set to assist steering. In the most extreme conditions the ship would ride out the storm completely bare-poled. Running rigging enabled the yards to be adjusted to the wind and the sails to be managed. The sails themselves were made from canvas, woven from hemp grown at such places as Bridport and King's Lynn, although much was imported from Brittany. On delivery, the rolls of canvas were cut and stitched in such a way that the sail had a natural ballooning shape when set, so that it could most readily take up the wind. On occasion, other materials had to be used. When the mast of John Smith's pinnace shattered in a storm on the Chesapeake in 1608 he had the tailor mend the sail with the crew's shirts; it was then bent onto a new mast formed from the felling of a tree on a nearby island.

Towards the end of the sixteenth century Britain's homegrown supply of masts and spars was much reduced and many were imported, especially from the Baltic. It is no wonder, therefore, that the tall upright timbers of Virginia and New England were seen as a useful commodity to ship home. Sadly for the settlers, such exports were not going to make their avaricious sponsors rich, and one can sense the scorn with which a cargo of masts rather than minerals was met. Even when loaded with such items, returning with them was sometimes not straightforward. In 1608, the master of *Gifte of God*, returning with scant provisions and the evacuees from the Popham colony, but laden with thirty-three masts of white pine and other timber, was forced to sell off the goods in the Azores in exchange for desperately needed food. Far from commiserating and commending the master, Sir Francis Popham and his mother took him to court to recover their losses. Fortunately the High Court of Admiralty dismissed the case.

Guns onboard the *Susan Constant*. At 120 tons, this heavily armed merchant ship, captained by the ex-pirate Christopher Newport, could probably have repelled any equivalent sized Spanish warship.

Mayflower on her return to England in 1621 did not even carry such a cargo, sailing empty from Plymouth. *Fortune*, following her home that same December, was, in response to criticism from the Merchant Adventurers, loaded with clapboard, suitable for barrels and wainscoting but not for ships' planking. She was seized by the French a few days out from the Western Approaches and all her cargo removed.

The fate of *Fortune* explains one fitting without which these ships would not have sailed – guns. Peace never existed at sea throughout this period and none could sail on the seas upon their lawful occasion without being prepared to respond with equal aggression to any assailant; even though nations might sign treaties, their seamen could never resist the opportunity to seize from the weaker vessel.

A whole range of weaponry was available to place on the decks of ships, ranging from cannon and culverin at the weightier end to sakers, minions, falcons and fowlers, in decreasing order of size. Naturally, light merchant ships could neither carry nor man the heavier weapons; they needed guns to use at close quarters to dissuade or disrupt an attempted boarding. Neither were the guns all pointed in the same direction, but mounted so that they could be brought to bear, either in succession, as the helmsman steered a gently curving course or, in the case of an assault, one after the other as the foe approached. With such small crews to man both the rigging and the weaponry, it is unlikely that they were reloaded, the master relying on deterrence and defiance to drive off the attackers.

For her size *Susan Constant* was well armed, carrying four minions and four falcons – the former firing a 4-pound shot, the latter one of 2 pounds, with each gun being provided with about four to six rounds. The guns, with barrels between six and seven feet long, were mounted on carriages which were themselves firmly secured by tackles to limit recoil and prevent any loose cannons causing destruction in rough weather. There would have been no separate magazine for powder, which would have been stowed in a couple of barrels in a forward storeroom. Given the limited amount of shot and powder, it is unlikely that gunnery practice ever took place. Merchant ships that wished to be heavily armed were at a disadvantage from similar-sized warships in that they needed to carry armament high up as their holds were often laden with cargo. This placing of heavy weights along the ship's side increased the vessel's instability, sometimes with fatal results. When Sir Humphrey Gilbert's *Squirrel* foundered in 'foul weather and terrible seas, breaking short and high, pyramidwise', on his return voyage

A replica of the Dutch ship *Onrust*, the first decked vessel to be built in the new world, showing the sprit rig.

in 1583, Edward Hayes, master of the accompanying *Golden Hind*, commented that the little ship was 'overcharged upon the decks with fights, netting and small artillery, too cumbersome for so small a boat that was to pass through the ocean'.

A ship had, of course, to be able to come to rest at journey's end, which generally meant anchoring, although the Jamestown vessels could tie up alongside the fort and secure themselves to tree trunks. Those offshore held fast with a suite of anchors, the number, size and mix of which was determined by a tried and tested ratio; the safety of the vessel would depend upon these great iron hooks once she was close inshore. Occasionally, the loss of an anchor required a passage plan to be amended. In July 1610, John Guy, bound for Newfoundland from Bristol, considered it expedient to put into Minehead after losing an anchor, and sailed six days later, presumably with a replacement secured. In 1612, having built the bark *Endeavour* in Newfoundland for the purpose, Guy undertook an inland voyage of discovery accompanied by a shallop. After riding out a night of foul weather in which the shallop sank, he weighed anchor, only to find the rocky seabed had 'worn asunder our hawse . . . for the anchor and twenty fathoms of the hawser were left behind'. Guy's ship survived, but losing anchors

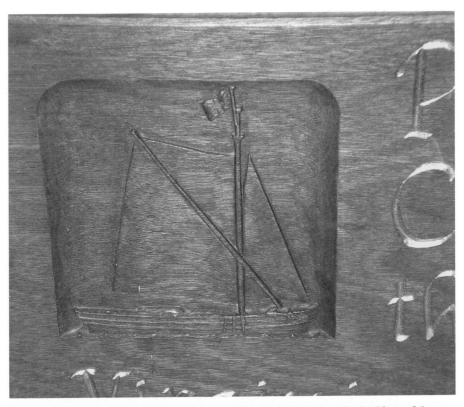

A carved pew back in the chapel of Compton Castle acknowledges the building of the *Virginia*, the first English vessel constructed in America, during Raleigh Gilbert's brief stay on the Sagadahoc River in Maine in 1607. It was sturdy enough to cross the Atlantic twice, surviving the storm that wrecked *Sea Venture*.

during an onshore gale could be disastrous. Guy preferred to 'put forth of Greene Bay, choosing rather to continue turning in the bay, than to ride in such a road, to the hazard of the loss of all our anchors'.

It was not only a naturally rocky bottom that threatened to wear away rope hawsers. Richard Whitbourne, commenting on the practice of fishing vessels anchored in Newfoundland harbours to embark many large stones to serve as presses in the production of train-oil, only to cast them overboard before they sailed, remarked that the rocks were 'to be seen lying in great heaps in some places, within three fathoms of water, to the great endangering of ships and cables'.

The need for a secure holding ground at which their resupply ships could ride in safety and in comfort close inshore should have dictated the choice of location for the initial landings. At Roanoke it did not, and the result, twice over, was disaster. Those outer rough seas continued to disturb and disrupt the presence of the ships attendant offshore. Weighing anchor by bringing the thick hawser home turn by turn upon a capstan required most of the ship's company to push hard against the capstan bars. If, while this was being carried out, the hawser was alternately tensioning and slackening due to a sea swell, as was present off the Outer Banks, the task became all the more difficult and dangerous. In August 1587, Governor White, forced by a disagreement with Ferdinando to make his return journey in the accompanying flyboat, reported that, on weighing anchor:

> twelve of the men which were in the flyboat were thrown from the capstan, which by means of a bar that broke, came so fast about upon them, that the other two bars thereof struck and hurt most of them so sore, that some of them never recovered it: nevertheless they assayed presently again to weigh their anchor, but being so weakened with the first fling, they were not able to weigh it, but were thrown down, and hurt the second time. Whereof, having in all but fifteen men aboard and most of them by this unfortunate beginning so bruised, and hurt, they were forced to cut their cable and lose their anchor.

Building in Bermuda

The vessels referred to above, with their agreed dimensions and ratios, were built in yards around England under the watchful supervision of experienced shipwrights. They needed to be, for they represented by far the most complicated exercise in design, construction and engineering and investment known up to that time and for centuries to come. Yet, it was not long before the settlers in America were building their own ships. In Newfoundland John Guy built *Endeavour* to explore the area while, even before that, in 1607, the men of the short-lived Popham colony built the pinnace *Virginia* so well that she crossed the Atlantic and then sailed for Virginia with the third resupply, surviving the hurricane that drove *Sea Venture* ashore on the Bermudas, leading to the most amazing of the shipbuilding sagas.

Sea Venture grounded on 28 July 1609, but was so skilfully manoeuvred in her final moments that she became solidly and unbrokenly wedged close enough to the shore for her to be abandoned without loss of life. Perhaps that feat alone should indicate the mettle of those onboard and their determination to escape from their rather pleasant desert isle. They began with caution and failure, converting the ship's boat to a decked vessel seaworthy enough for a voyage to America. On 30 August, under the command of *Sea Venture*'s master's mate, Henry Ravens, and having conducted two days of sea-trials while circumnavigating Bermuda, six of the survivors set sail to raise the alarm in Jamestown. Their fate remains unknown.

Back on Bermuda, a salvage and survival operation was being overseen by the shipwright Richard Frobisher. While some men waded out to the wreck and stripped her of her timbers, others rough-hewed them into a new vessel at a point now known as Buildings Bay. Unlike the division between gentry and labourers which was bedevilling Jamestown, here all worked, from Sir Thomas Gates down. As the new vessel, *Deliverance*, took shape it became obvious to the admiral, Sir George Somers, that at eighty tons and forty foot long, she would be unable to carry all the 144 survivors over to Virginia (142 in the end, as two mutineers chose to remain behind). Rather than spend time arguing or debating the issue, Somers was given his own team of twenty to build a smaller ship, a pinnace, which would be named *Patience*.

The task they had set themselves might have seemed extraordinary but they were helped, not only by good leadership, but by the fact that this was a pleasant isle with no native population to harass them, an abundance of fish in the sea and plenty of berries on the bushes; in short, an ideal place to be shipwrecked. Too ideal for some of the men, who in mid-September mutinied because they had no wish to sail away! Their plot and their punishment was well handled and caused no real disruption of the building work. The work was spiced up by an element of competition, with Somers at a double disadvantage, not only in having started later but in that his team had to fell and cut to size their timbers from the great cedars that grew on the island. *Patience* was to be secured by treenails; Gates gave Somers just one iron bolt, which was used to help secure the keelson to the keel.

Winter storms threatened the work, with the *Deliverance* team being forced to erect a dam rapidly around their ship on its stocks to prevent high and heavy seas pounding her hull to pieces. She survived, and in February she was caulked to await the next high tide, which came at the end of March, when she was dragged forward to meet the water in which she was buoyed up and towed by a small island-built boat to a deep but secure spot where she could be ballasted and fitted out. A month later she was joined by the twenty-nine-foot *Patience*. Over the centuries myriads of shipbuilders have stood back and watched their efforts bob proudly on the water, but it is unlikely that any stood more overjoyed and with chests more swelled with just and joyous pride than did the Bermuda builders that April day.

Thanks to the writings of William Strachey, we also have one of the few records of the dimensions of ships built at that time. That of *Deliverance* appears at the head of this chapter, while of *Patience* he noted: 'she was by the keel nine and twenty foot: at the beam fifteen foot and a half; at the loofe fourteen foot, at the transom nine, and she was eight foot deep, and drew six foot of water.'

Fitting out and victualling took another month, and it was not until 10 May that the survivors embarked on their voyage, which did not begin auspiciously. First, the wind died, meaning that the ships had to be towed through the narrow channels, then *Deliverance* ran aground, but luckily onto soft coral which powdered under her weight. If pride had been the common emotion in April, anxiety must have gripped them all that day in May. Two things now worked in their favour. The first was that the winds were steady but never strong: the second was that in Captain Newport they had a skilled navigator who knew these seas well. On 21 May he brought his small fleet into the Chesapeake to complete a journey the like of which can seldom have been equalled. Sadly, the state of the colony, which they had expended so much genius and backbreaking effort to reach so dutifully, must have shocked and hurt them, and many must have thought that life would have been better had they remained in Bermuda. Nevertheless here they were and the ships they had built had further roles to undertake, once the decision to abandon Jamestown had been overturned by the arrival of Lord De La Warr.

Patience was to see Bermuda again, carrying Sir George Somers there to pick up supplies to take back to Virginia. However, the admiral died on the island and his nephew sailed on for England, taking his noble uncle with him to be buried at his ancestral village, Whitchurch Canonicorum, near Lyme Regis. Thus, a small pinnace built for a short spring voyage proved herself sturdy enough to endure a 3,000-mile transatlantic voyage. What credit. For a short while the islands on which Sir George had so valiantly laboured were named, with a delightful double entendre, the Somers Isles, but the term fell into disuse and it is the name Bermuda that has endured. *Deliverance* also faded into history, her fate unknown. Her replica, built as a tourist attraction in Bermuda, was also in danger of disappearing following storm damage in 2007. Luckily, funding was forthcoming to effect repairs and she is once again open to the public.

The amazing story of the Bermuda shipbuilders did not end with the departure of *Deliverance* and *Patience*. In 1616 five 'plain and simple fellows' in the now established colony decided that they had had enough of life in Bermuda and wanted to return to England. Knowing that they would be refused permission to depart, they planned a getaway as bold and ingenious as those used centuries later to escape from German POW camps. First they got permission and enthusiastic assistance from the Governor to build a two-ton decked fishing boat. Like the 'wooden horse' of Stalag Luft III, this was built in the open and became so dear to the Governor's heart that he decided that no finer vessel was available to row him out to say farewell to *George*, the ship in which he had arrived. But when those that were sent to get the boat arrived at her berth they found that the boat had gone. The disgruntled five had 'shaped, as near as their small skill would serve them for England, being a voyage of about three thousand five hundred miles, having a huge and vast sea to traverse, and full many a dangerous and horrible tempest to escape'. After a month at sea they fell in with a French rover who 'inhumanely and barbarously' robbed them of their cargo of tobacco and cast them off again. After seven weeks they had exhausted their victuals but their main danger was, possibly, a unique one, for they had hewn away about half of the knees of their vessel to use as firewood, thus almost causing a foundering from within. However, they eventually came ashore near the mouth of the Shannon, where their story and their cockle of a craft so impressed the Earl of Thomond that he had the boat hoisted up and mounted on the walls of Drumoland Castle.

Tiller of the pinnace *Discovery*. Unlike larger vessels, pinnaces were steered by direct movement of the tiller, giving greater manoeuvrability but still needing tackles in rough weather.

Coastal and Inshore Boats

Throughout the period, voyages took place up rivers and along the coasts between Jamestown and Newfoundland. They had a variety of aims, of which the most encouraged and least valuable was to seek for a passage to Cathay. This occupied much of Christopher Newport's time in Jamestown and, although John Smith made better use of his inland voyages, he too hankered after finding a through-channel that would bring him fame. Yet, locally based craft were required for a much more useful purpose – survival.

Guy's Newfoundland journey in *Endeavour* is just one example of how important smaller vessels were for carrying out the numerous inshore waters tasks necessary to support an isolated coastal community. These ranged from foraging and fishing – by far the most important – to trading, exploring and, when necessary, raids on neighbouring settlements. For many of these tasks pinnaces proved ideal. These were single-decked vessels, like *Discovery*, which, on long voyages, might even be towed astern of a ship or carried in a kit form. For major amphibious operations they acted as the landing craft to take the soldiers ashore: on his 1595 voyage, Drake took fourteen prefabricated pinnaces, while a further eleven sailed independently. They joined together for his unsuccessful night attack on San Juan in Puerto Rico, his last assault before his death in January 1596 off Nombre Dios, which he had captured in 1572 with just three pinnaces. As with so many wooden sailing vessels, there was no firm definition of these light craft; they could carry either one or two masts and, although many were fitted with oars, some were not.

Pinnaces were unsuitable for work in creeks and the upper reaches of the rivers. Here, one-masted open rowing boats called shallops were employed. It was in a shallop that Christopher Newport made his initial journey upstream and John Smith his trip up the Chickahominy that resulted in his capture by the Powhatans and his life being saved by Pocahontas. It was in a slightly different version of the shallop, the light horseman, that Ralph Lane carried out his raid from Roanoke. Smith had his moments of excitement when storms whipped across the bay, but taking an open shallop out to sea was foolhardy. This was especially so for the Plymouth colony, where smaller vessels could meet mighty seas the moment they cleared the shelter of Cape Cod Bay which could itself be very choppy.

To replace the unseaworthy *Speedwell*, which would have remained in America to serve the settlers as a fishing and general-purpose vessel, had she managed the crossing, the Merchant Venturers dispatched, in the summer of 1623, the forty-four-ton pinnace *Little James* as her substitute. Later that year, returning from a trading trip to the Narragansett Amerindians, her anchors dragged and she drifted into the shallows off Brown's Island, close to Plymouth harbour, necessitating the cutting away of her mainmast to reduce her windage and relieve the strain on the anchors. This done, she held, but the following year, when on a fishing trip to Maine, her luck ran out. Anchored near Damariscove Island, where Sir Ferdinando Gorges had established a small fishing colony the previous year, she was battered by a gale which 'drove her against great rocks, which beat such a hole in her bulk, as a horse and cart might have gone in, and after drove her into deep water where she sank'. She was raised but, as described later, even after her resurrection she remained unlucky. She was not the last little ship to be castaway: Governor Bradford's account of the establishment of the Plymouth settlement lists several more. In 1626, desperate for a craft to replace the sunken pinnace, he recorded:

> Finding they ran great hazard to go on long voyages in a small open boat, especially in the winter season, they began to think how they might get a small pinnace . . . and took one of the biggest of their shallops and sawed her in the middle, and so lengthened her by some five to six foot, and strengthened her with timbers, and so built her up and laid a deck on her; and so made her a convenient, and wholesome vessel, very fit and comfortable for their use, which served them seven years.

Four centuries after Roanoke and Jamestown were first settled, the estuarine and rivers of the region are still lined with trees stretching well inland. Much of this is secondary woodland but it still gives a clear idea of the dense coverage of primeval forest that existed, albeit with signs of slash and burn clearings, when the colonists first arrived. Even today it is possible to lose a sense of direction on Jamestown Island or at the Roanoke site of Fort Raleigh, where one can easily stumble upon wide swamps or creeks too deep to wade across. The first settlers, with no idea of the geography of the surrounding land, would have been similarly disorientated, and they had also the fear of the native peoples to add to their woes. Indeed, it would be not too inaccurate to state that the majority of overland expeditions ended in failure while those undertaken by boat were usually successful.

In short, the English had established beachheads from which the most logical and defensible route out was by water. What is more, with an inability to clear sufficient land to establish their own protected fields, the year-round harvest of the sea offered the best resource to prevent their starvation. For this they needed armed fishing boats, supported by a larger vessel that could be used either for loading bushels of corn foraged from the Amerindians, or to sail to the northern fishing banks. In addition, a warship, at the least capable of frightening off pirates, at best defending against the Spanish, would have strengthened both morale and the beachheads from the Carolinas to Newfoundland. Yet the investors, from Ralegh to the Virginia Company, did not provide such ships. Had they done so, the durability of Lane at Roanoke might have been extended and the ordeal endured at Jamestown been reduced.

In the end it was a matter of investment. The issue of Charters meant that the Crown did not have to provide much for something that did not meet its approval. Elizabeth, having lost her investment in Lok's Company of Cathay through false assaying, had no wish to be similarly burnt, preferring to be an accomplice in the theft of recognizable, realizable, wealth that others had conveniently gathered together. A clear indication of the Crown's priorities becomes evident when one compares the investment and returns from various enterprises beyond Europe (Appendix 4). In his long reign, Henry VIII, who had created a large standing navy, released just one vessel, *Mary Guildford*, to sail across the Atlantic. Other than for raiding, Elizabeth, with a similar-sized fleet, loaned *Ayde* to Frobisher and *Tyger* to Ralegh. She was content to lend her sobriquet but not her sovereigns or her ships for establishing settlements. James, even cannier with his cash, provided not one ship, giving his name to a river and a fort but little else besides. Had either monarch shared the enthusiasm of the few advocates for invasion, they could have provided the ships and resources that would have secured the settlements.

CHAPTER 6

Pilotage and Navigation

For it is not unknown to your wisdom, how necessary for service of wars arithmetic and geometry are, and for our new discoveries and long voyages by sea, the art of navigation is one which is composed of many parts of the aforementioned science.

Richard Hakluyt to Sir Francis Walsingham, Paris, 1584

THE HAVEN-FINDING ART

As this work is being finished the newspapers and televisions are full of pictures of the wreck of the Italian cruise-ship *Costa Concordia* lying on her side in shallow well-known and well-charted waters unable, despite the presence of every modern navigational aid, to keep clear of the rocks. How much should we therefore admire those who, with neither charts nor sophisticated aids, managed to sail safely to America and back? How much more should we sympathize with and understand those who got it wrong?

For the English sailing masters, crossing the Atlantic in the sixteenth century was analogous to feeling their way across an unfamiliar darkened room in which the occasional piece of furniture lay waiting to trip them up on the way over, and with no certain knowledge as to when they might bump into the wall at the far end. All they had to confirm, roughly, where they were was, as far as the lateral walls were concerned, an occasional glimpse of the sun at midday and a pinprick of light from the Pole Star at night. Neither of these gave any indication of their proximity to the great bulwark that lay across their path.

Of equal importance was the fact that in the sixteenth century most English vessels sailed to standard European ports along traditional tracks. This meant that, by the time he achieved command, although a master had served a long apprenticeship in which he 'learned the ropes', he only knew, intimately, his standard route and ports of call. One such master was Captain Christopher Jones who was hired, along with his own vessel, *Mayflower*, to take the Pilgrims across the Atlantic. Records show that, prior to his voyage to Cape Cod, Captain Christopher Jones, had sailed *Mayflower*:

In 1609: to Trondheim in Norway, with a cargo of hats, hemp, salt, hops, vinegar on the outward journey and returning with tar, deal and herring.

In 1612: to La Rochelle in France with cloth, stockings, iron, pewter and virginals.

In 1614: from Hamburg with a cargo of taffeta, satin, sarsenet [silk fabric] and lawn [fine linen from Laon].

In 1615: inbound from La Rochelle, with Gascon and Cognac wines

These trips would have represented a typical record for many ships and most masters. Given a contented monarch, a wealth-satiated nobility and a well-rewarded merchant-class, there was little incentive to encourage voyages further afield, and so, for the most part, English ship masters were coastal sailors whose navigational requirements were, for the most part, satisfied by glancing at their own notebook, or the one they had inherited from the retiring master. Standard printed pilots, even had they needed one, just did not exist; neither could charts be purchased to plan a passage to an unknown port. On his known routes the requirements for making a safe voyage were few, but they were, in the hands of the trained, sufficient. So confident were the masters in their own skill at managing this limited hand that they were reported to have scorned those that would seek greater knowledge of the haven-finding arts. William Bourne condemned these men for their parochialism. While admitting that 'a simple Fisher-man of Barking knoweth Barking Creeke, better than the best Navigator or Master in this land,' he pointed out that, 'if they should come out of the Ocean sea to seek our channel . . . I am of the opinion that a number of them, doth but grope as a blind man doth.' What would be needed, at the far side of the Atlantic, was sufficient inshore information to make a Barking Creek of the Chesapeake for, while oceans allow errors, leniency is not an attribute of shallow waters.

Other than a trained eye, English mariners required few aids to conduct a safe passage in known coastal waters. They would have carried at least one magnetic compass, which served to give the helmsman a course to steer and an aid to holding the ship steady on

Modern replicas of a traverse board, log and line, compass binnacle and sand glass. With the addition of a sounding lead, these would have been all the instruments required for safe coastal pilotage in known waters.

that course. A traverse board, into which pegs were inserted at the change of watch, acted as a plot for the ship's track, while the vessel's speed through the water could be gauged by either throwing a log overboard and timing its movement aft with a half-minute sand glass, or by trailing the more sophisticated log and line, which was knotted at an appropriate distance to give an easy reading of nautical miles, knots, made good.

As he turned inshore at journey's end, the master would order a leadsman to take soundings up forward and report both the depth and, because the lead was 'armed' with tallow onto which a sample of the seabed could adhere, the nature of the seabed, to assist with establishing the ship's position.

Another important fact that the master needed to know was the phases of the moon so that he could predict the time and height of tide, which affected not only his choice of when to enter or leave harbour but could help him to know when to anchor in the Channel so as not to be carried back by an opposing current when the lack of wind or its adverse direction was also impeding progress. Luckily, a lunar almanac was simple to produce and interpolations of the data reasonably formulaic.

In summary, in his notebook, or rutter, a competent master would have recorded:

The tidal streams around the coast
Routes and courses to steer between ports
Entering and leaving harbour directions
Location and distances between harbours
Soundings to be anticipated and the nature of the seabed
The distances between headlands in 'kennings' of twenty miles
Flood and ebb tides and lunar data.

None of these would be available for those arriving off America for the first time. The result was the publication of both narratives and detailed descriptions of pilotage observations. However, before they could arrive safely, the masters needed to learn how to travel successfully by learning how to use astronomical instruments and data, a task that William Bourne felt was beyond their competence, when he wrote:

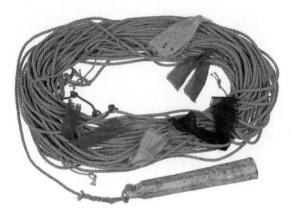

A modern copy of a log line, showing the knots clearly marked every fifty-one feet to give a reading of the ship's speed in nautical miles per hour (knots). (National Maritime Museum)

Costumed interpreters from *Mary Rose* demonstrating how a log and line was deployed from the stern of a sailing ship.

I do hope that in these days, that the knowledge of the Masters of ships is very well mended, for I have known within this twenty years that them that were ancient masters of ships hath derided and mocked they that have occupied their Cards and Plots, and also the observation of the altitude of the Pole, saying that they care not for their sheep's skins, for he could keep better account onboard.

And when that they did take the latitude, they would call them star shooters and Sun shooters, and would ask if they had struck it . . . And yet these simple people will make no small brag of themselves . . . what notable fellows they themselves are.

In succinct summary, what Bourne was commentating on was a very well-known navigational saw, which might prove to be the case with the *Costa Concordia*: that a ship is in greatest danger when her master is in error but not in doubt.

The Ocean-Crossing Science

The sixteenth century had seen several advances in the science of navigation but it was still a subject in which English seamen were several classes behind their more intrepid fellow mariners from the Iberian Peninsula, mainly because they were less adventurous. It is of note that one of the voyages that Hakluyt deemed worthy of inclusion in his *Principal Navigations, Voyages and Discoveries of the English Nation*, first published in 1589, was the voyage of Roger Bodenham in the bark *Archer* to Crete and Cos, undertaken in 1550. The equivalent Portuguese work, Camoëns's epic poem *The Lusiads*, published in 1572, tells of Vasco da Gama's epic voyage around Africa to India, undertaken in 1497. Magellan sailed on his voyage of circumnavigation in 1519, Drake on his in 1577. This sixty-year time-lag between competing maritime nations was something that the English Atlantic voyages helped to reduce.

The latter half of the century saw a number of works being published in English on the subject of navigation. Many were translations from the Spanish or Portuguese. A number of those involved in writing these works had interests in American voyages: John Dee's *The Perfect Arte of Navigation* was published in 1577; the northern waters explorer John Davies's *Seaman's Secrets* was published in 1594; George Waymouth's *The Jewell of Artes*, published in 1604, was in part based on the considerable practical navigational skills he had accrued during his 1602 voyage to discover the northwest passage. Advice on practical seamanship was published by John Smith in his *A Sea Grammar* of 1627; similar works included *Boteler's Dialogues* written by Nathaniel Butler, who had been Governor of Bermuda, and the observations of Mainwaring, the one-time Newfoundland pirate.

Textbooks by themselves did not create competent navigators. As Robert Hues wrote in his *Treatise on the Globe* in 1592, the efforts of Englishmen would have achieved more, 'had they but taken along with them a very reasonable competency of skill in Geometry and Astronomy, they had by this gotten themselves a far more honourable name at Sea'. Yet, as Dee found with his dull student, Martin Frobisher, it was vanity to teach a master mathematics and astronomy if the latter could not grasp the fundamentals of what was both a new and a complicated discipline, involving the use of unfamiliar

An advance on the cross-staff and back-staff, the quadrant was still an awkward instrument with which to measure the angle subtended between a heavenly body and the horizon, from which the ship's latitude could be calculated. It was not easy to use on a rolling deck. (National Maritime Museum)

The astrolabe marked a great leap forward in astronomical observation as it allowed the sun to cast its light through two pin-holes without the pilot having to squint directly at the sun itself. Many ornate and sophisticated instruments were produced, but most masters would have been content to carry a robust, no-frills version. This example dates from about 1588 and may have come from one of the wrecks of the Spanish Armada. (National Maritime Museum)

instruments. Of course, not all English mariners were slow learners: the self-taught Drake's successful and highly competent circumnavigation is a clear contrast to the fumbles of Frobisher. Once again, the Crown showed little inclination to lead the way for, unlike either Spain or Portugal, it did not sponsor a school of navigation, although a good case was put to Elizabeth by William Borough following his visit to Spain in Mary's reign.

LATITUDE

The transatlantic navigator had only to determine two things: his latitude and his longitude. For the former, instruments such as the cross-staff, back-staff and astrolabe existed with which to measure the angle from the horizon of a chosen heavenly body. Once this had been observed, the ship's latitude could be worked out by interpolation from tables of declination, provided the user was aware of the formula that needed to be applied, depending on the time of year and the relative positions of the ship, the sun and the equator, an exercise in spherical trigonometry that can still tax the brain of modern students of navigation. This, of course, assumed that the sun was visible at the critical moment of midday and that the rolling movement of the ship allowed for a reasonably accurate series of measurements to be taken.

The simplest, and often the safest, passage was one in which the master sailed to the known latitude of his destination and then, through observation, ran down that line until the destination was reached. Thus Humphrey Gilbert instructed his expedition to 'keep to the height of forty six degrees', while Frobisher, when returning from his quests for the northwest passage, had his fleet run down to the requisite latitude before turning east for the Channel. However, prevailing winds, ocean currents and lack of experience and confidence meant that, apart from the Newfoundland and northwest passage voyages, the English were initially content to follow the island-hopping tracks that the Spanish, and their own pioneer, John Hawkins, had taken to the West Indies, before turning north to reach Virginia. Such a semi-circular route also brought with it the chance to water ship and revictual among the islands and, in many a commander's mind, the opportunity to take a prize or two and so 'make' the voyage.

As more and more experience was gained, so pilots were able to collect a library of books of reference for their instruction. John Smith produced a suggested list after the following common sense guidance:

To learn to observe the Altitude, Latitude, Longitude, Amplitude, the variation of the Compass, the Sun's azimuth and Almicanter [the altitude of stars]; to shift the sun and moon, and to know your tides, your Rhumbs [lines on the chart enabling the shortest route to be plotted], prick your card, say your compass, get some of these books – but practice is best:

Master Wright's errors of Navigation
Master Tapp's seamen's calendar

The Art of Navigation
A Regiment for the Sea
The Seamen's Secrets
A Waggoner
Master Gunter's work
The Seamen's Glass for the scale
The New attractor for the variation
Master Wright, for the use of the globe
Master Hughes, for the same.

LONGITUDE

There was another good reason, apart from the fierce grip of weather and currents and the opportunity for refreshment, which encouraged English ships to sail circuitously to Virginia. It meant that they could establish their longitude in the West Indies with comparative safety and then approach the haven-lacking shores of North America at a gentle angle rather than have their position confirmed by driving upon that coast in the dark of night. Throughout the century the ascertaining of a ship's longitude was to prove intractable, although many suggestions were made as to how this might be done. The pithiest summary of the position was that offered up in *Boteler's Dialogues*:

Admiral: 'You have told me what the longitude is; let me also know how it is to be taken.'
Captain: 'I can more readily and surely tell you how it is not taken (or rather that it cannot be taken at all).'

The Captain then lists in long paragraphs four possible but very complicated and unproven ways of ascertaining longitude, involving: the eclipse of the moon; a reliable clock or glass; observation of the distance between the moon and another celestial object; and differences between the moon and the sun's positions. At the end of this the Captain's succinct summary is: 'whoever practised it had need to be very curious and a better arithmetician than most of our common masters.'

Bourne was similarly unimpressed by all the ways suggested to measure longitude, recommending that 'no seamen trouble themselves with this rule, but according to their accustomed manner, let them keep a perfect accord and reckoning of the way of his ship, whether the ship goeth to leeward or maketh her way good, considering whatever thing be against him or with him: as tides, currents, winds, or such like.'

With no method for working out longitude, meaning that opportunities for disaster were frequent, masters had to put a great deal of faith in their dead reckoning skills, their ability to estimate where the ship was through estimating the distance she had covered over the past hours. This was an art, for none of the variables involved in the dead reckoning of one's position was the product of empirical observation. The master could plot out his courses steered and the time spent on each leg; he could use a log and line to estimate the ship's speed and he could make allowances for drift, but he could not be on watch himself twenty-four hours a day and neither could he be sure of such influences as the currents, leeway, steerage error, compass variations and bad weather. Yet, with no certainty that the land that one was seeking was located at the longitude suggested on a chart, the opportunity for a precipitous and unexpected arrival remained, and dead reckoning was never, and rightly so, considered to be foolproof. The Dutch, who lost several ships on the reefs of Australasia, referred to dead reckoning as 'a blind and stupid pilot'.

With such imprecise instruments and methods of making an accurate landfall, many masters would have chosen to have aimed well north or south of their destination so they could alter course confidently once they reached the coast and run down to their to desired port. A most significant use of this method may well have been employed by the inexperienced ocean navigator Christopher Jones in 1620 to compensate for the strong winds and cloudy skies that he had experienced during his voyage to the Hudson. Making a landfall at Cape Cod, just some ninety miles laterally from his intended destination, and only forty miles from the northern end of Long Island Sound, represented an excellent feat of navigation after sixty-five days at sea that would have been crowned with a successful arrival off Manhattan a few days after Jones turned southwest to head for the Hudson. However, this was the moment when navigation turned into pilotage, and *Mayflower* did not carry appropriate charts to conduct a passage in inshore waters with any degree of safety, especially as Jones knew of, and could see ahead of him, the aptly named eddies of Pollack's Rip and Tucker's Terror, of which peril Bradford wrote later:

> But after they had sailed the course about half a day, they fell among dangerous shoals and roaring breakers, and they were so far entangled there with them that they conceived themselves in great danger; and the wind shrieking upon them withal, they resolved to bear up again for the Cape, and thought themselves happy to get out of these dangers before night overtook them, as by God's providence they did.

Both Bartholomew Gosnold and Samuel de Champlain had passed this way earlier in the century. Hudson had stood out to sea when heading south in 1610 to avoid the rips, but Christopher Levett had made a direct passage as recently as 1619. However, given his circumstances, Jones made the sensible navigational choice and turned away. The compiler of the modern *Admiralty Sailing Directions for the East Coast of the United States* would have approved his decision, for it states that the waters off Maine are freckled with islands, creating a maze for any navigator to pass through and record with accuracy, as are the Nantucket Shoals south of Cape Cod, which 'are subject to change in depth and position' and hence 'mariners should seek local knowledge before entering' them. Rather than take the risk, *Mayflower* in 1620 famously went about and, shortly and significantly, anchored in the one harbour of which all mariners wax lyrical, Provincetown, which the pilot states 'is one of the best on the Atlantic coast of the United States, having a large anchorage area with excellent holding ground [providing] shelter in it from gales from any direction.'

Jones's route to America was not unprecedented. In 1617, the widowed John Rolfe, returning to Virginia from England in *George*, reported that, after twenty-one days at sea, they lost contact with their admiral, *Treasurer*, which was commanded by the experienced Samuel Argall, and some twenty days later found themselves on 'the dangerous shoulder of Cape Cod running in one glass from twenty to five and four fathoms'. Their anxiety was heightened by the presence of thick fog which reduced visibility to half a cable. Wisely they anchored, and, having got underway again, arrived in the Chesapeake without further incident, having made 'a speedy passage.'

New World Pilotage

When they reached Virginia the English were presented with a coastline which few had visited, none had charted and which for hundreds of miles was either low-lying and featureless in the south or island strewn and rock bespattered in the north, factors that signalled danger for the approaching chartless navigator. Thus, the first decades of English voyages to the new world provide us with a glimpse of how a body of pilotage knowledge was gradually constructed and disseminated.

At the beginning of 1498, John Day, a Spanish spy resident in Bristol, sent to Columbus a short account of Cabot's voyage, enclosing a copy of a map that the latter had made. It would not have been accurate, for Cabot knew neither his latitude or longitude when he reached land, so that his actual landfall remains the subject of guesswork. Day stated:

> in it are named the capes of the mainland and the islands, and thus you will see where the land was first sighted, since most of the land was discovered after turning back. Thus your Lordship will know that the cape nearest Ireland is 1800 miles west of Dursey Head, which is in Ireland, and the southernmost part of the Island of the Seven Cities is west of Bordeaux River . . .

The account does little but confirm that a large lump of land lies on the other side of the Atlantic Ocean.

Almost a hundred years later, in 1584, when Amadas and Barlowe sailed to reconnoitre the Americas for a suitable site to colonize, the latter's report was more detailed:

> the second of July, we found shoal water, where we smelt so sweet, and so strong a smell, as if we had been in the midst of some delicate garden abounding with all kind of odoriferous flowers, by which we were assured, that the land could not be far distant: and keeping good watch, and bearing but slack sail, the fourth of the same month we arrived upon the coast, which we supposed to be a continent and firm land, and we sailed along the same a hundred and twenty English miles before we could find any entrance, or river issuing into the Sea. The first that appeared unto us, we entered, though not without some difficulty and cast anchor about three harquebus-shot within the haven's mouth, on the left hand of the same: and after thanks given to God for our safe arrival thither, we manned our boats, and went to view the land next adjoining.

This is an excellent summary of the cautious approach to be followed by a professional navigator when closing an unknown shore and the signs to be observed to indicate the proximity of land, smell being one indicator that has all but disappeared in the age of power-driven vessels. Barlowe went on to describe the inshore waters that he had seen:

> When we first had sight of this Country, some thought the first land we saw to be the continent: but after we entered into the haven, we saw before us another mighty long Sea: for there lieth along the coast a tract of Islands, two hundred miles in length, adjoining to the Ocean sea, and between the Islands, two or three entrances: when you are entered between them (these Islands being very narrow, for the most part, as in most places six miles broad, in some places less, in few more) then there appeareth another great Sea, containing in breadth in some places, forty, and in some fifty, in some twenty miles over, before you come to the continent . . .

These few lines contain sufficient detail for a subsequent voyager to appreciate when he had entered the region described by Barlowe. There is also enough information, which it must be assumed was backed up by personal debriefing, to indicate that the passage through the outer islands into the inner sea needed to be undertaken with caution.

Captain Christopher Levett was also cautious on his offshore journeys. In what could be an excellent summary of the pilot's art, he recalled one voyage off New England, when:

> About four leagues further east, there is another harbour called Sawco. Before we could recover the harbour a great fog or mist took us that we could not see a hundred yards from us. I perceiving the fog to come upon the Sea, called for a Compass and set the Cape land, by which we knew how to steer our course, which was no sooner done but we lost sight of land, and my other boat, and the wind blew fresh against us, so that we were enforced to strike sail and betake us to our oars which we used with all the wit and strength we had, but by no means could we recover the shore that night, being embayed and compassed round with breaches, which roared in a most fearful manner on every side of us; we took counsel in this extremity one of another what to do to save our lives, at length we resolved that to put to sea again in the night was no fit course, the storm being great, and the wind blowing right off the shore, and to run our boat on the shore amongst the breaches, (which roared in a most fearful manner) and cast her away and endanger ourselves we were loath to do, seeing no land nor knowing where we were. At length I caused our killick (which was all the anchor we had) to be cast forth, and one continually to hold his hand upon the rope or cable, by which we knew whether our anchor held or no: which being done we commended ourselves to God by prayer, & put on a resolution to be as comfortable as we could, and so fell to our victuals. Thus we spent that night, and the next morning, with much ado we got into Sawco, where I found my other boat.

NAVIGATIONAL ERRORS

Unfortunately, the pilot who sailed on all three of the early Roanoke voyages, Simon Ferdinando, was brash, over-confident and incapable of caution; his errors of judgement and faults in character cost the would-be colonists dear, even to the loss of their lives. So, although the skill and professionalism of the masters that brought ships safely across the Atlantic to Virginia deserves record and praise, their abilities might best be appreciated by studying the misfortunes of those who were unlucky enough to take passage with one evidently less skilled.

Ferdinando made his first recorded voyage towards the Americas when he sailed as pilot under Walter Ralegh in *Falcon*, one of the ships in Sir Humphrey Gilbert's fleet that was driven back to Devon by September's equinoctial gales. Ralegh stayed at sea and tried his hand at piracy, only to be taught a lesson by the Spaniards he tried to board. He moved on, but the following year Ferdinando made an exploratory voyage to America on behalf of Humphrey Gilbert before being employed as pilot of the admiral for the 1584 exploratory voyage undertaken by Barlowe and Amadas. For the succeeding voyages to be successful they would have needed a detailed preliminary report on coastal waters and options for havens secure both from the elements and the Spanish. This they did not get; as Barlowe acknowledged in his narrative sent to Walter Ralegh, 'I think it a matter both unnecessary, for the manifest discovery of the Country, as also for tediousness sake, to remember unto you the diurnal of our course, sailing thither, and returning . . .' However, Ferdinando, who – it is clearly stated by Barlowe – took part in the expeditions by boat to explore the inland waters, should, knowing their purpose, have made copious observations and notes for future use. He does not appear to have done so, perhaps assuming that he could remember sufficient and that, if he retained all in his own mind, he would be guaranteed employment in the subsequent voyage which, sadly, he was.

Duly appointed as Grenville's master and pilot for the transport of the settlers in 1585, Ferdinando was both complicit in and contributory to the errors that led to Ralph Lane's colonists failing to establish their beachhead to their best advantage. In the first instance, he seems to have done little to hasten Grenville's passage through the West Indies, where the English dawdled and delighted in the land's abundance and, surprisingly, Spanish hospitality. Barlowe, sailing on 27 April, reached the Carolina Outer Banks in early July; Grenville, sailing on 19 April the following year, grounded on those banks on 29 June, having taken eighty-one days for the same journey. This slow passage would be insignificant were it not for the fact that, to survive the winter in good shape, Lane's men needed to have cleared ground and harvested a crop before the onset of the cold. Planting at the end of July, which was when Lane's men landed on Roanoke, gave them no chance of a successful yield. The passage could have been considerably shorter; on 6 July, reconnoitring Croatoan Island, they 'found two of our men left there with 30 others by Captain Reymond, some 20 days before'.

What is more, on 20 June Ferdinando had almost run the fleet aground off Cape Fear; before, on 29 June, attempting to pass through the narrow channel at Wokoton (modern Ocrocoke) into Pamlico Sound, *Tyger*, 'through the unskilfulness of the Master . . . struck the ground and sank'. Well, she did not really sink, she only grounded, but with sufficient force to split her seams so that 'the salt water came so abundantly into her, that the most part of his corn, salt, meat, rice, biscuit, and other provisions that he should have left with them that remained behind him in the country was spoiled'.

Tyger was refloated and able to sail a few days later when the fleet moved up the coast beyond Cape Hatteras and to an offshore anchorage on the Atlantic side of Roanoke Island, but the damage had been done. Poor pilotage practice meant that Lane's 107 men were landed, ill provisioned, to fend for themselves until a relief supply arrived. Thus began the English malpractice of scrounging, demanding and forcibly removing scarce provisions from the neighbouring native peoples, who soon tired of having bullying beggars on their land.

Whatever his professional shortcomings, Ferdinando was reappointed master for the 1587 Virginia voyage. John White was soon suspicious of both his competence and motives from early in the passage when Ferdinando appeared to abandon the fleet's flyboat, 'leaving her distressed in the Bay of Portugal'. Once across the Atlantic, Ferdinando directed a victualling party to an island which he reported to be full of sheep, only for none to be found there; he also told the voyagers that the island on which they were refreshing themselves was free of 'savages' when their presence was most evident. Later, a watering stop with only a trickle of water, so that they drank more beer there than they replenished with water, was followed by an unsatisfactory call to collect salt, which was abandoned when Ferdinando 'caused the lead to be cast, and

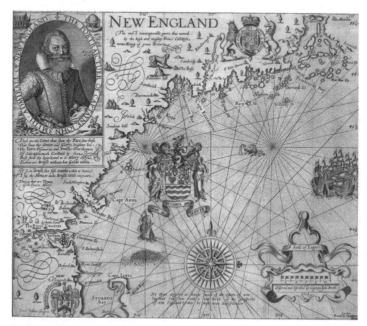

John Smith was a stern critic of any rival cartographer. That he spoke from strength is clearly indicated in this most competent map of New England. Note the large shoal of fish off Cape James, yet to be renamed Cape Cod.

having craftily brought the ship in three fathoms, and a half water, he suddenly began to swear . . . dissembling great danger, crying to him at the helm, "bear up hard, bear up hard", so we went off, and were disappointed of our salt, by his means.'

Then, with Virginia in sight, Ferdinando misrecognized his landmarks and had them anchor off what he reported to be Croatoan Island, only to admit his error and then almost to repeat his mistake of two years earlier when, during the night, they narrowly missed being 'cast away upon the beaches, called the Cape of Fear, for we were come within two cables' length upon it: such was the carelessness and ignorance of our Master'.

Even after the settlers had arrived in Virginia, Ferdinando played one more cruel trick on them. The original intention had been to land at Roanoke to see if any of the fifteen 'volunteers' that Grenville had left behind were still there, and then to sail on up to the more promising sites on the Chesapeake. But, once White had climbed onboard the pinnace to sail to Roanoke, Ferdinando hailed the crew and told them not to return with any of the planters, stating that the season was now too late (it was 22 July) to move on to any other location.

Confined to Roanoke, where the absence of Grenville's men and the destruction of their fortifications were clear indications of the dangers of the location, White had just two events to lift him out of despondency: the birth of his granddaughter and the

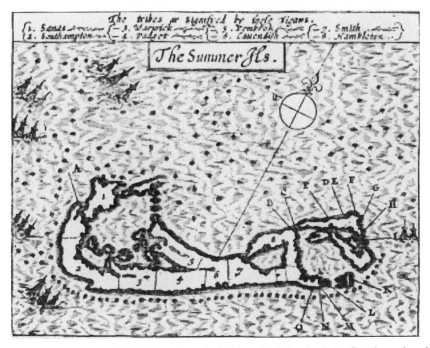

In addition to mapping the Chesapeake and New England, in 1624 John Smith produced the first accurate map of the new English colony of Bermuda. The dangerous reefs and many fortifications built to defend the island made it probably the best-defended settlement in the new world.

arrival of the abandoned flyboat, 'to the great joy and comfort of our whole company: but the Master of our Admiral, Ferdinando, grieved greatly at their safe coming . . . hoping that the Master thereof, Edward Spicer, for that he had never been in Virginia, would hardly find the place, or else being left in so dangerous a place as that was, by means of so many men of war, as at that time were abroad, they should surely be taken or slain.'

The underlying praise for Spicer's navigational skills emphasizes the contempt in which White held Ferdinando's professional ability. Indeed, Spicer's achievements in making a safe voyage deserved praise, but, so competent were so many of these Tudor and Stuart masters, it was by no means a unique act of seamanship. Whatever justice there might be in White's unproven darker suspicions, this whole episode of the voyage, both outward and inward, does demonstrate the dangers that those early settlers put themselves into when they had to put their faith in just one man to afford them a safe passage. The case of Ferdinando the traitor is unproven, but the case of Ferdinando the incompetent is most obvious, as is that of Ferdinando the callous.

Of course, not all navigational errors ended in disaster; some finished in farce. On 10 May 1603, Bartholomew Gilbert sailed from Plymouth in the fifty-ton *Elizabeth*, bound for America. He missed sighting Madeira and from those latitudes 'haled over to the West Indies'. His next sighting of land they took to be the Bermudas, although it was actually St Lucia, some fifteen degrees (or 900 miles) to the south! Wide seas forgive even such gross miscalculations, narrow channels do not. On his return from his expedition, George Waymouth found soundings for the Channel at dusk on 14 July but, 'for want of sight of the sun and stars, to make true observations: and with contrary winds we were constrained to beat up and down till Tuesday 16 July when at five of the clock in the morning we made Scilly.' One can imagine the frustration of the mariners anxious to step ashore once more but being compelled by their professional master to drift in deep waters until he was certain he could enter harbour safely.

Errors obviously could arise because the information before the pilot was not accurate. John Smith, never slow to criticize, wrote that he had six or seven plots of the northern parts of America so unlike each other or resemblance to the country that they were so much waste paper. He did his utmost to provide detailed and accurate drawings, but even his observations were only as good as his instrumentation would allow. Nevertheless, in an attempt to avoid 'dangerous ignorant hazard', he drew his maps 'from point to point, isle to isle and harbour to harbour, with the soundings, sounds, rocks and land-marks as I passed close aboard the shore in a little boat – it will serve to direct any that shall go that way to safe harbours.' A clearer definition of the practice and purpose of hydrography would be hard to find.

COMING SAFE TO SHORE

On his 1590 voyage, John White's ships anchored off a breach in the Outer Banks at the northeast end of Croatan Island, where he supposed the abandoned settlers might just be, and in the morning:

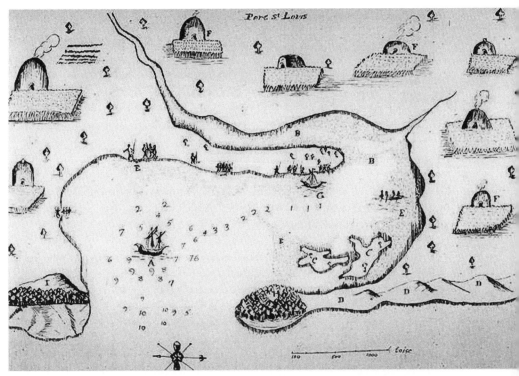

In 1605 when Champlain visited Port St Louis (Plymouth Bay) it was clearly a place of many villages producing much corn. By the time *Mayflower* arrived in 1620, imported diseases had led to many villages being abandoned and a catastrophic decline in population.

The earliest English map of the James River was drawn by John Smith's companion, Robert Tindall, in 1607. By 1608 a copy was in the possession of the King of Spain.

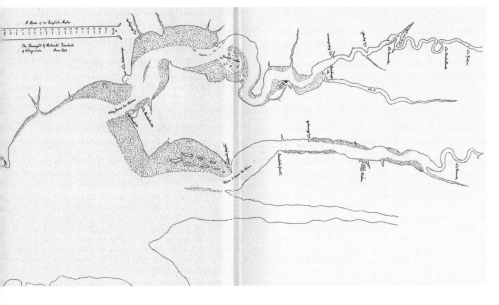

before we weighed our anchors, our boats were sent to sound this breach: our ships riding on the side thereof at 5 fathoms; and a ship's length from us we found but 4 and a quarter, and then deepening and shallowing for the space of two miles, so that sometimes we found 5 fathoms and by and by 7, and within two casts with the lead 9, and then 8, next cast 5, and then 6, and then 4, and then 9 again, and deeper; but in 3 fathoms was the least, 2 leagues off from shore. This breach is in 35 degrees and a half [actually 35° 16' North], and lieth at the very Northeast point of Croatoan, whereas goeth an inlet out of the main sea into the Inner waters . . .

It is a paragraph full of sensible practice and excellent hydrographic information.

Later, and further up the coast, James Rosier recounts that, in Waymouth's reconnaissance expedition of 1605, on:

Monday 13th May, about eleven a clock afore noon, our Captain, judging we were not far from land, sounded, and had a soft ooze in 160 fathoms. At four a clock after noon we sounded again, and had the same ooze in 100 fathoms. From ten a clock that night until three a clock in the morning our Captain took in all sails and lay a hull, being desirous to fall in with the land in the day time, because it was an unknown coast . . . otherwise we run our ship upon the hidden rocks and all perish. For when we set sail we sounded in 100 fathoms: and by eight a clock, having not made about five or six leagues, our Captain upon a sudden change of water (supposing verily he saw the sand) presently sounded, and had but five fathoms. Much marvelling because we saw no land, he sent one to the top, who then descried a whitish sandy cliff which bare West North West about six leagues off.

Having cautiously approached the shore and seeking for an inlet through the dunes, rather than sail for the widest entrance, Waymouth:

thought best to hoist out his ship's boat and sound it. Which if he had not done, we had been in great danger, for he bore up the ship as near he durst after the boat: until Thomas Cam, his mate, being in the boat, called him to tack about and stand off, for in this breach he had very shoaly water, two fathoms and less upon rocks, and sometimes they supposed they saw the rocks within three or four foot.

Not all groundings ended in disaster, for most ships were sturdily built and could be grounded with care – which they sometimes were to careen and clear their bottom of weed and worm. Hudson went aground in Delaware Bay on successive days of August in 1609 and then proceeded to scrape across a number of sandbanks in the Hudson, which did not harm *Half Moon* in the slightest, but which Jouet, Hudson's mate, recorded in his journal for the benefit of future voyagers.

Hydrography

In 1577 John Dee, in *The Perfect Arte of Navigation*, wrote:

> Hydrography, delivereth to our knowledge, on globe or plain, the perfect analogical description of the ocean sea coasts, through the whole world: or in the chief and principal parts thereof: with the isles and chief particular places of dangers, contained within the bounds of the sea coast described: as of quicksands, banks, pits, rocks, races, counter tides, whirlpools etc . . . Hydrography requireth a particular register of certain landmarks . . . from the sea, well able to be skried, in what point of the sea compass they appear, and what apparent form . . .

Now, with an unknown coast lying before them, the masters, pilots, artists and penmen of the American voyages were in a position to put Dee's description into practice. Their efforts not only represent the first systematic efforts by Englishmen to practise the hydrographic art but also created the bedrock on which future generations were to build the greatest and most exploratory hydrographic service the world has witnessed.

This desire to inform and aid is very apparent in George Waymouth's work, *The Jewell of Artes*, which he presented to King James in 1604. It was a wide-ranging work, including chapters on navigation, shipbuilding and artillery, and one on fortifications, specifically linked to those Waymouth thought necessary to protect new settlements in North America. Waymouth made the purpose of his book plain, writing:

> It were much to be wished that all those that do undertake to make Discovery of any strange countries or passages: had some skill in all these arts comprehended in this my present book, as first in Instruments of navigation they ought to know both the making and use of so many as is possible, for if they know not how their instruments ought to be made then may they be so faulty as they shall not be anything profited by them . . . good instruments make a good navigator, without the which it is impossible for him to do any good in performance of any profitable voyage at sea: in discovering of strange countries, or passages again if they never be exactly made yet if seamen want skill how to use them as have them.

Yet what they measured and recorded was not always what was reported and disseminated, for this was still an age of European rivalry and mistrust. Barlowe would, of course, have reported back the latitude and possible longitude of his landfall, but these would not have been broadcast beyond a close and trusted circle of adventurers and sponsors; as the earlier example of John Day makes clear, this was an age when rivalry between states was manifest in the use of spies and, most worryingly, when the hint of the location of a settlement could bring forth a wrathful raid from jealous Spain. This caution remained; in James Rosier's account of Waymouth's voyage to New England in 1605 he stated:

> After these purposed designs were concluded, I was animated to publish this brief relation, and not before; because some foreign nations (being fully assured of the

fruitfulness of the country) have hope would hereby to gain some knowledge of the place . . . and this is the cause that I have neither written of the latitude or variation most exactly observed . . .

Hydrography requires an honest eye and a disinterested dialogue, however well or badly this might reflect on the surveyor's national strategic interest. Thus the mature integrity of Cook, Vancouver and Fitzroy was absent in its infancy, while it was being raised by Rosier, Smith, Hakluyt and others. Nonetheless, the fact that it emerged upright and accurate and available to all seafarers owes much to the work of these early voyagers. Waymouth, in particular, seems to have wished to record with exactitude his whereabouts; as Rosier noted, during the 1605 voyage:

> Our Captain upon the rock in the middle of the harbour [Pentecost Harbour, Allen Island] observed the height, latitude, and variation exactly upon his instruments.

> 1. Astolabe.
> 2. Semisphere.
> 3. Ring instrument.
> 4. Cross Staffe.
> 5. And an excellent compass made for variation.

> The certainty whereof, together with the particularities of every depth and sounding, as well at our falling with the land, as in the discovery, and at our departure from the coast; I refer to his own relation in the Map of his Geographical description, *which for the benefit of others*, he intendeth most exactly to publish. [author's italics; the map is sadly lost]

In Newfoundland, John Guy continued this work, explaining in great detail – in a letter of 6 October 1610 to Sir Percival Willoughby, a major shareholder in the Company – that he had, by careful celestial observation, noted with exactitude the location of Cupid's Cove :

> the sun was elevated above the horizon at noon being in the meridian, thirty and eight degrees, the declination then was in the meridian of London to the southwards four degrees and twenty minutes but noon being here about three hours after, therefore the declination was three minutes more so that the Equinoctial is elevated above the horizon here 42 degrees and 23 minutes which deducted out of 90; there resteth 47 degrees and 37 minutes in the elevation of the pole . . .

There can be no clearer indication of the progress made in hydrographic practice than a study of the charts themselves. In 1576 Humphrey Gilbert produced a map to support his *Discourse of a Discovery for a New Passage to Cathay*, which did just that, optimistically showing a short passage around the top of America that led on directly to Japan. Two years later George Best's *True Discourse* was even more optimistic; here the channel is even wider and it disembogues directly upon the coast of Cathay. Then,

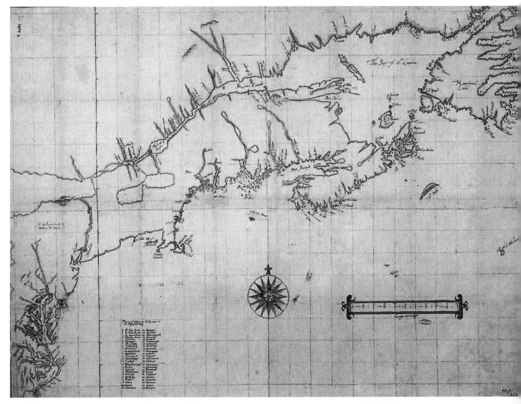

Known as the Velasco map after the Spanish ambassador to the court of King James, this 1610 English map took just three years to come into the possession of the Spanish king.

in 1625, *Purchas His Pilgrimes* included a copy of Henry Briggs's map of North America, most recognizable for what it was and with no fantasies to embellish its portrayal of geographical reality as Briggs had painstakingly worked it out to be from studying the detailed work of both John White and John Smith. Along the way John Dee had also made his contribution, although, with his desire to discover the Northwest Passage, the bias of belief infects the charts. Dee's major contribution to the North America project was the disregarded truth that ice barred the way of an easy northern passage to Cathay. Dee, who also claimed erroneously to have discovered a way of determining longitude, simply moved the through-route to Cathay further south, first to the St Lawrence and then, as an insurance, to the rivers that led inland from Virginia. Coupled with his conviction that gold ore must be present in the hills, Dee's authority and influence ensured that the sponsors would weigh their settlers down with an unmanageable burden of contrary and unachievable aims. Perhaps one can be fair to Dee by stating that he was considered to be a cosmographer, a word more at home in the period when art, science and imagination mixed more freely, and which has been superseded by the term 'cartographer', which assumes a commitment to objective recording.

Most of the records of the crossings that survive are journals, often written some while after the voyage that they describe. Surviving ships' logs, recording daily events as they occurred, are rare. Of those that are available that of Robert Juet, Henry Hudson's mate on his third voyage in 1609, gives a clear idea of all the navigational techniques discussed in this chapter.

Winds and Hurricanoes

When Shakespeare has King Lear, in his raging speech on the blasted heath, challenge the elements to:

> Blow, winds, and crack your cheeks! Rage! blow!
> You cataracts and hurricanoes . . .

he was using a word that had only recently entered the English language. 'Hurricane' is a Spanish adaption of a Taino word, *hurakan*, from *hura*, meaning wind. The Taino, part of the Arawakan tribal family, lived on the Greater Antilles and Bahamas, and thus on the track of many of those great winds which frequently moved on up the coast to the Carolinas, where, when Drake and Lane experienced one in 1586, neither man had probably heard the word nor knew when such storms were likely to fall upon that coast, although Drake had been battered by just such a wind in the Caribbean in 1568. The weather, abetted by the poor port provision, played a crucial part in the failure of the first English colony on the North American shore. For the settlers to ride out the storms they needed to have selected their base with skill and to have an understanding of the very different meteorological and climatological conditions that pertained in the new world.

Of all of a seaman's accumulative knowledge, the movement of the winds was the last to be codified. Beaufort's windscale was not introduced to the navy until 1835, some years before the Meteorological Department was formed in 1854, while weather forecasting, developed by its first director, Fitzroy of the *Beagle*, was still in its infancy. It is no wonder, therefore, that Walter Bigges's statement, in his account of Drake's West Indies voyage, that the great storm was 'extraordinary and very strange' shows an understandable lack of knowledge of the weather systems in the area. The hurricane season lasts from 1 June to 30 November, and during this period the Carolina Outer Banks have a storm pass close by every two years, with a direct hit about every seven years when average wind speeds reach ninety-seven miles per hour. Until the English found a safer anchorage within the Chesapeake, reinforcement and resupply was bound to be a worrying arrangement.

Certainly John White found it so and, for all the other frustrations that beset his several voyages, bad weather in the hurricane season made a major contribution to his failures. On the 1590 voyage, 'exceeding foul' weather struck them off Wokokon on 1 August, with 'much rain, thundering and great spouts', which did not abate for over a week. On 17 August, White recorded that the wind 'blew at Northeast and direct into the harbour so great a gale, that the Sea broke extremely on the bar and the tide went very forcibly at the entrance'.

This satellite picture of Hurricane Isabel arriving off the Carolinas in September 2003 clearly illustrates the enormous power such storms unleashed on the unsuspecting English at anchor off the Outer Banks. (NASA)

Despite these conditions, captains Cocke and Spicer took boats from their ships, which were anchored off the sandbanks, with the intention of passing through a breach into the inner sound, aiming to make a passage towards Roanoke. The narrow shallow breach was causing the waves to build up to an alarming height but Cocke's boat, although it shipped much water, came safely ashore. Spicer was not so lucky; as he steered to pass through the breach the following sea slewed his boat sideways and overturned it, throwing many of the occupants into the sea and forcing the remainder to try and right the boat or just to hold on in the hope that they would be carried ashore by the pounding waves. In this thunderous surf Captain Spicer and the coxwain Ralph Skinner were drowned, along with five others. The other four might also have lost their lives had not Captain Cocke, with four volunteers, bravely relaunched his own boat and rowed over to pull the survivors to safety. White states, understandably, that the incident dampened down the mariners' enthusiasm to spend more time on the coast looking for the lost planters, and the search was ended prematurely as soon as they had found the word CROATOAN carved on a stake in the abandoned fort, giving an indication as to where the settlers might, voluntarily, have departed.

By the time they returned onboard, the gale had become worse and the ships took the precaution of laying out additional anchors. Even so, as White related, the next morning, when they had agreed to sail down to Croatoan, in almost a repeat of the accident that happened on his departure from the colony in 1587:

> they brought the cable to the Capstan . . . when the Anchor was almost on deck, the cable broke, by means of whereof we lost another anchor, where with we drove so fast ashore, that we were forced to let fall a third Anchor; which came so fast home the ship was almost aground by Kendricks Mounts: so that we were forced to let slip the Cable end for end. And if it had not chanced that we had fallen into a channel of deeper water, closer by the shore then we accounted of, we could never have gone clear of the point that lieth to the Southwards . . . Being this clear of some dangers, and gotten into deeper waters, but not without some loss; for we had but on Cable and Anchor left us of four, and the weather grew to be fouler and fouler; our victuals scarce, and our cask and fresh water lost [having been abandoned ashore] it was therefore determined that we should go . . . to the Southward for fresh water.

The weather did not ameliorate and, with their ships ill-provisioned and leaky and the coast so tragically hostile, the two ships turned for the Azores and home, ending all hope of solving the mystery of the missing colony. White never returned, his long years of endeavour wrecked by the winds which made that coast the graveyard of hundreds of vessels in the years to come. What the Virginians were experiencing was a paradox unknown to them. This was that if they delayed sailing from England until the season was right for ships to cross the Atlantic – April and May – they would arrive, inevitably, on the American coast during the hurricane season when, as the *Admiralty Sailing Directions* advise, 'None of the harbours in the area . . . can be considered as safe havens during hurricane force winds. Ships should therefore put to sea to evade a hurricane,' a policy first practised by Drake in 1586. If one adds to the above information the fact that the preferred southern route sailed by the English to Virginia, until 1609, took them along the course of the north-flowing hurricanes, then the meteorological problems they faced can be seen clearly.

Yet foul weather could also be quoted to advantage. The rogue Sir Ralph Bingley preferring to take *Triall* a-pirating for his own benefit rather than sail to Virginia in 1606, as ordered, wrote the most magnificent lying letter of excuses to the Earl of Salisbury on 5 April 1608, in which he records the 'great distress' caused to his company by having to endure 'a most terrible storm . . . six weeks together upon the coast of Spain', after which they were forced to save their lives by boarding a French ship.

The great storms that battered Virginia were no strangers to Bermuda. Indeed, the colony traces its origins to the hurricane which drove *Sea Venture* onto its sharp and unforgiving shores. Neither was she the first or the last ship to end her days wrecked on the Bermudas. Even those who sought shelter in the harbours there were not immune from the gales. In 1619, *Garland*, having come within sight of the island, was driven south for three weeks and her crew so reduced by death and sickness that only revictualling by a passing Dutchman saved them from being lost. When she eventually made Bermuda she anchored below Kings Castle, which lay open to the northwest winds. When such a wind arose she was forced, for her own safety, to cut her mainmast down at deck level and 'to ride it out for her life'. She was luckier than the supply ship *Warwick*, which, with 'all her anchors coming home was driven upon the rocks and unrecoverably lost' with all the year's crop of tobacco onboard. This being Bermuda, plans were put in place to build a new ship to replace *Warwick* but, professional advice being heeded, it was decided to use *Garland* and not the new build as the replacement store ship. Then, around Christmas, another great gale struck the island and *Garland*:

> all her help giving way and so being upon drift, she fully within a cable length of the ruining rocks and had undoubtedly perished, but that one of her main anchors, fastened to an excellent new cable, by great good chance, hit foul betwixt two rocks, the which thereby fastening the whole stress and weight of the ship, so kept her alive the remainder of that huge gust.

Not just a lucky chance, the incident illustrates the principle that no ship adrift should ever ground with her anchors still home – many do. It was certainly some 'huge gust' that struck *Garland*; the great blockhouse on the hill that was the Governor's pride and joy was blown clean over.

Yet, even in more favourable locations, strong winds in shallow waters could cause great anxiety. In December 1620, with *Mayflower* anchored in the cosy enclosing comfort of Provincetown on the hook of Cape Cod, William Bradford took their reconstructed shallop away on an exploratory mission along the inner shoreline of the cape to seek out a suitable harbour which Robert Coppin, the ship's pilot, who had visited the area before, knew existed. It was not a good time to be in an open boat off an unknown shore. Driving sleet both reduced visibility and made steering difficult. In the end the latter proved impossible as a mighty sea lifted the rudder off its gudgeons, reducing the crew to using a pair of steering oars. Then Coppin, misidentifying his headmark as Thievish Harbour, had them run, with their mainsail set, straight towards the shallows of The Gurnet, a narrow peninsula that forms the northern limit of the entrance to Plymouth Harbour. Luckily, at this moment the strain proved too much for the mast, which splintered, bringing the sail down and into the water, where it formed a temporary sea-anchor to slow their progress towards destruction. By the time that they had stowed the sail, cleared away the splintered mast and taken up the oars, Coppin had realized his error and, although they were still being driven shoreward, a superhuman effort by the oarsman turned the boat into the wind and enabled them to round the headland and enter the calmer waters of the bay on whose shores they would soon settle.

The linked science of climatology was also in its infancy, and thus the English fell victim to a most understandable assumption: that the weather that they would experience would be similar to that encountered in the same latitudes in Europe. The contrast between the climate on the eastern edge of a vast continent and the balmier conditions of islands washed by the Gulf Stream was one that they would learn only through the bitter experience of enduring a winter for which they were ill prepared.

There was an added cruelty to the winter chill in that for much of the period of the settlements the world was going through a mini ice age, so that the harsher than normal winter conditions in Virginia even took the native population by surprise. Even, the realist John Smith, wrote of Virginia:

> The summer is hot as in Spain; the winter cold as in France or England. The heat of summer is in June, July and August, but commonly the cold breezes assuage the vehemency of the heat. The chief of winter is half December, January, February and half March. The cold is extreme sharp, but here the proverb is true, that no extreme long continueth.

In doing so he failed to highlight the hot humidity of summer to which, further north, would be added the bone-biting chill of winter.

In much the same way as the Elizabethan and Jacobean reigns saw a flourishing of the written arts, utilizing a language that burst forth in glorious full flower from a dull bud, so, at the same time, maritime England, cautious and coast-creeping until this time, suddenly broke from its shallow moorings and set out for a new world, ignorant but open-eyed, to cross blue waters where it met, accepted and overcame the challenges before it. In so doing, it played midwife to the birth of anthropology, geography and botany, sired the science of hydrography and succoured the infant British Empire. It delivered, mostly safely, those who would change the English diet for good, its smoking habits for bad, and on those far shores establish those freedoms of worship, liberty and democracy that the mother state was later, grudgingly, to adopt and call its own. It is not a bad achievement for those who went down to the sea and conducted their business in ships not much larger than a double-decker bus.

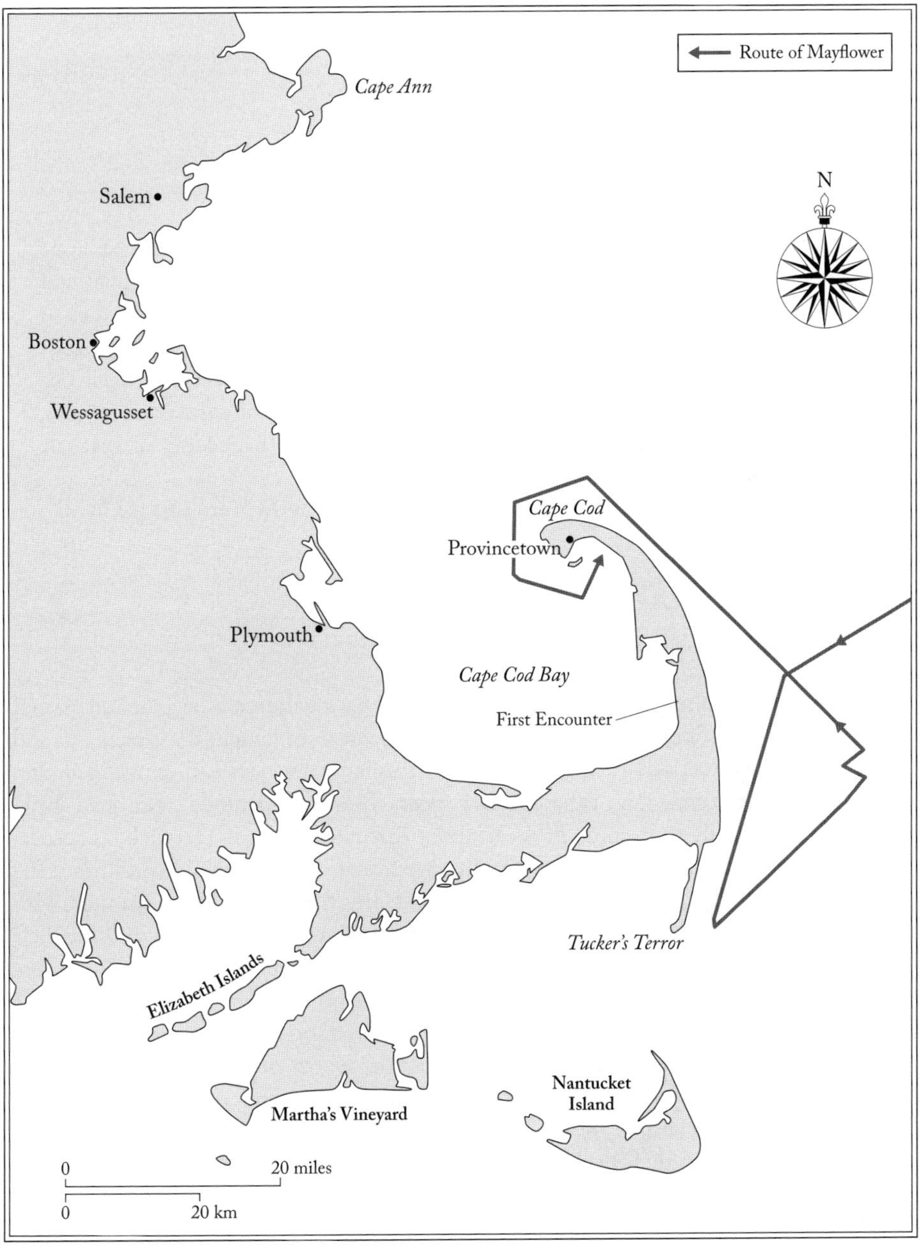
Route of Mayflower
Cape Ann
N
Salem
Boston
Wessagusset
Cape Cod
Provincetown
Plymouth
Cape Cod Bay
First Encounter
Tucker's Terror
Elizabeth Islands
Martha's Vineyard
Nantucket Island
0
20 miles
0
20 km

Map 4: New England, 1620–30

CHAPTER 7

The Crossings

we went from Falmouth, being in all two & thirty persons, in a small barke of Dartmouth called *Concord*, holding a course for the north part of Virginia: and although by chance the wind favoured us not at first as we wished, but enforced us so far to the southward, as we fell with S. Marie, one of the islands of the Azores (which was not much out of our way) but holding course directly from thence, we made our journey shorter (than hitherto accustomed) by the better part of a thousand leagues, yet were we longer in our passage than we expected; which happened, for that our bark being weak, we were loath to press her with much sail . . .

Brereton, *A Briefe and True Relation of the Discovery of the North part of Virginia*, 1602

TREMBLING AT THE OUTSKIRTS

On 31 May 1577 a horsethief, a highwayman, a robber, a perjurer, a beggar, and several more of England's finest, destined to form a stay-behind settlement on Greenland and Baffin Island, were set ashore at Harwich, having sailed a few days earlier from London with Frobisher's three-ship expeditionary fleet. These condemned men had been pardoned specifically to become colonists; their disembarkation at Harwich, as surplus to requirement, rather than in the icy north, saved them from death a second time. The next year the attempt at colonization was repeated. This time it was better planned, with a party of 100 men, under the command of Edward Fenton, specially selected for their mining backgrounds, being assembled to sail for the 'gold' mines that glistened more in the minds of Frobisher and his backers than in the ground. The preparation for this second settlement included the embarking of a large prefabricated house, its constituent parts spread among the fleet, and eighteen months worth of rations that have been estimated as being able to provide each man with some 6,000 calories a day, which showed a clear awareness of the needs of those labouring in sub-zero conditions. This time the men reached their destination and were even disembarked to begin work, but they too were saved from certain death from Inuit attack, scurvy or mutiny, and possibly cannibalism, by the intervention of nature. On the night of 2 July the bulk of the fleet was trapped in a lake of water surrounded by ice (a polynya). Although all but one of them managed to extricate themselves, the bark *Denys* was holed by an iceberg and sunk. Her crew was rescued but she took to the bottom with her the main frame of the miners' house. Many other parts of the building were used to fend off the encroaching ice, which meant that there was little chance of erecting the winter quarters. Instead, Fenton's men built a stone hut in which they left some trade goods to encourage friendly relations with the Inuit when they returned the following year – they never did.

The replica of *Matthew* under sail. The original of this three-masted carvel required a crew of about twenty for her thirty-five-day voyage from Bristol to Newfoundland.

This faint-hearted flirtation, which began with Cabot's timid touch, continued for a long while. It was not so throughout the American continent, where Spain, despite many setbacks to its own expeditionary forces, had fixed a wide choker around the whole of Central and South America. Then, in 1578, by which time there was a strong suspicion that Frobisher's efforts were going to yield little or no reward, Elizabeth at long last granted Humphrey Gilbert a Charter to establish an English presence in the new world.

Gilbert's first expedition, of 1578, was a West Country affair, with his fleet of ten ships mustered at Dartmouth, where it could prepare to depart despite a prohibition issued in London to prevent their sailing until they had paid restitution to a Spanish vessel whose cargo of Seville oranges they had illegally seized. This delayed their sailing untiil 26 September, just in time to for them run straight into the equinoctial gales, which drove them ingloriously into Plymouth just forty miles down the coast, a short journey that, for similar reasons, *Mayflower* would repeat 142 years later.

Rather than use the time in Plymouth for bonding with his team, Gilbert seems to have given them a tongue lashing for incompetence, as a result of which three ships stayed behind when he led the remainder to sea again on 19 November, only to be blown back to Dartmouth, where the voyage was abandoned. One ship continued: *Falcon*, the Queen's ship commanded by Walter Ralegh, in which that young gallant seemed to have taken the team-talk to heart, for he ploughed on into the gales to seek glory through plunder, his preferred source of income, whether by land or sea. In this, his first attempt, he fared not well and when he eventually returned to harbour it was in a damaged vessel and with several of his crew dead or injured, having been worsted by Spanish adversaries.

Over the next few years Ralegh courted his Queen with so much success that, when Gilbert was ready to try again for new world glory in 1583, he was able to do so in large part because his favoured half-brother had funds and shipping available, including his own *Bark Ralegh*, a well-armed and provisioned 200-ton ship, which demonstrates, along with a £2,000 loan, how rapid had been young Walter's progress.

Yet, although well-provisioned, *Bark Ralegh* had no stomach for the voyage and two days out in June 1583, Captain Butler, in the face of gales, turned her head for home. The rest of the fleet made it to St John's, Newfoundland, which Gilbert claimed for his Queen on 5 August 1583, along with the land lying 600 miles to the north and south, much to the bemusement of the fishermen he summoned to witness his claim and from whom he scrounged much-needed supplies. By this time the usual problems of sickness and desertion had taken their toll, so *Swallow* was detached to England as a hospital ship. This left Gilbert with just three ships to continue his voyage south: the 120-ton *Delight*, the forty-ton *Golden Hind* and the diminutive ten-ton *Squirrel*, in

This cutaway model gives some idea of the internal spaces of the first generation of the ships that carried colonists to North America.

which Gilbert chose to sail. On 29 August, during rough seas and fog, *Delight*, 'keeping so ill watch, that they knew not the danger, before they felt the same, too late to recover it', was cast away on the coast, bringing the expedition to a premature and tragic end for, as Gilbert said: 'Be content, we have seen enough, and take no care of expenses past: I will set you forth royally next spring, if God send us safe home. Therefore, I pray you, let us no longer strive here, where we fight against the elements.' For him and his hopes there was to be no 'next spring': he was last seen seated calmly reading his book while great waves built up around *Squirrel* so that, at midnight on Monday 9 September, she lost her fight against the elements and 'was devoured and swallowed up of the sea'.

RECONNAISSANCE

It is a strange fact that, although reconnaissance voyages were made prior to the establishment of both the Roanoke and the Popham colony in New England, neither settlement was a success. On the other hand, the enduring Jamestown and Plymouth sites were only reconnoitred once their settlers had arrived in America. In the first case, the rapture with which Amadas and Barlowe reported back, and the confirmation in Harriot's detailed description, served to hide the faults of the site selected. The reports on the New England voyages from 1602 to 1607 did likewise, emphasizing the positive while not remaining in the region long enough to discover the negatives, such as the cold winters.

Yet there was a more invidious problem caused by the lack of independent reconnaissance. The actions taken by Christopher Newport on entering the Chesapeake in 1607 and Christopher Jones sailing into Cape Cod Bay in 1620 were remarkably similar. Both masters anchored with caution and sent out teams to feel their way along the shoreline. In Newport's case eighteen days were to pass between the initial landing at Cape Henry and the decision to disembark at Jamestown while, in New England, *Mayflower* remained anchored at Provincetown for thirty-six days before sailing across to discharge her passengers at Plymouth. Once the settlers had landed, both ships remained behind. At Jamestown, Newport stayed on from 14 May to 22 June, carrying out the exploration ordered by the Company and, rather more importantly, consuming much of the already scant provisions. *Mayflower* remained at Plymouth from 16 December until 5 April, a staggering 146 days anchored off, during which time Captain Jones lost his boatswain, gunner, cook and fifteen of the crew to disease, for which weakness caused by malnourishment would have contributed. In neither case were the quantity and 'sell-by' date of the provisions loaded in the ship's holds sufficient to sustain both the crew and the settlers, who were not only having to undertake strenuous manual labour, felling trees and constructing defences, but were having to do so while weakened by the length of their ocean voyage. In the case of Jamestown, prior reconnaissance, including selection of a site and contact with the Amerindians, would have made an invaluable contribution to the viability of the colony, but so also would have been a decision by the Virginia Company to concentrate on one objective – the establishment of a safe and secure beachhead

Draped sheets provide limited privacy around one of the bunks on the crowded lower deck of the *Susan Constant* replica.

from which expeditions could be mounted at a more propitious time – rather than attempting to 'make' the initial voyage immediately by discovering a passage to the Pacific.

The case of *Mayflower* is, of course, very different, as the passengers disembarked far from their intended destination, making any earlier reconnaissance irrelevant. Nevertheless, the similar scenarios and similar woes were the result of inadequate preparation and the delayed departure of the ships.

By the end of the reign of the flirtatious but untouchable monarch, Elizabeth, the country which she had graciously allowed to be named Virginia after her revered goddess-like state was almost as chaste as she. Ralegh, her favourite, had cautiously plucked at the bodice-button of Roanoke, but let his men's fingers stray no further. In King James's reign settlers dared to penetrate further but cautiously withdrew the moment they saw themselves obstructed by the line of falls that marked the boundary between the coastal plain and the piedmont.

The English New England voyages were a continuation of this cautious courting. Between 1602 and 1608 twenty-five direct crossings were made in one direction or the other without a single ship being lost, apart from *Richard*, which was seized in the Florida Channel in 1607. The written reports of the voyages indicate that a high standard of navigation and pilotage was by now the rule rather than the exception, so there was no reason to expect that any colony could not have been well supported from England. Instead, the result of all this professional seamanship was a settlement at the mouth of the Sagadahoc River that lasted one year.

The further north along the coast the mariners moved, the closer they were to their home ports. This was an advantage that those who advocated the settlement of Newfoundland in preference to Virginia were at pains to emphasize.

John Mason, who stayed for three years and seven months on the island between 1616 and 1620, indicated his appreciation of its advantage of proximity in his *A Brief Discourse of the New-Found-Land*, in which he stated that the main reason why it was to be preferred to Virginia as a place of plantation was:

> the nearness to our own home, which naturally we are so much addicted unto, being but half of the way to Virginia, having a convenient passage for three seasonable months, March, April and May, which always accommodate fair winds to pass thither, sometimes in 14 to 20 days, seldom in thirty days. Likewise the commodious return in June, July, August, September, October and November, sometimes 12, 16, 20 and now and then thirty days.

Richard Whitbourne, in his *Discourse*, gave a seaman's chest full of reasons why England should support the settlement of Newfoundland, including it being the 'fittest place from whence to proceed' to the discovery of the northwest passage, and that it lay on the return route from Virginia so that 'your Majesty's subjects sailing to and from Virginia, New England and the Bermuda Islands, might in any extremity (having spent a mast or yard, or when any leak is sprung) be relieved and at other times refresh themselves in their voyages.'

Whitbourne was also well aware that anxious colonists might feel abandoned if anticipated support shipping failed to materialize so, with an obvious side swipe at Ralegh, he wrote:

> And as Newfoundland is nearer to us by more than 300 leagues than Virginia; and far from any of the plantations of the King of Spain, which peradventure might make the business the more difficult; so those of this plantation will have a great comfort and encouragement above all others, in that they shall not be left desolate in a remote country, to shift for themselves, as some have been but after five months past, they shall again see great numbers of their countrymen, and also of other nations, and have their company the rest of the year.

THE PASSAGE

Whitbourne was very aware of the time it could take to reach the Americas, with most voyages taking between two and three months, although contrary winds in the Channel could delay both departure and arrival by several weeks: *Mayflower* was sixty-five days continually at sea between Plymouth and Provincetown but, prior to that, spent another fifty days on passage or in port between London and Plymouth.

The route favoured by the early voyagers to Virginia was the southern one by way of Madeira, the Azores and the West Indies, for which no English rutter existed until Hakluyt printed two Spanish ones in the third edition of *Principal Navigations* in 1600: one for the West Indies and one that provided sailing directions, outward, from Sanlúcar at the mouth of the Guadalquivir, via the Canaries to the Antilles, Puerto Rico, Hispaniola and Cuba and then, inward, from Havana and the Bahamas Channel to Spain.

From the start there was debate as to whether a northern or southern route was the most advantageous. Before Gilbert set sail in 1583 he discussed the relative merits with his commanders and masters; sailing late in the season, he reasoned that:

> it seemed first very doubtful by what way to shape our course, and to begin our intended discovery, either from the south northward or from the north southward. The first . . . was the likeliest, wherein we were assured to have commodity of the current which from Cape Florida setteth northward, and would have furthered greatly our navigation, discovering from the foresaid cape along towards Cape Breton, and all those lands lying to the north. Also, the year being far spent, and arrived to the month of June, we were not to spend time in northerly courses, where we should be surprised with timely winter, but to covet the south, which we had space enough then to have attained, and there might with less detriment have wintered . . . These and other like reasons alleged in favour of the southern course first to be taken, to the contrary was inferred that forasmuch as both our victuals and many other needful provisions were diminished and left insufficient for so long a voyage and for the wintering of so many men, we ought to shape a course most likely to minister supply: and that was to take the Newfoundland in our way, which was but 700 leagues from our English coast. Where being usually at that time of year . . . a multitude of ships . . . we should be relieved abundantly with many necessaries . . . Not staying long upon that Newland coast, we might proceed southward, and follow still the sun, until we arrived at places more temperate to our content.

The longer southern route was the favoured option for voyages to Virginia until peace with Spain in 1604 removed the opportunities for plunder but left the Spanish free to attack any foreign intruders. Thus, Henry Challons in *Richard*, the first ship chartered by the Virginia Company following the grant of its Charter, had been taken in the Florida Channel on 10 November 1606, when she found she had sailed into the middle of a fleet of well-armed Spanish merchantmen. Her capture was reported to Cecil, the Secretary of State, in early February 1607 and he, anxious to retain good relations with Spain, no doubt, much favoured the testing of a more northerly route.

The Virginia Company was also eager to speed up the time taken on passage so, in 1609, it appointed Captain Samuel Argall to sail a course that would:

> avoid all danger of quarrel with the subjects of the King of Spain – not to touch upon his dominions . . . and to shape his course free from the road of pirates . . . and to attempt a direct and clear passage by leaving the Canaries to the east, and from

thence to run in a straight western course or some point thereunto; and so to make an experience of the winds and currents which have affrighted all undertakers.

Or, as the Dutch commentator Emanuel van Meteren wrote:

to discover a more convenient route or passage there so as to shun the worrisome route of the southern indies course and quarrels with the Spaniards over their express command nowhere to touch Spanish territory, and to fix a course away from the roadsteads frequented by pirates, who lie just off shore and in narrow passages; but since there is a direct straight passage from the Canaries in the east, to run a direct westerly course from there, or so nearly as possible, and thus to seek out the winds, watercourses, or currents which have hindered and bedevilled all who have investigated the northern course. Through such discoveries there should result greater security and convenience for the Company and all causes for offence will be avoided, while half of the costs would be saved in victuals and delays, which they must spend uselessly for the southern passage.

Argall was neither the first nor the fastest to sail this new route. In 1602, Bartholomew Gosnold, as recorded at the head of this chapter, also 'turned right' at the Azores, reaching Virginia just fifty days after leaving Falmouth. Argall departed from Portsmouth on 5 May and arrived off Virginia on 23 July, a voyage of just under ten weeks, which included two weeks lying becalmed in mid-Atlantic. It almost halved the time it had taken the voyagers of 1607. Argall put that time saved to good use. Before even arriving at Jamestown he sighted, hounded and drove out of the bay a Spanish ship commanded by Captain Francisco Fernández de Ēcija, which had been sent to spy on the English settlement. Just as well, for Ēcija would have discovered, as did Argall, the Jamestown settlers starving, disillusioned, disunited and in no fit state to defend themselves against a Spanish assault. Argall provisioned them as best he could and departed in the early autumn.

In the meantime, the Virginia Company, assuming that Argall would have succeeded, dispatched the next resupply convoy, carrying the new Deputy Governor, under the same sailing instructions as given to pioneer Argall but, where Argall had calms, they met storms which resulted in the flagship *Sea Venture* grounding at Bermuda, a mishap that led to the establishment of a new and successful British colony, and the near-abandonment of the older and unsuccessful one at Jamestown.

Scotland, late in coming to the potentially beneficial opportunities that might accrue from the export of its citizenry, found that citizenry failed to appreciate the opportunity offered by Sir William Alexander's Charter of 1621. Neither volunteers, ship nor crew proved ideal for the first crossing to Nova Scotia. The account of Alexander Fraser is pithy enough:

A Presbyterian clergyman and one artisan only joined the party of farm labourers at Kirkcudbright and the vessel left in June, 1622, less than a year after the date of the Charter. The party was detained at the Isle of Man until the month of August, and the promised land was not sighted until about the middle of September, when a storm prevented a landing and the vessel was driven back to Newfoundland, where the passengers wintered. The ship had been meagerly fitted out; money was scarce, and provisions short, so it was necessary to send the vessel back to England for fresh supplies. The clergyman and the artisan died; the labourers scattered to find employment among the fisheries, and the next year, when a ship arrived at St John with additional settlers the original party could not be assembled. A party of ten was selected to visit New Scotland and to report on the prospects of settlement. The result was encouraging, and they returned to England. These two attempts at colonizing practically ruined Sir William financially and the estimated loss of £6,000 sterling was made a public charge on the exchequer, but never was discharged.

The Passengers

An impression of miniaturization persists as one walks onboard the replica settler ships berthed at Jamestown. The scale seems to make giants of the well-informed costumed interpreters that act as guides. Most days there are not crowds clambering onboard and,

The ship's officers would have been loath to share or surrender the comfort of their own bunks in their own cabins.

besides, health and safety regulations limit the number of people allowed to explore the ships at any one time. Even so, politely passing other visitors in passageways gives one some idea of what it must have been like when seventy-one passengers and crew were crammed in *Susan Constant* in 1606, with a further fifty-two in *Godspeed* and twenty-one on the twenty-ton *Discovery*.

The guides know. Questioned by a young girl as to what it was like for the passengers, one of them asked her if she had ever flown in a crowded airliner. She had. 'Did she feel she had room to get up and move about?' he asked. She did not. 'Had she been invited to help with the chores?' he asked. She had not. 'That', he said, 'is what it was like, but they were there for four months, not four hours.' It would be difficult to find a more apposite analogy unless it was of a crowded open-top double-decker bus travelling a bumpy road in driving rain.

The ships were not designed to carry what the crew referred to, somewhat disparagingly but accurately, as 'light freight'. To sail, steer, store, stow, sleep and defend such ships, every square metre of space had a purpose: access and neatness were all-important. Moving cargo, be it casks, loose cannon, slaves or passengers, created problems, best avoided if only they could be securely strapped down.

There is one other link between modern planes and those ships: in just the same way that few travel writers today describe in detail the plane that has flown them to their destination, so very few of the settlers left behind any firsthand accounts of life onboard the ships in which they sailed. This is sad but perhaps understandable if conditions onboard were as unpleasant as they surely were on a lengthy, crowded voyage which resulted in many of the passengers disembarking in such a poor physical condition that they would not recover on the meagre rations available ashore.

Even when an emigrating group was distributed between ships, conditions for the passengers were not ideal. Most had to sleep in hammocks or on the deck, with some privacy afforded the women; only gentlemen could expect cabins. Brian Lavery estimated that the outward-bound *Susan Constant* was overcrowded even by the standards of her time, when two tons per passenger seems to have been a norm. Given the composition of her crew and passengers, Lavery considers that the ship would have had been temporarily partitioned into: upper deck after cabins for the captain, mates, the carpenter and the chart room; six further cabins in the gunroom aft for the gunner and six gentlemen; further space for the bulk of the crew beneath the forecastle; leaving space on the gundeck for double cabins for the remaining gentlemen and an open area to be shared by the forty-seven remaining artisans and labourers. All of this allocation was made easier by the fact that this was a single-sex ship: once women and children started to be carried the problem increased.

A similar exercise to that undertaken by Lavery was carried out many years earlier by W. Sears Nickerson to calculate where the passengers and crew of *Mayflower* might have been accommodated. His plan divided the area of the poop deck into two and fitted three tiers of double bunks on either side, with another three at the stern for passengers, leaving the forward end of the poop clear for the officers. Below that, the cabin deck might have had two lengths of double bunks three tiers deep on each side, with another tier athwartships aft and forward. In this cosy area, Nickerson would have housed the married couples, the unmarried young women and the children too small to be separated from their parents. The unaccompanied men and older boys would then have been invited to sling their hammocks or place their palliasses on the gundeck. They would not have rested comfortably on their rolling beds. Above them the seamen would have pattered day and night along the decks while obeying shouted orders to adjust sails, while, on all but the most recently refitted vessels, water would have flowed or dripped through the planks of that deck until the seamen found time to hammer in more oakum. Their own clothes, inevitably wet after a visit to the upper deck, would remain damp and the salt water caked on their unwashed skin. The young would soon have become bored, with few toys to play with and too many feet over which to trip. Yet, although, to a modern eye, living arrangements onboard the settler ships appear to be very cramped, there were two groups of almost contemporary travellers who sailed under more crowded conditions. The ships of the Royal Navy, when fully manned, crammed their sailors between decks like sardines. In a typical 74-gun vessel 500 men were accommodated in an area of some 6,000 square feet, with a maximum width between hammocks of fourteen inches. The conditions onboard slavers were, naturally, much, much worse.

SEASICKNESS

The cramped conditions and stale fare were as nothing to these landlubbers, which included nearly all the settlers, as the miseries they endured from seasickness. The best description of the effects of this dreadful malady was recorded by John Donne, who wrote his poem, 'The Storm', having sailed with Essex to the Azores:

> Some coffin'd in their cabins lye, equally
> Griev'd that they are not dead, and yet must die.
> And as sin-burd'ned soules from grave will creepe,
> At the last day, some forth their cabins peepe:
> And tremblingly aske what newes, and doe heare so,
> Like jealous husbands, what they would not know.
> Some sitting on the hatches, would seeme there,
> With hideous gazing to feare away feare.
> Then note they the ship's sicknesses, the Mast
> Shak'd with an ague, and the Hold and Wast
> With a salt dropsie clog'd, and all our tacklings
> Snapping, like too- high-stretched treble strings.
> And from our tatter'd sailes, ragges drop downe so,
> As from one hang'd in chaines a year agoe.
> Even our Ordnance plac'd for our defence,
> Strive to breake loose, and scape away from thence.
> Pumping hath tir'd our men, and what's the gaine?
> Seas into seas throwne, we suck in againe.

Onboard Victualling

Another anxiety that was frequently expressed concerned the availability and condition of the food. This would have been purchased cheaply and in bulk, which meant that it started monotonously and ended stale, putrid and in short supply. Oat biscuit, dried or buttered peas, salted beef and pork and hard cheese might have been supplemented with milk or eggs, providing goats (and, because these were settler voyages, the occasional cow) and hens were making the voyage. Dried or fresh fish would have provided a change. Frustratingly, as the daily fare dried out and decayed, thus needing to be washed down, so the beer turned stale and the water foul. Cooking in the one small galley range available would, for the most part, have been carried out on a family-by-family basis and been impossible in rough seas, when hot food was most needed. A succinct, sad summary of the conditions that had to be endured is provided by Hanserd Knollys, a preacher who underwent a fourteen-week return voyage to England: 'By the way my little child died with convulsion fits, our beer and water stank, our biscuit was green, yellow and blue, moulded and rotten, and our cheese also, so that we suffered much hardship . . .'

There was little reason, other than parsimony, for providing poor or scanty rations. The Royal Navy had come into permanent being in the reign of Henry VIII, not because Cardinal Wolsey found ways of providing sufficient money to build ships but because he had the genius to introduce a scheme whereby he could keep thousands of seamen and accompanying soldiers victualled at sea. The period for which Wolsey, and his successors, felt it expedient to store the King's ships was a minimum of three months. One of those successors, Edward Baeshe, undertook in 1565, for an annual payment equivalent to four and a half pence per man per day, to provide every sailor with the following minimum weekly allowance, which would be augmented by each ship's purser:

Flesh Days: Sunday, Monday, Tuesday, Thursday,
    2 lb fresh beef or ½ lb salt beef or ½lb bacon
    1 lb biscuit or bread and 1 gallon of beer
Fish Days: Wednesday, Friday, Saturday
    ¼ of stockfish or 4 herring
    1 lb biscuit and 1 gallon of beer.

This would have provided each voyager, at a very reasonable cost, a daily calorific value of about 4,500 calories. Indeed, an analysis of very similar rations provided for Frobisher's crews in 1577, but with the addition of 4½ lbs of peas a week, indicated a calorific value of 6,000 units a day. Given the length of an Atlantic crossing, the amount of stowage available and the number of crew and passengers embarked, it would have been simple to have victualled to the naval scale; simple but not standard. *Mayflower*'s passengers had to surrender three or four firkins of butter (one firkin = 56 lbs) to pay for repairs to the unseaworthy *Speedwell* and up to their departure from Southampton they were still expressing their grievance that their money had been frittered away, or stolen, stating: 'We are in such straits at present as we are forced to sell £60 worth of our

Within the brick oven a cauldron, two-thirds full of water and suspended over a small fire, provided a versatile cooker, with food tied in muslin being cooked in the boiling water while bread was proved on the bricks and baked in the corners once the flames had died down.

(facing page) The upper deck of the *Elizabeth II*. Even without passengers there was little room on the ships' upper decks for the seamen to man the ropes and set the sails.

provisions to clear the port and withal to put ourselves upon great extremities, scarce having any butter, [and] no oil . . .' A few days later, Robert Cushman, who abandoned the voyage in Plymouth, anticipated that, due to malpractice: 'Our victuals will be half eaten up . . . before we go from the coast of England, and if our voyage last long we shall not have a month's victuals when we come to the country.'

Cushman was not alone in stating his grievances. For his third voyage of 1578, the mining settlement one, Frobisher was appointed both victualler and commander, not a good decision by the Commissioners in London, who knew that they owed him a great deal of money. The resultant malfeasance is thus not unexpected:

> At the beginning of this third voyage Captain Frobisher was sent by the Commissioners from London to Bristol to furnish and dispatch from thence the ships *Ayde* and *Gabriel* for this voyage, wherein he was made victualler of the ship *Ayde*, for the which victuals he had £500 delivered to him beforehand, but he did so evil victual the same ship, that whereas the Company allowed him money for to victual her with flesh four days of the week, he served the men only three days and two days in the week therewith and the rest of the week with fish and that so evil and so scarce, that thereby much sickness grew, and divers died, as the men do report.
>
> He was sent into the West Country to provide 120 miners, for this voyage, for whose furniture he had money from the company beforehand for their wages, £240, which is 40s for each man, but thereof he paid these men, to some 20s, to some 13s 4d, and to some nothing, as his accomplice declares . . .

That would be damming enough, were it not for the thread of rumour and innuendo that runs through it.

Travelling in Company

Although some of the early voyages were made by single ships, and some of the later – like that by *Mayflower* – ended up as solo voyages, travelling in company had several advantages such as: mutual support against attack; distribution of supplies; alternative transport in the event of accident; and exchange of ideas and proposals. What it did mean, however, was the imposition of a command structure and the selection of a rendezvous in case of dispersal. As regards the first of these, the orders agreed upon by the captains and masters of Humphrey Gilbert's fleet in 1583 can serve as a template:

> First, The Admiral to carry his flag by day, and his light by night.
> Second, Item, if the admiral shall shorten his sail by night, then to show two lights until he be answered again by every ship showing one light for a short time.
> Three, Item, if the admiral after his shortening of sail, as aforesaid, shall make more sail again; then he is to show three lights one above another.
> Four, Item, if the admiral shall happen to hull in the night, then to make a wavering light over his other light, wavering the light upon a pole.

Mayflower II at sea. The approach of ships under sail awed many of the watchers from the shore, who saw something otherworldly in these moving islands of clouds and were thus quite prepared to treat the occupants with reverence. (Plimouth Plantation)

Five, Item, if the fleet should happen to be scattered by weather, or other mishap, then so soon as one shall descry another, to hoist both topsails twice, if the weather will serve, and to strike them twice again; but if the weather serve not, then to hoist the maintopsail twice, and forthwith strike it twice again.

Six, Item, if it shall happen a great fog to fall, then presently every ship to bear up with the admiral, if there be wind; but if it be calm, then every ship to hull, and so to lie at hull till it clear. And if the fog do continue long, then the admiral to shoot off two pieces every evening, and every ship to answer it with one shot; and every man bearing to the ship to leeward so near as he may.

Seven, Item, every master to give charge unto the watch to look well, for laying aboard one of another in the night, and in fogs.

Eight, Item, every evening every ship to hail the Admiral, and so to fall astern him, sailing through the ocean; and being on the coast, every ship to hail him both morning and evening.

Nine, Item, if any ship be in danger in any way, by leak or otherwise, then she to shoot off a piece, and presently to bring out one light; whereupon every man to bear towards her, answering her with one light for a short time, and so put it out again; thereby to give knowledge that they have seen her token.

Ten, Item, whensoever the admiral shall hang out her ensign in the main shrouds, then every man to come aboard her as a token of counsel.

Eleven, Item, if there happen any storm or contrary wind to the fleet after the discovery, whereby they are separated; then every ship to repair unto their last good port, there to meet again.

These rules may seem a bit quaint but they served well, indeed the loss of Gilbert's *Delight* might be directly attributed to the failure to observe several of these simple rules, mainly Item Six.

In 1578 Frobisher had issued similar, but shorter, rules requiring his nine consorts to remain at all times within one mile of the admiral, *Ayde*, which was the only ship that would carry a stern light at night. Each evening a captains' briefing would be held at 1900 in *Ayde*, while any ship that became detached was to make her way first to 'Friesland' and then to the straits, the exact latitude of which captains were informed separately. Frobisher also planned for an enemy attack, with his fleet being divided into three divisions led by *Ayde*, *Judith* and *Thomas Allen*.

Given the vagaries of weather and the response of individual ships and their captains to adverse conditions, the need for a rendezvous was paramount. Gilbert asserted that:

The course first to be taken for the discovery is to bear directly to Cape Race, the most southerly cape of Newfoundland; and there to harbour ourselves either in Rogneux or Fermous, being the places appointed for our rendezvous . . . and, therefore, every ship separated from the fleet to repair to that place so fast as God shall permit . . . and there to stay for the meeting of the whole fleet the space of ten days; and when you depart, to leave marks.

The most famous of these marks, and the shortest and most tragic, was, as already recounted, the message left by the Roanoke colonists of 1585 when they abandoned their settlement leaving, for John White to find, when he eventually returned in 1590, on a tall post with 'the bark taken off and five foot from the ground in fair capital letters' the one word CROATOAN, 'without any cross or sign of distress.'

In some voyages the fleet managed to stay remarkably close together despite encountering violent storms, while others seem to have had great difficulty keeping in contact. Thus Grenville sailed in 1585 with a fleet consisting of his flagship, *Tyger*; the vice-admiral *Roebuck*; the *Lion*, a 100-ton merchant vessel; the fifty-ton *Elizabeth*, with the experienced circumnavigator Thomas Cavendish in command; and, also at fifty tons, *Dorothy*, captained by Arthur Barlowe, who had sailed on the previous year's reconnaissance. Finally, there were two pinnaces, tenders to the larger vessels. The fleet departed from Plymouth on 19 April but was scattered by a storm off Portugal in which *Tyger*'s pinnace sank. The admiral continued the journey alone, making a fast passage to the Indies, where she anchored in the Bay of Guayanilla, Puerto Rico, the agreed rendezvous, on 15 May. Eight days later Cavendish brought *Elizabeth* into the bay, by which time Grenville's crew had built a replacement pinnace. On the 29th, after leaving a message nailed to a post, which he optimistically assumed the Spanish would not remove, the fleet of three sailed on to indulge in a little piracy and prize-taking, at the end of which five ships sailed on to Hispaniola. Further dalliance meant that they did not arrive off the Carolina Outer Banks until the last week of June.

Meanwhile, *Lion* kept company with the other pinnace and, having probably drawn in a fight with a French ship off Jamaica, ran aground on the north shore of that island. After being refloated, a shortage of victuals led to Captain Raymond landing twenty soldiers on that deserted coast to fend for themselves. *Lion*, now in company with *Dorothy*, sailed on to the Carolinas, where, on 17 June, Raymond set another group of thirty-two men ashore on Croatoan Island, from where two were recovered on 6 July by a reconnaissance party landed by Grenville. Around this time *Roebuck* also rejoined; thus it had taken the fleet some ten weeks to reform following the storm. Grenville's laxity as a fleet commander was made more manifest on the return voyage, which he completed alone, to his evident pleasure as he took a rich prize, the profit from which he thus did not have to share with the other captains.

By way of contrast, the same size fleet making up the 1609 resupply, having lost sight of the admiral *Sea Venture*, which eventually struck the Bermudas, kept on course, with four of them, *Lion*, *Falcon*, *Unity* and *Blessing* entering the James River together on 11 August, followed a few days later by the vice-admiral, *Diamond*, and then, three days later by *Swallow* and *Virginia*, the last of the surviving ships, a remarkable feat for any group scattered by storms.

DISEMBARKATION RATIONS

The weary survivors of the third resupply stumbling ashore at Jamestown would immediately have been aware of the importance of the supplies that were carried in their ships' holds to the survival of the starving settlers. It was the same story along the whole littoral, while the choice of which victuals to carry for the period from arrival to relief was made more difficult by the problems of preservation, the lack of cleared land and/or time enough to sow and harvest; and an over-optimistic view of what could be gleaned from the wild or traded with the Amerindians. The southern colony seems to have been poorer at loading provisions, and better at spoiling them, than were their compatriots further north, where the inclement weather was a known factor. By way of comparison, in the 1620s the Virginia Company considered that the victuals to be provided for a whole year for one man should consist of:

Two bushels of peas	Two bushels of oatmeal
One gallon of aquavitae	One gallon of oil
Two gallons of vinegar	

Whereas the experienced Newfoundland settler John Guy recommended to Sir Henry Salisbury in 1623 that a group of eight people in that plantation would need:

Four cwt of biscuit	Six barrels of beer
Four cwt dried fish	Nine bushels of dried wheat
Ninety bushels of malt	Forty five cwt hops
Sixteen bushels of peas	One bushel of beans for planting
Four kinterkins butter	Three cwt cheese
One kinterkin vinegar	Four cwt pork
Ten cwt salted beef	Six flitches of bacon
Six gallons of oil	Two gallons of honey
Ten dozen lbs candles	Four bushels of oatmeal
A firkin of aquavitae	A firkin of Canary wine
A firkin of methaglyne (mead)	A peck of mustard seed

Plus rice, sugar, currants, raisens, pepper, cloves, mace, ginger, nutmeg and cinnamon.

To supplement this very full list the settlers were to be provided with fishing nets, seed for the garden, two rams and ten female goats, as well as a boar and a sow.

The difference is startling, as is the detail that accompanies it concerning the working and support of a small fishing unit of three boats manned by thirteen men and a boy. Even more impressive are the lists drawn up by Richard Whitbourne in *A Discourse and Discovery of Newfoundland*, printed in 1622. As a result, although aristocratic investors such as William Vaughan, Lord Baltimore and Lord Falkland more or less lost interest in the Newfoundland settlers, the latter, clustered together in this bleak land, survived, thanks in part to their early and sensible provisioning and the constant intercourse with the visiting fishing vessels.

Those who dispatched the settlers should have been aware of the effect that unloading insufficient victuals would have on their fragile beachheads. Ralegh might have been lulled by the report of Amadas and Barlowe into thinking that Virginia was so bountiful that self-sufficiency was going to be the natural condition. Indeed, despite the spoilage of much of the stores carried onboard *Tyger* when she ran aground, Lane does seem to have kept his party, if not well fed, certainly safe from starvation. This was to be, however, an exception. Death struck the Jamestown settlers of 1607 very early.

Christopher Newport sailed away on 22 June, leaving the colonists with a daily ration for each man of half a pint of soaked barley and half a pint of wheat, in both of which weevils were already feasting. Just six weeks later Percy was recording in his journal:

> The sixth of August there died John Ashby of the bloody flux, the ninth died George Flower of the swelling. The Tenth day died William Brewster, gentleman, of a wound given by the savages and was buried the eleventh day. The fourteenth day, Jerome Alicock Ancient, died of a wound, the same day Francis Midwinter, Edward Morris, corporal, died suddenly. The fifteenth day, there died Edward Browne and Stephen Galthorpe. The sixteenth day, there died Thomas Gower, gentleman. The seventeenth day, there died Thomas Mounslic. The eighteenth day, there died . . .

The list goes on: a wastage of bubonic plague proportions, which Percy considered to have been caused by 'swellings, fluxes, burning fevers, and by wars, but for the most part they died of mere famine'.

The traditional blame for this death rate is placed squarely on: the selection of low-lying, marshy, mosquito-infested Jamestown; the poor administration of Wingfield; the idleness of the settlers themselves; and the drinking of river water. Although the James River, tidal and slow flowing as it passed the island, might mutely have to accept some culpability, the equally brackish drinking water of low-lying Roanoke seem to have been swallowed without great harm. Indeed, by 1609, John Smith wrote, 'we digged a fair well of fresh water in the Fort of excellent sweet water which until then was wanting.' Incompetent Wingfield might have been, but to have led so many men, uninjured by warfare, to their graves in so short a time, even if they dwelt on the marshy site he had selected, exceeds any scale of poor leadership. Rather, the blame, or less emotively, the explanation, for so many early deaths through 'mere famine' must be shared by the contribution of that which was not stored in the holds of the three ships before they left London.

STORES

Along with the stowage of the food, the settler ships had to carry both arms and artisanal equipment. Most of those travelling as tradesmen could contain their tools within a large wooden chest. Harquebuses and other weapons, often rejects from English armouries, would also have been boxed up, while barrels of gunpowder would have been most carefully placed well away from any source of heat. The Virginia Company laid down that every man voyaging to the colony should be fitted with: one suit of armour, one musket, one belt and bandolier, twenty pounds of powder and sixty pounds of shot. Once armed, the head of household was also expected to equip himself with numerous hoes, axes, hand-saws, hammers, shovels, spades, augers, chisels, awls, gimlets, hatchets, hand-bills, nails, pickaxes, along with pots, pans and plates for his family kitchen. To this domestic bill of lading Virginia seems to have paid greater attention, but once again the detail provided by Richard Whitbourne by way of guidance for Newfoundland immigrants is a far better inventory.

CROSSING BACK

Prevailing winds and a favourable current, as well as being unencumbered with puking and complaining passengers, made for swifter and less troublesome homeward voyages, although, if the ships were forced to embark evacuees, things could become more difficult. There were other exceptions as well.

In 1578, *Endeavour*, one of Frobisher's fleet, having barely escaped the ice off Baffin Island, found herself spending weeks unable to get around Ireland. She eventually grounded at Smerwick, where her cargo of worthless ore was later utilized in the defences of that fort against the assault in 1580, which ended in the whole Spanish garrison and its supporters being slaughtered by Ralegh after surrendering.

John White's return trip in the flyboat in 1587 was another horrendous journey resulting in the death of many of the crew from malnourishment. In December 1607 *Gifte of God* departed from Fort St George on the Sagadahoc with timber and an

Half Moon, in which Hudson sailed up the Hudson River in 1610, was a sturdy vessel to whose seaworthiness the master and his mate, Jouett, made no little contribution through their very professional seamanship

evacuation party of sick settlers for whom six weeks' rations had been scraped together. They barely made it to the Azores, where the cargo was sold for sufficient rations to continue their voyage to Topsham. The master, John Havercombe, was later sued, unsuccessfully, by Sir Francis Popham for the value of the timber, some £33!

Yet the conditions onboard are of less importance than the cargo being carried, which clearly showed both the main interest, or obsession, of the investors and the inability of the settlers to deliver what those investors most desired. Thus, despite Harriot indicating that this virgin land would yield an amazing opulent bounty from its fruitful womb, the first commercial crop that was sent back from Virginia was useless sassafras. Once that market had been exhausted, little interest was shown in holds laden with shipmast and board while, unlike for the French in the north, furs and skins were lacking in both quantity and quality to 'make' a voyage. What the investors wanted was gold, and this is what they instructed their men to find.

So, the first cargo to cross back from the new world was ore, or it was not, although the first intended settlers of any significance were miners. These poor men laboured in the long northern summer days to fill ship hold after ship hold with nothing better than aggregate, which Frobisher and his backers insisted would yield gold. With nothing learned from this experience, the Virginia Company required Christopher Newport to manage a mini gold rush in the gardens of Jamestown, thus creating the opportunity for famine to afflict the stay-behinds once he had sailed away with gravel and not gold in his hold. And still the investors did not learn. Most famously, farcically and tragically of all was the double journey of the founder of Virginia, Walter Ralegh, who caught gold fever so badly that he led two expeditions, based solely on the myth of El Dorado, up the Orinoco, losing both his son and his head to the lure of gold.

Gold, when it did arrive, did so in the form of gold leaf – Virginian gold leaf – the result of the careful nurturing of good-quality tobacco plants by John Rolfe, to whose attention to detail and excellent husbandry the survival of the Virginia settlement owed a great deal. At long last the colonies had something valuable to export; something it was worth merchants sending ships over the Atlantic to collect; something which the colonists could claim they had developed themselves; something for which they would insist they received a just reward. Ralegh might have flirted with tobacco, but it was Rolfe who wooed the weed and to whom later generations of Virginians owed their inheritance, rather than the man who had only wished to lord over the land.

More valuable to the investors at the start of the invasion than the goods in the hold of the vessels returning was the good news by letter or word of mouth sent by those who had seen little but imagined much. These adulatory reports about Virginia, New England and Newfoundland show that most fell for the charms of the new land but, like a besotted suitor, were blind to its obvious faults. While many more, at home in England, expressed an interest from a distance, both groups were united in under-achievement. The Atlantic, which in Cabot, Gilbert and Frobisher's time had proved to be a voracious swallower of ships, had been tamed; now it was the land that required the same zeal and attention from the settlers as the seamen had accomplished by education and endeavour. They had provided the bucking wooden steeds to carry their passengers across the ocean, yet those they landed on its shores with authority to 'conquer, occupy and possess' remained too scared of this beckoning, beautiful and bountiful land to penetrate beyond the coastal petticoats. Until they were man enough so to do they would woo but never win.

Before 1630, most crossings to America had been organized by either individuals or joint-stock companies as speculative ventures to increase their own wealth while, at the same time, offering a sop to settlers sufficiently dipped in honey to encourage them to walk down to the docks and embark. By having a financial interest in the whole venture these investors were quite willing to skimp in certain areas if it meant minimizing their early losses. They were also oblivious to the need to unload the maximum of stores to be consumed by the minimum of people, allowing the crossing vessels to remain far too long, superfluous to requirement but depleting the stores. It was not until the commissioning of the ships was separated either from the work being carried on ashore or was itself ordered and arranged by the settlers themselves that an acceptable, agreed, scheduled and lasting standard of transatlantic shipping service could come into being. When it arrived it proved to be the co-founder, along with the East India Company ships, of the oceangoing merchant marine with which Britain was to dominate maritime trade up until the end of the Second World War.

CHAPTER 8

Fortress America

> yet might the practice of fortifications now, as necessarily be employed in the land
> of Florida in those parts thereof which long have been in possession of our English
> nation . . . for that country being but weakly planted with the English, and more
> weakly defended from the invasions of the heathen, amongst whom they dwell . . .
> those parts I say might easily be fortified . . .
>
> George Waymouth, *The Jewell of Artes*, 1604

The most obvious iconic structure whose very form identifies America today is the
skyscraper, its symbolism poignantly reinforced by the destruction through enemy
action of the Twin Towers in New York in 2001. Yet skyscrapers still occupy only a
fraction of the land, their distribution far less widespread than that of the structure that
came to represent both the foreshore and the frontier of manifest destiny – the fort.
In the three hundred years it took the Europeans to complete their conquest of North
America, forts were built to protect and deprive from sea to shining sea. Turn to the
index of any reasonably detailed atlas of the world, look up 'Fort' and the long column
will show that it is dominated by place names in America, many of which are redolent
of American history and the way the newly arrived culture took hold of the land. By
their location and names these forts relate the story of the invasion and struggle to
possess America.

In the far north Anglo-French rivalry had been there from the beginning so, before
his 1578 voyage to Baffin Island, Martin Frobisher gave his commissioners:

> many arguments and reasons, how requisite and needful it was to fortify and to inhabit
> in that new country, and to urge . . . a greater furniture of shipping for his dominion
> [having discovered] how that the French king did arm presently twelve ships to pass
> to the same new country, to take possession of the straits and to fortify at the mines
> there . . .

At the other end of the continent, in support of Ralegh's vision, Hakluyt wrote that
a 'strong order of fortification' would be needed to hold the ground and annoy any
'weary power . . . that shall seek to arrive'. Francis Bacon in 1601 wished to see an armed
group, very similar to the one Ralegh first dispatched, sent to establish a colony. In New
England, Brereton in 1602 echoed that view and suggested that 'men most skilful in
the art of fortification' be encouraged to fortify both river mouths and islands in the
approaches. Waymouth went as far as to produce diagrams of fortified towns in his
1604 *The Jewell of Artes*, while, as late as 1623, Calvert, planning for his Newfoundland
settlement, was instructed to 'build and fortify castles'.

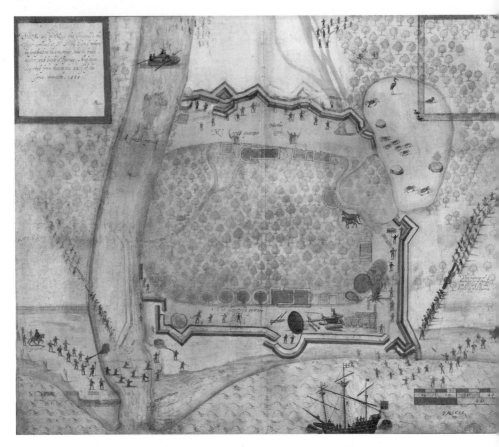

Ralph Lane's fort at Guayanilla Bay, Puerto Rico. The fort was wisely built to protect the English while they built a pinnace and watered their ships. The Spanish horsemen sent out to investigate chose not to attack. (British Museum)

Yet, despite the preparations and the alarms, only in Nova Scotia were the forts ever required to be manned to repel an attacking European force. Elsewhere it was the Amerindians who were to be the enemy at the gates. This did not prevent most advice being predicated on a European threat, the Jamestown settlers being told to ensure that their beachhead was not as open to a Spanish assault such as that which had destroyed the French settlement at Fort Caroline.

The first building erected in the Americas by the Europeans in the Columbian era was a fort at La Navidad in modern-day Haiti. It was built in December 1492 from the timbers of Columbus's *Santa María*, wrecked through careless watchkeeping some four miles offshore. Columbus manned the fort with an inadequate garrison of thirty-nine soldiers and abandoned them. Their fate, which was to be killed by the native people while the fort itself was razed, was mirrored by the fate of the few left behind to man a fort by Grenville at Roanoke in 1586.

Ralph Lane's fort near Cape Rojo, Puerto Rico, was built to enclose a hill of salt, and likewise not attacked by the Spanish troops who arrived in force to drive off the intruders. Given the time available for its construction, the fine lines are probably an ingratiating exaggeration by the force artist, John White. (British Museum)

Likewise, the first structures erected by the English in the new world were also to be forts, beginning with Frobisher's temporary palisade of earth-filled casks in Baffin Island in 1577, which was followed by a more substantial stockade constructed by Ralph Lane in Guayanilla Bay, St John's Island, off Puerto Rico, begun on 15 May 1585. This was built in a most defensible position, being provided with protection by a river on one side, the sea on another and dense woodland on the other two sides. It was a wise decision by Grenville to build the structure, behind which the English could construct their new pinnace and refresh themselves, for the Spanish soon came to investigate and remonstrate, and presumably would have substituted weapons for words had the English not taken such precautions. As it was, the Spanish withdrew, having promised to supply the transient camp with victuals, a promise which, 'keeping to their old customs for perjury and breach of promise came not'. Hot-headed Grenville then fired the woods by way of demonstrating his disappointment and on 29 May 'retired to our Fort, which was the same day fired, and each man came onboard', and watched Ralph Lane's work go up in smoke before they sailed away. They left behind, carved into a tree trunk, a record of their time there as a guidance to any who might be following after them. They may well have had in mind the fleet under the command of Bernard Drake, which, ready to depart with supplies for the new colony in June, was diverted to warn the English fishermen off Newfoundland not to land their catch in Spain, or they might have been thinking of Francis Drake's expeditionary force which was following them to the Indies.

Lane's second landing, and second fort, was erected a few days later at Salinas Bay near Cape Rojo, Puerto Rico, where he had been sent to gather salt. Once again his fortifications, which, from John White's drawing, appear both considerable and skilfully built, were timely, for no sooner had they been constructed than a Spanish force, which Lane estimated to consist of forty cavalry and 300 foot soldiers, arrived, but strangely, given the odds in their favour, did not attack.

Having put his skills to use on temporary structures, Lane was next responsible, at Roanoke, for the building of a fort strong enough to deter or drive off a determined Spanish force detached specifically to destroy his settlement and the men within. In fact he planned two structures: the main fort and a seaward warning station protected by the natural barrier of the Carolina Outer Banks and located so as to guard the best entrance into their harbour of Port Ferdinando. Of its siting Lane wrote to Walsingham:

> This . . . has a bar at twelve foot at high water: and the bar very short, being within three, four and five fathom water: so as this port at the point of the land being fortified with a sconce, it is not to be entered by all the force of Spain can make, we having the force of God.

Across the waters of Pamlico Sound, Lane began work on the first English fort to be built on mainland America. It was soon done, with work beginning on 27 July 1585 and completed by 17 August. The time taken, compared with that to erect the temporary forts in the West Indies, coupled with the easy to work sandy Roanoke soil, indicates that the defences were well planned and well constructed. Unfortunately Lane neither described nor did White draw this historically most significant building. The former

Fort Ralegh: this small reconstructed earthwork stands forlorn in the woods of Roanoke – a reminder of the fate that befell the settlers that White left behind.

An artist's impression of the first fort at Jamestown as it was about 1614. (Courtesy National Park Service, Colonial National Historical Park)

spent more time writing inflammatory criticisms of Grenville than he did in describing his own work – an irrational behaviour that also set a trend whereby the English put as much fervour into finding fault with each other as they did in fighting their true foes. However, on 3 September 1585, Lane ended a letter to Richard Hakluyt with the words 'From the new Fort in Virginia'.

Today, at Fort Raleigh on Roanoke, a small earthen rampart has been constructed close to the site where archaeology has shown evidence that a similar sixteenth-century structure existed. This one is about twelve yards square and surrounded by ditches about five foot deep and twelve foot wide. It seems just too small to have housed the settlers. Much of what was recovered from the dig suggests that, instead of this being Lane's fort, it was built to protect Harriot's scientific and mineral assessing laboratory, but he makes no mention of this earthwork in his lengthy narrative. In any case, even this structure would have required many man hours to erect, and Lane would have been unlikely to have spared his men for such an endeavour. There could be a third explanation in that it marks the spot where White's abandoned colonists gathered to make their last stand. Whatever its origins, the evocative little mound, lying among the towering trees, is a powerful mute testimony to the smallness of the original settlement groups and the immensity and fearsomeness of the land surrounding them which they were expected to tame.

The earthwork also bears little relation to the layout proposed for a fort which was offered as advice to Ralegh when he was planning his expedition. This was that it should be:

> a pentangle in this manner. With five large bulwarks, the casements of the bulwarks large and open with a way out of the bulwarks and the other into the street. The collionsides or ocrechons [cullions or shoulders/excretions] large and long, the curtains somewhat slant, that the earth may lie the faster and the ramparts of the curtains very broad. Every bulwark shall have by it a cavalier to beat the field . . .
>
> The ditch I would have large with walls, beyond the ditch a twenty foot from the ditch I would have a wall of four foot high with a rail on the top so as to top of this should be within a three foot height by cause it shall prevent any sudden scallado [assault].
>
> The fort should be where a landing of reinforcements would always be possible and among its servants should be; a physician, a good geographer and excellent painter, an apothecary, surgeons and 'a general to command absolutely within the fort and without on all matters marshal' and a Justice, whose decisions were binding, a High Treasurer and an Admiral.

The choice of Roanoke left Lane with two tasks instead of one if, as he told Walsingham, he and his men were 'as resolute rather to lose our lives than to defer a possession to her Majesty'. Having met his first priority, to provide a robust fortification for his company, he had then to find a better site for a privateering lair. That he achieved this despite having so few men with him gives great credit for one about whom commentators, because of his decision to abandon the project, have been less than kind. His plan for moving north into the Chesapeake was also creditable:

My meaning was further at the head of the river in the place of my descent where I would have left my boats to have raised a sconce with a small trench, and a palisade upon the top of it, in the which, and in the guard of my boats I would have left five and twenty, or thirty men. With the rest would I have marched with as much victual as every man could have carried, with their furniture, mattocks, spades and axes, two days' journey. In the end of my march upon some convenient plot would I have raised another sconce according to the former, where I would have left 15 or 20. And if it would have fallen out conveniently in the way I would have raised my said sconce upon some corn field that my company might have lived upon it. And so I would have holden this course of ensconcing every two days march, until I had arrived at the Bay or Port he spoke of: which finding to be worth the possession, I would there have raised a main fort, both for the defence of the harbours and our shipping also, and would have reduced our whole habitation from Roanoke and from the harbour and port thereof.

Apart from the obviously inflammatory plan to commandeer the native corn, the concept was reasonably sound and would have led to the establishment of a better site for White's colony of 1587. Unfortunately, the weather prevented the project's inception, so that White's inadequately defended villagers suffered accordingly. Yet, what made their fate more certain was the fact that, by the time they sailed from Plymouth on 8 May 1587, the protective fort had, first, been abandoned by Lane, then inadequately garrisoned by Grenville with fifteen soldiers who were driven out by the Amerindians. The likelihood of failure became evident from the moment White set his eyes on the only recently evacuated Roanoke fort, of which he wrote:

> The 23 July, the Governor, with divers of his company, walked to the North end of the Island [Roanoke], where Master Rolfe Lane had his fort, with sundry necessary and decent dwelling houses, made by his men about it the year before, where we hoped to find some signs, or certain knowledge of our fifteen men. When we came thither, we found the fort razed down, but with all the houses standing unhurt, saving the nether rooms of them, and also of the fort were overgrown with melons of divers sorts, and deer within them, feeding on the melons: so we returned to our company, without hope of ever seeing any of the fifteen men living.
>
> The same day order was given, that every man should be employed for the repairing of these houses, which we found standing, and also to make other new cottages, for such as should need.

Once the new arrivals realized that Ferdinando was determined to leave them on Roanoke, where Grenville's fifteen soldiers had met their grisly end, they must have felt that a similar doom could be their most likely fate. That they all did not clamour to re-embark with White says much for the human spirit but not a lot for its intelligence. With Roanoke being written off in 1587, a new King, James I, was on the throne before the English considered returning to the new world. They would come under different leadership, for James had thrown Ralegh into prison under sentence of death for treason. Now, for the moment, the new world entrepreneurs would be businessmen, not favourites, but the aims of their umbrella organization, the Virginia Company of London and Bristol, remained much the same, as did their instructions to the first settler groups, which included building sure defences against the wrath of Spain.

Thus the appointment of a military engineer as the first President of the northern settlement was not a singular act. For this enterprise, George Waymouth, closely involved in the preliminary investigations leading to the new settlements, had drawn up plans for various versions of fortified colonial towns, many geometrically as complicated as knot gardens, but all based around the idea that he expostulated: that any settlement in the new world would have to be fortified if it were to stand a chance of surviving. Before Waymouth had expressed his views in print, Bartholomew Gosnold had completed an exploratory voyage in 1602 and selected an island in a lake on Elizabeth's Isle (now Cuttyhunk) on which to build a fortified trading post. In Brereton's account this was none too soon for, on the second day of this three-week task, eleven canoes were sighted heading for them. So they abandoned work: 'being loath they should discover our fortification, we went out on the sea to meet them'. After the Amerindians had attempted some pilfering, only to be reprimanded by their own leader, a friendly exchange of goods took place over a three-day period, giving Brereton the chance to write a detailed and favourable pen-picture of these people, whom he considered, 'exceeding courteous, gentle of disposition, and well-conditioned, excelling all others that we have seen'.

That favourable impression was not enough for Gosnold's original volunteers to retain their desire to overwinter at the fort. The decision of the reluctant twelve would have been influenced by an Amerindian attack on a foraging party, one of whom was injured by an arrow. More influential was Bartholomew Gilbert's refusal to land sufficient supplies to ensure they did not starve in the winter. So, on 18 June 1602, yet another British fort was abandoned as *Concord* departed with her full company.

Shortly after Gosnold had returned and reported on his voyage, Martin Pring sailed from Bristol, on 20 March 1603, in the fifty-ton *Speedwell* with her consort the twenty-six-ton *Discoverer*. This short trip – having left a stormbound Milford Haven on 10 April 1603, they were back in Bristol on 2 October – was also a trading and exploratory voyage with an outward cargo of 'Hats of divers colours, green, blue and yellow, apparel of coarse kersey and canvas readymade, stockings and shoes, saws, pickaxes, spades and shovels, axes, hatchets, hooks, knives, scissors, hammers, chisels, fish-hooks, bells, beads, bugles, looking-glasses, thimbles, pins, needles, thread and such like.' As this was exchanged for the totally useless sassafras root, the Amerindians got the better bargain. The trading followed a similar course to that experienced by Gosnold, with the locals, near Provincetown, Cape Cod, behaving in a friendly fashion until, near the time of the visitors' departure, they seemed to turn hostile. Pring, however, had taken precautions and constructed a 'small baricado' from which 'to keep diligent watch'. When the Amerindians arrived armed, a 'piece of Ordnance' was shot off 'to give terror to the Indians, and a warning to our men'. A much more effective weapon was the two 'great and fearful mastiffs', Fool and Gallant, whose appearance caused even greater trepidation. A bite to their bark was provided by George Waymouth's kidnapping of six Pemaquid people in 1605, which ensured the continuation of mutual distrust even after the Amerindians were returned home unharmed.

So, when George Popham led his settlement group ashore at the mouth of the Sagadahoc River on 18 August 1607, they fully appreciated that a fort was essential to protect against both the native population and other rival European powers. Thus the spot that they chose for their plantation was a peninsula which could be readily and rapidly made defensible. From the 20 August onwards, while 'most of the hands laboured hard about the fort', others carried out some preliminary exploration, finding another spot 'most fit to fortify on being by nature fortified on two sides, with a spring of water under it'. Work continued under the gaze of friendly visiting Amerindians, until completion in early October, by which time an area of some 5,000 square metres had been enclosed by an irregularly shaped rectangular fortification of clay, rock and sand, tied together by timbers. Several sturdy bastions were also erected to house the eight heavier guns, while a small protected pier was included at which the settlement's pinnace, *Virginia*, could be secured. The sides of the fort measured roughly seventy metres from north to south, with a thirty-metre northward-pointing pan-handle, and 100 metres on the east–west wall alongside the river. Outside the walls a fenced garden was laid out; inside, it was claimed, fifty dwellings were built, as well as a church and a storehouse. Ironically, this well-constructed fort lasted just a season while that lethargically begun at Jamestown a few months earlier became a permanent settlement.

The London Council's *Instructions Given by Way of Advice* to the south Virginia colony quoted earlier also recommended that, upstream, having somehow ensured that none of the 'natural people of the country inhabit between you and the sea coast', the invaders employ forty men to fortify their settlement. One can therefore imagine the settlers' consternation when their leader, the weak Edward Wingfield, decided not to do this, preferring, to follow the views of Bartholomew Gosnold, who advised against raising barricades so as not to alarm the Amerindians, in accordance with their orders 'to have great care not to offend the naturals'. A flimsy compromise was reached, with George Kendall erecting a simple fence at the narrowest part of the peninsula to enclose the settlement where they had landed on 14 May 1607. Before the end of the month the Amerindians attacked in force and, 'had it not chanced a cross bar shot from the ships struck down a bough from a tree amongst them, that caused them to retire, our men had all been slain, being securely all at work and their arms in dry fats [stowed]'. Knowing that the defending fleet would soon sail brought about a change of heart, and Wingfield then ordered the settlement to be 'palisadoed'. One still gets the impression that he understood neither the threat nor the countermeasures necessary to repel it for, a few days later, a friendly native suggested that the settlers might do well to mow down the long grass beyond the palisades through which the attackers could, had and continued, to approach the fort unobserved.

In 1610, at the time of the evacuation, Jamestown Fort was described as being:

rather as the ruins of some ancient fortifications, than that any people living might inhabit it. The palisade . . . torn down, the ports open, the gates from the hinges, the church ruined and unfrequented, empty houses (whose owners untimely death had taken newly from them) rent up and burnt, the living not able . . . to step into the woods to gather other firewood.

Yet, shortly after De La Warr had arrived, William Strachey was impressed by the fort, describing it as being in:

> the form of a triangle and so palisaded . . . At every angle or corner, where the lines meet, a bulwark or watch tower is raised and in each bulwark a piece of ordnance or two well mounted. To every side . . . is a settled street of houses . . . In the midst is a market place, a store house, and a corp de garde . . . And thus enclosed with a palisade of planks and strong posts . . . The fort is called, in honour of His Majesty, Jamestown.

The mosquitoes that infested low-lying Jamestown appear to have injected a lethargy into many of the settlers as far as self-protection was concerned; they allowed both their fortifications and their persons to rot once they had sent the injured but still ardent John Smith home in early September. By March 1610, after the 'Starving Time' of a cruel winter, only 60 out of 500 colonists were left alive. When they made the decision to depart they left behind a fort whose very gates had come off their hinges and whose fortifications they had to be prevented from burning down. Ordered back by a man with some backbone, they returned to rebuild that which they had abandoned, and did so with such effect that when Amerindian resentment finally boiled over into massacre in 1622, the inhabitants of Jamestown repulsed an assault while those in the outstations were ripped apart.

Among those outstations was Henricus, which Sir Thomas Dale ordered to be built in May 1611, following instructions from the Virginia Company, that a new town was to be founded to replace Jamestown as the centre of government. Two earlier attempts had failed: the first, under the limp-wristed leadership of Francis West, mainly because John Smith's advice had been rejected; the second, organized and directed in person by De La Warr, because of persistent Amerindian attacks during the winter. Dale sailed upstream in September. Determined not to repeat West's mistakes, he first prepared 'timber, pales, posts and rails' to impale the town and 'to secure himself and men from the malice and treachery of the Indians'. The site was well chosen defensively, for it was built 'upon a neck of very high land, three parts thereof environed with the main River', with the land approach secured by a palisade. It needed to be: without mounting an assault, the Amerindians took frequent bow-and-arrow pot shots at the builders.

Yet, mainly because the new settlers were keener on creating their own largeholdings than living under the surly eye of Dale, few chose to move into the completed fortified town. Ironically, their land grabbing for tobacco planting acted as the catalyst for the catastrophe which Dale was endeavouring to avoid. It came on 22 March 1622, when Opechancanough, Powhatan's younger brother and successor, ordered a coordinated attack on the British settlements the length of the James River. Henricus was destroyed. Jamestown itself, forewarned, repulsed the attack, but settlers in more isolated settlements were slaughtered. There is some inverse correlation between the scale of defences and the success of the attacks, but there is also a random pattern to the deaths, depending very much on the speed of response by the settlers as much as the determination of the Amerindians to kill. Thus, although Bermuda City was reported to be the best fortified point in the colony, situated on high ground with natural cliff defences as well as a trench and palisade with 'great timber blockhouses' which was built to be 'an impregnable retreat against any foreign invasion, however powerful', and with a two-mile pale stretching from the banks of the Appomattox to the James, it was temporarily abandoned following the attack.

Even with the growing awareness that the local population was not friendly, the English did not forget that their European rivals Spain posed an absent danger. For this reason the entrance to the Chesapeake and the James River were soon fortified, with the added advantage that these palisaded settlements could provide outstations to where some of Jamestown's settlers could be dispersed at times of famine. Thus came into being Forts Algernon, Henry and Charles, which served well in their unspectacular role as lookouts and outstations, although the company at Fort Algernon drew George Percy's wrath when, at the end of the Starving Time, he sailed down to see the garrison and found them living well off shellfish and pork-fed crab, which 'would have been a great relief unto us and saved many of our lives'. This ability to live well lasted. In 1614 Ralph Hamor described the forts as 'goodly seats and much corn ground around them, abounding with the commodities of fish, fowl, deer and fruits, whereby the men live, with half that maintenance out of the store, which in other places was allowed'.

Thomas Hamor (Ralph's brother) was less sure as to the fort's defences, exclaiming, 'we cannot secure it, if a foreign enemy, as we have just cause to expect daily should attempt it.' Yet, when called upon so to do, Fort Algernon acquitted itself well. When that enemy, in the form of Don Diego de Molina, arrived in the Bay in April 1611 to carry out a reconnaissance as ordered by Philip III, he was seized and imprisoned and his ship, rather than hazarding an exchange with the fort, fled without its leader.

The eastern shore of the Chesapeake was also fortified against foreign aggression, with the added advantage that the local Accomacks, ruled over by the 'laughing' King Debedeavon, were friendly and cooperative. A small salt works was established here for a few years before it was abandoned, but by 1625 the fort was well manned and on muster found to contain thirty-five firearms, three swords, twenty-eight suits of armour, 155 pounds of powder and 646 pound of shot.

To 'defend against the invasion of a foreign enemy', an upstream fort was ordered to be built in 1623 at Warrascoyack, the site of great slaughter the previous year, but, despite a report that 'the fort is abuilding apace', the 1625 census lists it as having just two palisades, nine suits of armour and thirteen [unspecified] 'fixed pieces', with very few men to man them. This would indicate a well-judged complacency, for no foreign fleet ever entered the Chesapeake in strength and the downstream settlements became very successful, giving rise to what were to become the main centres of population (Newport News, Hampton and Elizabeth City) in the years to come.

Indeed, the success of the downstream fortifications as settlements should have encouraged a consolidation of the land between them and Jamestown rather than attempting the move inland. This would have fulfilled one of the few sensible instructions issued by the Virginia Company: to ensure that no hostile Amerindians held the land between the settlement and the sea. Until this was achieved, every settler working outside a defended settlement had to keep one eye warily on the surrounding woods. So, to overcome this fear, and following the massacre of 1622, another iconic American structure was erected – the frontier. The concept of shutting out the Amerindians from the peninsula lying between the James and York Rivers had been mooted as early as 1611 but had been shelved as a result of the peace settlement following on from the marriage of Pocahontas and John Rolfe. It was revived in 1623 when Governor Wyatt wrote to the Earl of Southampton that the colonists planned 'winning the forest' through building a pale between those rivers.

It was not until the early 1630s that the work began, but by 1634 a six-mile frontier was in existence, described as:

> a strong palisade . . . upon a straight between both rivers and . . . a sufficient force of men to defence of the same, whereby all the lower part of Virginia have a range for their cattle, near forty miles in length and in most places twelve miles broad. The palisade is very near six miles long, bounded in by two large creeks . . . in this manner to take also in all the ground between those two Rivers, and so utterly excluded the Indians from thence; which work is conceived to be of extraordinary benefit to the country . . .

The English had created America's first frontier but, after 1644, with the Powhatan Confederacy no longer considered a threat, the palisade fell into disrepair, with almost all traces eventually disappearing. Not so the concept: in 1634 no one had any idea how far that first frontier would stretch or how long it would last.

In New England the *Mayflower* settlers were only a short time ashore at Plymouth before they realized that they faced a potential Amerindian threat. Their initial response

Burial Hill fort. Although the Plymouth settlers spent much time and effort on building their stockades, they were never subject to the continuous hostility experienced by those at Jamestown, meaning that they could work outside the palisades without fear of attack.

was to train and practise with their arms and to form a defensive ring whenever the alarm was raised. Then in February 1621, in response to their coming under observation, they hauled their six large guns up a nearby hill as the first step in creating a defensible position. Then, lulled by reaching a mutual defence agreement with Massasoit, the Pokanoket *sachem*, little further advance was made in fortifying the settlement until it was recognized that reaching agreement with one tribe almost automatically put them in jeopardy with another, in this case the Narragansett, who went so far as to deliver to the settlers a challenge in the form of a number of arrows wrapped up in a snakeskin. They hardly needed their 'liaison officer', Squanto, to explain the seriousness of the threat made, even more so when, in response, Bradford returned the skin refilled with gunpowder and shot. Then, realizing that war might not be far off, Bradford ordered an eight-foot-high palisade to be constructed around the settlement, a distance that exceeded half a mile. Fired by necessity, fewer than fifty half-starved men felled trees, sided off the branches, dug postholes and trenches and dragged the twelve-foot timbers to the ditch and hauled them upright. Slowly, like an emerging giant millipede, their defences wound around their houses. It took a month and, in that time, Miles Standish created a military structure to man the defences, with four companies drilled and assigned posts, while another group acted as a mobile reserve and fire-fighting force. When completed, the fort included three entrances which, standing proud of the walls, provided platforms that commanded the palisade itself. It was not the only fort being built here at that time. The Wassagusset wild bunch had begun constructing their fort immediately on arrival. They were wise to have done so, for their own behaviour in stealing the produce of the nearby Massachusetts settlement to supplement their own meagre rations provoked in the villagers a desire to rid themselves of these obnoxious new neighbours.

Hearing of the plot, which included the destruction of both settlements, and that even the once-friendly Massasoit 'began again to cast forth many insulting speeches, glorifying in our weakness and giving out how easy it would be ere long to cut us off', the Plymouth settlers decided to build a fort within the perimeter palisade on the top of Mount Hill 'from whence a few might easily secure the town from any assault'. The fort reinforced the existing gun-platform and provided a site where a 'continual watch' could be kept so that 'no Indian can come near thereabouts but he is presently seen'.

The Amerindian threat in Newfoundland was soon found to be non-existent, both from the scarcity of the indigenous Beothuk inhabitants and their nomadic way of life. Here the ever-feared, and ever-present, threat came from pirates and the French, often the same people. They required the same response, and the Charter of Avalon authorized George Calvert 'to build and fortify castles, forts and other places of strength, for the public and their own private defence'. In addition, Calvert was authorized to impose martial law and to exercise 'law military against mutinous and seditious persons, such as shall refuse to submit themselves to his, or their Government, or shall refuse to serve in the wars, or shall fly to the enemy, or forsake their ensign . . .' In other words this was a military colony and expected to be run on military lines. Yet, unlike its southern sisters, forts and troops were not what Newfoundland needed for its defence. Here the fighting, when it came, would be at sea and it was in the provision of warships that Government advice and provision was defective.

The Scottish forts in Nova Scotia (French Acadia) had the shortest occupancy of all the early defences; here the Scots found themselves living in close proximity to the rival French, with whom they were to exchange forts on numerous unneighbourly occasions. Although Sir William Alexander had been granted his Charter in 1621, it was not until 1629 that his son, along with seventy-two settlers, arrived in the region of Port Royal on the sheltered western coast of the Nova Scotia peninsula. Here, on a scenic but also defensible site, they established, near modern Annapolis Royal, Fort Charles, 'in forme of a pentagon, with many horne works good both for offence and defence'. It mounted eight pieces of ordnance: 'four demie culvering and four minion'. The settlers and ships' crews also erected a house for Alexander and a storehouse, and settled down to die from scurvy and malnutrition, thirty of them failing to survive the winter, a bitter experience which young William did not share, having gone home. He returned in the late spring in the company of the powerful privateering Kirke brothers, whose aim was to wrest control of the St Lawrence pelt trade from the French.

To further that strategic aim, in 1629 Sir James Stewart of Killeith, Lord Ochiltree, landed a garrison of sixty Scotsmen at Port aux Baleines in Cape Breton, where they planted Lord Ochiltree's settlement, protected by another wooden fort, Fort Rosemar. The fort was well defended, not only with cannon that had been transported but with the addition of several weapons taken ashore from a captured Portuguese vessel. Nevertheless, that autumn, Captain Charles Daniel, a Frenchman who had

The reconstructed entrance of the French fort at Port Royal.

been dispatched to resupply the besieged Champlain in Quebec, having been blown off course and landing at Sainte Anne's Bay, Cape Breton, sighted the Scottish fort and decided, although outnumbered, to attack. On 8 September, Fort Rosemar fell to a combined bombardment from the sea and a frontal assault by Daniel's sailors. The captives were marched off to build a French fort, Sainte Anne, and then shipped across the Atlantic, the majority being landed at Falmouth while those for whom a ransom might be raised, including Ochiltree, were imprisoned in France. Sadly, the released Ochiltree was to spend another twenty years in a Scottish prison after falsely accusing a fellow countryman of treason.

In the meantime, Port Royal was surviving well enough to be considered a site of permanence. Then, following lengthy diplomatic discussions, after the signing of the 1629 Treaty of Susa between England and France, the terms of which restored Acadia to France, Sir George Howe, the governor in residence at Port Royal, was ordered in 1631 to 'remove all the people, goods, ordnance, ammunition, cattle and other things belonging to the colony, and to leave the bounds thereof altogether waste and unpeopled as it was when [William Alexander] first landed there'. Surrender it they might be forced to do, but there was no reason why the French should benefit from four years of Scottish endeavour! Fort Charles itself remained garrisoned until 1632, when those who did not wish to transfer their allegiance to the French camp were carried home after being paid compensation for their eviction.

AMERINDIAN FORTS

Although neither Cabot nor subsequent adventurers would find native castles to subdue and occupy, the Amerindians did fortify their settlements. Arthur Barlowe stated in his discourse that a nearby village of nine houses was 'fortified round about with sharp trees, to keep out their enemies, and the entrance into it made like a turnpike very artificially [i.e. cunningly]', but White's drawing of Pomeiooc shows defences built to protect more from prowling beasts than assaulting foes, a view supported by Thomas Harriot, who described the few villages that were fortified as being 'only done with barks of trees made fast to stakes, or else with poles only fixed upright, and close one by another'.

At first, the French appear to have had a similar experience with Amerindian fortifications. A woodcut showing Champlain opening up with his harquebus on Iroquois warriors near Ticonderoga – of lasting fortress fame – shows a small circular wooden palisade behind the defending Iroquois, along with the trees that were felled to construct it and a couple of hammocks, suggesting that this was a temporary camp. Elsewhere, more permanent Amerindian fortified villages could present a more formidable structure. In September 1615 Champlain led a small party of Frenchmen with a force of 500 Hurons, Montagnois and Ottawas on a punitive raid on the Onodagas settled on the eastern end of Lake Ontario. Surprise was lost when the Huron war-whooped upon a group of village women and children out tending their fields. The alarm was raised, which gave the defenders time to run back inside their village and man the walls. When the pursuing French broke into the clearing they

John White's drawing of Pomeiooc Amerindian village, showing the simple stockade, more use for deterring marauding animals than for keeping out determined attackers. (British Museum)

were stunned by what they saw. On the far side of a deep moat rose a massive palisade consisting of two rows of well-embedded tree trunks leaning towards each other and crossing about five metres above the ground. The space between was filled with logs and tamped-down earth, while at the bound crossing place a line of planks provided the gathering defenders with a walkway from which to fire arrows down on their attackers. The overhasty Huron charged on and were driven back. Champlain was forced to resort to his schoolboy history lessons by having a siege tower built to overtop the walls. However, even this failed to achieve the desired result when the Onodagas realized how long it took a Frenchman to reload his musket and lost all fear of these firearms. In the end Champlain's force retreated, much fearing pursuit.

The Onodaga fort had been built to local design, but in many areas the Amerindians witnessed and copied what they saw as advantageous to their aggressors. However, the erection of forts into which the warriors and their families retreated removed their main tactical weapons, which were concealment, mobility and surprise. The story of their forlorn attempts at fortress defence lies outside the period of this account but needs to be recorded briefly to balance the account.

In New England, during the Pequot War of 1637 the Puritans, to what should be their eternal shame, fell upon a so-called Pequot fort on the Mystic River and, brushing the defences and the defenders aside, slaughtered some 400 men, women and children. The new English allies, the Narragansett, were horrified by what they saw and, realizing that soon they also could one day be attacked in a similar way, took steps to avoid a similar fate and joined a fatal anti-settler confederation.

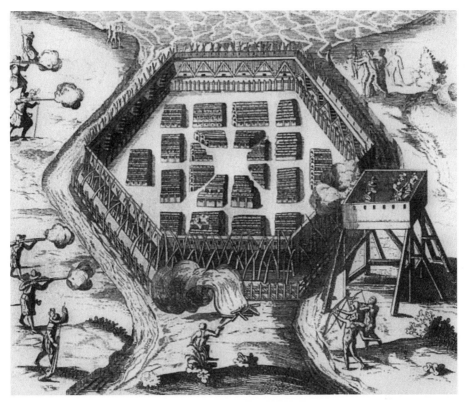

The Iroquois Fort at Onondaga under siege by Champlain, 1615. Note the use of a natural moat and the double palisade. Champlain was forced to build a siege tower and employ his Indian allies to fire the fort.

Similar defences were overridden in Virginia, where, at the time of the third Anglo-Powhatan War of 1644, the Powhatan leader Opechancanough, constructed a fort on the Pamukey River, from which he launched some initially successful attacks. However, having rallied, the settlers took the fort, along with Opechancanough, with comparative ease, thus ending the resistance which had begun with the wounding by arrows of Bartholomew Gosnold on the first day that the Jamestown settlers ventured ashore.

BERMUDA

Although warfare had become endemic along the American littoral as the Amerindians tried both to negotiate with and to drive away the invaders, the greatest concentration of fortifications during the first century of colonization lay offshore, on the Bermudas. On these uninhabited islands the first priority had been the construction of *Deliverance* and *Patience,* in which the survivors of the wreck of *Sea Venture* continued their voyage to Virginia. However, they left behind two 'mutineers' who, roaming the island, discovered a large lump of ambergris, a sweet smelling intestinal product of the sperm whale which was much desired by perfumers, who would be prepared to pay a good price for it. With this in mind, and probably thinking that no help would ever arrive, they set about building their own boat, only for the arrival of Richard Moore as Governor in *Plough* to end their project and provide them with the headache of smuggling their lump of ambergris home unobserved, which they failed to do.

News of the arrival of the ambergris and its source soon came to the attention of Spanish spies in London, who reported the find back to Madrid with suggestions that an assault on the Isle of Devils by the Spaniards might be worthwhile. Realizing this, the English dispatched *Plough* for Bermuda and included in her instructions orders to build a fort and the wherewithal so to do. In siting these fortifications the planners were aided by nature, for the very reefs on which *Sea Venture* struck in 1609 provided a razor-sharp glacis on the outer side of a sea moat which offered little chance of a landing from either the north or west. The harbour before the main settlement at St George's could be entered by several channels, but these were shallow and required a slow passage, even in those ships with shallow draught which could pass this way. Thus the main anchorage came to be Castle Harbour, whose very name attests to the defences that were rapidly constructed to protect this one weak point where the channels, like breaches in a castle's defences, invited access to an invading force. Thus a series of garrisoned redoubts were hastily constructed on the islets that beaded across the entrance, with the one on Castle Island receiving a cannon salvaged from *Sea Venture*. Its neighbouring fort on King's Island is now the oldest extant British fort in the new world, while the Captain's House, built inside the walls in 1621, is similarly the oldest British home. Soon other forts, most named after members of the British aristocracy who knew little about this mid-Atlantic colony, added to a formidable collection of defences: Devonshire Redoubt, Landward Fort, Southampton Fort, Charles Fort, Pembroke Fort and Fort Bruere, numbering some ninety by the time building work ended 325 years later.

For most of the time the greatest excitement available to the somewhat bored garrison was provided by fishing, but in 1614 there was a call to arms when two long-expected Spanish ships approached the harbour. Two shots from King's Castle, both of which splashed into the sea, convinced the Spanish that the defenders were well prepared for their assault and they turned away, which was considered fortunate, for that salvo used up two-thirds of the fort's ordnance.

The survival of many of these forts to the present day owes much to the fact that, unlike all other new world forts of the time, these were constructed in stone. It was just as well. On 21 October 1619, Captain Butler, newly arrived as Governor of Bermuda in *Warwick*, carried out an inspection of the first King's Castle, the only fort built of wood. As he departed, the gunner, desirous to impress, loaded the ordnance and fired a salute to the Governor, before following him down to *Warwick*. He left behind him a smouldering linstock lying on the gun platform. This, in turn, fell through the planks and set the whole building 'to kindle' and a pile of ash. One presumes that this bonfire deprived the unfortunate gunner of any credit won from the salute. Still, it would have been a sweet-smelling blaze: Bermuda cedar, *juniperus bermudiana*, once plentiful but now endangered as a result of both overuse in shipbuilding, house construction and furniture (it repels moths) and fungal attack, has a wonderfully aromatic scent.

The building and successful defence of their forts was one of the few positives that emerge from the early years of colonial plantation. In this respect due praise must be given to Ralph Lane's settlement, for he alone among all who followed was the leader who kept his men fit and well enough to avoid death from disease or malnutrition. His was also the only truly military colony, suggesting that, if the English state had been prepared to send further soldiers to man garrisons in America, then the civilian settlers may well have endured less harsh conditions under which to attempt to cling on to life and livelihood. As it was, for most days throughout the long century of invasion, few felt that they could venture more than a fledgling's flutter from their fort without fear of assault.

Not many sea miles up the Chesapeake from Hampton Creek where Forts Henry and Charles were built in 1610, lies Fort McHenry, built to defend Baltimore against the returning British. During the short and unnecessary Anglo-American war of 1812 an event occurred here which should guarantee the iconic status of 'the fort' in the American psyche. Following a fierce naval bombardment by the British fleet, it was after he had witnessed, in the dawn's early light, the star-spangled banner still proudly waving above the battlements, that Francis Scott Key was moved to write, to the perpetual embarrassment of the British, the song that would become the American national anthem.

CHAPTER 9

Reinforcement and Resupply

There were never Englishmen left in a foreign Country in such misery as we were in this new discovered Virginia. We watched every three nights lying on the bare cold ground what weather soever came warded all the next day, which brought our men to be most feeble wretches, our food was but a small can of barley soaked in water to five men a day, our drink cold water taken out of the River, which was at a flood very salty, at a low tide full of slime and filth, which was the destruction of many of our men. Thus, we lived for the space of five months in this miserable distress, not having five able men to man our Bulwarks upon any occasion. If it had not pleased God to have put a terror in the Savages' hearts, we had all perished by those wild and cruel Pagans, being in that weak estate as we were.

George Percy, from Jamestown, 1608

On 19 November 1578 Sir Humphrey Gilbert departed from Plymouth with seven ships, well armed and crewed, and victualled for 'a long voyage of one whole year'. On 20 December Sir John Gilbert of the support party staying behind, informing Sir Francis Walsingham, the Queen's Secretary, of this fact, assured him that, although it was reported in Court that his brother had been 'not victualled to any effectual purpose for such a voyage', he could swear that each ship sailed well 'victualled with bread, beef, fish, beans, peas, bacon, meal and such other that was requisite'. Strange then that in the same letter, he reported that they had put into Ireland 'to continue the first proportion' and that on 7 February the Spanish ambassador, Don Bernardino de Mendoza wrote to the King of Spain that the expedition had 'returned under stress of weather to Ireland, where they are revictualling in order to resume their voyage'.

English merchants knew how to victual their ships for their normal short-haul voyages. During the reign of Henry VIII, Thomas Wolsey ensured that a standing navy could be created by developing a system to keep the royal fleet victualled for several months at a time. Drake, Hawkins and other long-distant corsairs also learned how best to keep their crew fed, as did the skippers of the small fishing boats now sailing to the Newfoundland Banks. Unfortunately for the invasion parties, their sponsors had no such experience since many came from military backgrounds, which were notoriously poor at provisioning their men.

Sixteenth- and seventeenth-century armies advanced with a victualling train, and when its supplies ran out, or turned putrid, they lived off the land, which is one of the first military euphemisms for a process that began with purchase and ended with pillage as local produce failed to keep up with demand and the native population saw their vital supplies dwindling. Once the last fruits of someone else's harvest had been gathered in, the campaign season ended and the armies returned home to rest and recuperate and rearm. Even this simple requirement proved too difficult for the English. Henry VIII began his reign by ill-provisioning an expeditionary force he sent to Navarre. He ended it by laying siege to Boulogne in northern France, relying on baggage trains from Flanders and Calais to keep his force supplied. This source proved inadequate, and the Duke of Norfolk was forced to send foraging parties deep into the French countryside. Unescorted troops fared badly. In one orchard, not far from the British camp, it was reported that the bodies of some men were found hanging from the branches 'after the French had crammed their jaws and bosoms with cherries'. Similar mocking executions would take place in Virginia, with bread rather than cherry stuffing, for the same reason. As autumn moved into winter, the English soldiery wasted away from starvation, dysentery, plague, cholera and all the contagions of a sodden camp.

It was not only the English that found resupply so difficult; in the Thirty Years War that raged across central Europe between 1618 and 1648, every participating army was devastated by want, as was every occupied town or village. With a change of names the same miserable circumstances could be applied to the new world, where poorly victualled settlers tried to stay alive by forcing ill-provisioned locals to hand over their own limited resources. It was not an age of surplus on either side of the Atlantic; one year of plenty could be followed by seven lean ones. In England towns and villages had Poor Laws which gave them the right to drive out the indigent itinerant into the next parish, using force if necessary, so that soldiers and sailors returning from the wars required passports to prevent them receiving the same treatment.

If the great powers of the state were incapable of provisioning either its citizenry or its main forces in sight of their own shores, how less capable would private individuals or companies be able to support, for four seasons, an outstation many months away? Ralegh's expeditions provided the answer, Jamestown the evidence, that the requirement was brushed over and the lessons of the state would not be learned.

The frequent failure to establish a viable beachhead in America owed as much to the maladministration of those who were responsible for succouring the infant settlements as it did to the behaviour of those who first landed, for no major amphibious landing can achieve success without the timely arrival of follow-up forces bringing in reserves of stores and personnel; the arrival of the latter without the former is a certain precursor of failure. The adventurers who dispatched the American settlers knew this and planned accordingly but often failed to adjust to circumstance to ensure that resupplies were delivered in a timely and competent fashion. As a result, the landing party was often left clinging to the coast in desperate straits.

It began right at the beginning, with Ralegh's lack of commitment and failure to invest in a sizeable expeditionary force. Lane landed with 107 men. Compared with the expeditions that Ralegh was personally to lead to Guiana this was ludicrously small, especially bearing in mind that the Guiana expeditions were not intended to involve settlement. Nevertheless, Ralegh raised the sum of £60,000 to finance his thirty-day search up the Orinoco for El Dorado in 1595, while in 1617 he sailed with fourteen ships and 1,000 men to repeat his folly and failure. Such investment in Virginia would have secured a firm fortress.

Small though his force was, Ralph Lane was probably competent and capable enough to continue holding Roanoke for another season provided his men's morale did not fall because they felt that they had been abandoned and under-resourced. Indeed, after the grounding of *Tyger* had led to the ruination of much of their stores, John Arundell had been ordered back to England on 5 August specifically to report on the dearth of both arms and provisions. His fast passage earned him a knighthood in October but does not seem to have speeded up the resupply, for the much-needed provisions did not leave England until well after their scheduled delivery date, which was itself an optimistic one. Lane was expecting relief by Easter (3 April 1586) but was prepared to allow for some delay, and had planned for future operations accordingly:

> Hereupon I resolved with myself that if your [Ralegh] supply had come before the end of April, and that you had sent any store of boats or men, to have had them made in any reasonable time, with a sufficient number of men and victuals to have found us until the new corn were come in, I would have sent a small bark with two pinnaces about by sea to the northward to have found out the Bay . . . and to have sounded the bar.

If the expedition to the Chesapeake had taken place then White's party would have had a better site to establish the City of Ralegh, and Ferdinando a more secure harbour in which to anchor.

FORAGING

Foraging was very much a feature of foreign deployments and, with the loss of *Tyger*'s stores, Lane's party would have needed to forage early. That he was able so to do in a reasonably peaceful manner is a credit, especially as his arrival had been heralded by the hot-headed Grenville setting fire to the houses and crops of the Pamlico Sound town of Aquascogoc because someone had stolen a silver cup. Lane was also helped, initially, because the need for 'liaison' had been foreseen and catered for by the removal of the Amerindians, Manteo and Wanchese, by Arthur Barlowe the previous year, specifically so that they could be taught English, become 'civilized' and act as go-betweens. This was a task that Wanchese fled from but which Manteo did his best to deliver.

As in Europe, foraging began amiably enough with the exchange of trade goods for grain. It was only when, with the onset of winter and the exhaustion of supplies on both sides, the English were exposed as bullying beggars that the hospitality offered to the invader dissipated.

Foraging could also involve living off the land, its wild fruits, nuts, berries and fish. This was another method of staving off starvation that Lane introduced successfully and which was to be copied by Jamestown. Lane, however, suspected that the 'savages' were cunningly forcing him to disperse his forces this way for he wrote:

> By this means [the withdrawal of supplies] the King stood assured, that I must be enforced for lack of sustenance, there to disband my company into sundry places to live upon shellfish, for so the savages themselves do, going to Hatorask, Croatoan, and other places fishing and hunting, whilst their grounds be in sowing, and their corn growing . . .

Now used as an ingredient for root beer, the sweet-smelling sassafras root had a short-lived demand as a cure for syphilis, for which, it was soon realized, it was not efficacious.

Once John Rolfe had managed to grow good-quality tobacco in Virginia, the future of the southern colony was assured as long as the settlers obtained mastery over the local population.

For the famine grew to extreme among us, our weirs failing us of fish, that I was enforced to send Captain Stafford with twenty with him to Croatoan . . . to feed his company and also to keep watch, if any shipping came upon the coast . . . I sent Master Prideox with the pinnace to Otterasco, and with him the Provost Marshall to live there, and also to wait for shipping: also I sent every week sixteen or so of the rest of the company to the main over against us, to live off cassava and others.

This policy kept everyone alive, but at the cost of reducing significantly the strength of the garrison at a time when an assault was presently expected. Lane had little option, therefore, but to launch a pre-emptive strike, which was carried out with a swift brutality just before Drake hove into sight.

By the time Drake had arrived, Lane knew his party had overstayed their welcome on Roanoke and for that reason, as well as the simple imperative of finding a better harbour, the settlement needed to move north to a site on the Chesapeake, which is where, thanks to his advice, Jamestown would be established.

Yet Jamestown was no bread-basket, and the settlers were very soon surviving on a daily input of about 500 calories, a dietary deficiency that encouraged the onset of disease and famine. Even so, they were slow to respond by organizing foraging parties but when they did they were blessed that, in Captain John Smith, they had a forager of genius. Smith was one who seldom saw any circumstance without rapidly working it to advantage. Shooed away from the shore by the Kecoughtans as a 'famished' man, Smith turned the table by kidnapping their idol, only releasing it once his boat was filled with corn, turkey, wildfowl and venison. Other bluffs worked as well, aided by the arrival of migrating wildfowl in late November 1607, until Smith was seized by the Powhatans and only saved from execution by the dramatic intervention of Pocahontas. Even this turn of events proved to be of calorific value as, following his release, Powhatan sent daily supplies of food down to the fort.

After Smith's departure in October 1609 the foraging arrangements that he put in place, or their replacements, failed disastrously. On Dumpling Island, where Smith had sent John Martin to live among the Nansemond, the English, in an effort to establish good relations, 'beat the savages out of the island, burnt their houses, ransacked their temples . . . and carried away their pearls'. The outpost could not therefore have been surprised when they found one of their number pincushioned with arrows like Saint Sebastian. In response, their leader, Martin, fled back to Jamestown, leaving Michael Sicklemore, 'a very honest, valiant and dedicated soldier', in command. Yet, however valiant Sicklemore was, his men were both starving and scared. Seventeen of them mutinied and stole a boat to sail over to ask for food from the villagers of Kecoughtan. When they did not return Sicklemore led a party out to search for them. Unlike the mutineers, who went missing, presumed killed, the bodies of the Sicklemore party were discovered, each with a loaf of bread contemptuously crammed into his mouth.

In another initiative, Percy dispatched John Ratcliffe, who had previously performed poor service as the president, to the mouth of the James River to build a fort on the north bank at Point Comfort, which was to be named Fort Algernon after Percy's nephew, son of his elder brother the earl. Here Ratcliffe might have dwelt securely had he not, strangely, received a message sometime in November from Powhatan,

The complacent English thought that their possession of a few superior firearms would ensure that the natives lived in awe of them. They were, however, never masters of the woodland terrain and only comfortable venturing away from their stockades embarked in their boats.

inviting him to sail on a trading mission up to the chief's town of Orapakes on the Chickahominy River. With Percy's approval, Ratcliffe, and between fifty and twenty-five companions – the accounts are contradictory – sailed upstream; with Powhatan's approval, most did not sail down. All but two of the shore party were killed, Ratcliffe himself being tortured to death. Many in the accompanying pinnace also died; those that did return came back empty handed.

In another foray, Captain Francis West sallied forth with thirty-six men embarked to trade with the friendly Patawomecks in the Chesapeake and managed to fill his pinnace with corn, after beheading several Amerindians, but, knowing the ghastly conditions back at Jamestown, he then turned east and headed for England; since he was an aristocrat his desertion was rewarded not by execution but by his later elevation to Governor.

This woeful effort changed abruptly with the arrival of De La Warr, an experienced military man who could stiffen his severity with troops. An offensive against the neighbouring tribes, regardless of their allegiance, led to villages being burnt and sufficient corn being seized not only to fill the English stomachs and stores but also to leave inadequate seed for the Amerindians to sow for the next year's harvest. Harsh this might appear, but it was a method of warfare that would have been recognized and approved by any of the warring factions that were being deployed around Europe, not only at this time but in the centuries that followed, up to and including the Second World War.

To take one example (selected purely at random from my son's bookshelf), in 1918 the British, meeting opposition to their policy of forcibly recruiting Kuki tribesmen from northeast India to serve on the Western Front, blockaded their fields, forcing them to surrender because, had they not done so, the Kuki 'would have been too late to prepare the ground for the next harvest, and would in consequence have been faced with famine'. A total of 128 villages were burnt during the operation.

RESUPPLY

In early April 1586, Ralegh's first resupply vessel cleared the Channel and arrived at Port Ferdinando in the latter part of June. She was 'freighted with all manner of things in most plentiful manner for the supply and relief of the colony' which had just departed with Drake. A few weeks later, Grenville, with his much larger force, delivered an equally futile freightage. He had endeavoured to clear Bideford harbour on 16 April, but claimed that low water at the bar delayed his sailing until 2 May. Even this tardy departure did not deter him from making a leisurely crossing, with sufficient time available to capture and relieve several ships of their cargo, including *Angel of Topsham*, *Brave* and *Peter and Julia*, which were probably English vessels. Seventy-five days later the fleet of two large and four smaller vessels anchored off the Carolinas to find the colony abandoned. Grenville was in a position to leave a new and substantial group behind, but instead chose to land fifteen soldiers. Fifteen! It was a ridiculously small number, and the thought arises that these might have been marooned troublemakers rather than willing volunteers, for it is unlikely that his company, however ill-informed, included fifteen would-be suicides. Yet, to have landed a viable number of settlers would have left Grenville shorthanded in pursuit of what he most wanted, which was to intercept and seize Spanish ships in the *flota*. In fact he missed them off the Azores but, instead of turning for home, he sailed off to Newfoundland, without calling in to check on the Roanoke fifteen, before returning to the Azores, from where, hope of booty ended, he sailed back home.

The fact that there were now fifteen isolated soldiers left at Roanoke where, had Ralegh's plans been successful, there should have been some 300 settlers, did not prevent him pressing ahead with the next stage of settlement, which was to dispatch a domestic group, basically an English village, out to Virginia. Its extirpation can fairly be blamed on the failure to provide logistic support.

White's endeavours to provide just such support between 1587 and 1590 were farcically tragic. They began at the moment of his departure from Roanoke on 27 August 1587, when he left the fragile colony to fend for itself while he returned home to seek out urgent resupplies, and to inform Ralegh that, thanks to Ferdinando, he had established the colony at Roanoke and not further up the Chesapeake. Ferdinando refused to embark him in *Lion*, forcing him to sail in the much smaller and less well provisioned flyboat, which managed to limp unseaworthily into Smerwick, where the ship's boatswain, boatswain's mate and steward died from their deprivations. White, having made arrangements for his surviving sick, then continued his journey in *Monkey* to Southampton, where he landed on 8 November and discovered, much to his fury, that *Lion*, also with dead and dying onboard, had come into Portsmouth three weeks earlier.

On arriving in London, White must have been deflated to realize that the deteriorating relations with Spain had changed the strategic importance of the Virginia settlements, and that Ralegh, whom he met on 28 November, although he responded to the plea for assistance, might also be considering other activities of equal significance to his overall aim of self-aggrandizement. Nevertheless, it appears that Ralegh was prepared to send a pinnace immediately with essential supplies and to follow this up in early 1588 with another fleet led yet again by Grenville, and thus incorporating a privateering aim. Strategic necessity meant that it needed to be a substantial force and it was, consisting of the 250-ton *Galleon Dudley*, the 200-ton *Virgin God Save Her*, a refitted *Tyger* and some smaller vessels, including *Golden Hind*, *St Leger* and the thirty-ton bark *Brave* and twenty-five-ton pinnace *Roe*. However, on 9 October 1587, as a result of the threat from a Spanish invasion, a stay on departing vessels was imposed, and when the Privy Council discovered that Ralegh intended to ignore this directive they sent Grenville an order on 31 March that he was 'to forbear to go on his intended voyage' and 'to send presently to Sir Francis Drake such ships as were of greatest burthen and fittest for service'. It was not a blanket embargo, for the Privy Council went on to decree that 'such as Sir Francis should not think fit to be retained, he [Grenville] might dispose of and employ in his intended voyage', although 'her Majesty considered the danger of this present time and his knowledge and experience in martial affairs did think it convenient he himself should remain'. This suited Grenville, who would not even have considered it worth his while sailing in the diminutive *Brave*, which – along with *Roe* – were the two vessels released to take White, supplies and just fifteen men and women to reinforce the colony.

The two ships departed Bideford on 22 April 1588. Unfortunately, the sea commander was Captain Arthur Facy, a pirate and privateering companion of Grenville who had, along with the latter, wrongly seized a Dutch ship during the return from the abortive relief voyage of 1587. The smallness of his hulls did not deter Facy from fancying his chances of prizes during the outward voyage so, ignoring White's desire for a swift passage, a few days out, he boarded and seized goods from both a passing Scottish and a Breton ship. He then chased whatever sails he sighted in his passage across Biscay until he found himself being pursued by two larger Frenchmen on 6 May. *Brave* was battered and boarded and fortunate not to be taken as a prize, but the bruising she received left her in no fit state to continue and she turned back to Bideford to be rejoined a few days later by *Roe*, which had separated from her before the fight. The frustrated John White arrived back in England on 23 May, his failure later summed up pithily by Richard Hakluyt: 'The fifth voyage intended for the supply of the Colony planted in Virginia by John White which being undertaken in the year 1588 by casualty took no effect.' Behind the scenes there seems to have been, if not a falling-out or open hostility, a problem between Drake and Grenville. The former may have been piqued, if accounts are true, by the Queen's poor view of his removal of the Ralph Lane settlement, just weeks before relief arrived, making Grenville's voyage a wasted one. Grenville and Ralegh, on the other hand, might have felt out of sorts for receiving only subsidiary roles in the command structure furnished to meet the Spanish Armada. Whatever the cause, there is little doubt that a determined approach would have garnered some ships' release from England to make a Virginia voyage. The Spanish threat provided either a reason or an excuse not to respond as was so obviously necessary. Drake had certainly stated that he had more than enough vessels to meet the threat, but still White found great difficulty in getting to sea.

The appointment of Facy to captain the resupply fleet was glaringly incompetent. Grenville might have argued that, given the embargo, he was limited in both choice of ship and commander, but other more viable and reliable hulls were available. A Government order of 1 April 1588 directed the ports to equip and supply ships over sixty tons to join the defending navy. Even so, ports such as Teignmouth and Barnstable pleaded poverty and stated that they could not provide the two ships and one pinnace that each of them had been ordered to dispatch. They were not alone among the Devon

The waters of the Chesapeake and Cape Cod swarmed with fish but the English most often failed miserably to catch many and had to rely on Indian generosity or barter to secure sufficient for their needs. Based on one of John White's drawings, this reconstruction shows the simple but tasty way the Indians prepared their fish, which were caught either in nets or in traps built along the river edges.

and Cornwall ports, most of which continued to send out their fishing fleet to the Newfoundland Banks. Not only their vital return cargo but also their size, mostly between twenty-five and fifty tons, left them unaffected by the Government's decree. When, a few years later, the case was being made to establish a permanent settlement in Newfoundland, one of the supportive arguments was that such settlements would enable the fishing fleet to take passage outbound laden with goods for the colonists rather than sailing empty. Ralegh had connections with all these ports and most skippers would have welcomed the opportunity to earn additional income. What is more, they would not have been diverted from their task by the desire to take prizes. In 1589, when no resupply voyage was undertaken, the port records of Exeter alone list eleven fishing vessels landing from Newfoundland yet, ignoring this source of reliable hulls, the 1590 resupply voyage also involved both pirate captains and another Privy Council stay on shipping.

In January 1590 the privateering entrepreneur John Watts fitted out three ships in the Thames: *Hopewell* of 150 tons, *Little John* of 100 tons and the pinnace *John Evangelist*. They were both heavily armed and well-crewed, with Captain Abraham Cocke commanding in *Hopewell*, while captaining *Little John* was Christopher Newport, who would become heavily involved with the establishment of the Jamestown settlement in eighteen years' time. On 1 February, in almost a repeat of the 1587 resupply preparations, the Privy Council, in response to a renewed threat from Spain, placed a stay on all shipping. The desperate White rushed off to see Ralegh with the proposal that, should Watts agree to his fleet diverting to Roanoke, they might be allowed to sail. The idea found favour and Watts was released, only to break the agreement before sailing by refusing to embark either settlers or stores, although there is reason to suppose that these might have been embarked in *Moonlight*, an eighty-ton merchant ship belonging to Ralegh's backer William Sanderson and commanded by Captain Spicer, which was a late addition to the fleet. White sailed alone.

Arriving in the Indies at the end of April, the fleet dispersed to increase their chances of falling in with a prize. Unsuccessful endeavours prolonged their sojourn, and it was not until 15 August that *Hopewell* and *Moonlight* came to anchor some way off Port Ferdinando. Rising smoke from shore gave cause for hope but investigations found no evidence of the settlers where they first searched.

When, on 17 August the surf breaking over the harbour bar overturned *Moonlight*'s boat, drowning Captain Spicer and six of his men, the disheartened seekers gave up their search having found nothing but the word CROATOAN carved on a post to indicate where the lost colony had gone. With the weather driving them south and eventually forcing them to abandon a plan to winter in the Indies and return to the Carolinas in the spring, White was forced to realize that he would never find his lost children.

Further attempts were made to discover the fate of the Roanoke settlers, but the limited evidence links them more to Ralegh's concern that his Charter was time-expired and the rule that there could be no ownership without occupation. The first two such ventures failed to reach their destination, while the third, commanded by Captain Samuel Mace, ended when, as frequently occurred, 'the principal ground tackle' was lost in foul weather. In 1602 Mace, with Bartholomew Gilbert in company, tried again, taking with them many items for which they believed the colonists might by now be in short supply. Driven apart by strong winds, they made independent landfalls. Gilbert's crew, landing first in Chesapeake Bay, were severely mauled by the Amerindians, and had to abandon the search. Mace may have fared better, but we do not know as much for, when he reached London to report back, Ralegh was in the Tower accused of treason and his 'private court' had dispersed quietly to avoid being caught in the storm. It is known that Mace did bring some Amerindians back with him, and it has been conjectured that they were able to report that some of the original colonists had survived. Rumour spread through the gossip shops of London and, like all good stories, found its way to the stage, where, in the 1605 play *Eastward Ho*, it is bawdily suggested that 'They have married with the Indians'. This appears to have been King James's view, for he was also content to poor ridicule on the colonial schemes, believing that any sailing that way to settle would end up in 'vile' Virginia, naked except for feathers in his hair.

Although White, and to a certain extent Lane, have been lambasted for lack of leadership or staying power, the simple logic is that the Roanoke settlement failed because its protagonist preferred the profit to be had from piracy and plunder than to persevere with simple settlements on an alien shore until they were truly established for, unless an amphibious force achieves total control and establishes an economy capable of maintaining an invading army, its survival hinges on the provision of adequate and timely reinforcement and resupply. In America, to begin with, this did not happen, as

Although as accurate a reconstruction as it has been possible to make, the interior of Jamestown fort lacks the stench and squalor of the earlier settlement, especially during the dark months of the 'Starving Time.'

the investors failed to provide the follow-up and the funding for those whom they had dispatched.

Jamestown nearly went the same way, coming within one day of being abandoned. That it clung on might be attributed in part to the fact that privateering was no longer an easy, cruise meandering, option and that a more direct crossing to Virginia had been demonstrated as possible. It also owed something to the fact that the project was now one supported by a Company with investors anxious to make a return, who were not, as a joint body, content to be deflected by the latest scheme available for their own personal profit. Yet, above all, where White was unlucky, the Jamestown settlers were fortunate.

Having landed the Jamestown settlers in May 1607 and ensured to his satisfaction that they were competently protected and provisioned, Captain Newport sailed back to England with *Susan Constant* and *Godspeed* on 22 June 1607, leaving *Discovery* behind to do what her name suggested and to provide both a floating fort and a prison hulk. Before sailing, he confirmed with the colonists his intention to return within six months. He was one week late, arriving on 2 January as promised, but only just in time to save John Smith from possible execution and to revive a colony that, through its own grievous

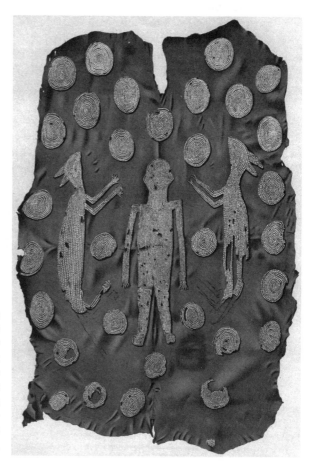

The trappings of even the most important of chiefs were simple; their authority lay much more in their personality and power to command. It was a cloak such as this that Powhatan presented to Christopher Newport after his 'coronation'.

wrangling and incompetence, had barely survived. Now, for the first time, new settlers, sixty of them, arrived to supplement rather than replace the old, a joyous occasion somewhat marred a few days later when, on 7 January, one of the newcomers set fire to his house, which burnt down along with many of the other lodgings and the storehouse with its newly landed supplies, leaving Jamestown in much the same position as had been Roanoke in 1585 after *Tyger* had grounded. A few unloaded provisions secure in *John and Francis* were all that was left. The settlement was saved by trading with the Amerindians and the open generosity of Powhatan. Having spent too long in Virginia, eating scarce rations, Newport turned again for England on 10 April, his hold loaded with what he suspected was gold ore and which John Smith knew was not.

Ten days after Newport's departure, Captain Nelson arrived in *Phoenix* which, having been considered lost, had, like her namesake, risen from the ashes. Nelson, having experienced similar weather to that which had driven White and Cocke south from the Chesapeake in 1590, had taken similar action but, instead of diverting to the Azores, had done what the earlier voyagers intended and wintered in the Indies so that he was now delivering sixty healthy well-fed colonists as well as a ship laded with fresh supplies. Of all the many resupply vessels, *Phoenix* proved to be the best, bringing forth from the normally begrudging Smith the comment, 'Now we thought ourselves as well fitted as our hearts could wish both with a competent number of men, as also for all other needful provisions, should come to us.' Nelson, one must admire him, delivered and departed. Onboard he had a cargo of boring but useful timber and a paper nugget worth far more than all of Newport's ores. This was John Smith's brilliant firsthand account of the settlement, *A True Relation of Such Occurrences and Accidents of Note as Hath Happened in Virginia since the First Planting of that Colony which is Now Resident in the South Part Thereof till the Last Return from Thence.*

His work safely dispatched, Smith set out on a seven-week expedition from which he returned to find the colony yet again in dire straits through mismanagement by Ratcliffe, to whose office Smith himself succeeded on 10 September 1608. At the end of the month Newport's second resupply arrived. This time he landed seventy new colonists, including the first two women to be brought over, one of whom, the unmarried Anne Burras, was not long a single female, for she married before Christmas. In his first resupply Newport had brought over two gold refiners and two goldsmiths, this time the useless element of his cargo included a crown and bed for Powhatan, the placing of which on his head and under his back respectively, increased his own feeling of self-worth at the expense of Smith and his fellow colonists. Newport had also been ordered to return with something of value, such as a report of a gold mine, a passage to Cathay or the discovery of the Roanoke settlers. Brave pirate and most able navigator that he was, he seems to have been unable to stand up to the unreasonable demands of the Company and to tell them the facts as he could both readily witness himself or be briefed on by Smith, who had no such false respect.

On 8 June 1609, having endured a week of gales sheltering in Falmouth, the most remarkable of all the resupply voyages, a fleet of nine vessels commanded by Admiral Sir George Somers, cleared the Channel. Onboard the flagship, *Sea Venture*, which was commanded by the now veteran master Christopher Newport, was the colony's new Lieutenant Governor, Sir Thomas Gates, who had been instructed by the Virginia

Company to decide, following 'counsel with the Masters and Pilots and men of the best experience what way is safest and fittest for you to take, because we hold it dangerous that you should keep the old course of Dominico and Nevis lest you fall into the hand of the Spaniard'. The prevailing weather systems of the Atlantic precluded the fleet from sailing in a straight line from the western approaches, at latitude 49° North to the mouth of the Chesapeake at 37° North; instead, for a few weeks the nine ships kept comfortable company, heading first below the Azores, from where they could run the requisite latitude to bring them to a landfall on the Florida coast, from where they could turn north and run up to the Chesapeake. For seven eventless weeks all went according to plan, but as July entered its last week the weather changed radically as an intense tropical storm tracked rapidly down onto the fleet, which was unable to turn from its wave-rearing path. All semblance of keeping in company ceased as individual masters used every skill that they possessed to handle their own vessel in a way that would maximize their chance of survival. And that was the position in which they found themselves, for this was no ordinary storm but one that made a darkness of the day and replaced the air with spume and spray and raised upon the sea great white watery hills with yawning fearsome ship-swallowing valleys in between. William Strachey, a landsman, recorded what he saw and felt in a letter home whose most vivid phrases found eternal life when they were used by William Shakespeare for the opening of his aptly entitled play *The Tempest*.

In this tempest *Sea Venture* played the role that Shakespeare adapted for his play, grounding in raging sea on the reefs of the Bermudas, while Saint Elmo's fire lit up her rigging. The seven other scattered ships sailed slowly on, entering the Chesapeake in mid-August where, once they were secured by their hawsers to the living bollards of trees, they began unloading their 400 passengers, several horses and the much-needed supplies that were not storm damaged. If the ships had survived, the same could not be said of many of their passengers. Illness, possibly plague, carried away thirty-two of those onboard *Diamond* and *Swallow*, while two babies born during the storm died shortly after birth.

With the non-arrival and suspected loss of *Sea Venture*, one of the dilemmas of reinforcement and resupply became very rapidly apparent. The seven ships had transported the reinforcement but, without the supplies loaded in *Sea Venture*, the stores that they unloaded were inadequate to replenish and cater for both the established settlers and their new companions. This shortfall, coupled with mismanagement, was to lead to the one of the most harrowing periods endured by any settlement along the entire coast. Prior to the resupply arriving, John Smith had enforced a policy of dispersing groups of settlers to other areas, where they might survive on untapped local food supplies, including shellfish, for few were capable of fishing. This had worked reasonably well and, with the arrival of hundreds of new colonists, this scheme was continued by Smith's less-able successor George Percy, even when the wounded Smith had been shipped home and the Powhatans had been thus emboldened, rightly realizing that there was none now left able to command their cautious respect.

With a swelling demand for Jamestown's few rat-infested resources, the Amerindians inflicted further dearth by raiding Hog Island and slaughtering all the colony's pigs. Cats, dogs, rats and mice were their substitute, while all those who ventured out to hunt and grub up roots ran the risk of being killed by the gleefully watching Amerindians. Inside the palisade the survivors boiled and gnawed at their shoe-leather and even dug up the dead to chew on their bones. One colonist murdered his pregnant wife and chopped her up into salted joints, some of which he consumed before the crime was discovered and he, having confessed, was roasted alive, but presumably not eaten.

The Starving Time continued, aided by the many inadequacies of the incompetent who were not even capable of fishing from the well-stocked river and bay. It need not have been so bad; when Percy visited Point Comfort he found that the men under Captain James Davies were faring so well that he hatched a plan to send his Jamestown people down to the coast in relays for rest and recuperation. That plan, one of his more sensible, did not take place because, as it was being hatched, two ships were sighted entering the Chesapeake. After the usual immediate panic and suspicion that they were Spanish it was discovered that they were *Patience* and *Discovery*, the two vessels built in Bermuda from the remains of the wrecked *Sea Venture*. They were, of course, no longer a part of the resupply convoy that had sailed so many months earlier from England. Now they carried a human cargo of 142 new settlers, all anxious to restart their lives in this promised land after the enforced delay ashore in Bermuda. Yet, instead

A replica of *Mayflower*'s shallop. Even in the more sheltered waters of Cape Cod Bay *Mayflower*'s shallop came into danger of sinking in the storm that preceded the crew's arrival in Plymouth Bay. It was from the bows of this boat that, according to legend, the first settlers stepped ashore on Plymouth Rock. (Plimouth Plantation)

of being welcomed by well-fed and content fellow countrymen, they saw bedraggled starving creatures with staring eyes that had witnessed vile horrors. Even the new town where they soon disembarked resembled a village bedevilled by famine, illness and the ravages of war, populated, once the enfeebled had stirred themselves to rise and greet the newcomers, by people who stuck their claw-like hands out and exclaimed, 'We are starved, we are starved.' Soon they would have been informed that of the 600 settlers who would had seen John Smith depart from Jamestown on 4 October 1609, now – 20 May 1610 – only sixty were left clinging precariously to life. Captain Newport, who had now returned in *Deliverance*, was probably the man to whom Sir Thomas Gates turned for advice rather than the dishevelled and discredited George Percy. The recommendation must have been obvious but, before accepting it, Gates tried by instilling discipline, organizing fishing expeditions and reopening trade negotiations with the Amerindians to avoid the inevitable, but with Powhatan implacable the sad decision was made, after a fortnight, to evacuate the colony.

Both Roanoke and Jamestown thus failed in their nascent days because of the shortcomings in reinforcement and resupply. Elsewhere the continuing sea deliveries were as critical but their delay or non-appearance was never as tragic as it proved to be in southern Virginia.

The native staples of maize, beans and squash grew symbiotically, with the maize (Indian corn) providing a stalk for the beans to wind around while the squashes acted as a green moisture-retaining mulch and kept weeds at bay. The English chose to ignore such evidence of stable settlement.

The 1607 Norumbega (New England) settlement at Fort St George on the Sagadahoc River was almost too short lived to warrant resupply but, although little is known about its support, it was certainly timely, after difficulties at the start. Sir Ferdinando Gorges was keen to point out these problems to the Earl of Salisbury, to whom he wrote in December 1607:

> It seems to be most certain that there is no enterprise, (how well so ever intended) but hath his particular impediments meeting with many oppositions, and infinite crosses, as in this small attempt, (begun by my Lord Chief Justice out of a noble zeal to his prince and country, among many others), it is experienced for first as he was honourable himself, so he thought all others were, believing what they told him, and trusting to what, they promised, by which means, his Lordship was not a little deceived of what he expected, for neither were his provisions answerable to his charge bestowed, nor the persons employed such as they ought.

The letter continues in a similar self-justifying vein, making sure that all other than Gorges can be held responsible for the failure of the colony, if it indeed were to fail. Yet, the winter blew the dark clouds away and in March 1608 Gorges was writing to the Earl reporting the dispatch of resupply ships to the colony: 'As concerning our Plantation, we have found the means to encourage ourselves anew and have sent two ships from Topsham for the supplies of those that be there, with victuals and other necessaries, having set down the means how we shall be able, by May next, to send one more of 200 tunnes.' He continues by extolling both the 'excellent country' and the 'several commodities that a fertile soil will yield, when art and industry shall be used for the ease of nature, the which seems to show herself exceeding bountiful in that place'.

There is no record of that ship promised in May arriving at the colony. If it did not, that might explain why, when *Mary and John*, the ship that had ferried the original settlers to Maine in 1607, arrived at Fort St George in the autumn, the colonists decided to abandon their settlement and clamber onboard with their leader, Raleigh Gilbert, who used the excuse of returning to claim his inheritance as a reason to depart. So, as had happened in Roanoke and Jamestown, a resupply vessel was turned around to become an evacuation ship. Even further north in the bleak coves of Newfoundland, where thin acidic soils and brutal winter weather gave settlers few opportunities to establish a self-sufficient community, resupply was most vital.

Back in Virginia short rations were often the order of the day and would be while the settlement relied on resupply rather than harvesting its own produce, which remained subject to Amerindian attack until the Powhatans were neutralized. Thus, in 1623, Richard Frethorne, an indentured servant who arrived at Martin's Hundred a year after the massacre, described the bleak scene he found in a request to a London friend for succour:

> those servants that were there before us were almost Pined, and then they fell to feeding so hard of our provision that it killed them that were old Virginians as fast, as the scurvy & bloody flux did kill us new Virginians: for they were in such a Case by reason of the murder done all over the land that they Could not plant anything at

all, and at every Plantation all of them for the most part were slain and their houses & goods burnt. some, the Indians kept alive and took them away with them, and now these two Indians that they have taken doe tell us that the Indians have 15 alive with them . . . thus through their Roguery the land is ruinated and spoiled, and it will not be so strong again not this 12 years, for at our Plantation of seven score, there was but 22 left alive, and of all their houses there is butt 2 left and a piece of a Church, and our master doth say that 3000 pounds will not make good our Plantation again . . .

In the end it was trade, not resupply, that ensured the survival of the colonies. Without nations to conquer, foes to vanquish or fortunes to be made, resupply of the colonies required a costly one-way flow of funds. Ironically, for settlements that were constantly on the verge of starvation, it was not a foodstuff that saved the settlement but an inedible plant, tobacco, and an indigestible animal part, fur. Even more ironically, the enthusiastic adoption of tobacco from the Amerindians would eventually kill far more of the European invaders than they in their turn slew Amerindians, with the first death from lung cancer being that of Thomas Harriot, one of the few invaders who appreciated the native way of life his fellow nationalists would destroy.

On 18 October 1781, less than 175 years after John Smith and the Jamestown settlers had landed in Virginia, just a few miles away by road from the original settlement, and a bit further by water, the great English plantation idea was brought to an ignominious end when General Cornwallis was forced to surrender to the besieging American rebels. The reason for his ordering his troops to lay down their arms? The failure of the fleet to deliver reinforcements and resupply. Some lessons are a long time in the learning.

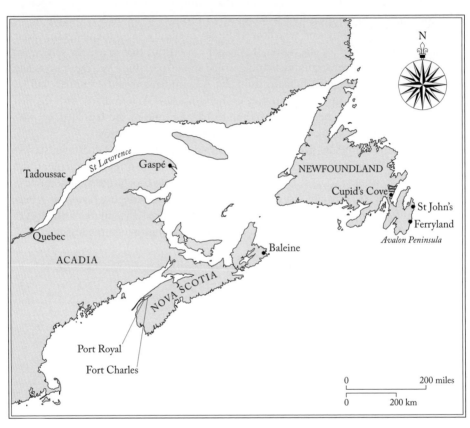

Map 5: Newfoundland, Nova Scotia and the St Lawrence

CHAPTER 10

Extirpation, Evacuation, Eviction and Abandonment

and to the end that you be not surprized as the French were in *Florida* by *Melindus*, and the *Spaniard* in the same place by the *French*, you shall do well to make this double provision. First, erect a little stoure at the mouth of the river that might lodge some ten men; with whom you shall leave a light boat, that when any fleet shall be in sight, they may come with speed to give you warning . . .

Virginia Company of London, *Instructions by Way of Advice*, 1606

THE EXTIRPATION OF OTHERS

It was not only the English who found their virginalling fingers brushed away from the fringes of North America. Even those who penetrated deeper and with more force found themselves spurned by a continent that would not yield its favours willingly.

The glittering success of the Spaniards in Mexico and the south casts a shadow over the series of disasters that struck them further north, where a series of expeditions yielded little of value at great human loss. In February 1521 the elderly and experienced Juan Ponce de Léon landed on the land he had discovered and named on *Pascua Florida* – Flowering Easter – with 200 potential settlers. They were repulsed by the Amerindians and Ponce de Léon fatally wounded. Five years later, after years of planning, Lucas Vásquez de Ayllón sailed from Santo Domingo with six ships carrying 500 men and women and numerous domestic animals. They landed in present-day South Carolina. By mid-October over half of them, including de Ayllón, were dead of disease and skirmish wounds. After a mutiny, the survivors re-embarked: only 150 returned to Santo Domingo.

The following year many hundreds more tried their luck in a venture led by Pánfilo de Narváez, a jealous rival of Cortés. Leaving a group to construct a fort at Tampa Bay, de Narváez led his force inland to discover a city of gold. Their epic march of over a 1,000 miles ended six years later when just four survivors struggled into the small Spanish settlement of Sinaloa on the Gulf of California. Back at Tampa Bay the fort builders abandoned their defences after one year and sailed home, leaving just one man behind to surprise and greet yet another expedition in 1539 when, undeterred by stories of failure, or blinded by gold greed, Hernando de Soto led an even larger expedition into the wilderness. They marched further, some 6,000 miles, and survived better – over 300 returned four years later – but they achieved the same result: zero. The Spanish persisted. In 1559 some 1,500 would-be colonists left Veracruz under the command of Don Tristan de Luna y Arellano and landed near present-day Pensacola, Florida, where they laid out the town of Ochuse. Two years later it was abandoned after a series of mutinies, during one of which Luna ordered all his men to be hanged, only to fall on his knees and beg forgiveness. With that abject failure the Spanish decided enough was enough, only for the French to replace them as suitors.

The first French attempt at settling on the southern coast of North America was made in 1562, when the French corsair, Jean Ribault, landed two dozen men to build a pirate base at Charlesfort in Port Royal Sound, South Carolina. After months of waiting for a promised resupply, the men built a makeshift boat and sailed away, to be rescued from a certain death by drowning, starvation and further cannibalism by a passing English vessel. Two years later, a larger group of Huguenots, led by René de Laudonnière, sailed over to Florida and landed further south than previously, near present-day Jacksonville, and constructed the settlement of Fort Caroline. Unusually, the French established friendly relations with the native Amerindians, even marrying a number of their women, but the usual discontent surfaced, leading to the attempted murder of Laudonnière and the abandonment of the project by many who preferred to turn privateer. It was their success that brought about the failure of the Fort Caroline

The building of Fort Caroline by the French in 1564. The favoured triangular shape is clearly evident as is the use of an island site for further protection. Drawing by Le Moyne, engraving by de Bry, 1591.

project but, ironically, before that happened this small colony was offered salvation when John Hawkins called in July 1565 and offered to evacuate the distressed settlers. Laudonnière, his own plans for evacuation well advanced, refused, but gratefully accepted life-saving provisions and the gift of a fifty-ton bark. Then, on 20 September 1565, acting on orders from his king, Don Pedro Menéndez de Avilés, pausing only to establish his own base at Fort Augustine forty miles to the south, descended on the settlement, which, with further irony, would have been evacuated had not the arrival of Ribault with 500 more colonists delayed departure. However, instead of fortifying the settlement, Ribault's ships, with many of the crew ashore, fled when challenged in the night by the Spanish armada, and then failed to carry out a counterattack on Fort Augustine. Instead, a violent storm drove the vessels south and they were unable to offer any support when Menéndez fell on the colony, slaughtering 140 of the settlers even after they had surrendered. A handful, including Laudonnière and the artist Le Moyne, escaped onboard a French vessel fortuitously anchored off the coast.

This was not the end of the affair. Ribault's ships had been wrecked and the survivors had begun the long walk north towards Fort Caroline. They were intercepted by

Fort Caroline under attack by the Spanish. After the defenders had surrendered, most were massacred by order of Pedro Menendez in September 1565, just days after John Hawkins had offered to evacuate the settlement.

Menéndez, who once again tricked them into surrendering before tying them up in batches of ten to be led behind some sand dunes, where they were murdered by the Spanish soldiery. Some 350 died this way; others fled, most to suffer a more lingering fate. To this day the spot where this ghastly massacre took place is known as Matanzas, Slaughter.

Saint Augustine, its rivals razed, was not itself successful. Mutinies and desertions, disease and failed crops gave it a hesitant future. In 1568, the Frenchman Dominique de Gourges assaulted the site of Fort Caroline, renamed San Mateo, and exacted a total revenge by massacring the 380 members of its garrison.

In 1586, when the settlers at Fort Augustine might have felt that they had overcome the enormous difficulties inherent in establishing their colony and could look forward to developing a viable township, the sea again delivered a savage blow. This time it was Sir Francis Drake and his fleet, sailing home to England via the Virginia settlement, who anchored offshore, concerned that this small beachhead could be a threat to their countrymen settled in similar circumstances many miles to the north.

Drake sighted the Spanish lookout tower on 27 March and landed the next day to assault the Fort of San Juan. Their first attack was repulsed but the Governor and

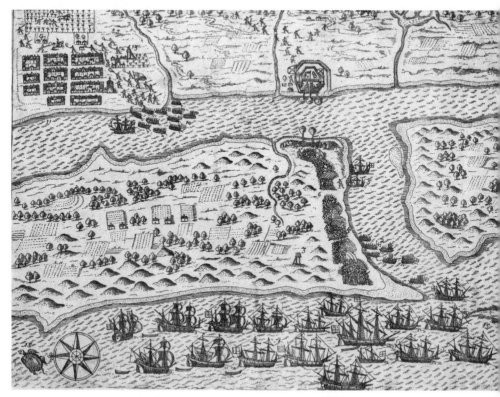

Drake capturing St Augustine, 7 June 1586. Unlike the Spanish at Fort Caroline, Drake made no attempt to massacre the inhabitants of St Augustine, being content just to drive them away and raze their fortifications. (National Maritime Museum)

his men crept away at night, leaving, as well as the usual ordnance, a strongbox with a useful £2,000 of the townsmen's money in it. The fort was put to the flames, as was the small settlement of Saint Augustine, although the inhabitants, who had fled, were not pursued. Neither did Drake attack the nearby Amerindian villagers, although they had turned out to help the Spaniards repel the attackers. Most notably, Drake did not pursue to the death the defeated citizenry, demonstrating a humanity that was very much his own; a Grenville, Ralegh or Gilbert would most likely have copied Spanish practices in such circumstances.

Being repulsed so bloodily in the south did not deter the French from attempting to establish themselves in the far north. Not that the French settlements here, established by Champlain and others, amounted to much more than religious missions or trading stations perched precariously on a climatically inhospitable coast or riverbank. They began with a longhouse, built as a fur trading post, in 1600 at Tadoussac at the mouth of the Saguenay River, a tributary of the St Lawrence. After one winter the majority of those housed there had died and Champlain, whose first visit to North America in 1603 involved reconnoitring from this site, returned to France with the suggestion that Acadia, later Nova Scotia, would be a better area on which to establish settlements. His advice was followed and, in May 1604, a settlement was sited at Port au Mouton with a winter colony established on the Île Saint Croix (Dochet Island). Champlain also discovered a potential settlement site at Port Royal, now Annapolis Royal, at the head of the Bay of Fundy. After a destructive winter in which thirty-five of the seventy-five settlers died, Champlain continued his exploration, which included the first survey of Cape Cod and Plymouth Bay. Upon his return, the colony was moved to the Port Royal site, where it remained until 1607 when, with the withdrawal of their Charter, the settlers returned to France.

EVACUATION AND ABANDONMENT

For the English, the much-feared Spanish attack failed to materialize. Instead famine and disease, supported by winter, were the greatest present danger. Nevertheless, they were right to plan to repel the Spanish for, whereas an Amerindian attack might have decimated but could usually be dispersed, a Spanish assault would have exterminated. Luckily, the Spanish seadogs sniffed, growled but never bit the trespassers within their master's domain, and he, when informed of their presence, considered them too distant to deserve the attention of his mastiffs.

With recklessness verging on stupidity the English had, from the start, teased those terriers by announcing their intentions to establish a toehold on the continent Spain considered was its own territory. In 1585 Grenville made no attempt to waft through the Caribbean with silent sails. In response, the authorities, despite an outward display of hospitality, voiced their concerns about his intentions to King Philip. If the Spanish had any doubts that Grenville's arrival was nothing other than a passing visit, they were swiftly disabused. On 7 June 1585 Grenville's fleet 'departed with great good will from the Spaniards from the Island of Hispaniola'; on 1 January 1586 Drake sacked Santo Domingo on the southern shore of that same island. Then, after further sackings

James Fort, built on the original site of Jamestown. This picture shows clearly the somewhat flimsy palisade and the frame for one of the first houses built within the stockade.

and ransoming and marauding mayhem, Drake followed Grenville's route north through the Florida Straits, stopping off to raze Saint Augustine before reaching the desperate disheartened English colony on 9 June. A greater indication of the threat that an English presence in the Americas posed to Spanish trade and settlements it would be hard to conceive, and this at a time when the fledgling colony in Virginia needed support and peace if it was to be established successfully. Indeed, throughout Elizabeth's reign, England's aggressive foreign policy was quite contrary to that which should have been pursued if the aim of colonizing Virginia was a priority in Elizabeth's plans. It was not, and the plantings failed.

The evacuation of the first Roanoke settlement was, however, not due to the Spanish threat. The enemy outside the walls was the local Amerindian one, whose initial friendliness had turned to aggression as a result of both misunderstanding and mishandling by Lane. By June 1586 his party had been ashore at Roanoke for a few weeks short of one year. During this time they had secured just a small beachhead, where they now lay invested by an enemy whose presence they were not strong enough to dislodge although they could fend off even the fiercest of attacks, provided that they were regularly reinforced and resupplied from the sea. In time, as happened later, the siege could be lifted and the slow advance from sea to shining sea could get underway, but until the prerequisites of security and self-sufficiency were reached it was to the sea not to the hills that they had to lift their eyes, for it was from there and only there cameth their help.

They had done remarkably well. All but one of the original number remained alive thanks not only to the limited provisions that they themselves had brought over but also through trading with the Amerindians, who had been prepared to barter and even help plant crops, but with greater and greater reluctance as the harsh winter dried up their own supplies. Spring had brought about a thaw in the relationship that enabled the colonists to sow seed and venture out in search of game without fear of attack but, with the failure of the relief fleet to arrive, desperation set in and made itself madly manifest when, on 1 June 1586, Lane put the colony at greatest risk by launching a pre-emptive attack on those dwelling in the belligerent, but temporary quiescent, native settlement. Before reprisals were organized a great fleet was espied in the offing which, possibly surprisingly, turned out not to be hostile and Spanish but friendly and English: Francis Drake, true to his word, had deviated from a direct passage home from his raid in the West Indies to check on and replenish the little colony.

Drake, who must have been much disheartened by the open roadstead which offered his ships no abiding stay, began nevertheless on a positive note, gifting Lane four months' supplies together with sufficient ships and the men that he had recruited in the West Indies with which to move the colony north to the more protected harbours which Lane had identified. This would have been a positive evacuation and one with the added, but unforeseen, advantage that in the time it took to embark, the resupply ships might have hove into sight.

It was the elements that made the decision for them. By the time that the storm had passed on, the few ships suitable for an inland voyage had either been sunk or scattered and the alternative transports were not considered viable. Lane brought his men out. The evacuation, free from opportunistic Amerindian attack, was a successful conclusion for what remained the most effective attempt at settlement for half a century. Evacuated they may have been, but as they had returned undefeated, and with both White's marvellous drawings and Harriot's enthusiastic account of a year in America, Ralegh could still believe that Virginia was beckoning him back with the promise of success.

Yet it was in the failure of the second Roanoke colony that Spain achieved its one success in eradicating an English settlement in North America and even that was not accomplished by a vicious Virginian vendetta but through a campaign Spain fought and lost on the other side of the Atlantic – the Armada enterprise against England. Fell circumstance meant that, while Ralegh and White were petitioning for permission to dispatch a relief squadron to Roanoke, England was gathering every available ship it had to repulse the great fleet which Philip II had assembled to ferry his much-feared soldiery across the Channel. Had they landed, England's amateur army would have been defeated; the nation's only hope lay in mustering a large enough fleet to defeat the enemy at sea. Meanwhile, in response to the needs of Roanoke, Ralegh was organizing 'a good supply of shipping and men with sufficiency of all things needful, which he intended, God willing, should be with them the summer following. Which pinnace and fleet were accordingly prepared in the west country at Bideford under the charge of Sir Richard Grenville.'

The clear and present danger of the Armada meant that an embargo was placed on this fleet and all shipping movements, while Grenville was hastened away for military service. With the turning back of the two small vessels that White still managed to

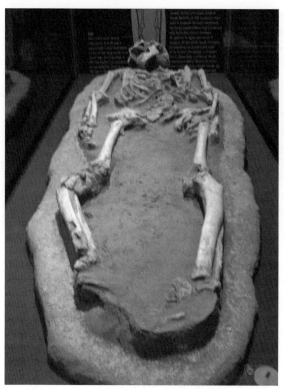

Accident or murder? This skeleton of a young man, recovered from the burial site within Jamestown fort is considered to be that of Stephen Calthorp, who died on 15 August 1607. Strangely, he appears to have died from an untreated injured leg in which an English lead musket ball was lodged.

wheedle out of Ralegh, the thirty-ton *Brave* and the twenty-five-ton *Roe*, the Roanoke colony was, for all practical purposes, abandoned. All voyages after that were made to salve White's conscience and keep Ralegh's Charter claims alive.

The return of the English to Virginia in 1607 might have ended in a very similar fashion to Ralegh's Roanoke settlements. That it did not is due more to coincidence than accomplishment. As it was, it led to the shortest evacuation in English history. On 23 May 1610, Sir Thomas Gates arrived in Jamestown with the survivors from the *Sea Venture*, to be faced with a landwreck far more precarious than that which they had endured at sea. Skeletal figures, just sixty of them from a group of 500 settlers alive just six month earlier, witnessed with the sunken-eyed lethargy of the starving his well-fed cohort march into their once overcrowded camp that was being throttled by Amerindian pressure.

Having left a paradise, mostly of their own creation, in Bermuda, Gates and his people must have thought that they had sailed into the heart of darkness. To escape this monstrous sight and stench must have been the wish of them all, as well as that of the inmates of this foul fort. Gates and Somers endeavoured to turn the tide by encouraging fishing and scavenging, but to no avail, and after ten days they realized that there was no possibility of an abiding stay and instigated an orderly evacuation. So on 6 June 1610, around midday, having dissuaded the bitter colonists from burning down their dwellings, Gates ordered *Virginia*, *Discovery*, *Patience* and *Deliverance* to cast off from their berths at Jamestown with the few starving survivors of the besieged

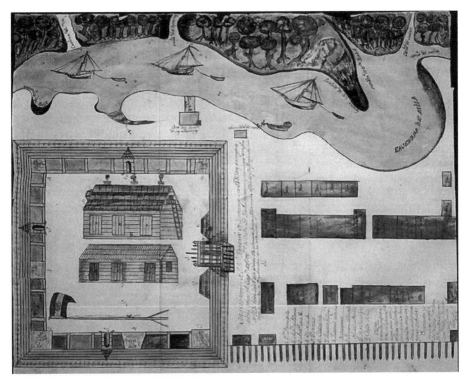

The four-square nature of this Spanish fort would indicate that they feared no foreign assault on their townships in the new world.

colony onboard. That night they anchored off Hog Island, just six miles downstream, but when they weighed the next day, with the intention of clearing the river, they were intercepted by a sailing boat carrying a message from the new Governor, Lord De La Warr, newly arrived in the Chesapeake, instructing them to turn again. So, on the night of 8 June they once again moored to the tree trunks on the Jamestown shoreline, disembarked and awaited their Governor. De La Warr appears to have been a man whose reputation preceded him. Although the settlers would have grumbled exceedingly that their salvation, as they saw it, had been snatched away from them, there seems to have been neither petition nor even mutiny about the change of plan. Many must have known it was a gamble which having extra mouths to feed would not assist. Indeed the meagre ration of seven pounds of meal a week for each man was not a working allowance, while the five pounds for women ensured that they remained the weaker sex. The one thing that must have united them all in labour was the realization that, like the passengers and crew onboard *Sea Venture*, they would sink or swim solely by their own exertions. With De La Warr in command there would be no more talk of evacuation.

Timing, as so often in early Virginia, had been the most critical element. Once news of the events of that summer of 1610 reached England, the Virginia Company stated that:

If God had not sent Sir Thomas Gates from the Bermudas within four days, they had all been famished . . . If they had abandoned the fort [any earlier] and had not so soon returned, questionless the Indians would have destroyed the fort . . . If they had set sail sooner and had launched into the vast ocean, who could have promised that they should have encountered the fleet of Lord La-ware?

The Popham Colony

Further north it was the elements rather than the Amerindians that persuaded the early settlers to withdraw after a promising preparation, for if reconnaissance and planning were the perquisites for a successful plantation, then the Popham colony established at the mouth of the Sagadahoc River by Sir George Popham in 1607 should have flourished. Gosnold in 1602, Pring in 1603 and 1606, and Waymouth in 1605 had explored, charted and reported back on the New England coast around the point of settlement. What is more, Waymouth had returned with a number of Amerindians to be trained as translators and to act as liaison officers. The team of 100 that set sail in *Gifte of God* and *Mary and John* included a fair mix of skilled artisans, farmers and soldiers, although fifteen 'gentlemen' may have been twice as many as was necessary to manage such a group. The record also indicates that many of the settlers were 'pressed to that enterprise', possibly by Lord Justice Popham as an alternative to jail. It began well. The crossing was incident free and the landing smooth, with little interference from the

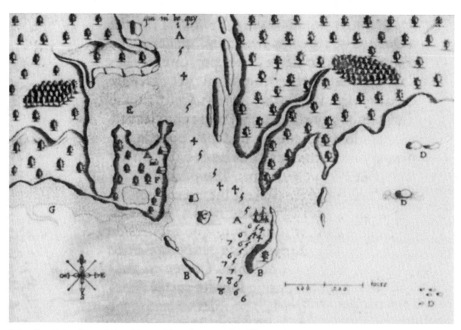

Mouth of the Sagadahoc River. This drawing by Champlain shows the site of Fort St George, which was built on the tip of the right ear of the cat's face formation of land on the west bank of the river.

Amerindians who witnessed the fort being erected. Why then did such a promising beginning endure for such a short time?

Logistics, as so often in such endeavours, was the most evident flaw. The colonists arrived with too little, planted too late and traded too inefficiently to gain what they needed from the Amerindians, who were content to leave them miserable to their own means, with even the interpreter, Skidwarres, confusing and deceiving them. Having landed on 18 August 1607, fifty colonists were evacuated back to England in *Gifte of God* in mid-December. Because they could not be fed, their journey home, via the Azores, in a ill-provisioned ship, led to the death of two of them before they arrived weak in Plymouth, bringing a pompous letter from George Popham with them in which their Governor's optimism is clearly out of keeping with the evidence of the returning evacuees.

The remaining members of the colony clung on, their circumstances made worse by the foul winter that was gripping Maine and their inability to trade for warming furs until the spring. Then, just as the weather started improving, George Popham died and was succeeded by Raleigh Gilbert. This changeover should have had no material effect on the plantation, which was in reasonable shape to start the New Year afresh, although the anticipated presence of rich minerals had not materialized. Fresh supplies arrived from Topsham in March, but the resupply also brought the news that the colony's chief sponsor, Sir John Popham, had died. Another death, that of Sir John Gilbert, was reported in July 1608 when *Mary and John* anchored off the fort. That news meant that Raleigh Gilbert, instead of being the leader of a small, almost destitute body of men,

Compton Castle, the home of the Gilbert family for centuries. In 1608 Raleigh Gilbert was faced with the option of remaining at Fort St George on the Sagadahoc River or returning to claim his inheritance. Understandably, he chose the latter, bringing the remaining colonists home with him.

stranded on a distant seashore, found himself heir to a great and established English estate, including the wonderful Compton Castle in South Devon. The choice was simple: homeward he came, and the remaining colonists with him. Sagadahoc colony had failed entirely with the help of its own resources.

In 1623 Christopher Levett, an associate of Ferdinando Gorges who had just been granted a Charter to establish the Province of Maine, sailed to settle a 6,000-acre estate at York, near present-day Portland. Here he built a stone house in which he placed a group of Yorkshiremen, promising to return with supplies a few months later. Instead he found himself commanding a naval ship at the assault of Cadiz in 1625 and only sailed back to America in 1630 to meet with Winthrop at Salem, dying at sea on the return voyage. No written record or trace remains to give a clue as what happened to the abandoned settlers.

Not all evacuations ended with the disillusioned settlers being returned home. Some tried resettlement, often successfully. In 1624 the Reverend John White and 118 Dorchester worthies dispatched a group of fishing farmers to the bleak shores of Cape Ann. They clung on for three years before quitting, unable to either scrape a living or provide a return on the investment. Yet, some twenty-five of them, led by Roger Conant, liked the life, and, with White's distant encouragement, sailed south to Naumkeag, which became the original settlement of Salem. In 1628, White persuaded a further group of fifty settlers to join Conant. The next year another 300 disembarked at Naumkeag, their occupancy strengthened by the issue, after a liberal greasing of palms, of the royal Charter for the Massachusetts Bay Company, which would follow them in Governor Winthrop's ship. Yet the site of Naumkeag did not find favour with Winthrop and he was soon a-boat again, sailing into a bay fifteen miles down the coast where, on the peninsula between the Mystic and Charles rivers a number of villages were established which coalesced into Boston, a city on a hill and an abiding stay.

Newfoundland

Evacuation, abandonment and resettlement were also key features of the colonizing process in Newfoundland and Nova Scotia as the English, Welsh, Scots and Irish tried to come to terms with the harsh environment. Their one advantage was that the annual fishing fleet kept them in contact with their homeland and could be approached for both provisions and trade. What these spring arrivals could not do was mitigate against the memory of the scarcely endurable harsh winters. After the bitter winter of 1613 the Cupid's Cove settlement in Newfoundland, which had been founded in 1610, was reduced to just thirty souls, which did not include its Governor and leaders, who had abandoned it. Nevertheless, while shareholders complained about returns and settlers moaned about hardships, the survivors clung on with perverse perseverance. Outside the limited shelter of Conception Bay, the Welsh colony established at Aquafort on the Atlantic coast of the Avalon peninsula in 1617 was unable to muster the same bloody-minded tenacity. The settlers huddled together in abandoned hovels and did little to improve their lot through labour. In 1618 their first Governor, Richard Whitbourne, moved them to the harbour of Renews, much favoured by fishermen, but, frustrated by their lethargy, he abandoned the place, leaving just six settlers behind for a few months before they too saw error in their ways and came home. Yet, instead of washing his hands of the idea of colonization, Whitbourne sat down and wrote one of the most authoritative, enthusiastic and useful guidebooks about Newfoundland. *A Discourse and Discovery of Newfoundland* ran to three editions by 1623, its lucid, matter-of-fact style, popular with those who might claim to have all the necessary attributes of a prospective planter except get-up-and-go. On the propaganda side it showed the government how fishing and settlement could work together. On the practical side it explained how, by chartering a small boat, settlers could establish their own small business.

The next attempt at establishing a colony in Newfoundland was in 1623 and was initiated by Henry Cary, Lord Falkland, as a plantation for the English Catholics of Ireland. As a consequence of the time Whitbourne and Lord Falkland's man, known only by the initials T.C., spent together in planning the initiative, this was to be one of the best organized of all settlements along the whole American littoral. The settlers even sailed with clear direction being given to them by Lord Falkland himself. Yet, by 1628, the south Falkland colony, adjacent to Renews, had also been abandoned.

A few years earlier another man with Irish interests, George Calvert, Baron Baltimore, purchased land in Avalon, Newfoundland, for which he received a royal Charter in 1623. Calvert's first move had been to send the Welshman Edward Winne out to establish a settlement at Ferryland, which was done, but not without creating friction between landsmen and visiting fishermen. The colony appeared to thrive and became a destination for a number of Catholics, both priests and laity seeking freedom of worship. Thirty-two people survived the winter of 1622/1623 at the site and, encouraged by their endeavour, Calvert expanded his landholding.

Then, in 1625, an old difficulty re-emerged, with the government staying English ships in port because of the threat from Spain. Amazingly, Calvert appears to have had more influence in Court than did Ralegh in similar circumstances in 1587, for he was allowed to dispatch his ships with the proviso that they returned laden with fish for the navy. Once war broke out, the nation's demands for both ships and seamen superseded Calvert's own requirements, making him nervous enough about the colony's position to make a personal visit to Ferryland in 1627. He found the settlement had lost its early zest but did not appear to be about to disintegrate. Having arrived, he led from the front, including launching several successful anti-piracy patrols. He even considered moving his family to Ferryland, but the winter of 1628/1629 endured in 'the coldest harbour of the land' convinced him that his future lay further south. Realizing the falseness of the favourable reports, through the famine and the frostbite, he wrote to King Charles that he was going:

> to quit my residence, and to shift to some other warmer climate of this new world, where the winters be shorter and less rigorous . . . [for] I have found by too dear bought experience, which other men for their private interests always concealed from me that from the middest of October to the middest of May there is a sad face of winter upon all this land . . . .

Calvert's house, he reported, 'hath been an hospital . . . of 100 persons, 50 sick at a time, myself being one of them and nine or ten of them died'. He therefore abandoned 'this place to fishermen that are able to encounter storms and hard weather'. So south he sailed with forty others, leaving behind a settlement that he had striven for and enriched with the building of many jetties and boats, many of which he had protected from the French. Neither need he have felt a failure in those harsh lands: his survival rate of 90 per cent in the harsh winter that drove him away was far better than that achieved either at Plymouth or Jamestown, where conditions were far more favourable.

His decision brought forth the caustic comment that 'the air of Newfoundland agrees perfectly well with all God's creatures except Jesuits and schismatics'; abandoned by their patron, the few remaining Ferryland settlers clung on, for they too had invested much in this new life and could not afford to depart with the apparent insouciance of a George Calvert to a new land in the south. Over their heads would rage land claims between Calvert and the Kirke family, but they were too busy earning a livelihood to pay too much attention. Their survival against the odds is a mute fanfare for the endurance of the common man more interested in family than fortune.

DESERTION

Not all abandonments were the result of the failures of sponsors back in England. In many cases it was the settlers themselves who decided when enough was enough. In some cases, like the German Dutch in Jamestown in 1608, they joined the natives, in other instances they wheedled a passage back on one of the ships. Occasionally their decision to return home amounted to desertion, as in the case of the obnoxious and cowardly Francis West, who, when food and fighting men were in most demand at Jamestown in the winter of 1609, sailed his pinnace full of forage back to England. A year later, Sir George Somers's nephew, with his uncle dead on the shores of Bermuda, also decided to sail on to England rather than return with provender to Jamestown.

These are two of the more dastardly examples, but all through the period of initial occupation a steady trickle, occasionally a stream, of settlers decided that the new world was not going to offer them a decent new life. Few could dispute the moral right of the disillusioned to return. The Virginia Company did, and thus failed to endorse its own propaganda that a land of opportunity awaited all who had the courage to venture forth.

By the time of the third Charter of 1611, desertion had grown to be such a major problem that several paragraphs were devoted to the discouragement of both reluctant emigrants and disappointed returnees.

And furthermore, whereas We have been certified, That divers lewd and ill disposed Persons, both Sailors, Soldiers, Artificers, Husbandmen, Labourers and others, having received Wages, Apparel and other Entertainment, from the said Company, or having contracted and agreed with the said Company to go, or to serve, or to be employed in the said Plantation of the said first Colony in Virginia, have afterwards either withdrawn, hid, or concealed themselves, or have refused to go thither, after they have been so entertained and agreed withal: And that divers and sundry Persons also, which have been sent and employed in the said Plantation of the said first Colony in Virginia, at and upon the Charge of the said Company, and having there misbehaved themselves by Mutinies, Sedition, or other notorious Misdemeanours, or having been employed or sent abroad by the Governor of Virginia, or his Deputy, with some Ship or Pinnace, for our Provision of the said Colony, or for some Discovery, or other Business and All airs concerning the same, have from thence most treacherously either come back again, and returned into our Realm of England, by Stealth, or without Licence of our Governor of our said Colony in Virginia, for the Time being, or have been sent thither as Misdoers and Offenders: And that many also of those Persons after their Return from thence, having been questioned by our Council here, for such their Misbehaviours and Offences, by their Insolent and Contemptuous Carriage in the Presence of our said Council, have showed little Respect and Reverence either to the Place or Authority in which we have placed and appointed them; And others for the colouring of their Lewdness and Misdemeanours committed in Virginia, have endeavoured by most vile and slanderous Reports made and divulged, as well of the Country of Virginia, as also of the Government and Estate of the said Plantation and Colony, as much as in them lay, to bring the said Voyage and Plantation into Disgrace and Contempt: By Means whereof, not only the Adventurers and Planters already engaged in the said Plantation, have been exceedingly abused and hindered, and a great Number of other, our loving and well-disposed Subjects, otherwise well affected and inclined to join and adventure in so noble, Christian, and worthy an Action, have been discouraged from the same; but also the utter overthrow and Ruin of the said Enterprise hath been greatly endangered, which cannot miscarry without some Dishonour to Us, and our Kingdom.

Now, forasmuch as it appeareth unto us, that these Insolences, Misdemeanours, and Abuses, not to be tolerated in any civil Government, have, for the most part, grown and proceeded, in regard our said Council have not any direct Power and Authority, by any express Words in our former Letters-patents, to correct and chastise such Offenders; We therefore, for more speedy Reformation of so great and enormous Abuses and Misdemeanours heretofore practised and committed, and for the preventing of the like hereafter, do by these Presents for Us, our Heirs, and Successors, GIVE and GRANT, to the said Treasurer and Company, and their Successors for ever, that it shall, and may be lawful for our said Council for the first Colony in Virginia, or any two of them (whereof the said Treasurer or his Deputy for the Time being, to be always one) by Warrant under their Hands, to send for, or cause to be apprehended, all, and every such Person or Persons, who shall be noted, or accused, or found at any Time or Times hereafter, to offend or misbehave themselves, in any the Offences before mentioned and expressed.

By 1622 settlements had spread along both banks of the James River up to the natural obstruction of the Falls. Although wary, and all settlers never moved far from their firearms, most felt that the Amerindians had, however grudgingly, acknowledged their presence and even their right to be there. Lulled deliberately to lower their guard, few anticipated the 'skyfall' of 22 March 1622 when Opechancanough launched his Powhatan confederacy in a coordinated assault on the settlements. The result was the temporary abandonment of many of the outlying plantations, although some, like Henricus, never recovered. It was a short-lived ebb, for the tide of people flowing westward was too strong to be dammed by a limited hiatus which provided an excuse to deal more savagely with the 'savages'. It would not be too long before it was the Amerindians who were forced to abandon their lands, and then their removal would be not a temporary but a permanent eviction.

EVICTION

Deterring the Spanish

Whatever Philip II might have wished to achieve with his great Armada against England, his representatives in New Spain felt that a solitary ship might be able to seek out and destroy the Roanoke settlement. In May 1588, as the Armada prepared to sail from Spain, Captain Vicente González was deployed from Saint Augustine on a three-month voyage north to seek out any English heretics who had had the temerity to settle in Virginia. A summary of his report, penned by Father Luis de Oré, gave a geographically accurate and glowing account of the land around the Chesapeake but did not report finding any settlements. Some evidence of their presence came to light, in that they did discover a slipway and some casks serving as rainwater butts, which González took for signs of temporary rather than established settlement. They sailed away but, if that visit had been observed by the stranded community at Roanoke, it might have been the catalyst that made them either depart for the presumed safer site at Croatoan, or even to surrender to the Spanish rather than fall into the hands of the 'savages'.

The accession of the less dogmatic, more pragmatic and broke Philip III increased the frustration felt by Spanish ambassadors and courtiers, who itched to persuade their King of the threat posed by an English presence in North America. Even when the two nations were not at war, they advised that there was just cause and no impediment to the destruction of these usurping, piratical, Protestant dens. The Spanish ambassador in London, Don Pedro de Zúñiga, as a good ambassador should, spied and bribed his way to the information he needed, and then warned both the English and the Spanish King of the consequences of the English action. To Philip III he urged early action before the English settlement got too large to be easily dislodged and, when this failed to stir, changed tack to suggest that the Virginia venture was designed to establish a pirate base rather than a settlement. In parallel, he had an audience with King James in which he stated how much 'against good friendship and brotherliness it was for his vassals to dare to people Virginia, since it is a part of the Indies belonging to Castille'. He even threatened 'inconvenient results'. Neither king took any notice, but in July 1609 Samuel Argall encountered a Spanish vessel on a reconnaissance mission in Chesapeake Bay. Its reported presence caused investor alarum, for many thought that it presaged a Spanish plan to, in the words of the Venetian ambassador, 'make the same slaughter of these as they did of the French in the same Indies'.

For the next two years the settlement lay low, but when in 1611 the hard-strapped Virginia Company was given permission to raise funds through a lottery, it could obviously not keep quiet about its ambitions or intentions, one of which was to dispatch a group of settlers so powerful that it would not fear the threat of Spanish assault. The success of the lottery alarmed de Zúñiga and he wrote to Philip that, 'they have collected in twenty days an amount of money for this voyage that frightens me'. This seems to have grazed the mark, for the next reported Spanish presence in Virginia came in 1611, when a caravel on a spying mission anchored off Port Comfort and sent three people ashore. They were promptly arrested and interned. One died a few months later, while the other two, Don Diego de Molina and Francis Lenbri, endured nearly five years of captivity, not being shipped until April 1616, when they sailed with Sir Thomas Dale, onboard *Treasurer*, commanded by Samuel Argall. During the passage Dale discovered Lenbri to be English and hanged him as a spy, so only Molina made it home. He had, however, managed to forward a letter concerning his observations in which he stated that the English were establishing the 'Algiers of America', a reference to the corsairs that plagued the Mediterranean, for, like Algiers, Virginia was 'very suitable for a gathering-place of all European pirates'. Molina considered that it was high time to 'stop this hydra in its infancy', which could be done by sending 800 to 1,000 of the King's soldiers 'to reduce the place with great ease'. Molina thought the fortifications of 'boards . . . so weak that a kick would break them down and once arrived at the ramparts those without would have the advantage over those within because its beams and loopholes are common to both parts'. These were, in his opinion, fortifications built without skill and made by unskilled men who were 'poorly drilled and not prepared for military action'. Yet Molina did not think force the only option available for removing this pestilential settlement. He had seen the living conditions endured by the settlers and the harsh rule under which they were being managed. Thus he thought them 'desirous that a fleet should come from Spain to take them out of their misery' and that, should such a fleet appear to give them passage, not 'a single person would take up arms'.

Molina might have misjudged the mood as far as the acceptance of a free passage to Spain was concerned; fear of the Inquisition was ever in the English mind, but the massacre of March 1622 would soon confirm his views on the weakness of the English fortifications, and his estimate of the numbers needed to overcome them was probably very accurate.

Mainland America was not the only site where the Spanish railed against English settlement. Bermuda became another place ripe for extirpation, especially after Philip III received a report of the ambergris found in the Bermudas by the 'mutineers' from the shipwrecked *Sea Venture*, which had sold at £10,000 a pound on the London market in 1613. So, in March 1614 two Spanish ships arrived off the settlement, presumably with hostile intent. The colonists were ready for them and, with a few well-aimed cannon shots, encouraged them to sail away.

Evicting the French

The Spanish threatened much and delivered little. Not so the French, with whom the English, and Scots, were to develop a long-lasting intimate antagonism in their struggle for commercial and political control of Canada, Newfoundland and Nova Scotia, their claims and counter-claims based around Charters and grants of arguable legality.

In 1610 Port Royal was again occupied, as was Mount Desert Island, on which a Jesuit mission was established at a spot they called Saint-Sauveur. It was this settlement that first drew down on itself the wrath of the English, and on 28 June 1613 the Admiral of Virginia, Captain Samuel Argall, sailed north from Jamestown in his fourteen-gun ship, *Treasurer*, to wipe out the settlements. But the fierce Argall displayed a softer side when dealing with the intruders than ever did the Spanish. Only three of the new colonists were killed, while the three wounded and fourteen other prisoners transported back to Jamestown were well treated.

However, having landed his prisoners, Argall was ordered north again by the Governor, Sir Thomas Gates, to complete his work of eradication, which he did by razing the buildings on Mount Desert and at Saint Croix and Port Royal. During the voyage he also became the first Englishman to land at Manhattan.

A number of the inhabitants of Port Royal had been absent from the fort when Argall fell upon it and had to endure another starving winter until relief arrived in

Argall attacks the French settlements in Nova Scotia, 1613. On an extirpation mission, Argall removed the French from both Port Royal and the Jesuit base at Saint Sauveur on Mount Desert Island.

March 1614. Not surprisingly, all but a handful of the colonists opted to return to France, but the number left behind was too small to further infuriate the English and, as if to symbolize his belief in the finality of Argall's action, James I renamed the Acadian peninsula Nova Scotia, and granted a Charter to the Scot, Sir William Alexander, to exploit it. Among the dispossessed Frenchmen was Claude de la Tour, who, rather than returning to France, chose to slip across the Bay of Fundy and establish a fortified trading post, Fort Penagoet, at the mouth of the Penobscot River. The Virginian English arrived in 1626 to dispossess him and take over the site, which they renamed after the river on which it stood.

Deep inland, and far away from the coastal fracas, Samuel de Champlain had founded Quebec in 1608. Investors' concerns that settlers might endeavour to seize a slice of the seasonal lucrative fur trade had led to limitations on both the number and type of person who was sent out to Quebec, so its growth was not as rapid as it might have been, and, by 1620 when Champlain was joined by his wife, only forty-six settlers occupied the site. It was to Quebec that the piratical Kirke brothers were drawn in 1628, as recounted later. Sufficient to relate here is that they captured the outpost in 1629, holding it until 1632, when, by treaty between England and France, it was returned to the latter until General Wolfe finally seized it in 1759.

Threatening the Dutch

The Dutch arrived stealthily in America. Reconnaissance in 1609 by Henry Hudson, an Englishman in their employ, led them to fancy the shores of the island of Manhattan and the banks of the river Mohicanituck, later to be renamed after its first European explorer. In 1610 they began to traffic with the Amerindians, and in 1613 they built a trading post at the head of navigation on the Hudson, where Albany is now situated, its riverbank enhanced by a replica of Hudson's *Half Moon*. However, most of the trade took place over the ships' sides, and when Samuel Argall arrived off Manhattan on his return from evicting the French from Port Royal, he chanced to see very few Dutch traders standing around a flagpole on which their national flag had been raised. Argall, whose natural character appears to have been prickly and acquisitive, seems on this occasion to have been unusually friendly towards the interlopers for, after ordering them to lower the flag and leave, it was he who departed, leaving the Dutch to continue trading both here and, briefly, on the Delaware.

In 1619 Thomas Dermer passed that way again and, noticing that the Dutch seemed well established and wealthy, reported the fact to Argall, now the Governor of Virginia. This time, instead of resorting to force, Argall invited the British Government to dispute the Dutch West India Company's rights to Manhattan and the Hudson in the courts. In its 1621 defence the States-General deployed evasion and obfuscation, stating that they had never authorized any settlement on the Hudson and, even if they had, it was only for twenty-four years, but the English had to wait a further forty-three years before they were able to remove the Dutch. The whole episode indicates with clarity that even territorial disputes could be settled without bloodshed or violence.

ESTABLISHMENT

The ever-present Amerindian threat was never conclusively resolved until the second quarter of the seventeenth century, when a harsher pragmatism saw war as a justifiable and expedient tool. Until that time, which could not be before the beachheads were properly secured, the broad Atlantic, lying between the settlers and the source of resupply, created a great gap between potential and realizable development of the colonies. It is a simple fact that these early settlers did not achieve self-sufficiency either in food or protection. Without relief supplies being delivered from England, all the settlements would have failed. The record of evacuations and abandonments that took place is simply the tangible proof of this discrepancy.

Yet not all moved away from these charnel houses that had unexpectedly become their homes, and there is an interesting contrast between many who did leave, or never came out, and the brave few that stayed on. In the first category can be placed the propagandists Ralegh, Hakluyt and Dee and investors such as Thomas Smythe; the short-term settlers include such wealthy and aristocratic names as Gates, De La Warr, Calvert, Vaughan, Ralegh Gilbert, Gorges and Falkland. The stayers-on were men such as John Smith, untimely ripped from the land he loved, John Rolfe and the mostly anonymous brave and hardy souls who clung on in Newfoundland, as well as the entire body of the Plymouth settlers. Above all, it was when those who ventured were promised a just reward for their labours, rather than being sent to serve absentee investors, that the determination to make good became manifest. The Virginia Company was late, too late for its own survival, to appreciate this truth which the *Mayflower* voyagers knew to be self-evident from the start. There are, indeed, few better illustrations of the effect that the change in the terms had than in the different responses to the offer of evacuation from Lane's Roanoke garrison in 1586 and the Jamestown settlers of 1608, and that of the *Mayflower* Pilgrims, none of whom wished to sail home. Unlike the southern Virginians, they had landed with a common purpose, a shared belief (mostly) and, of course, no real home to which they could make a welcome return.

CHAPTER II

The Amphibious Campaign

Because in so remote a country, and situate among so many barbarous nations, the incursions as well of the savages themselves as of other enemies, pirates and robbers, may probably be feared, therefore we . . . do give power . . . to levy, muster and train all sorts of men whatsoever . . . to make war and prosecute the enemies and robbers aforesaid, as well by sea as land, yea even without the limits of the said Province, and by God's assistance to vanquish and take them, and being taken to put them to death.

The Charter of Avalon, 7 April 1623

Of all military operations an amphibious assault ranks with the most difficult. It requires a joint, cooperative and coordinated command; a good reconnaissance of a hostile shoreline; transport of sufficient forces to secure and hold a beachhead, yet compatible with the cramped and often limited transport available; the landing of enough materiel and victuals to make the force initially self-sufficient, yet with the guarantee of regular and scheduled reinforcement and resupply; and, above all, a clear aim and a realistic target. Not surprisingly, given the complexity of the evolution, the long sixteenth century had its fair share of failures.

Henry VIII began his reign by dispatching an expeditionary force to northern Spain to support an attack by his father-in-law, Ferdinand, on Navarre. With nothing achieved, the Marquis of Dorset returned with his mutinous horde, leaving behind thousands who had died of dysentery and overdrinking brought about by ill-discipline and the absence of victuals and tentage. At the end of Henry's reign similar disasters were to happen, under the command of another aristocrat, Henry Howard, at the siege of Boulogne. Elizabeth's commanders continued the underachievement in many amphibious deployments, most notably in Ireland and the Low Countries, while, finally, King Charles was to have his own amphibious failures off Cadiz in 1625 and before La Rochelle in 1627. The Tudors' greatest successes were Drake's raid on Cadiz in 1587 and the return visit to that port by Effingham, holding the reins of Ralegh and Essex in 1596. However, Drake was to fail before Lisbon in 1589 and in the West Indies in 1595. If the professionals, usually carrying troops sufficient for success, could have such a poor record, it is not surprising that the English amateurs without state support and with few men available – and they untrained – did not do well after landing in North America.

Just one contrast in the approach to colonial settlement between the state-backed Spanish and the investor-backed English should suffice. In 1493 Columbus decided to found the city of La Isabella at a poorly chosen site on the northern coast of Hispaniola. Five years later the disillusioned survivors moved over to the southern shore and founded a new and lasting capital, Santo Domingo. But then 1,500 settlers had disembarked at the proposed site of La Isabella, and had built for themselves a strong structure in stone, their numbers and their ramparts able to withstand any attack that might be launched against them. By contrast, in 1587 the grandiloquently and egotistically named corporate body, the Governor and Assistants of the City of Ralegh, appointed an adynamic artist, John White, to lead 110 people to the new world, where he endeavoured to establish the new city at Roanoke, where he knew it was not meant to be. Five years later, probably far less, it was no more.

The Aim

To say that the English assault on America was an invasion that lacked a realistic military aim is to state the obvious inadequacy of the enterprise. This flawed approach stemmed from the top. The Charters granted to the expedition planners were grandiloquent and unrealistic, based as they were on approving the conquest of a continent with a company of untrained men. Even to begin the enforced occupation of another land required, at the very least, local supremacy in numbers and a steady stream of reinforcements. The execution involved little groups of settlers being transported, to huddle on an inhospitable coast thousands of miles from friendly succour; those who did not succumb to disease could have been snuffed out at any time of choosing by either the Spanish by sea, or the natives by land.

The Threat

In America, as in Europe, the main threat to the survival of expeditionary forces was disease, brought about by a combination of malnutrition, malpractice and poor medicine, and its malevolent effects far outweighed those incurred by enemy action. It would, therefore, be thought obvious that forces should be deployed with sufficient food and medicine to meet the main threat. This did not happen, and campaign after campaign failed because of the impact of often preventable disease. It was to be the same in America.

The human threat to the invaders was forecast to come from: the Spanish, the French, the Amerindians and pirates. Of these it was the Spanish that were the settlers' principal concern until it was realized that they were better at writing and issuing threats than delivering deeds. The French, having been massacred in Florida and moving into the interior of Canada, were more interlopers than enemy, except in Nova Scotia and Newfoundland, which was also the region preferred by the pirates. This meant that, for greater Virginia, it was logically the people whose land was being seized who objected the most and fought back the hardest and longest.

However, although aware that they were entering disputed territory, the resentment that the English anticipated was not that of the native population but from the Spaniards, whom they knew would bridle at any intrusion into the world over which they claimed hegemony and in defence of which they had demonstrated great ruthlessness. It was the Spaniards too who were forewarned of the English intentions and who kept many spies and couriers employed snooping out and reporting on future intentions. So it was the Spaniards whom the English feared, fortified against and to whom they fed false information about their settlements. They were also very clear in their advice to the settlers, quoted earlier, not only about the danger of the Spanish threat but that it was of more substance than that which would be posed by the 'naturals', although – and this was a warning that the Plymouth Pilgrims also took heed of – the advice to Jamestown stated that:

> Above all things, do not advertise the killing of any of your men, that the country people may know it; if they perceive that they are but common men, and that with the loss of many of theirs they diminish any part of yours, they will make many adventures upon you. If the country be populous, you shall do well also, not to let them see or know of your sick men, if you have any; which may also encourage them to make many enterprises

How far removed from reality this prioritizing was can be illustrated by a simple comparison: on the American mainland disease and famine killed thousands of the English invaders; the Amerindians killed many hundreds; the Spaniards not one. The reason is not difficult to comprehend. Spain held vast global estates, on the far-flung edges of which the English were rumoured to be camped illegally; yet that distant campsite was in the Amerindians' backyard. Such warnings were prescient but did not suggest that a 'massacre' such as happened in 1622 was even a remote possibility. Events would demonstrate that, if the Spanish responded to the settlers as intruders, the Amerindians viewed them as invaders but, in dealing with the Amerindians' reaction, the English could draw on their experiences far closer to home.

Strategy

The English did not anticipate trouble. Their propagandists had even ensured that the emptiness of the land to which they were heading was either enshrined in its very name, Virginia, or meant to sound homely, as with New England. Yet, when they discovered that the natives were not quiescent they knew just what to do, for the English had form. It had begun in the shadowy period when the Anglo-Saxons forced the Celts to flee into the wild parts of Wales or kettled them into the confined corners of Cornwall. The English response to opposition was soon to make itself apparent in Ireland. In the *Remonstrance of the Princes*, King Donal O'Neill of Ulster wrote to Pope John XXII in 1318, in words that could be transposed to the mouths of either Powhatan or Massoit in America:

> There is no hope whatever of having peace with them [the English] for such is their arrogance and excessive lusts to lord it over us and so great is our due and natural desire to throw off the unbearable yoke of their slavery and to recover our inheritance wickedly seized upon by them, that . . . there cannot now be, or ever henceforth be established, sincere good will between them and us . . . for we have such a natural

hostility to each other rising from the mutual malignant and incessant slaying of fathers, brothers, nephews and other near relatives that we can have no inclination to reciprocal friendship . . .

In Elizabeth's reign, frustrated that the Irish did not seem to understand the benefits of subjection, and disdainful of their race and despising the religion, the English decided to settle the Irish question once and for all. Those who were dispatched to enact this civilizing process, angered that the Irish were able to ambush English forces and assault English settlements, responded with atrocities of their own. Among those present at such cold killings were Francis Drake, Humphrey Gilbert and Walter Ralegh. The latter combined his military role, which included the bloody execution of the Spanish garrison of Smerwick after their surrender, with a land-grabbing opportunity, being granted great plantations by his besotted Queen to which he endeavoured to transport some 100 settlers. Truly, Ireland served as the template for Virginia, except that in Ireland the English invasion was supported by thousands of troops.

Yet for all the troops and senior leadership that the English sent over to Ireland the result was often unsatisfactory, as few were competent to issue and enforce a coherent strategic plan. This same lack of direction is most evident in America where, without the presence of a military force of any size and the absence of local intelligence, the lack of a strategic plan is most understandable and regrettable. The need was simple: to

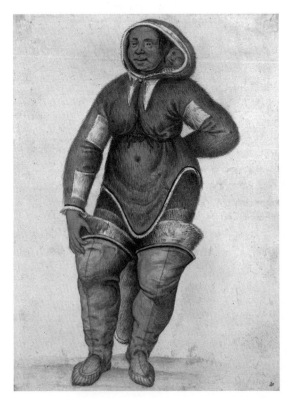

An Inuit woman and child. Brought to England as objects of curiosity, like so many kidnapped Amerindians, Arnaq and Nutaaq did not long survive the germs and general unhygienic conditions of Tudor England. (British Museum)

establish a beachhead and control the waterways, but that would not produce income. Thus many would be doomed to march by ambushed arms and many more would see their personal and collective strategy based on one simple word – survival.

INTELLIGENCE

Geographic Intelligence

We are so used to setting off for a destination, the direction and distance of which we know from maps or experience, and which is indicated, while we travel along well-surfaced roads, by signposts and GPS, that it is difficult to imagine not only a journey without maps but one through a trackless land. Look up at a nearby hill and imagine what it would be like if one did not know what lay on the other side: it could be a river too deep to ford; a lake too wide to cross; a swamp too marshy to traverse; a gorge too wide to bridge; even an ocean leading to Cathay, while the land itself could be inhabited by both savage animals and hostile tribes. That was the world awaiting the English in America, the coastline, the only known feature, an inky squiggle on a chart separating the blank and broad Atlantic from the even blanker inland America, where the unknown lay one tree trunk's width beyond the beach.

With so much of their new world map blank, it is not surprising that imagination seduced when information was absent. The longest, most fruitless imposition of imagination over intelligence was in the search for a passage to Cathay, either through the frozen north or along the continental river system, such as was tried by both Hudson and Newport. Dreams they were, little else, and, as with Ralegh's two expeditions in search of El Dorado, they could soon turn to nightmares.

Yet Ralegh had had the foresight to send spies out to view his promised land of Virginia, only to have them return enthusiastic about the country, but in error about the best point of entry. The Virginia Company of London chose not to carry out such a preliminary and, as a result, its settlers at Jamestown would suffer accordingly. On the other hand, the northern Virginia investors did much coastal investigation but, as with the Nova Scotia and Newfoundland settlements, failed to appreciate the adverse weather conditions that their colonists would have to overcome. Similarly, the *Mayflower* group knew neither the lie of the land, nor the climatic conditions, nor the reaction that they might expect from the local population although having landed in the wrong spot, their lack of intelligence is understandable.

Once ashore there were two sorts of intelligence gathering that the invaders pursued. The first was exploration. Ralph Lane realized the necessity of discovering more about the geography of the surrounding land as soon as he saw the shortcomings of the shallow-watered Roanoke settlement, and his northern investigations are what led to the move to the Chesapeake in 1607. In so doing he was aided by John White, whose map of Virginia, copied by Theodore de Bry for publication in Harriot's *Briefe and True Report*, is a jewel of its genre. Once established in Jamestown, however, imagination again imposed its debilitating, temptingly vacant parchment before the force leaders. Newport wasted resources endeavouring to track a route into the interior and onward to Cathay, while the much more cartographically competent John Smith, produced a beautiful chart of his own inland voyages that could claim to be the basis for future hydrography but, more importantly, aimed to locate alternative sources of food for the besieged settlers. Once published, these maps served greatly to enforce the English claim for ownership by right of occupation and exploration of these lands, but the time spent in compiling them might have better been put to use getting to know the more immediate neighbourhood.

Spanish Intelligence

In the Simancas archive in Spain, two maps of the James and Chesapeake and a detailed sketch of Fort Saint George, all drawn by Englishmen, provide dusty evidence of the extent of Spanish espionage. It was present from the first. Cabot may have only have taken one small step in the new world, but to the Spanish it was a giant one, as in the report sent to the Duke of Milan on 24 August 1498 stating that 'His Majesty sent out a Venetian who is a very good mariner and skilled in discovering new islands. He has returned safe and has found two very large and fertile new islands. He has also discovered the seven cities, 400 leagues from England on the western passage [to Cathay].'

Exaggeration and lies were to become a staple in the reports by the American adventurers and, as can be seen from the above, such dissembling was not limited to the explorers and their backers. The Duke of Milan was impressed and equally so by his feeling that Henry had, 'gained a part of Asia without a stroke of his sword'.

Elizabeth's spymaster Walsingham has rightly won admiration for managing a spider's web of intelligence gatherers that trapped every foul foreign or domestic fly. Yet, he was not unique in an age in which secrets were seldom cloaked with security. Spanish ambassadors flooded their sovereign with information throughout the period of the English invasion, often exaggerating in hope of a response. Thus on 26 April 1582, Don Bernandine de Mendoza wrote to Philip II, stating:

> I have had news today that the ships, which I wrote about to your Majesty were ready to sail have now left and also that Onxiginberto [Humphrey Gilbert] is fitting out three more with which to go to Florida and settle there in a place where Stukeley was and Jean Ribault (the man whom Pedro Menéndez beheaded) with the French. When he asked for the Queen's assistance he was answered in Council that he might go and that when he had landed and fortified the Queen would send 10,000 men to conquer the territory and safeguard the port.

Yet not all of the reports called for action. Following Drake's assault on San Augustine, Alonso Suarez de Toledo wrote to the Crown on 3 July 1586:

> To maintain Florida is merely to incur expense because it is and has been entirely unprofitable nor can it sustain its own population. Everything must be brought from outside. If, although your Majesty possesses San Domingo, Puerto Rico, Cuba,

Yucatan and New Spain, the garrison of Florida has nevertheless suffered actual hunger, what would happen to foreigners there who must bring their sustenance from a great distance to an inhospitable coast? The land itself would wage war upon them! To say that they can maintain a base there from which to damage the fleets is idle talk because from Cape Canaveral (which is at the end of the Bahamas Channel) to Saint Augustine is a bay of fifty leagues and dangerous coast. Let your Majesty improve the harbour instead and fortify it.

All they desired, as Pedro Menéndez Marquéz wrote from the razed Saint Augustine, was for 'His Majesty . . . to send relief quickly or at least to combine the forts in one, which will be reasonably strong, although the corsair is so powerful that everything else is puny in comparison'.

Menéndez Marquéz might not have had the frontier spirit; when he was goaded into taking action, he informed the King that he had 'sailed from Saint Augustine in the same ship which brought the dispatch and with two small boats to carry out these orders', but when he met strong winds which sank a boat and blew him off course he abandoned his journey and returned home, promising to try again the following year. However, the first recorded spying mission that entered the Chesapeake was led by Vincente González in 1588, who, as mentioned above, found evidence of European visits in the form of a slipway, and water butts, but no sign of a permanent settlement.

Even with the peace that followed shortly after James I's succession, the Spanish continued to send probes northward, entering the Chesapeake on several occasions when they were, as discussed earlier, persuaded to depart. Yet, coincident with James's accession in England, Spain was heading into a recessional and political quagmire that necessitated it to concentrate efforts on the European theatre. What is more, Philip III lacked the fiery zeal of his predecessor and thus preferred to ignore rather than act upon intelligence concerning overseas activities that posed no threat to his European domains. Nevertheless, every time sails were sighted in the Chesapeake, the settlers responded with alarm as if the Don was descending on them. Yet, when Spanish spy ships arrived, they were either driven away, as in 1609 when Argall threatened the snooping intruder Francisco de Écija, or had their leading spy captured, as happened when Don Diego de Molina landed off Fort Algernon in 1611. Yet, none of the anticipated assaults took place. Then, in 1618, Spain became embroiled in the Thirty Years War in Europe, which drained both its money and its manpower. It was a struggle that devastated Europe but saved Jamestown.

Local Knowledge

Spanish intelligence gathering was accurate, consistent, regular and a failure; that provided for the English was none of these things and was, ultimately, a success. Few great endeavours in history have begun with so little knowledge of what was achievable, so limited information as to the challenges to be met, and so few resources to achieve success. The English investors and landing parties were succoured (even suckered) by propaganda and seduced by favourable intelligence reports.

Arthur Barlowe, having had his feet and clothes washed by attentive Amerindian maidens, considered his reconnaissance party to have been 'entertained with all love and kindness', by a people who were, 'most gentle, loving and faithful, void of all guile, and treason, and such as lived after the manner of the golden age'. Thomas Harriot reinforced Barlowe's fatal views, stating that that the native peoples, 'in respect of troubling our inhabiting and plantation, are not to be feared, but that they shall have cause both to fear and love us, that shall inhabit with them'.

Harriot also believed that the Amerindians quite appreciated that, when they were slain by the settlers, they had, like naughty schoolboys, deserved their just fate so that 'there is good hope that they may be brought through discreet dealings and government to the embracing of the truth, and consequently to honour, obey, fear and love us'. But not, it should be noted, the other way round.

Amadas and Barlowe, as sojourners, posed little threat to the local population and were thus treated with instinctive hospitality. In a telling couple of sentences, James Axtell summarizes the Amerindian position in relation to the arrival and encroachment of the invaders:

> in every 'Indian' war in colonial America, the warring Indians invariably *reacted* to European provocations, usurpations, or desecrations, arrogations much more specific and serious than mere trespassing on Indian soil. Because quickly outnumbered by the prolific and technologically superior newcomers, the warring tribes or confederacy had to have their collective back to the wall or their stoical patience exhausted before they would risk armed conflict.
>
> Their caution and forbearance were well placed, for once the aggressing colonists felt the sting of attack, they became in their own minds, aggrieved victims, with holy vengeance for their cause. Their retaliations were usually savage, if not particularly swift: their lack of defensive preparations was predicated on their disbelief that anyone could doubt their innocence.

Gaining local knowledge was a major part of intelligence gathering, and in America this was usually provided by young Amerindians who had been kidnapped or otherwise persuaded to sail away with the reconnaissance party to be taught English, civilized, converted and sent back as liaison officers and interpreters. This policy caused two problems: it was difficult for those who had witnessed such events to differentiate between seizure for slavery and kidnapping for conversion, if indeed there was much. In addition, those snatchings that did take place were clustered around the areas identified as possible trading and settlement sites and, although limited in scope, were often brutish in execution, when opportunist raiders, in the absence of readily portable pillage, chose to kidnap people as the only commodity which might attract cash at home. This resulted in both hatred and distrust, a legacy which those who came after were obliged to bear. The practice was widespread. Frobisher on his first voyage of discovery had leant over his ship's side and, with his great strength, hoisted an Inuit, kayak and all, bodily onboard to take back with him. In 1584 Amadas and Barlowe 'brought home also two of the savages being lusty men, whose names were Wanchese and Manteo'.

Further north, Edward Harlow made a typical raiding voyage in 1611, returning to exhibit in London a 'savage' taken from the St Lawrence. His example was followed by Thomas Hunt, who had sailed with John Smith, and kidnapped as many native captives as his ship could hold to sell as slaves to the Spanish. In response, in 1615, the Amerindians fell upon the crew of a French ship wrecked off Cape Cod and either slew or enslaved the survivors.

Four years later Thomas Dermer crossed to New England carrying a survivor of Thomas Hunt's raid, Squanto, who was to prove to be an able interpreter and negotiator for the Plymouth settlers in the following year, although greed and local native politics led to his downfall. Dermer's 1619 voyage was one of the few amicable ones, with goods being exchanged to mutual satisfaction, so much so that Dermer returned the following year, a few months ahead of the Pilgrim Fathers. But this time his reception was far different. In the intervening months another English ship had anchored offshore, invited the Amerindians onboard to trade and then murdered them. To Dermer was meted out revenge; in a series of fights he lost many of his crew and, ultimately, his own life – just one of the many ships' captains who were slain in America.

The second problem for the invaders was whether individuals such as Manteo at Roanoke and Squanto at Plymouth had been truly converted or whether their loyalties still lay with their tribes. This seems to have been the case with Skidwarres who, having been kidnapped by Waymouth in 1605, returned as part of the Fort St George colony on the Sagadahoc River, where he paid back his captors' trust by warning away trading Amerindians and giving false advice to the exploring Englishmen. Squanto appears to have used his position as interpreter and liaison officer between New Plymouth and the *sachem* Massasoit to further his own tribal aspirations, a fence-balancing act that won him the distrust of both sides.

It seems strange that, given the limited understanding of local language, alliances and political and military practices, the English were often able to launch pre-emptive strikes. In 1586 Lane organized a brutal assault against the local *weroance*, or chief, Pemisapan, who, he claimed, was going to attack Fort Ralegh. Yet Lane's intelligence was gathered from a youth called Skyco, the son of King Menatonon, whom he had held imprisoned and shackled for many months as a hostage for his father's good behaviour. Just how Skyco learned of the plan from his closely guarded cell – having twice endeavoured to escape – is not clear, but any information he did give could have either been extracted by duress or freely offered as an ingratiating get-out-of-jail card. Whatever the source or its accuracy, it gave Lane an excuse to lead an amphibious assault on Pemisapan's forces who were gathered across the sound and to kill and behead the King and several of his followers. The following year John White, in a repeat of Lane's pre-emptive strike, made a night raid by water on an Amerindian encampment which turned into a disaster when they discovered that they had opened fire on a group of friendly natives, as described in more detail below.

Such drastic reaction to uncertain intelligence continued and was often justified by reference to the need to strike first, after which the asking of questions was not encouraged. Thus Standish's raid on the Massachusetts, who it was claimed were threatening both Wessagusset and Plymouth, was encouraged by Massasoit, the *sachem* of the rival Pokanoket tribe and the settlers' ally, who would gain much prestige and authority from the destruction of his rivals. The English gained little; their assault and head-severing caused panic among potentially friendly and forage-providing tribes, all of whom now fled into the interior, leaving fields unsown and produce unexchanged, of which the most important for the future prosperity of the settlement was fur. Away from the front line the sagest comment on the un-wisdom of the colonists' action was that passed by their elderly pastor, John Robinson, who wrote to them, 'Oh, how happy a thing had it been if you had converted some before you had killed any! Besides, where blood is once spilled, it is seldom staunched of a long time after. You say they deserved it. I grant it; but upon what provocations and incitements . . .?'

Robinson, who drew his intelligence from wisdom, forecast more war to come, foreseeing that the English would continue throughout Virginia with the morally wrong concept of punishing many for the sins of a few, which would create 'a kind of ruffling course in the world'. Events would prove him right. Unable to live in harmony with their neighbours, time and again the English would use poor intelligence as an excuse for brutal war.

Yet, even when the strife was fiercest the 'heathen people among whom we live' were never spoken of with the vitriol that the English reserved for their fellow Europeans and countrymen of a different persuasion. Nothing, for example, matches these words written by Thomas Windebank, who was serving in King Charles's army during the disastrous invasion of Scotland in 1639:

> We have had a most cold, wet and long time of living in the field but kept ourselves warm with the hope of rubbing, fubbing and scrubbing those scurvy, filthy dirty, lousy, itchy, scabby, shitten, stinking, slovenly, snotty-nosed, logger-headed, foolish, insolent, proud, beggarly, impertinent, absurd, grout-headed, villainous, barbarous, bestial, false, lying, roguish, devilish, long-eared, short-haired, damnable, atheistical, puritanical crew of the Scottish Covenant.

Such a diatribe was infrequent in America, possibly because, with their habit of washing daily, many of such comments would not stick to the smooth-skinned Amerindians.

While the English had limited knowledge of the land that lay before them, the Amerindians had an equally limited understanding of the threat that they were now facing. Few had seen a white man or a sailing ship, heard a cannon's roar or a musket's discharge, watched an axe or a sword cut deep or, most importantly, been subject to a method of warfare that lay well outside their moral ken. In time, although they would glean tactical information, they were never able to extract strategic intelligence, and this was the cause of irreparable harm. However, they soon realized that false intelligence, sprinkled with the temptation of gain, was a favourite food for greedy Englishmen, who could then be used as allies to further local aims, which became more and more important as the demand for initially plentiful products such as furs outstripped local supplies, forcing native trappers to move into the territory of rival tribes. In such ways did European coastal settlements affect alliances far inland.

The Naval Element

The naval element of the amphibious operation was almost a total success, but it did not deserve to be. For a force that had just cause to be wary of the threat from Spain, the first English amphibious force behaved with recklessness: not only sailing into the Spanish-controlled waters of the West Indies but also throwing down a gauntlet by seizing ships and stores. All this was reported back to Spain both by an anxious Governor of Havana, Diego Hernandez de Quiñones, and by one of those hostages taken in the frigate, Don Fernando de Altamirano. Luckily for Lane, their reports indicate that Grenville's company succeeded in disguising from the Spanish both their destination and their purpose. Be that as it may, the presence of a fox in the golden-egg-laying hen house caused great panic, which turned out to be all cluck and no beak.

Yet, given that for many years the preferred British route to Virginia passed through the Spanish West Indies, it is surprising that the settlers and their resupply convoys did not meet much opposition while at sea in those waters, for the Spanish were quite capable of mounting patrols and deploying larger fleets for this purpose, as they did when they endeavoured to destroy the fleet that had sailed under Drake on his last voyage before it could clear the Caribbean into the open waters of the Atlantic. Here, off Cuba in 1596, arguably the first modern sea battle was fought between the English – with Hawkins and Drake both having died weeks previously – under the command of Baskerville and a Spanish fleet of eight galleons and thirteen armed merchantmen. It ended in a goalless draw.

Yet the Spanish never patrolled the Florida Channel where, it was proved, vessels on passage could be taken with ease. On 12 August 1606 Captain Henry Challons sailed from Plymouth in *Richard*, bound for Norumbega (New England), the first ship so to do, following the chartering of the Virginia Company. He chose to follow the traditional southern route and had a quiet passage until, at dawn on 10 November, he found *Richard* surrounded by a fleet of Spanish merchantmen which were also transiting the Florida Channel. Challons produced his papers, expecting to be allowed to continue, but past depredations meant that he and his company were treated as privateers, seized and distributed around the Spanish fleet which, on its homeward voyage, was scattered by storms so that some of the crew were landed and released at Bordeaux while others, much unluckier, found themselves sent to the galleys, where they remained until, after intense negotiations, they were released in November 1608.

Hostilities in southern waters continued, but with the frequency and effect of occasional nettle rash. In February 1620 Anthony Chester, captaining the 160-ton *Margaret and John*, a ship armed with eight cannon and a falconet, and carrying passengers for Virginia, closed Guadeloupe to water, and noticed two vessels lying in the anchorage flying Dutch flags. The wily Chester, suspecting a trick, sent a boat over to investigate, which, on returning, reported that the ships were in fact Spanish men-of-war. Needing time to restow his stores so that his guns could be manned, Chester sent his boat over once again to parley, but this time they were called upon to surrender, which they did not, despite being fired on with such accuracy that some of their oars were smashed.

Shortly afterwards the Spanish admiral weighed anchor and opened hostilities with an exchange of words and a battery of demands which, being refused, caused him to grapple his ship to *Margaret and John* and attempt a boarding which was repulsed with such vigour that his men had to retreat and watch as their grappling lines were axed. Three times the Spanish attacked and three times they were driven off until finally they withdrew, leaving Chester free to engage the consort, which also retired having been blasted by Chester's four available cannon. The next morning an exchange of fierce stares was also won by the British and the Spanish sailed away, their manner of departure indicating to Chester that they had lost many of their crew. *Margaret and John* had eight dead, two mortally wounded and fourteen of her crew badly injured. If we are to believe Chester's description of his adversaries as each being of 300 tons and carrying twenty-two and sixteen guns respectively, then his was a gallant victory over great odds.

Where the sailors were not an asset was ashore. On many occasions they became just idle extra mouths to feed who were quite capable of undermining the shore party by trading with the enemy. Strachey's vitriol is a fair summary:

And for this misgovernment chiefly our colony is much bound to the mariners, who never yet in any voyage hither but have made a prey of our poor people in want, insomuch as unless they might advance four or five for one, how assured soever of the payments of their bills of exchange, they would not spare them a dust of corn nor a pint of beer to give unto them the least comfort or relief, although that beer purloined and stolen perhaps either from some particular supply or from the general store, so uncharitable a parcel of people they be and ill conditioned . . . Besides, to do us more villainy and mischief, they would send off their longboats full by night, and well guarded make out to the neighbour villages and towns and there, contrary to the articles of the fort, which now pronounce death for a trespass of that quality, truck with the Indians giving for their trifles otter skins, beavers, racoon furs, bears' skins, etc., so large a quantity and measure of copper as when the truck master for the colony in the daytime offered trade, the Indians would laugh and scorn the same, telling what bargains they met withal by night . . . I may boldly say they have been a consequent cause this last year to the death and starving of many a worthy spirit.

The criticism, fair as it might be, must be set against the greater truth that, had it not been for the mariners' constant resupply, there would have been many more deaths and starvings.

THE LANDINGS

Once ashore, the invasion force on the whole was badly led and thwarted by failure. In part this is due to the fact that the landings were not considered invasions, for those who waded ashore were not disciplined warriors, led by competent generals with the aim of establishing local military supremacy, but a mishmash of quarrelsome individuals unwelcoming of order, unwilling to work and uncertain of their aims.

The need for an organized soldiery was ignored despite the fact that, in the parallel occupation of Ireland, such a force was deemed essential if the English were to repulse or rout the Irish rebel rabble or, if summoned, to restore and revenge. The better-organized Amerindian clans were not, because they were considered 'savages', felt to offer a serious threat nor expected to feel seriously grieved by the foreign intrusion. The absence of the military in any numbers meant that, in America, every man had to carry weapons for self-defence, a fact which created a citizen militia whose rights to bear arms were eventually enshrined in the controversial Second Amendment to the Bill of Rights. The native peoples, who understandably objected to the seizure of their lands and the sharing of limited resources in time of scarcity, were condemned as obstructive and unhelpful for just the sort of behaviour one might expect from a population witnessing the arrival of an occupying force.

Although no repelling force assembled to challenge the English, they had little reason to misinterpret the response to their arrival. On 20 August 1576, Inuit seized five of Frobisher's men, who were never seen again. On 28 June 1587, just days after they had reoccupied the fort at Roanoke, George Howe, one of White's men, was ambushed while crabbing and pierced by sixteen arrows before being clubbed to death. Coming ashore at Cape Henry on 26 April 1607, Newport's landing party of thirty armed men were charged by the Amerindians, whose arrows wounded Gabriel Archer in both hands and Matthew Morton, a sailor, 'in two places of the body very dangerous'. And this was before the English had done anything to 'offend the naturals', which the Virginia Company had warned them against doing.

In New England similar hostility was created, as it so often was, in response to the offhanded brutishness of casual but constant coastal contacts. In 1501 Gaspar Corte-Real kidnapped over fifty Amerindians from Norumbega; unnamed French traders did likewise and sometimes paid for their behaviour with the loss of both their ships and their lives. In 1614 Thomas Hunt seized twenty-seven natives to sell into slavery while, in 1619, English sailors landed in the region of Cape Cod and killed some of the people of Massasoit, the local ruler. In response the Amerindians had attacked a party landed by Thomas Dermer, who had sailed down the coast from Maine. Although all these Europeans sailed away, they left behind a deadly biological weapon – plague – for in a very short space of time a once-populous shore had become almost empty of people, with deserted villages evidence of the deadly disease.

So, when the *Mayflower* party sent out exploratory groups from Provincetown in November 1620, they could have anticipated an unfriendly encounter. It was a while coming, with both their first and second expeditions discovering evidence of settlement but making no contact with the native population. Then, on their third expedition, which departed in early December and discovered Plymouth Harbour, they landed one evening near where Amerindians had been sighted and decided to raise a barricade about their camp. It was just as well: a false alarm overnight was followed by a dawn assault by Amerindians who loosed off many arrows at the travellers but injured none. Thus, when they returned to *Mayflower*, the news that they had found a settlement site had to be tempered by the report that the first encounter with the natives had not been a friendly one.

FIREPOWER VERSUS STRINGPOWER

Arrogance is a thin armour against assault, yet it provided the breastplate for many of the early invaders. Amadas and Barlowe reported that:

> When we discharged any piece, were it but a harquebus, they would tremble thereat for fear, and for the strangeness of the same: for the weapons which themselves use, are bows and arrows: the arrows are but of small canes, headed with a sharp shell, or tooth of a fish sufficient enough to kill a naked man.
>
> Their swords are of wood hardened: likewise they use wooden breastplates for their defence. They have besides a kind of club, in the end whereof they fasten the sharp horns of a stag, or other beast.

This complacent position was reinforced by Thomas Harriot, who stated:

> If there fall out any wars between us and them, what their fight is likely to be, we having the advantages against them in so many matters, as by our discipline, our

Cannonballs and caltrops. Large-calibre weapons never featured in the English land arsenal, but the sound and fury of the cannon they possessed did much to dissuade would-be attackers, especially when fired from supporting vessels.

strange weapons and devices else, especially ordinance great and small, it may easily be imagined, by the experience we have had in some places, the turning up of their heels against us in running away was their best defence.

No wonder that the English felt supremely confident. Yet, a few days after the 1607 landing at Jamestown, the settlers were in danger of being overwhelmed by this stick-wielding populace and were saved only by a quick-witted sailor discharging a ship's cannon loaded with cross-bar shot that brought down a large branch and scattered the assailants, who fled, leaving most of the defenders with wounds to lick. Conflict had come with *Susan Constant* and would be a perennial attendant, lying dormant for periods of time, but always ready to leap back into life. When it did so, the English would learn that the Amerindians could fight not only with arrows and wooden swords, but held within their armoury weapons such as siege, hunger, fire, ambush and cunning, while the forest with its trees and swamps was as protective of them as any palisade.

In time, both sides appreciated the shortcomings in each other's weaponry. In 1602, two of Gosnold's men wandered away to go crabbing and were 'assaulted by four Indians, who with arrows did shoot and hurt one of the two in his side, the other, a lusty and nimble fellow, leapt in and cut their bow-strings whereupon they fled'.

On the other hand, in 1607, Davies reported that during Raleigh Gilbert's exploratory voyage up the Sagadahoc River, as they pushed off from the shore:

the savages perceiving so much subtly devised how they might put out the fire in the shallop by which means they saw they should be free from the danger of our men's pieces, and to perform the same, one of the savages came into the shallop, and taking the fire brand which one of our company held in his hand, to light the matches . . . as soon as he had gotten it into his hand, he presently threw it into the water and leapt out of the shallop.

It was not many years earlier that archery practice had been compulsory in England for boys from the age of seven. The settlers should thus have well understood the fact that such training was also commonplace in America, with Amerindian mothers not serving their sons breakfast until they had managed to strike the target during their morning archery practice.

It took many years for the English to comprehend and adopt the Amerindian tactics. Woodfighting, with its essential creed of march thin and scatter, was not written up as guidance until Captain Benjamin Church, the very successful New England Amerindian fighter, published his memoirs in 1716. Then in 1757, the founder of the Rangers, Richard Rogers, laid down his rules for this specialist form of warfare in a way that has led to them being described as 'the first written manual of irregular warfare in the New World'. Those gathered at Jamestown and Plymouth had no such guidance and too few men with which to risk experimentation. For them the water was far safer than the woods.

THE WAR OF THE WATERWAYS

So, although in Mexico and Peru Cortés and Pizzaro disembarked and marched their small band of soldiers inland to achieve gold and glory, in North America this option was never available to the invaders, who remained beleaguered at the beachheads, fearful of marching inland where they would never become the Amerindians' equal or masters in fieldcraft. Yet, if fear was the first fruit in every forest, where each narrow track promised ambush, there was one area where, in the words of Richard Hakluyt 'we are the lords of navigation and they are not.' The selection of Roanoke, Jamestown and even Plymouth as settlement sites might have been subjected to criticism but they could not be faulted in being, in regard to the above notion, strategically sound. As rulers of the rivers, the English could use them to trade in time of peace and invade in time of war. The open country of the waterways also gave their marksmen sighting lines that the wooded land would never make available. So it was to the waterways they took whenever there was a need to move away from the protection of their palisades.

Moving by boat had many advantages. Apart from removing the fear of ambuscade, it allowed a reasonable body of men to travel together swiftly and, to some extent in secrecy, without being weighed down by their weapons and supplies. It meant that a small group of men could be inserted close to an objective to carry out an incisive raid and then be withdrawn, without fear of retaliation and before the opposition could respond in force. For the English, the shallop assumed much the same role as the helicopter does today for similar operations.

From his fort on Roanoke Island, Lane had little option other than to respond to a suspected build-up of native forces on the mainland by launching a pre-emptive strike. With the numbers that he had been led to believe were gathering, had he allowed them to cross over to the island there would have been very little likelihood of the colony surviving. He thus ordered the surreptitious destruction of all the Amerindian canoes in the area after sunset to separate the groups on the island from those gathering on the mainland. On this ruse being discovered, Lane decided he must deliver a *coup de main* at the camp of King Pemisapan, where he arrived by boat the next day with all the signs of being on a peaceful mission. However, once disembarked and satisfied with the balance of forces, Lane issued a password at which his men opened fire on the assembled company, causing them to flee. Pemisapan, despite being injured, also attempted to get away but was overhauled in the woods and beheaded, his dripping head being carried back to Lane, a grisly precedent for several other royal killings to come.

A few days later Lane was organizing the evacuation of his troop from Roanoke onboard the ships of Drake's fleet, so there is no way of telling if his strike would have dissuaded the Amerindians from launching another attack. Yet, the following year, the luckless White, who had witnessed Lane's raid, launched a similar operation as an act of revenge for the death of Grenville's soldiers the previous year and the killing of George Howe, ambushed while crabbing. Neither killing could be pinned on the group upon whom White launched his night raid. Rowing quietly towards their small encampment, White led his men through the rushes to the perimeter of the small clearing, from where they opened fire on their enemy, silhouetted around a fire. Except they were not their enemy but friendly Croatoans on a foraging trip, many of whom, including a mother and child, were injured before the English realized their mistake. White reported that there were no hard feelings, an unlikely summary since friendly fire, especially that which harms women and children, has never been easy to forgive, and although the loss of White's people sometime over the next few weeks or months can never be attributed to this incident, it would certainly not have won the invaders allies in a place where they were in sore need of support.

The Jamestown settlers continued the policy of foraging and raiding by water. Time and again the English slipped away from Roanoke or Jamestown to fetch forage that was too dangerous to collect by pathway or to raid a village too difficult to reach overland. John Smith used to conduct negotiations with villagers from the safety of his shallop, persuading them to fill his boat with corn rather than arrows while not being adverse to inflicting damage on those who needed extra encouragement to trade. Negotiations ended, he could slip safely away by water.

There were only two occasions when this dominance of the waterways was challenged. During his exploration voyages up the Chesapeake and its rivers, Smith soon discovered that attack from 'nimble Indians', such as the Rappahannocks, determined to porcupine them and their boats, was most likely in the shallow narrow headwaters where his boats came within easy range of their attackers' arrows. They were even encouraged by signs of friendship to enter such waters where their enemy felt they might be best dealt with. The Nansemond tried this subterfuge, enticing Smith into a narrow passage into which they launched eight canoes filled with warriors to cut off the explorers' retreat while hundreds more lined both banks in anticipation of them being driven ashore. Once more, the advantage of firepower, without the obstacle of trees, proved itself, and Smith, having first driven away the canoeists, opened fire on those on the shoreline to such effect that, on landing, he was able to demand, against the threat of burning the village, 400 baskets of corn, with which he returned triumphantly to Jamestown the following day.

Such narrow escapes did not happen every time. In March 1623, Captain Henry Spelman, a man previously respected by the Patawomecks, among whom he had once lived, sailed up the Potomac to trade. He was met with violence, for, the previous year, a Captain Maddison had kidnapped the local *weroance* (chief) and killed some thirty of his subjects. Spelman and some twenty of his men died, as did the crew of his shallop, which the Amerindians captured. Only the pinnace *Tiger*, standing further offshore, was able to escape, but only after fighting off a determined assault mounted from sixty pursuing canoes.

Breaking Out

If, in Virginia and New England, the English remained confined to their beachheads, they would have had to admit defeat and retreat. Theirs were neither trading posts nor self-sufficient homesteads; they had both mouths to feed and investors to satisfy. To do so they needed to break out, and to do so soon.

In May 1607, President Wingfield gave one of his first, and last, positive instructions when he ordered Captain Newport to take an expeditionary party to explore upstream from Jamestown. Six days, and some eighty miles later, they reached the head of navigation at a place they called the Falls. Here, 'upon one of the little islets at the mouth of the falls [they] set up a cross'. This was not just a symbolic gesture; command of the Falls would be a strategic necessity for those wishing to exercise authority over the lower James. Well aware of this, the English endeavoured to establish themselves here by building a major settlement which they would name Henricus. Many tried, none succeeded. All were defeated by the local tribes.

In the early autumn of 1608 John Smith ordered a well-provisioned Francis West and 140 men upstream to stake a claim to the region. When Smith himself came up to inspect the work he was amazed to find that West, who was absent at the time of his arrival, had selected a site subject to frequent inundation. Unimpressed, he negotiated with the Amerindians to take over an old settlement of theirs built on higher ground, which he named 'Nonsuch'. West reversed that decision, only to find that his 'West Fort' came under such constant attack that it had to be abandoned, having lost many men both in skirmishes and through drowning.

In 1610 De La Warr decided to revive the construction of a fort at the head of the river. He naturally moved his force by water but unwisely ordered some men to travel independently. Thirty-five miles from Jamestown the company were beguiled:

ashore by the savages and beginning to fill their barricoes with water were easily thereunto induced and after enticed by the savages up to their houses pretending to feast them but our men forgetting their subtleties like greedy fools accepted thereof, more esteeming of a little food than their own lives and safety for when the Indians had them in their houses and found a fitting time when they least dreaded any danger did fall upon them slew divers and wounded all the rest who within two days after also died. Only Dowse the Taborer who flying to their boat was hardly pursued but gaining the same he made a virtue of necessity using the Rudder instead of a target to keep their arrows out of his body. And so sculling off by little and little got out of their reach and freed himself.

There is no better indication as to how the balance of power lay between the opposing forces. The English ruled the water, the Powhatans the woods. In the war unleashed by De La Warr, three strategic aims thus emerge, although he did not spell them out: to secure the tideway; to break out of the beachhead and to drive the natives out of the area being occupied by the English. The first was simply the application of one of the *Instructions by Way of Advice* issued by the Virginia Company in 1606, which stated that the settlers 'must in no case suffer any of the natives people of the country to inhabit between you and the sea coast, for you cannot carry yourselves towards them, but they will grow discontent with your habitation . . . if you neglect this, you neglect your safety.'

In May 1611 Dale, returning as Governor, took little time to turn this advice into activity when he transported a force of 100 men by water to assault the Nansemond who dwelt near the mouth of the James. Unusually, the fight was fought in the open, where the English proved to the Amerindians that the tribe could not defeat men with muskets wearing body armour, the efficacy of which was proved when Dale avoided having his head split open by an arrow when it slid off his helmet. Many of the other English, including Francis West and John Martin, were injured, but the Amerindian warriors were slaughtered and their crops and houses burnt. The triumphant English returned to Jamestown by boat.

With the seashore secure, the next stage in these tidewater clearances was the move upstream to construct the new proposed principal town of Henricus, close to where Francis West and De La Warr had had so little success earlier. Dale wished now to obtain a psychological ascendance over the opposition so, in the late summer of 1611, instead of detaching Captain Edward Brewster and his 350 men by boat – which would have been the easier and safer option – he had them march up the riverbank, where they came under constant but ineffective attack from the Amerindians, led by the charismatic Nemattanew, known to the English as 'Jack of the Feathers' for his battle robes of swan's wings and feathered cloaks. Dale himself travelled with the heavy goods, by boat.

Dale chose to build what he wished to be the new capital, on a defensible peninsula jutting into the river. In fifteen days he constructed America's first frontier, as described earlier; it was not just for show, as Strachey explained, for when the Amerindians, 'still continuing their malice against us sent some as spies to our fort who being apprehended my Lord caused one to have his hand cut off and so sent unto his fellows to give them a warning for attempting the like'.

Further fortified settlements were to be established in the area. On the opposite bank to Henricus, Thomas Dale impaled twelve acres at a site he named Coxendale, for which he provided the added protection of four forts which were named Charity, Elizabeth, Patience and Mount Malado. At the mouth of the Appomattox, Bermuda City and Bermuda Hundred were impaled, also from 'river to river', and became the foci for much artisanal activity, but for their main industrial activity the English returned to the Falls, to which, in 1619, some 150 workers were dispatched from England to establish an ironworks. Sadly, there was little iron available for them to work.

When to all this settlement is added the 10,000 acres set aside to create the College Lands, where it was intended to establish a school for the native population, it might be presumed that, by the end of the second decade of the seventeenth century, the English had broken out successfully from the Jamestown beachhead and could claim control of the James River region. They could not.

The Counter-Offensive

Unable to defeat the English in uncoordinated skirmishes, the Powhatans lulled their foes into a sense of security by keeping to the terms of a truce agreed at the time of John Rolfe's marriage to Pocahontas. Behind the bushes they schemed, with their new leader, Opechancanough, even assuring the settlers in early March 1622, in the now-infamous phrase, that, 'the sky should sooner fall than peace be broken . . .' Then, on 22 March, the sky fell when a force of some 600 Powhatan and allied warriors, moving along both banks of the James, slaughtered some 347 settlers in both small and well-populated sites. They destroyed what remained of the almost-abandoned settlement

The well-coordinated Powhatan assault on the James River settlements in March 1622 may well have succeeded in driving the English away for a short period had the attackers laid siege to Jamestown itself. (National Maritime Museum)

of Henricus, killed eighteen people on the College Lands, twenty-seven more at the ironworks, thirteen at nearby Sheffield's plantation, several more at Coxendale; and 'utterly demolished' Bermuda Hundred. Few of the upriver settlements survived the attack; most were voluntarily or forcibly abandoned. The breakout had failed. Elsewhere along the littoral it was not even tried. The shocked survivors fled to the safety of the core settlement at Jamestown which, having been forewarned by a Christian convert, shook off its attackers.

With the James basin secured, Opechanacanough and his men did little to consolidate their advantage. The so-called massacre passed along the river like a tidal bore and petered out. It was no tsunami. Opechanacanough left the survivors shocked and later starving, but undisturbed to plot their revenge. The reason for his failure to follow up his success remains a mystery. The real losers were the Powhatan people, against whom the settlers were now able to wage total retaliatory war without fear of criticism.

In England, the beleaguered Virginia Company acted hastily to pin the blame for the violence on the colonists themselves for their simplistic dealings with the sly savages, and thus divert attention from their own shortcomings. Their letter penned to the colony by return contained the following attribution of blame:

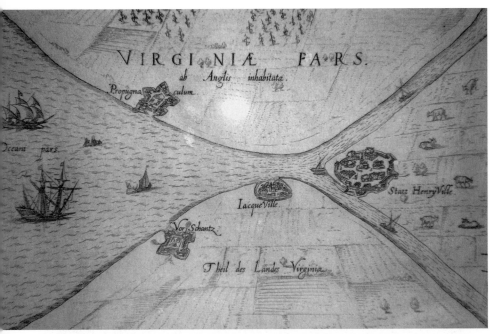

The Jacobus Francus map of 1613 clearly shows the major fortified settlements along the James River some nine years before the Indian massacre.

We have to our extreme grief understood of the great massacre executed on our people in Virginia, and that in such a manner as is more miserable than the death itself, to fall by the hands of men so contemptible; to be surprised by treachery in a time of known danger . . . and almost guilty of the destruction by a blindfold and stupid entertaining of it; which the least wisdom or courage sufficed to prevent.

It was an unsatisfactory state of affairs, which was acknowledged in the Virginia Company's official report by Edward Waterhouse, which stated that:

Because our hands which before were tied with gentleness and fair usage, are now set at liberty by the treacherous violence of the savages, not untying the knot, but cutting it: So that we, who hitherto have had possession of no more ground than their waste, and our purchase at a valuable consideration to their own contentment, gained; may now by right of war, and law of nations, invade the country and destroy them who sought to destroy us; whereby we shall enjoy their cultivated places, turning the laborious mattock into the victorious sword.

Thus, at long last, did the provoked English admit openly what they had long acknowledged privily: that they had invaded a foreign nation whose inhabitants, so different from themselves, they would have to subdue, slaughter, enslave or drive away if they were to establish a new world that was in keeping with their ambitions. In this there could be no compromise or integration.

The Government's reaction to the massacre gives a clear insight to the position that the colony held in the royal scheme of things. It was not great. In response to the killing of over 300 of his citizens, the King authorized the release from the royal armoury of 1,000 halberds, 700 light muskets, 300 harquebus, 300 pistols, some ancient suits of armour and 400 bows with 800 sheaves of arrows, which latter, for understandable concerns that they might fall into the wrong hands, were diverted to Bermuda. This cobwebbed materiel was acknowledged to consist of 'old cast arms . . . altogether unfit, and of no use for modern service'.

The anonymous advisor to Walter Ralegh had proposed, in 1584, the following humane laws should be applied when dealing with local population:

* First that no soldier do violate a woman.
* That no Indian be forced to labour unwillingly.
* That none may strike or misuse an Indian.
* That none shall enter any Indian house without his leave.

In close encounters Indian arrows did little damage to armoured Europeans who, knowing this, could, like Champlain in this drawing, close to lethal range with their muskets.

Apart from the first, the total war that was unleashed negated such desire for harmony. There was to be no more fraternization – the one policy that could have induced harmony – which, Wyatt reminded the Company in his reply, had formed part of the 'instructions you have formerly given us, to win the Indians to us by a kind entertaining of them in our houses, and if it were possible to cohabit with us . . .' Be that as it might have been, by 23 January 1623 Wyatt was able to report that the invaders:

> have slain divers, burnt their towns, destroyed their weirs and corn . . . It is most apparent that they are an enemy not suddenly to be destroyed with the sword by reason of their swiftness of foot, and advantages of the wood . . . but by the way of starving and all their means that we can possibly devise we will constantly pursue their extirpation.

After the heinous poisoning of the Amerindians who had gathered to discuss peace in May 1623 (discussed below), Virginia's southern colony assumed an ascendency over the Amerindians that they were not going to relinquish. Governor Wyatt declared, 'our first work is expulsion of the savages to gain free range of the country for it is infinitely better to have no heathen among us . . . than to be at peace and league with them.' In 1624 both sides met for the first time in what approximated to a conventional European battle. For this the Powhatans mustered 800 Pomunkey bowmen to meet just sixty Englishmen who had arrived, in comfort and without fear of ambuscade, by boat. The two-day battle ended with the survivors of the defeated tribe watching ruefully as their corn and their villages were put to the flame. The English then re-embarked for the safe passage home.

Although a two-year hiatus followed because of an English shortage gunpowder, there was no doubt that hostilities would be renewed, and in the summer of 1627 amphibious raiding parties landed all along the Chesapeake estuaries to scorch the earth around the Amerindian villages and to kill all who chose not to flee. Although fighting continued into the next decade, only ending in 1646, when the centenarian Opechancanough was captured and murdered in captivity, the war had been won on the morning of 23 March 1622 when the English survivors of the James River massacre took stock and found their assailants had slipped away, leaving them weakened in numbers but strong enough to plan and execute total revenge.

Back at Wessagusset the maverick settlers were now starving, for they had bartered all they had for handfuls of provisions, earning Amerindian scorn for their scavenging ways and willingness to enslave themselves for scraps of food. Some of them even moved from the fort to the wigwams in a form of forced adoption, none endeavoured to rally their indigent comrades. At least that is the conventional colonial record of their circumstances. It is as leaky a yarn as the elderly beech-bark Amerindian canoes that the reportedly despised Wessagusset community was repairing for their neighbours. However stark their circumstances, the settlers did not choose the simple option of re-embarking in *Swan* and sailing for the safety of Plymouth. In fact, Standish, arriving in response to the raised alarm, found the ship, which, moored in the harbour, offered the most secure protection for the threatened community, empty while the men, oblivious to any evil intent, wandered around the native village, which would indicate that their straits might not have been as dire as others wished to believe. Yet, as the rumour of an impending Amerindian attack spread, one man, Phineas Pratt, had fled from the fort and made the dangerous overland journey to Plymouth to seek support. Having 'been pursued for his life in time of frost and snow as a deer is chased by wolves', he arrived just ahead of the following braves and pleaded for support for his friends. The swift response might suggest that the Pilgrims had already decided on a pre-emptive strike, for on 25 March, the day after Pratt's dramatic arrival, Miles Standish, with eight men, embarked to sail the day-long journey to Wessagusset.

On disembarking, disgusted with the state of affairs, he first summoned the dispersed settlers and ordered them back inside the stockade, where a few handfuls of wheat from the boat staved off their hunger pangs. Standish then went in search of Pecksuot, the local chief, who reacted in a way made famous through the centuries by, amongst others, Longfellow's poem 'The Courtship of Miles Standish',

> Then he unsheathed his knife, and, whetting the blade on his left hand,
> Held it aloft, and displayed a woman's face on the handle,
> Saying, with bitter expression and look of sinister meaning:
> 'I have another at home, with the face of a man on the handle;
> By and by they shall marry; and there will be plenty of children!'

Both men, it seems, perfectly understood the veiled threat in Pecksuot's words and, in a pre-emptive *coup de main* Standish invited a delegation of four to return for dinner. Once they were seated Standish drew his knife and stabbed Pecksuot. Wituwamat and another Amerindian were also killed, while the fourth, an eighteen-year-old, was hanged. Standish then turned on the natives in the fort, killing seven while the eighth escaped, hotly pursued, to raise the alarm, allowing his friends to escape into the woods. Such ferocity quashed any plan for an Amerindian strike against Wessagusset which, nevertheless, was disbanded, with one group sailing in *Swan* to Maine while the other chose to return with Standish to Plymouth, where the head of Wituwamat was impaled on a stake beside the blockhouse. Thus ended what may have been the first genuine attempt of the two communities to live side by side, although Standish and his colleagues probably considered it to be more important that they had disposed of a settlement that was rival to their own.

From then on, until the civil rights dream became reality, the North American continent was a world at war, as people tried to convert this land from 'their land' to 'our land'. Timelines can list conflicts with both start and end dates, but the actuality was that in between periods of open warfare there were only times of uneasy truce observed from hostile camps. The English, convinced of the rightness of their cause, failed to grasp this inevitability, which meant that from their arrival in 1585 onwards, they neither regarded themselves as invaders, nor the Amerindians as defenders of this bountiful world whose brilliant potential future both could have shared.

War Crimes or Harsh Times

The English departing for America were leaving behind a killing continent across whose open spaces great armies had clashed for many centuries. Although the Church had endeavoured to assert some sort of moral code upon the combatants by defining a just war, this held little sway for two reasons. The first was that it did not apply to the 'heathen', the second was that the very size of these armies meant that they had to live off the land across which they moved, pillaging from the peasantry; where pillage took place so did slaughter and rape. Thus a continent that claimed to be the centre of civilization had the greatest concentration of armed, and often uncontrolled, force in the world. So, although Shakespeare could have the Welshman Fluellen exclaim in *Henry V* (published 1598): 'Kill the poys and the luggage! 'Tis expressly against the law of arms. 'Tis as arrant a piece of knavery . . . as can be offert. In your conscience now, is it not?' Few might have agreed with him: the 'gallant' King Henry's response was to cut the throats of all his prisoners.

In 1580 the Spanish garrison at Smerwick in Ireland surrendered to Lord Grey, who had all the 600 occupants slain, including the women and children. In charge of the slaughter was Walter Ralegh. It would be wrong, however, to consider that the atrocities came from one side only. In 1641 the Irish, rose up against their Protestant intruders and, at Portadown in County Armagh, they herded several hundred Protestant men, women and children to the banks of the river Bann, where they were forced to strip before being forced at pike-point into the icy water, where they either drowned or had their heads beaten in with oars. One survivor, Elizabeth Price, saw five of her children murdered in this way. Something similar happened in America, but not on the same scale.

In 1610, during De La Warr's savage war against the Powhatans, raiding parties were dispatched from Jamestown to fall without warning and with extreme violence on the neighbouring settlements. Among these was one led by George Percy, who, sailing to the mouth of the Chickahominy, led his men three miles inland to attack the Paspaheghs, fifteen or sixteen of whom they killed and decapitated, after which, having set fire to the village, they returned to the boats with the captured Queen and her two children. Once afloat Percy allowed his men to throw the children overboard and use them for musket practice, the soldiers 'shooting out their brains in the water.' Which left the Queen, whose living arrival so disgusted De La Warr, that he ordered her to be burnt. Shocked by such a callous inhumanity, Percy, her captor, decided it were better that his lieutenant take her into the woods and put her 'to the sword'.

There was one other incident which would stand out as a war crime in whatever age it was committed. On 23 May 1623 a small delegation of Jamestown settlers sailed up the Pamunkey River to solemnize a peace treaty and exchange prisoners with Opechancanough, who was waiting for them with a large contingent of his own tribe. After much speechifying and signs of bonhomie, William Tucker proposed a toast be drunk from a barrel of white wine that the colonists had brought with them. It had been laced with poison by Dr John Pott. Several hundred of the Amerindians died in agony, a further fifty, incapacitated, were shot. A clearer statement of intent by the now-dominant English could not have been made; from now on this was to be a war of extermination.

If it is considered that the English behaved deplorably towards the Amerindians because of any particular disrespect for them as 'savages', then a glance at what was happening at the same time in Europe provides a balance. In the Thirty Years War, from 1618 to 1648, Europeans perpetrated on civilian and soldiery, young and old, women and men, town, country, crops and livestock, such abominations that the term 'civilization' should forever be expunged from any reference to seventeenth-century Europe.

There is one atrocity, a constant companion of European warfare, that appears absent from America during the invasion, and that is battlefield rape. European soldiery considered it a reward for their work, and – if that were not bad enough – it was often accompanied by drink-inflamed added violence. To take but one, mild, example from the Thirty Years War:

> In Olmütz the daughters of the richest burghers were forcibly married to careerist army officers at the request of their colonel. In Thuringia a father who appealed for justice against a soldier who had raped and killed his daughter was coarsely informed by the commanding officer that if the girl had not been so niggard of her virginity she would still be alive.

Strangely, the Amerindians might have sympathized or identified with the colonel. Along the littoral a rule of war appears to have existed by which women and children were spared the club and taken into captivity as slaves, adoptees or wives, to boost the numbers reduced by disease and war. Yet the settlers appear not to have practised licentious rape, the fear of which Shakespeare reflected in *The Tempest*, with Caliban being accused by Prospero of seeking 'to violate the honour of my child'.

Anecdotal evidence would indicate that the European idea of extermination was as alien an introduction to America as was plague, smallpox and measles. Yet, like those dire diseases, there is no evidence that, in their treatment of their American foes the English introduced a way of behaviour that they were not familiar with in Europe. Indeed, as mentioned earlier, before the age of slavery there is much to suggest that the English hated none more than those who held to a different Christian creed, and it was for them – the Irish, the Scots, the recusants – for whom they reserved their most poisonous vitriol and most peculiar punishments.

The evidence indicates that the clashes during the early occupation of America, including the torching of villages and the 1622 'massacre' along the James River, were not abnormal for the period. They certainly did not involve unusual degrees of 'atrocity' or even 'genocide', as is sometimes stated. Sadly, there is little in the inhumanity of either side which did not fall within the range of the bestial norm that the age employed to mete out unpleasantness to a nation's enemies on either side of the ocean. A most succinct summary was made by William Strachey, who wrote: 'Certainly the miseries of war are never so bitter and many as when a whole nation, or great part of it, forsaking their own seats, labour to root out the established possessions of another land, making room for themselves, their wives and children . . . The merciless terms of this controversy arm both sides with desperate resolution.'

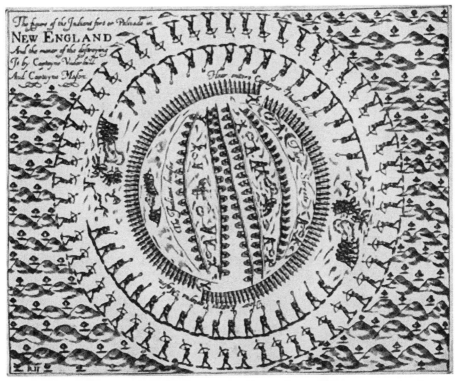

An incident in the Pequot War, 1637. John Underhill's drawing of the attack on the Pequot fort at Mystic shows the English, allied with Amerindians, opening fire on the defenders and those trying to escape. Interestingly, no Amerindians are shown armed with muskets. Over three hundred Pequot were slain at the cost of two English dead; even their allies protested that such warfare was wicked because 'it is too furious and slays too many men'.

Yet, at no time did the English admit that the Amerindians were fighting for the right to hold onto their land and their way of life. Rather, it was the invader who justified his behaviour, while those who would opposed his advance were considered scheming, cruel and untrustworthy rogues who had no right to call their own the land through which they merely roamed. Without such an acknowledgement the idea of a peace treaty between equals was a very difficult concept to grasp but, on occasions, such mutuality was attempted.

EARLY TREATIES

Of course, the English would have preferred to take what they wanted without having to fight for it but, although trade depends on mutual agreement, the occupation and acquisition of land leads inevitably to dispute, especially when both claim ownership by right. In Roanoke and early Jamestown, agreements were reached but not confirmed as treaties to be observed by both parties. Even the marriage of Rolfe and Pocahontas was seen as a reason for a truce rather than signifying a marriage contract that would unite two peoples, as would have been the case in a similar ceremony in Europe. Rather than following the biblical story of Ruth and Naomi, in which it was agreed that 'thy people shall be my people', the American way harked back to an earlier Eden when the Lord declared, 'I will put enmity between . . . thy seed and her seed.' Sadly, it would be disingenuous to consider that any treaty between the English and the Amerindians was entered into for any other reason than to gain time for the strength to overthrow the enemy. That is, all but one. The agreement reached between Governor Carver and Sachem Massasoit in March 1621 remains a fine example of how two potentially hostile people could live in peace if not mutual trust. A summary of its terms stated:

1. That neither Massasoit nor any of his men should do hurt to any of the settlers.
2. That if any of his did hurt any of theirs, he should send the offender, that they might punish him.
3. That if anything were taken away from any of theirs, he should cause it to be restored; and they should do the like to his.

A drawing by Champlain showing him leading his allies, the Algonquins, Hurons and Montagnais in July 1609, against the Iroquois, who, having exited their hastily built stockade, fled when two of their number were shot by Champlain.

4. If any did unjustly war against him, they would aid him; if any did war against them, he should aid them.
5. He should send to his neighbours and confederates to certify them of this, that they might not wrong them, but might be likewise compromised in the conditions of peace.
6. That when their men came to them, they should leave their bows and arrows behind them as we should do our pieces when we came to them.
7. That King James would esteem Massasoit as his friend and ally.

Edward Winslow, one of the senior members of the community and a leading and trusted negotiator with the Amerindians, concluded his account of the treaty signing as follows:

> We cannot yet conceive, but that he is willing to have peace with us, for they have seen our people sometimes alone two or three in the woods at work and fowling, when as they offered them no harm as they might easily have done, and especially because he hath a potent adversary the Narragansetts, that are at war with him, against whom he thinks we may be some strength to him . . .

The seven clauses of the treaty could have achieved a mutual peace had not the twin imps of land acquisition and local politics caused both sides to revoke their side of the bargain. Then, when things turned sour, a much older covenant was invoked to justify the invaders' behaviour now they had entered the land which they felt the Lord their God had given unto them. This was the Old Testament account of the children of Israel entering the Promised Land and the harsh way in which they dealt with the original occupants in response to the 'convenient' word of God.

Eight months after the treaty was signed with Massasoit the settlers found that, for all its peaceful intentions, an alliance with one tribe would mean, as Winslow forecast, a falling out with another. In November the Narragansett people delivered to them the unmistakable threat in the form of a bundle of arrows wrapped within a rattlesnake skin. Bradford's bold response in kind, as recounted earlier, gained the settlers time to build their palisade.

The men who had pallisaded Plymouth had no time to admire their efforts. In the spring of 1622, via a 'boat which came from the eastward . . . from a stranger of whose name they had never heard before, being a captain of a ship come there a-fishing', they received a letter by way of a warning telling them of the massacre of the Jamestown settlers. That 'stranger', Captain John Huddleston, also provided the settlers with bread to supplement their meagre ration as they strove, under Bradford's urging, to build a fort inside their stockade, which took most of the year to construct. At the same time, another tiny group of settlers, led by Thomas Weston, the Merchant Adventurer who had double-crossed the Pilgrims back in Europe, had arrived and moved twenty-two miles up the coast to Wessagusset, modern Weymouth. They too built a fort there in anticipation of trouble, which duly arrived by way of Amerindians gathering outside the walls and yelling threateningly at the cowed and hungry defenders. By now rumour was hard at work and the evidence mounting to indicate that the Massachusetts intended to massacre the inhabitants of both settlements in concurrent raids.

Standish, as has already been described, led a raiding party north from Plymouth to Wessagusset, where he perpetrated a bloody pre-emptive strike. Further killings followed, with the result that, although the threat was lifted, the settlers lost their trading partners while the Amerindians, driven into the marshes, forfeited their livelihood and lives. Standish returned in triumph with the head of his foe, Wituwamat, tied up in a blanket. He skewered it onto one of the posts of Plymouth Fort, thus continuing a bloody policy that had begun when Lane was presented with the head of King Pemisapan in 1586. Ninety years later, on 17 August 1676, the severed head of the quartered King Philip, sachem of the Pokanokets, was stuck on one of the palisades close to where that of Wituwamat had been displayed. It was to remain there for two decades, briefly joined by the heads of two of his leading warriors, Annawon and Tuspaquin. Not much had changed in the relationship between the invaders and the native peoples in these fifty-plus years, except that there could by now be no doubt, as there had been in the 1620's, as to the eventual outcome.

THE PRICE OF SUCCESS

The long recessional of the Amerindians lasted centuries, but the more immediate losses suffered by the settlers rank with the worst endured by any group of Britons standing into danger. In the Second World War Bomber Command lost 55,573 airmen out of a total force of 125,000 (44.4 per cent); the Merchant Navy lost about 32,000 from a total strength of 185,000 while in the Battle of Britain 17 per cent of British fighter pilots died in combat. By comparison: all 155 of those left behind at Roanoke in 1587 were presumed dead; the Jamestown settlement lost 70 of 108 settlers in its first year, and 440 out of 500 during the Starving Time, while, between 1619 and 1622, out of the 3,600 settlers transported by the Virginia Company, over 3,000 died in that same period. In 1619, of the 180 emigrants that sailed out of Emden under the leadership of Blackwell, 130 had died by the time they reached America.

Devastating though these losses were, the English could sustain them and replace the fallen. Not so the Amerindians, whose small tribes and loose-knit confederations were never able to engage in a war of attrition. Although they could adapt their tactics to minimize the effect of firearms, could even become better in their use than were the invaders, there were two enemies whom they could not surmount: disease and crop-plundering, both waterborne.

Once control of the sea approaches could be guaranteed so that supplies could be safely delivered, the outcome was inevitable, for the Amerindians could delay but not dam the incoming tide of Englishmen who, having arrived on the neap, ebbed only to return on the flood. Defeating the invader could only ever have been a temporary and local triumph for a population which was ill-prepared, loosely organized, too disunited and dispersed to do other than irritate rather than eradicate those who would destroy their way of life. And, to the shame of the invaders, it was the Amerindians' virtues rather than their vices, their innocence and hospitality, that were used against them, especially at those critical moments when the beachheads were being established. Yet, in the end it was micro-organisms, not military might, that led the main assault: while conflicts decimated, disease destroyed.

By 1630 the English still possessed only limited control of a small area of land. The Amerindians had had the chance to evict them even from these confined beachheads but had failed so to do. The opportunity would not come again. From then on they would wage wars that they could not win. These would be defensive and, increasingly, desperate, with the retention of pride not of land being their noble aim.

CHAPTER 12

Piracy

None make greater pirates than the English   Seventeeth-century saying

Throughout the Tudor and Stuart period the most dangerous place to meet an Englishman whilst on one's lawful occasion was upon the sea lanes that ran along the coast. Here morality was balanced by weight of shot, and fear of being caught no impediment in a nation where even the Lord High Admiral, the man charged with controlling and capturing corsairs, owned his own pirate fleet. From this pirate fleet's handsome returns the Admiral paid bribes to the Admiralty Court who were meant to pass judgment on maritime miscreants whose behaviour he well might have, earlier, condoned by presenting them with a royal letter of marque to give to their vessels a veneer of virtue. In this, the involvement of the Crown, which meant such men could be referred to as privateers rather than pirates, England showed itself to be more of a pariah state than present-day Somalia, whose pirates operate completely outside the authority and control of that ineffective state – legalized theft remains theft. Yet, these men, Effingham, Grenville, Ralegh, Drake, Frobisher and many less well known, have been the childhood heroes of many generations of English, who have been thrilled to hear of their exploits and read about their fictional versions in gems such as *Treasure Island*. However, they had their honour: the force that fought the Armada was led by these pirates, many of whom had made a major financial contribution to the nation's always-precarious coffers. Naturally, they made a fortune for themselves as well, and if, like the Earl of Cumberland, they also lost it, they did so in style, on wine and women and horses, after which – like any wild rover – they went to sea again

For the Spanish, trying to ship gold and silver from Potosi's mines and elsewhere to Seville, pirates were as ever present and annoying as the infernal mosquito. They cursed corsairs such as Drake, active in both their oceans, eliminated those like Oxenham, whom they captured, and formed convoys to deter and to defend their goods from the hated swarms. Not so the English, for whom piracy and privateering were as legitimate a way of gaining fame and fortune, and more reliable, as settling in a new world and seeking out their own mines. The English went fossicking in frigates as frequently as they sought their fortune in imagined mines, and with far greater success.

The maritime adventurers involved in the invasion of America were all privateers by profession and pirates by inclination. Cabot was an exception: coming from a mercantile state, he had built a career on honest trade. Drake amassed the wealth with which he returned from his circumnavigation from seized Spanish ships, not from the gold of California, which lay hidden for several more centuries. Frobisher, a reformed pirate, on his northern voyages, where plunder was not possible, returned home poor with just tons of worthless aggregate to show for his efforts. Ralegh, under strict instruction

This painting, dating from 1616, shows a fictional event with an English pirate ship attacking a Dutch vessel. Most such pirates swept their horizon for a sight of a homeward-bound Spaniard or Portuguese East Indiaman. (National Maritime Museum)

not to act the pirate on his second Guiana voyage, similarly arrived back broke. For the English the wealth of the new world lay, demonstrably, in the holds of other people's ships. And that wealth was not just in precious metals – a cargo of fish, removed from the rightful owner, could also 'make' a voyage.

The close link between piracy and plantations is clearly evident in the preparations that Humphrey Gilbert made for his first voyage, despite his vague instructions directing that if he committed any act of hostility by sea or land against any subjects of any ruler in amity with England he was to make restitution on pain of the annulment of his authority. Whatever his aims, whether to explore, settle or conquer, Mendoza, the Spanish ambassador, was convinced that they included an attack on the Indies. Certainly the eleven ships that Gilbert assembled, their previous deployments and their present owners all supported Mendoza's view that a harmless exploration was not the full intention.

That fleet had begun assembling in the spring. By the summer the notoriety of the commanders led the Privy Council to order a halt to the plans to prepare the fleet in a warlike manner. This concern was shared by the Commissioners for Piracy in Wales, who reported that *Elephant*, captained by the known pirate, John Callis, was being equipped in just such a way. As if to confirm with contempt those concerns, shortly after *Elephant* joined Gilbert in Dartmouth she sailed with Henry Knollys, Gilbert's second-in-command, into the Channel, where they seized the pirate Robert Holbourne and brought him and two of his well-laden prizes into Plymouth. The pirate they released, the goods they disposed of. This behaviour, along with Knollys's refusal to hand over to the authorities two of his men accused of murder, may have led to a breach with Gilbert, for on 18 November Knollys in *Francis*, in company with *Elephant* and *Bark Denyse*, sailed one day ahead of Gilbert's main body and, abandoning all intention to go exploring, carried out a pirating voyage off the coast of Ireland and Spain.

Gilbert's force did not behave thus, but they carried 122 guns and 409 men, sufficient strength to challenge any Spanish ships of war at sea or capture any cargo vessel that strayed into their path. They were not, however, ships with unblemished sails. The following year *Red Lion*, captained by Miles Morgan, was operating in company with Knollys when they seized the French ship *Mary*. A short while later *Red Lion* foundered and Morgan was drowned, but the French accused Gilbert of involvement in *Mary*'s seizure. With the voyage abandoned in 1578 and Gilbert determined to sail again, the Privy Council again intervened, in April 1579, 'revoking of him from his intended journey at the seas' because of the piratical behaviour of his associates. As if to cock a snook at the authorities, before his intended departure Gilbert's men made off from Dartmouth in a Spanish ship loaded with oranges and lemons. On 28 May the Council wrote to Gilbert and Ralegh telling them 'to surcease from proceeding any further and to remain at home and answer such as have been by their company damaged'. This was followed, three days later, by a letter to the Commissioner for Piracy, ordering him to carry out investigations into all the acts of piracy reported to have been committed by those who 'pretended to accompany' Gilbert and his team. In addition, the troublemaking expeditionary force was to be told to disperse to their homes. Eventually, implicitly acknowledging their impotency, the Privy Council hired Gilbert's force to sail to Ireland to intercept a continentally equipped group of Irishmen led by James Fitzmaurice, who were reported to be heading for Ireland. Gilbert used this opportunity to raid Galicia and thus he missed Fitzmaurice's force, which sailed unmolested to Kerry, where they reinforced the headland at Smerwick and where, the next year, they greeted further Spanish reinforcements who were later, every one of them, contrary to the rules of war, to be massacred.

On his final voyage of 1583 Gilbert sailed with five ships, of which only the smallest, *Squirrel*, was his own. *Swallow* he acquired through intercepting the pirate John Callis in the Channel returning home with two French prizes which Gilbert freed while seizing *Swallow*, which was the legal property of a Scottish merchant. However, Gilbert managed to mist over the waters of her whereabouts and retain her for his use. The third ship, *Golden Hind*, had spent 1580 and 1581 on piracy voyages, the sort of deployment that Ralegh envisaged for his own contribution to the expedition, *Bark Ralegh*. Only the ill-fated *Delight*, owned and commanded by William Winter, the son of the surveyor of the navy, Sir William Winter, could claim to be free of the pirate's stain. Yet, although the mission was non-piratical, old habits died hard and, off St John's, Newfoundland, *Swallow* stopped a ship to lighten her of the clothing and food she carried.

While Gilbert was sailing and failing, Ralegh's *Bark Ralegh*, having abandoned the expedition early on in the voyage, was making a fortune at sea from piracy. Others of his fleet such as *Bark Burton* brought home from one voyage alone goods to the value of £10,000 while *Pilgrim*, commanded by Ralegh's senior pirate, Jacob Whiddon, landed seized cargo valued at £500. *Ark Ralegh*, built as the flagship of Ralegh's pirate fleet and at the time the most powerful English ship afloat, was to win everlasting fame when, with her name changed to *Ark Royal*, she joined the royal fleet in time to fight the Spanish Armada. With such a fleet and with such sea captains available to him, it was most unlikely that Ralegh would turn his and their attention solely to settlement once he had been bitten by the Virginia bug.

Indeed they did not. Sir Richard Grenville, disregarding the need for caution, sailed the first colony fleet along a route on which he knew prizes might lie. He managed to seize two on the outward journey, preferring wealth to stealth, and on the homeward leg the voyage was 'made' when, for want of a conventional craft, he boarded a Spanish ship in a boat made hastily from a ship's chest, which fell apart as he scrambled up the side of the prize. The slapstick nature of its capture was forgotten when it was found that *Santa Maria* was 'richly laden with sugar, hides, spices and some quantity of gold, silver and pearl'. She was on lone passage because, although having been the flagship of a *flota* of seventeen when they had sailed out of Santo Domingo, rough weather had dispersed the fleet and she, being a poor sailer, had been unable to catch up with her companions. Seeing a sail bearing down on her she thought it was one of her scattered flock, only to discover – too late for her defence – that it was a foreign wolf and not a Spanish sheep which was snapping at her heels. The Spanish claimed that the gold, silver and pearl on their inventory were worth more than 40,000 ducats, while the sugar, hides and spices added another 120,000 ducats in value.

Grenville, either preferring the luxury of *Santa Maria*, or nervous about letting the treasure out of his sight despite transferring most of her victuals into *Tyger*, continued his journey in the prize. This involved masquerading as a Spaniard in order to obtain supplies at Flores where, having been provisioned, he released his captives and sailed for England. Here, finding a need to justify his behaviour, he wrote a most memorable tongue-in-cheek memorandum stating, 'In my way homewards I was encountered by a Spanish ship, whom assaulting me and offering me violence, God be thanked, with defence and safety of myself and all my company, after some fight I overcame and brought into England with me; her lading is ginger and sugar.'

The 400-ton *Santa Maria* was worth, even by Grenville's cautious estimate, some £15,000, while the Spanish exaggerated value of the cargo was placed at 160,000 ducats which, at six shillings to the ducat, would make it worth – let alone the ship and its fittings – £48,000 (about £6 million at today's rates). Even after the Lord Admiral had taken his tenth and Customs their share, and with the owners, victuallers and crew paid off, there was more than enough money to pay Lane and his men and still leave a profit of several million pounds (in today's money). By way of contrast, the sassafras unloaded by Archer in 1602, which was priced at 3s a pound, would have realized gross, £330. No clearer indication exists of the value of voyage plunder compared with the return from the settlements themselves.

Whatever the amount realized from the prize, and Grenville was determined to underestimate its worth, that one act of piracy clearly demonstrated to Ralegh that, for the moment, true fortune was to be made at sea. The next year, while Grenville was sailing on his relief mission to Roanoke, Ralegh dispatched *Mary Spark* and *Serpent* on a raid, the value of which belied the diminutive size of the vessels involved. Besides the cargo in the hold, the crew captured several high-ranking Spaniards, including Don

Pedro Sarmiento de Gamboa, who had the misfortune to be the Governor of cold and distant Patagonia. Ralegh's machinations and attempted double-dealings linked to Sarmiento's release lie outside this work, but what does not is that, during his time as Ralegh's guest, he introduced the greedy dreamer to the story of the 'great and golden city' of El Dorado that lay awaiting the bold adventurer up the Orinoco. Thirty years later this Sarmiento's nephew, Don Diego Sarmiento, Count Gondomar, while Spanish ambassador to the Court of King James, was instrumental in bringing about the former favourite's fall.

For the time being, Ralegh made golden hay with his deep-sea harvesters. In April 1591 some ships belonging to Peter de Hody, a merchant of Bayonne, returning from Newfoundland with 108,000 dry fish, 4,000 fresh fish and 14 hogsheads of train oil, with a total value of £1,500, were taken by a ship belonging to Ralegh and shepherded into Bristol where, despite correct pleas of foul play, the senior captain was held for eight months.

Ralegh, well aware of the bitter experiences that John White suffered while endeavouring to return to Roanoke, knew how much piracy was detrimental to colonial ambitions, but he continued with this money-creating option. By such behaviour he made a mockery of his epithet the 'Shepherd of the Ocean', behaving more like a wolf in sheep's clothing. The reciprocal response followed a predictable track and, in August 1592, Ralegh reported to the Privy Council that twenty ships of war were lying between Ushant and Scilly to intercept Newfoundland men and that this threat should be met by dispatching a fleet or else 'we shall lose all and be the scorn to all nations'. Decades of assault against the Newfoundland fishing fleet carried out by pirates of all nations, including the English, who had no qualms about preying on their own kind, were to follow.

In 1596, a Richard Clarke reported an act of piracy committed against his vessel in Newfoundland waters by a cunning Frenchman, Michael de Sancé, who began his escapade by inviting Captain Clarke to breakfast onboard his vessel and then agreeing to return to the Englishman's ship the next day for dinner. However, pleading sickness, the Frenchman, asked Clarke to return to minister to him and then, at a prearranged signal 'the Frenchmen crying "*Rend vouz, Rend vouz*"', Clarke and his men were taken and kept prisoners nine days'. When they eventually clambered back onboard their ship they found 'it was delivered up to them altogether unfurnished'.

The violence that was very early apparent in Newfoundland continued, with the main threat coming from two notorious English pirates, Peter Easton and Henry Mainwaring. On the side of law and order, an experienced sea captain, Richard Whitbourne, was engaged to deter the pirates. Whitbourne had not only been present at St John's to witness Humphrey Gilbert's historic claiming of the land for the Queen, but had also been part of Bernard Drake's force which had sailed to warn the fishermen in 1585 of the coming war with Spain, and incidentally to 'take many Portuguese ships, laden with fish and trayne oil'. He also claimed that, in 1611, he was abducted by 'that famous and Arch-Pirate' Peter Easton when the latter hauled over to Newfoundland with ten ships. Easton saw the fishery as a source of manpower and had intended to seize as many as 1,000 men with whom he could mount an attack on the Spanish *flota* as it sailed from the Indies richly laden for Spain. Whitbourne was held for eleven weeks and, if we are to believe his own evidence, not only persuaded Easton to 'desist from his evil course' but was promised much wealth by the pirate if, on his release, he were to return to England to seek a pardon for Easton. However, on arrival in London he found that the pardon had already been granted, which left Whitbourne without either riches or employment.

Shortly afterwards, in July 1613, the English pirate Gilbert Roope seized the fifty-ton Breton fishing boat, *Katherine of Olan*, off Newfoundland and brought her into Kinsale, only to be accused of offering 'violence and disturbance' to the French. Later that month the merchants trading with Newfoundland claimed losses of £20,400 caused by divers pirates and asked for a warship to protect the fishing fleets. The following year, Samuel Argall was accused by the French of outrage on the coast of Canada which involved emptying fully laden French fishing boats of their fish, train oil and whale blubber, and sending them home empty. This time the protestations reached the ear of the Crown and Sir Thomas Smythe, of the Virginia Company, was asked to explain Argall's behaviour. He, in turn, provided the disingenuous and delaying answer of a promise to take action once the facts were known.

Returning to Newfoundland in 1614, Whitbourne, stretching credulity in his honesty, complained that he was forced to 'spend much time' in the company of another notorious pirate, Henry Mainwaring, a graduate of Brasenose College who, after being apprenticed as a pirate, was given a commission in 1610 to seek and find Easton. Instead of pursuing this task Mainwaring used his ship *Resistance* on a privateering expedition against the Spanish until, in 1614, he realized that easier, although smellier, pickings could be had in plundering, skua-like, the Newfoundland fishing fleets.

As befitted a graduate of Brasenose, Mainwaring's onslaught of the fishing boats was well planned. First he established a base at Harbour Grace which could be well defended. He then recruited some fresh crews for his eight ships before letting them loose on, it is claimed, Spanish, French and Portuguese ships, which is probably, in truth, one nation too few. From these vessels he not only took the catch and provisions but 'perforst' every sixth man into his own fleet. Released from Mainwaring's clutches, Whitbourne returned again to Newfoundland in 1615, carrying with him, so he claimed, a commission from the High Court of Admiralty authorizing him to carry out an investigation into the abuses on the coast and to make recommendations for their correction. His advice, or so it seemed to him, was not heeded and the piracy continued.

Mainwaring, for his part, was better recompensed for his achievements, being offered a commission in the Spanish navy, which he turned down on being pardoned and promoted in 1616 by James as a reward for giving protection to the Newfoundland fleet which had been threatened while on a trading voyage off Gibraltar.

The French were also not quieted by Whitbourne's Commission and in 1616 that hapless gentleman had a 100-ton ship, bound for Lisbon, intercepted by the French pirate Daniel Tibolo, 'who rifles her, to the overthrow and loss of my voyage, in more than the sum of £860'. His luck continued to be bad. In 1618 Whitbourne, a Jonah among shipowners, had another of his vessels taken by Captain Whitney, who had sailed with Ralegh to Guiana and, following the disastrous final act of that farce, had mutinied and sailed to Newfoundland, where he intercepted the ship with which Whitbourne was establishing the bounds of William Vaughan's proposed colony. By removing the master, the bo'sun and some of the crew as well as the victuals, Whitney disrupted Vaughan's programme for what was always a marginal idea.

While Whitbourne's ill-luck at the hands of pirates continued through 1618, his nemesis, Mainwaring, was both knighted and appointed a Royal Navy Vice-Admiral, with duties not so onerous that they prevented him from serving as a Member of Parliament for Dover from 1621 to 1622. He also returned to his academic instincts by becoming a copious writer on naval matters, including piracy, and, in his *Discourse of Pirates* of 1622, he explained that the pirates sailed to Newfoundland for the summer season because in these months there was less chance of easy pickings elsewhere, as the Spanish and Flemish men-of-war were at sea in numbers and that, 'On the bank of Newfoundland they easily get bread, wine, cider and fish enough, with all the necessaries for shipping . . . In Newfoundland, if they be a good force they will command all the land, in regard that the fishermen will not stand to each other.' He also advised those trying to provide protection against pirates to concentrate on fortifying the main fishing ports rather than adopting the more expensive option of providing convoys.

Convoys were, however, a reasonable proposal for those concerned with shipping American goods back to England, for it was not only off the coast of the new world that the planters experienced the depredations of pirates. In 1621, seventeen Newfoundland fishing boats had been attacked by pirates on their way to the Mediterranean, where five years later a further seven were captured. This led to the very commendable suggestion that, rather than risk passing through the Straits of Gibraltar, the fishing fleet should land at Lisbon, where the lower prices would be recompensed by the certainty of a safe landfall. But that year it was not only southern waters where the threat lurked. In response to a demand from the Merchant Adventurers for saleable goods from Cape Cod, the Plymouth Pilgrims loaded their first resupply ship *Fortune* with sassafras, clapboard and beaver pelts, worth about £500, or the equivalent of half of their debt. *Fortune* sailed on 1 December 1621. In the Western Approaches she was stopped and boarded by a Frenchman who removed all her cargo. It was not the only loss that the Pilgrims would suffer. In 1625 *Little James*, heading home from New England with a fortune of 500 beaver pelts onboard, was taken by pirates and the skins sold in the souks of Algiers for just four pence each. With such misfortune it would not be an overstatement to suggest that the Plymouth colony could have been abandoned if the ravages of the pirates had been only a little more successful and enduring.

So Whitbourne's views on how to handle the 'injury of pirates' off Newfoundland voiced in his *Discourse* were both timely and authoritative. His lengthy, close and personal contact with them led him to believe that they could best be countered by 'maintaining two good ships of war, of 200 ton apiece, and two pinnaces of 40 ton apiece' on station for the duration of the summer season. To pay for this deployment Whitbourne proposed that each fisherman contribute 'the value of a good day's fishing', which sum would be more than recompensed by the freedom to fish without fear. In addition Whitbourne saw the warships not only acting as convoy escorts but deterrents against those who would 'come near the southern part of your Majesty's Kingdoms; neither to lie in wait in the course sailing to and from the Newfoundland'. A similar suggestion, the payment of 500 fish, or approximately one-fiftieth of each vessel's catch, had been made in 1620 by the Newfoundland Company and resulted in John Mason, the Governor of Cupid's Cove, being commissioned by the Lord Admiral to sail in command of a 320-ton warship which was to be deployed on anti-piracy patrols. If this voyage took place it does not seem to have become an established procedure, for the woes inflicted by piracy were again apparent a few years later.

In 1625, a twenty-seven-sail fleet of Barbary pirates sailed into the seas off the West Country. They timed their arrival to perfection, for all was chaos in Britain's maritime world. Part of the price King Charles I had had to pay for his marriage to the teenage Henrietta Maria of France was the loan of six warships, refitted at public expense, to support the Catholic assault on the Huguenots besieged at La Rochelle, a deployment of which neither the crews nor Parliament approved. At the same time, King Charles had exacted recompense for his earlier amorous rebuttal by the King of Spain's daughter through war against Spain, which culminated in the disastrous naval expedition against Cadiz in October 1625. Closer to home, pirates based in Dunkirk were causing chaos in the Channel and needed blockading in their port. With so many calls upon his navy and with ships being unmanned and mismanaged, the arrival of the Barbary fleet in the Western Approaches was most unwelcome. The great fear was that it would fall upon the returning Newfoundland fishing fleet, whose 250 ships and 4,000 to 5,000 men were, according to the Mayor of Poole's anxious note to the Privy Council, standing into danger as they approached home waters. While lurking in wait, the pirates raided Padstow and Lundy Island, where they seized some of the inhabitants for slavery, and similarly threatened Ilfracombe. Desperate Devon wives demanded something be done to release their captured menfolk. In response, the government dispatched Sir Francis Stewart to bring the pirates to blows but he complained that they just outran him. When he was accused of negligence he told Parliament that he wished that he had 'petitioned for an act to have a fair wind'. He followed this limp response by stating that '*Lion* is leaky, and the men are falling suddenly sick for want of clothing or vinegar to wash between decks', going on to remark that, 'as long as the Turks are supplied with necessities by the Flemish freebooters, and the Newfoundland fleet will not arm for their own defence, these picaroons will lie hankering upon the coast'. Wryly, Sir John Coke sent him a carpenter and a note stating, 'It was not intended to clothe the mariners in harbour to make them handsome to run away'.

George Calvert, like Whitbourne before him, was to gain a firsthand experience of the pirates of Newfoundland when in 1628 he felt forced to lead an assault on some piratical Frenchmen commanded by Raymond de la Rade, who had arrived off the coast with three ships manned with 400 men, including 'Gentlemen of quality and La fleur de la Jeunesse of Normandy'. Calvert reported his robust response to both the Duke of Buckingham and Charles I. Having been alerted to the French seizure of English vessels at Capreboile, a few miles down the coast from Calvert's own settlement at Ferryland, Calvert sailed in his well-armed *Benediction* of 360-tons, with her sixty-ton consort, but failed to surprise the alerted French, who slipped their cables and fled, leaving 67 of their number ashore to be captured. A few days later, Calvert again sailed to cut off the French in the Bay of Conception, only for them once more to be alerted and make their escape. In compensation for his troubles Calvert, aided this time by the armed merchantman *Victory*, took seven fully laden French boats in Tresspassy and sent them as prizes to England. This was no plain sailing. Unaided by *Victory*, *Benediction* had driven off four French men-of-war seeking to retake the prizes in the Atlantic and then, with *Victory* departing to enter Plymouth, had been forced alone to defend her squadron from 'a desperate Dunkirker in the Narrow Seas'.

Success at sea led to another fight, with Calvert having to go to court over the division of the spoils from his seven prizes; *Victory*'s London owners claiming legal rights to them, while Calvert's agents took the moral high ground, imploring that Lord Baltimore might have the portion he had earned:

> By preserving at least forty or fifty sail of English from the French.
> By chasing them away with his own ships and servants thereby neglecting his plantation and fishing to his prejudice almost £200.
> By discovering to the *Victory* the place and strength of those prizes.
> By the just performance of her part in taking them.
> By preserving them twice at sea when the *Victory* had abandoned them.

Regardless of the outcome of the legal struggle, Calvert yearned for better practical support to defend his colony, and the main point of his letters to Buckingham and the King was to request naval support for the 'safeguard of the gainful trade about which 300 ships are yearly occupied and now like to fall into great and imminent danger'. Other options were unlikely to respond to his call: for example, in March 1620 Bristol merchants stated that they could not raise funds to contribute against such depredations – having lost £8,000 in one year through shipwreck and piracy. As so often in the long century of initial settlement, the Crown was the only authority with pockets deep enough to underwrite the adventure.

Calvert, a friend of the King, had his request granted. Yet, in December 1628, his son-in-law, William Peaseley, writing on Calvert's behalf to the Lord Commissioners of the Lord Admiral, while admitting that the loan of *Esperance* was 'a great argument of his Majesty's and your Lordships' special favour and an evident sign of your care for the safety of many thousand Englishmen, who yearly resort with little or no strength to Newfoundland', followed up his flattering thanks with no-thanks by stating that *Esperance* 'requires a greater charge to fit her for sea then the freight of another ship will cost, or at the least a longer time to repair her, than the necessity of the service doth permit'. Once again the ploy worked and, instead of the unseaworthy *Esperance* a prizeship, *St Claude*, was appointed to serve the colony for six months.

Further south, the Jamestown settlement, once regarded as a potential haven for pirates, was itself untroubled by their depredations and, indeed, was benefiting from a trade in contraband tobacco being carried out at the mouth of the James River under the blind eye of the compliant governors.

In 1619, pirates were responsible for landing in Virginia a human cargo that were to be the first of many more unwilling passengers from far further afield than any settlers had so far travelled. While the Virginia colonists were learning to live in untrusting proximity with the native peoples, on the other side of the southern ocean, the Portuguese were forcibly removing the population of Angola to sell them as slaves in America. In mid-1619, some 350 slaves were shackled into the hold of *São João Bautista*, whose captain planned to sell them at Vera Cruz. Off the coast of Mexico the slaver was intercepted by the Dutch privateer *White Lion* and her consort, the Earl of Warwick's *Treasurer*, revictualled and illegally supported by Captain Samuel Argall, the shortly-to-be-removed Governor of Virginia. Some of the cargo was transferred and then traded throughout the West Indies until *White Lion* arrived at Jamestown with just '20 and odd Negroes' left, to be followed a day later into the Chesapeake by *Treasurer* with a further thirty of which to dispose. Only those in *White Lion* disembarked, being bought by Governor Yeardley in exchange for provisions. Daniel Elfrith, the captain of *Treasurer*, appears to have taken fright that he might himself be arrested for his unlicensed privateering activities and, having been refused trade at Kiccowtan, he quickly left harbour.

In the 1620 census of the colony the surviving Angolans from *White Lion* are listed as 'others not Christians in the service of the English'. What that service entailed and the conditions imposed or inflicted on those undertaking it we do not know, but these anonymous Africans were as important first-footers in their way as were those 'English' that had stepped ashore at Jamestown in 1606. By their labours the colony and its future neighbours would thrive in a way so different from the settlements further north that explosive fusion or fission would be the inevitable outcome.

THE KIRKES AND KIBEC

In 1603 the French explorer Champlain, voyaging up the St Lawrence, 'landed at a place which the Amerindians called Kibec, in their language signifying a strait'. It was a decision which would thrill many a future English schoolchild whose history lessons were enlivened with the tale of how, in 1759, General Wolfe, having led his army up the unscalable 'Heights of Abraham', fell on the French defences, only to die – as so many English heroes did – at the moment of victory. What few, if any, of those children would have known is that Quebec had fallen to the English before in a sea assault launched by pirates that was as thrilling as Wolfe's later siege.

Champlain's settlement grew slowly, but international rivalry over control of this potentially valuable St Lawrence waterway simmered with more vigour. In 1621 Sir William Alexander, the Nova Scotia Charter holder, formed the Adventurers of Canada, whose main aim was to displace the French from the St Lawrence and assume control of the wealthy trade in pelts. One of the men he recruited to his company was Gervaise Kirke, of an Anglo-Huguenot family, who just happened to have apprenticed his fistful of sins to be pirates. All the Adventurers needed was an excuse to act.

In 1627 in France the excuse was being prepared when a similar company was formed to exploit the wealth of Canada, but this one, the Company of New France, or, as it is better known, the Company of One Hundred Associates, was being driven by religious suspicion and intolerance, for one of the stated aims of its Charter was to ensure that only Catholics settled and traded with New France, a gauntlet flung down, although not aimed at, Gervaise Kirke. The challenge to England as a whole was even starker; Richelieu granted the Associates control of an area stretching from Florida to the Arctic Circle and inland to the source of the St Lawrence. To manage this estate they agreed to dispatch several hundred colonists in the first year and over 4,000 by 1643, supported by many missionaries.

By 1628 the French were busy planning to upset this rumoured intrusion by returning to the region in numbers. In 1629, English agents reported that there were twenty ships gathering at Dieppe, Newhaven and Honfleur, bound for Canada, St Kitts and Newfoundland, with another twenty expected to sail from Brittany and the Biscay ports. While this fleet was being assembled a storm cloud was gathering further down the coast at La Rochelle, where the fate of the besieged Huguenots led to England declaring war against France and launching Buckingham's flawed amphibious assault. The crisis at La Rochelle provided the English, and Gervaise Kirke in particular, with the excuse they needed, so, learning of the French deployment, he summoned his sons. The eldest, Captain David Kirke, a future Governor of Newfoundland, was ordered to sail with six ships and three pinnaces to 'reconter' the French. His letter of marque indicated that 'It would prove a good service and honour to our land . . . if some three or four men of war could be sent to the lord Baltimore whereby to withstand the enemy'.

However, The Adventurers had funds sufficient only to equip three vessels: of these, the admiral *Abigail* was to be commanded by David, while Lewis and Thomas captained the other two, with the younger brothers, James and John, going along for work experience. In his cabin David held his letters of marque and the written authority 'utterly to drive away and root out the French settlements in Nova Scotia and Canada'.

The Kirkes had a fine passage and began their Canadian work by capturing several Basque fishing vessels to replenish their own supplies and establishing a base at Tadoussac, a harbour sheltered by the udder-shaped hills after which it was named, lying at the confluence of the St Lawrence and Sagueny rivers. Here, while not planning how to harpoon the gathering minke whales, they plotted how they could best force

Tadoussac proved an ideal base from where David Kirke could mount an attack on Quebec while preventing relief supplies reaching the isolated settlement.

Quebec to capitulate. As with all the early settlements, it was known that victuals would be in short supply, so the first act of aggression undertaken by the Kirkes was to destroy the farm from which Quebec drew its supplies, at Cape Tourmente, some thirty miles downstream from their objective. That done, the Kirkes cleverly sent their prisoners to Champlain, thereby increasing the mouths he had to feed, and along with them went a letter inviting him to take the sensible course of action and surrender. Champlain declined the offer, stating incorrectly that his storehouses were full, gambling on the hope that a relief mission was on its way to replenish his desperately low stocks. It was to prevent this happy union that the Kirkes abandoned their siege and drifted downstream to await the French fleet.

They found them close inshore off Gaspé Point, which juts out at the point where the St Lawrence disembogues into the mouth of the Gulf of the same name. Claude de Roquemont's fleet of eighteen vessels must have given the Kirkes pause for thought, but not for long; the English piratical reputation was based on their boldness to attack prey far larger than themselves. And so it was that day and, although Kirke called on Roquemont to surrender, the moment the Frenchman showed that he was unwilling to do so without a fight *Abigail* and her sisters swooped. The deep-loaded Frenchmen could scarcely get to their guns, many of which had been stowed below to improve stability. After a few hours of warming them up at range *Abigail* moved swiftly in for

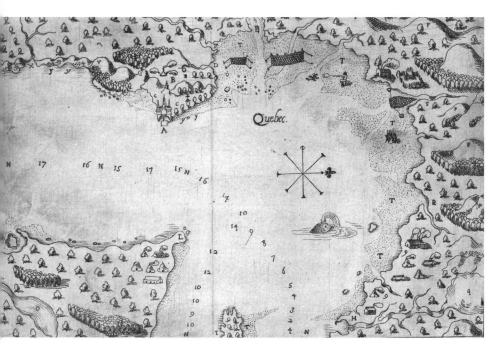

Champlain's drawing shows how small his first settlement at Quebec was: built in 1608, it consisted of just three two-storey buildings. Nevertheless, David Kirke avoided making an assault on the buildings. As well as sowing seed, the little group of settlers are shown having set fish nets and shooting wildfowl. As with all his maps, Champlain indicates the depth of water for navigation.

the kill, raking Roquemont's ship with lethal grape before grappling her to allow Kirke's well-trained boarding parties to swing onboard. The short fight was soon over, with the injured Roquemont surrendering to avoid further loss of life. In the middle distance David Kirke could see the other two warships hauling down their flags in response to his brothers' successful assault. The rest of the day the three sea-wolves spent rounding up and penning the fifteen merchant ships – none escaped. Having more hulls than he could manage, David Kirke decided to raze ten of them after he had removed the stores. He also had too many captured passengers and crew to risk retaining onboard the remaining prizes, so many of these he landed at a missionary station on St Pierre Island before he escorted his prize convoy back across the Atlantic to England, where their arrival gave rise to much rejoicing.

Quebec's winter of woes continued. A relief ship was hastily stored and dispatched from France, only to be wrecked off Canso Island where, luckily, there was a French fishing settlement. The survivors were able to board a passing trading vessel for the journey home, but this too was wrecked in the Bay of Biscay.

The Kirkes were faring better. In March 1629 David, still in *Abigail*, Lewis in *Willliam* and Thomas in *George* sailed in company with Captain Brewerton in *Gervaise*, two other ships and three pinnaces. On reaching the Canadian coast, all except *Abigail* and a consort were detached to destroy the French coastal settlements, while David entered the St Lawrence to renew his conversation with Champlain. Winter had been an English ally. Within days of his arrival, and without a shot being fired, the cross of St George was flying over the rickety wooden walls of Quebec, while her famished inhabitants were being mollified with a warm meal. In their place, deployed at both Quebec and Tadoussac, 150 English soldiers assumed guard of the stockades and the thirty out of eighty-five French who elected to remain behind. Champlain himself, one of the greatest of all American pioneers, was ferried to England in ships laden with furs which had been destined for France.

Champlain was not to be disconsolate for long. On arrival in England the Kirkes discovered that, even before Quebec had surrendered, England had signed a peace treaty with France, but the pirates chose, for as long as they could, to ignore the implications and continued making money from the fur trade over which they had, for the time being, a monopoly. But while they were getting rich illegally, King Charles I's coffers were heading in the other direction and, in 1632, to stave off bankruptcy, he agreed to return the sites seized from France in return for a large sum of money. The Adventurers of Canada were also required to pay compensation for the loot that they had taken after hostilities had ended on 24 April 1629. In an unwarranted act of vandalism the Kirkes abandoned Quebec only after they had razed the site to the ground, meaning that the last years of the returning Champlain – who died in 1635 – were spent restoring that which he had spent over twenty years of his life establishing. David Kirke also returned to the region, being granted, as Sir David, a Charter to develop Newfoundland.

If one places the pros and cons of piracy in the scales as far as they aided or detracted from the success of the invasion of America, the balance initially slumps heavily on the side of the pirates. This was a maritime enterprise that began not only without the support of the Royal Navy, but also without a cargo over which merchants would rival to fill their holds. Hiring empty hulls to ferry poor passengers was not an attractive proposition for either investors or shipping agents. The proposal that the opportunity for a little piracy was ever present was not just an added attraction, or bribe; it was the very reason why many of the earliest voyages were undertaken.

CHAPTER 13

Joint Command

What shall I say? But that we lost him, that in all his proceedings, made justice his first guide, and experience his second; ever hating baseness, sloth, pride, and indignity, more than any dangers; that never allowed more for himself, than his soldiers with him; that upon no danger would send them where he would not lead them himself; that would never see us in want of what either he had, or could by any means get us . . . whose adventures were our lives, and whose losses our deaths.

William Fettiplace (Symonds), eulogy written on John Smith's departure from Jamestown, 1612

THE PROBLEMS OF AMPHIBIOUS ASSAULT

If 100 illegal immigrants landed at Portsmouth and claimed hegemony over Hampshire, let alone the whole of England, they would be laughed back onboard their ferry. But, suppose their leaders had been named Hengist and Horsa and that there were more of them on their way. The UK Border Agency would call for reinforcements while parliamentarians would demand a debate. In America there was no united front to respond to the arriving threat but neither was the invasion being led by such as those ferocious Jute joint commanders.

One of the difficulties in both the planning and execution of an amphibious operation is that it requires the appointment of both land and sea commanders, with the latter transporting and providing logistical support to the former. In an age when authority was often based on lineage and title rather than experience or suitability, and where the nobility found quarrel in a straw if they felt their honour was at stake, the execution of such complicated acts as amphibious assaults was often thwarted by the arguments of those appointed to lead them. Yet, even when the commanders were in concord, things went awry.

The supreme exponent of amphibious operations in Elizabeth's reign was Sir Francis Drake. His Great West Indies Raid of 1585 to 1586 saw Santo Domingo and Cartagena fall readily to the swiftly executed onslaught by Christopher Carleill, whose troops were ferried ashore by Drake in the most expeditious place, while the fleet remained in close support throughout the assault. Yet even Drake could get it wrong. His 1589 attack on Lisbon failed mainly because he landed Sir John Norris and his men through the dangerous surf at Peniche, making them march forty-five miles south to reach their objective where, for four days they besieged the city unsupported by Drake who, inexplicably, failed to force a passage past the forts of Belem and into the Tagus to threaten Lisbon from the river. At the very end of 1595, days before his death, Drake, having failed to take San Juan de Puerto Rico, repeated that earlier error by landing

John Smith spent just two and a half years at Jamestown and yet his influence, initiative and leadership places him head and shoulders above all of the other early colonists. So it is right that he and he alone stands proudly on the original site of Jamestown, looking across the river whose uses he understood so well.

Sir Thomas Baskerville at Nombre de Dios, over thirty miles short of his objective, Panama, instead of sailing the fleet up the swollen Chagres River. Ill-shod and poorly clad, the troops struggled along muddy tracks for two days until they were repulsed by the Spanish dug well in on the final mountain pass. Once again, the physical separation of the shore and sea elements of the operation spelt failure.

However, in both triumph and disaster, Drake and his three land commanders seem to have remained on excellent professional terms. To a large extent this was due to the fact that all owed their appointments to their proven track record and not to their being favourites at Court, which meant that they could speak freely to each other as equals. It was not always so when proud and prickly personalities were required to work together. During his first attack on Cadiz, in 1587, Drake ordered the arrest of William Borough, his second-in-command, for querying his decisions. In the second attack on Cadiz, in 1596, it took all of Charles Howard's charm to keep Ralegh and Essex from allowing personal rivalry to detract from the common cause. When that governing wisdom was withdrawn, the antipathy between the two courtiers, acting as joint commanders, was responsible for the failure of the island voyage to the Azores in 1597. If such rivalry could cause such discord during a short deployment, how much more could it infect one of longer duration? No matter how high placed or deep pocketed the investors back in England were, it was upon the leadership in America that the success and safety of each of these ventures would depend.

FROBISHER AND FENTON

Although Frobisher did not manage to establish the first English colony destined for America on the bleak coast near Baffin Island, the 'might have been' gives an insight to the qualities of leadership that could make or break amphibious operations such as this one. Neither Frobisher, the admiral, nor Fenton, the land commander, were deep-minded individuals, and both resorted to violence when their views were challenged. Richard Madox, Fenton's chaplain on his ill-fated voyage of 1582, described his commander as unable to 'abide to be seen to learn anything of anybody, but his own proud mind', while Frobisher had been considered to be a man of 'furious humour of temper, swearing, outrageous and bullying behaviour'. Frobisher displayed this choleric element during the 1578 voyage when his navigational opinion was rightly questioned at the mouth of the Gulf that bears his name. The result was that the admiral led a part of his fleet on a lengthy detour 180 miles down the appropriately named Mistaken Straits before admitting his error and going about. With such a pair in joint command, the likelihood is that the attempt to establish a colony would not, even if the conditions and equipment had allowed for it, have been a success.

GRENVILLE AND LANE

The first amphibious assault on Virginia was led by Sir Richard Grenville, who was both the sea and, while in theatre, land commander, with Ralph Lane, a military professional purposely taken away from his duties in Ireland for this mission, very much his subordinate. The two men had differing priorities, with Grenville content to dally in the West Indies in the hope of taking a few prizes, while Lane was desperate to land at Roanoke well ahead of the winter. The result, given Grenville's position as supreme commander, was a debilitating delay and a quarrelsome relationship. It would also lead to the departing Grenville torching a whole village as a punishment for the theft of a cup, thereby establishing uneasy relations with the native population with which Lane, who was remaining behind, needed to be on good terms.

Twice during the voyage Lane is recorded as voicing his disquiet at Grenville's cavalier approach to the mission, but the arguments came to nothing at the time, leaving Lane to voice his frustration and resentment in several strongly worded letters written to Walsingham, Sydney and others. He refers to that time onboard when he believed that Grenville intended to have him swing for insubordination, writing: 'he hath not only purported but even propounded the same, to have brought me by indirect means and untrue surmises to the question for my life, and that only for an advice in public consultation by me given, which if it had been executed, had been for the great good of us all, but chiefly for himself.'

Lane, believing that Grenville, by reporting to Ralegh and the Court in person, would have a distinct advantage over his own point of view, wielded his pen like a trowel, laying it on that, although:

> it is not possible for men to behave themselves more faithfully and more industriously in our action . . . contrariwise Sir Richard Grenville, General, hath demeaned himself from the first day of his entry into government at Plymouth, until the day of his departure from hence over the bar at Port Ferdinando, far otherwise than my hope of him, though very agreeable to the expectations, and predictions of sundry wise and goodly persons of his own country, that knew him better than myself, and particularly how tyrannous an execution without any occasion of my part offered.

So consuming was Lane's rage against the Admiral (Lane slips into subordination by using the term 'General') that in a most damning phrase he desires his sponsors 'to give me their favours to be freed from that place where Sir Richard Grenville is to carry any authority in chief'. After which he concludes his diatribe by 'Assuring you, Sir, with all that the Lord has miraculously blessed this action, that in the time of his being amongst us, even though his intolerable pride, and insatiable ambition, it hath not at three several times taken a final overthrow'.

The Queen's Secretary would have received this letter sometime after Grenville's fleet made its leisurely return, having seized the wealthy prize *Santa Maria* while on a passage that took eight weeks, five days longer than John White took to reach Ireland from Roanoke in his unseaworthy shell two years later. The rich prize 'made' the voyage and would certainly been a persuasive defence against any charges of maladministration with which Lane wished Grenville to be confronted. Given the tight-knit group that formed the operational executive at Court, it seems most likely that the letter would have been shown to Walter Ralegh and its content conveyed to Grenville. The revelation of such criticism could only have been the result of a massive falling out and, given that, it is unlikely that Grenville returned to England either advocating an expeditious resupply or desiring to sail with alacrity once the logistics were in place.

Back in Roanoke, Lane would have had time to ponder on his letters posted in haste and in doing so he would have been less than human to not wonder whether his outburst had burnt the returning boats, especially when the much-anticipated sails failed to appear. Thus, when Drake arrived, a man who had no commitment to support the settlement, and offered both provisions and then a passage home, it is no wonder that Lane, who, ironically, had commanded the most successful of any of the earlier plantations with an almost miraculous survival rate amongst his men, accepted. Drake evacuated Lane's expeditionary force on 18 June 1586; Grenville, with both reinforcements and resupply a-plenty, arrived off the Carolina Outer Banks at the end of July. Given the strength of feeling between the two protagonists, that fatal gap could have opened because Lane did not trust Grenville to reappear and the latter made less effort than he might to arrive in a timely fashion.

WHITE AND FERDINANDO

Lessons in leadership were not learned from the first colony. Instead of finding two competent, charismatic and compatible commanders for the next voyage, Ralegh selected the artist White and the petulant Portuguese pilot, Ferdinando. They sailed for Virginia from Plymouth on 8 May 1587. A week later the relationship had soured so much that White claimed that Ferdinando 'forsooke our flyboat'. Given the vicissitudes of sailing in company this could have been an accident, but on 25 July, when the flyboat rejoined them off Hatorask, White recorded that she had arrived all safe:

> to the great joy and comfort of the whole company: but the Master of our Admiral, Fernando [sic], grieved greatly at their safe coming: for he purposely left them . . . hoping that the Master thereof, whose name was Edward Spicer, for that he never had been in Virginia, would hardly find the place, or else being left in so dangerous a place as that he was, by means of so many men of war, as at that time were abroad, they should surely be taken, or slain, but God disappointed his wicked pretences.

Sadly Spicer was to be lost on Lane's 1590 voyage when he drowned trying to take his boat through to those same shores of Hatorask where he had landed safely in 1587.

As in Lane's earlier correspondence, the key to the incompatibility between White and Ferdinando lies in the phrase 'Master of our Admiral'. At no time does White acknowledge the sea commander as being the expedition's admiral, rather he refers to him throughout just as being a master with no rank or responsibility other than to his own vessel.

That Ferdinando felt differently and resented White's criticism, either inferred or outspoken, is evident in the horrific way in which he virtually marooned the landing party on Roanoke, claiming that there was insufficient time to take then into the Chesapeake as had been tacitly agreed. If the Grenville–Lane relationship led to an evacuation, the White–Ferdinando fracas contributed to an extermination. Yet, strangely, Ferdinando did not disembark the colonists and then depart; he stayed anchored uncomfortably off the Outer Banks from 22 July to 28 August. Even when a hurricane forced him to cut his cable and stand out to sea on 21 August, giving him the ideal excuse to abandon the colonists and return home, he clawed his way back to the anchorage to collect White, duty, apparently, being stronger than the most evident mutual loathing.

In all these matters of divisive command it is not the cause but the effect that is important. Ferdinando and White returning together to put a joint case for immediate resupply would have presented a far more persuasive, almost irresistible, argument than could the diffident but insistent White by himself. Joint command works best but only if the commanders wish it so to do.

POPHAM AND GILBERT

Sir George Popham, the elderly gentleman selected to govern the first North Virginia colony under the 1606 Charter, of which he was a grantee, was an experienced and well-connected soldier. As second-in-command and 'admiral' he was supported by Raleigh Gilbert, whose name was his reflected glory. Socially, the two men should have had little problem with each other's pedigree; professionally, they should have respected each other's judgement; yet they were to lead one of the shortest-lived colonies settled on the coast of America. Their failings were both avoidable and personal. Above all else Popham was too old for his occupation and, if evidence can be deduced from his letters, possibly senile. His death on duty must have been foreseeable by both the Lord Chief Justice, Francis Popham, and Sir Ferdinando Gorges, the main sponsors of the expedition. If the leader was frail then it was vital that his deputy was firm: with Gilbert this was not so and his shortcomings came as no surprise for, in a character attack on both men, Gorges wrote to the Earl of Salisbury:

the President himself is an honest man, but old, and of an unwieldy body, and timorously fearful to offend, or contest with others that will or do oppose him, but otherwise a discreet careful man. Captain Gilbert is described to me from thence to be desirous of supremacy, and rule, a loose-life, prompt to sensuality, little zeal in Religion, humorous, head-strong, and of small judgement and experience, other ways valiant enough, but he holds that the king could not give away that, by Patent, to others, which his father had an Act of Parliament for, and that he will not be put out of it in haste.

Gilbert, if indeed he felt that he still had claim to the lands promised to his father, was in error. Sir Humphrey Gilbert's patent for six years would have expired in 1584, had not his drowning in 1583 effectively ended it prematurely, while its successor patent, that to Walter Ralegh, foreclosed in 1603. Yet, to appoint Raleigh Gilbert as second-in-command to an elderly unfit man, knowing that he held such disruptive views, was an act of folly, which it proved to be when Gilbert repaid his trust by returning to England once he was made aware that an easier, wealthier life awaited him as the family heir on the death of his elder brother. Gorges went as far as to suggest that Gilbert's mail be intercepted, read and delayed, which sheds light on the degree of trust that he had in his colony's admiral.

As for the President, George Popham, his character might best be extrapolated from the pompous, irresponsible, misinformed, over-optimistic letter that he wrote to King James from Fort St George in 1607. Devoted and daft was not a sound state of mind for one charged with taking the first small step on a mighty journey. Men there were who could have done a better job, but they stood without Gorges's small coterie, whose fatal desire was to control rather than encourage initiative from those whom they dispatched westward.

NEWPORT AND SMITH

If the two earlier Roanoke partnerships were flawed, that between Newport and Smith on the return to southern Virginia in 1607 was almost fatal for the latter, who was not, at the start, either the appointed or even the obvious choice for land commander. Yet neither was anybody else pre-selected for the post, thereby leaving much power to be wielded by the naval commander, Christopher Newport. Matters, as they did on the Roanoke voyages, came to a head during the Atlantic crossing. Smith, who would pick an argument at the slightest provocation, much upset his fellow passengers: so much so that he was arrested onboard *Susan Constant* and charged with the capital offence of mutiny. However much his fellow travellers might have loathed this 'unclubbable' upstart, he could not have been either tried or locked up without Newport's agreement. Neither could the gallows that were erected at Nevis to hang Smith have been raised without Newport's knowledge and yet, although Smith might later comment that 'he could not be persuaded to use' them, they would only have been denied their victim by Newport's intervention.

Newport did not, however, intervene to assist Smith to claim his rightful place on the Council, perhaps agreeing with Wingfield that, 'if he were in England, I would think scorn this man should be my companion'. Nevertheless he took him as one of only five settlers to augment the eighteen seamen who accompanied him on the first explorative journey that he made. That journey was the making of Smith. He seems to have proven his worth as a military man during the voyage while, back at Jamestown, the leaders left behind were demonstrating their own inadequacies, only just managing to stave off a fierce Amerindian attack planned to take place before the return of the explorers who were being, suspiciously in Smith's mind, detained by offers of hospitality.

After Newport's departure the settlers had to come to terms with the inadequacy of their leadership and the fact that Smith was de facto in charge but not in command, while the disastrous and later disgraced Ratcliffe held the post of President before, on 10 September 1608, Smith took the oath that placed him in the position he should have held all the time.

Smith appears to have been a contradictory but not a scheming colleague, much preferring to spend his time away from Jamestown exploring the country and getting to know the native people so that essential and beneficial trading links could be established. This had been at the risk of his own life, which was twice saved by the intervention of the princess Pocahontas. On the first and famous occasion, when Pocahontas threw herself over the prostrated Smith just before his head was smashed in by a club-wielding executioner, he returned to Jamestown only to be sentenced to death by his own people. In part this was due to the fact that he had found out that the leadership was intent on abandoning the colony and planning to sail back to England onboard *Discovery*. Smith took command of the others and together they trained every available weapon on the still secured ship. The mutineers, for so they were, slunk back ashore, only to accuse Smith of culpable manslaughter by allowing Thomas Emry and Jehu Robinson, the two men who had accompanied him on his journey, to be killed at the hands of the Amerindians. This time there seemed to be no escaping the council's sentence of death, but then Newport, in *John and Francis*, eased alongside on the evening tide of 3 January,

Samuel Argall forces Pocahontas aboard his ship, the most famous kidnap of them all. This drawing shows most aspects of the English campaign: ships and shallops nosing their way upstream; raiding parties firing Amerindian villages and, of course, the kidnapping itself. (National Maritime Museum)

bringing fresh supplies and a further sixty new colonists, and immediately ordered the release of Smith and the long-imprisoned Wingfield.

Newport had thus saved Smith's life at least twice. It did not mean that the military man was going to overlook the naval man's imperfections in his performance ashore. Smith was one of the few colonists who saw the Amerindians as partners in the successful establishment of the settlements with whom it was essential to have a working relationship based on respect and trust, and whom the English should come to dominate but not domineer. What he saw as counterproductive was either that the settlers should become bullying beggars whenever they were short of a bushel of bread, as would happen under Percy, or that naive traders were easily outsmarted, as Newport seemed content to let happen when he was in charge in dealing with Powhatan, even in one instance arming the Amerindian leader with twenty swords in exchange for the same number of turkeys. Smith did not and would not trade in this way, and it grieved him to have to stand by while the inexperienced and short-term visitor Newport undermined his authority in this way.

Smith had other reasons to despair at Newport's conduct, although these were based on the latter endeavouring to fulfil the demands of the Company who paid his wages. London backers were obsessed with the desire to discover gold, and Newport raised their hopes by filling his holds with hard-won valueless rocks at the expense of placing the colony on a more secure footing by encouraging defensive building and the clearing of ground to grow grain. In addition there was the desire to find a short passage nearby that would lead to a lake outflowing west to the Pacific. Neither of these aims had featured in the first Charter, appearing first in the *Instructions* issued by the Company, to whose members Smith had no hesitation in writing and explaining their own and their naval commander's shortcomings.

In a letter whose tone is set at the very beginning, he wrote that Newport was being paid too much for his work, at the expense of the settlers and, moreover, he, Smith, was obliged to follow that man's instructions to the detriment of all. He went on to pour scorn on the exploration up to the Falls, the search for gold (Smith having found and forwarded lumps of iron ore) and the attempts to establish industries at Jamestown. Not content with that, he considered Newport's coronation of and trading with Powhatan a farce and the long stay of the mariners a drain on severely limited resources. Given both Smith's strength of character and feelings, it is unlikely that he did not flex them against Newport. In so doing, of course, he would have done little to improve the bonded strength of the joint command.

Accurate though such a summary was, its accusations created an embarrassment that could not be ignored, leaving the Virginia Company little option but to appoint a senior figure, Lord De La Warr, as Governor to instil discipline and to enforce the Company's objectives. Yet the barbs directed against Newport also struck home and, when the third supply fleet sailed from England on 2 June 1609, the experienced navigator who had been the 'admiral' for the first voyage found himself only in command of one ship, *Sea Venture*, onboard which were travelling not only the acting Governor, Sir Thomas Gates, but also Newport's direct superior, the fleet admiral, Sir George Somers.

Smith and Newport had had similar freebooting backgrounds. The former had been a mercenary, a calling in which leaders had to win through success the respect of their

The capture of John Smith. A distinctly cowed John Smith is prodded towards his doom, where the presence of excited tribal elders in a smoke-induced trance, with a collection of clubs lying at their feet, makes his situation decidedly parlous. (National Maritime Museum)

men. This was also the case with Newport's piratical career, in which he lost his arm in the fight to take the *Madre de Dios*, the richest prize ever seized. Yet Newport had experience of command in the confines of a ship while Smith, usually as a subordinate, had the mercenary's freedom to take his labour elsewhere whenever he disagreed with the orders he was given. The next pair of commanders also included one seaman and one soldier, but both had served the state and understood both leadership, the role of follower and the call of duty. It was this reliability, combined with a proud professional background, along with their personal investment in the Company, that made them ideal candidates for the task of commanding Jamestown. They did not betray that trust.

SOMERS AND GATES

The quality of leadership is best exposed when events go badly wrong rather than when they proceed smoothly. Those embarked in *Sea Venture* in 1609 were to experience most of the perils of the sea: a badly leaking ship caught in a great storm; a shipwreck on a coral reef; and being marooned on the isolated Bermudas. Yet they were blessed in all these travails by the presence of two outstanding men who led by example, ruled with wisdom and, most importantly of all, acted with united authority. To some extent their joint rule was aided by the fact that they were both experienced, respected and, for the period, elderly gentlemen who were prepared to risk their lives as well as their investments in pursuit of the vision of a prosperous Virginia: a commitment and a duty that was not going to be interfered with by the nuisance of a shipwreck. Strachey, who was anxious to curry favour with Gates, under whom he had secured the post of Secretary, wrote of his boss that:

> it was happy for us, who had now run this fortune and were fallen into the bottom of this misery, that we both had our governor with us, and one so solicitous and careful, whose both example (as I said) and authority could lay shame and command upon our people. Else, I am persuaded, we had most of us finished our days there, so willing were the major part of the common sort (especially when they found such a plenty of victuals) to settle a foundation of ever inhabiting there; as well appeared by many practices of theirs (and perhaps of some of the better sort).

This praise could be applied equally to both men from the moment that the storm struck. Throughout the four-day battering that *Sea Venture* endured, sinking lower and lower into the water, Strachey recorded the gallant way the ever-vigilant Somers and the ever-active Gates strove to keep the ship afloat by example and exhorting the passengers and crew to work beyond exhaustion.

> Our governor upon the Tuesday morning (at what time, by such who had been below in the hold, the leak was first discovered) had caused the whole company (about 140, besides women) to be equally divided into three parts, and opening the ship in three places (under the forecastle, in the waist, and hard by the binnacle), appointed each man where to attend; and thereunto every man came duly upon his watch, took the bucket or pump for one hour, and rested another. Then men might be seen to labour, I may well say, for life; and the better sort (even our governor and admiral themselves), not refusing their turn and to spell each the other, to give example to other. The common sort, stripped naked as men in galleys, the easier both to hold out and to shrink from under the salt water which continually leapt in among them, kept their eyes waking and their thoughts and hands working with tired bodies and wasted spirits three days and four nights, destitute of outward comfort and desperate of any deliverance, testifying how mutually willing they were yet by labour to keep each other from drowning, albeit each one drowned whilst he laboured.
>
> One thing: it is not without his wonder (whether it were the fear of death in so great a storm, or that it pleased God to be gracious unto us), there was not a passenger,

gentleman or other, after he began to stir and labour, but was able to relieve his fellow and make good his course. And it is most true, such as in all their lifetimes had never done hour's work before (their minds now helping their bodies) were able twice forty-eight hours together to toil with the best.

Once land had been sighted and Somers had directed the ship towards the sharp-rocked shore, it was luck that she struck and wedged where she did, but it was a luck brought about by excellent and confident seamanship. Then calm confidence quelled the rush to scramble over the side and head for shore so that *Sea Venture* was abandoned in an orderly way and without the loss of life that might have been expected in such dire circumstances.

Once ashore, Gates assumed the full panoply of command, leaving Somers to manage the seamen in a way that would prevent them turning into an 'awkward squad', which sailors stranded ashore so often become. So he gave them seamanlike tasks: they were first charged with unloading stores from the wreck; then in charting the bays of Bermuda and fishing. Finally, Somers employed them in the building the second of the craft in which they would continue their voyage to Virginia. Both men knew that they were unlikely to be rescued, but before long they also realized that to many, both passengers and crew, the Somers Isles (as they were briefly called) offered far better opportunities than those that lay awaiting them in Virginia. As well as the fish, the island was full of strange edible fowl, hundreds of wild hogs, and berries and roots that could keep the whole company well fed in a pleasant climate, free from disease and pesky native people. It was, therefore, no wonder that Strachey reported:

Lo, what are our affections and passions, if not rightly squared? How irreligious and irregular they express us! Not perhaps so ill as we would be, but yet as we are. Some dangerous and secret discontents nourished amongst us had like to have been the parents of bloody issues and mischiefs. They began first in the seamen, who in time had fastened unto them (by false baits) many of our landmen likewise, and some of whom (for opinion of their religion) was carried an extraordinary and good respect. The angles wherewith chiefly they thus hooked in these disquieted pools were how that in Virginia nothing but wretchedness and labour must be expected, with many wants and a churlish entreaty, there being neither that fish, flesh, nor fowl which here (without wasting on the one part, or watching on theirs, or any threatening and art of authority) at ease and pleasure might be enjoyed. And since both in the one and the other place they were (for the time) to lose the fruition, both of their friends and country, as good and better were it for them to repose and seat them where they should have the least outward wants the while.

This, thus preached and published each to other, though by such who never had been more onward toward Virginia than (before this voyage) a sculler could happily row him (and what hath a more adamantine power to draw unto it the consent and attraction of the idle, untoward, and wretched number of the many than liberty and fullness of sensuality?), begat such a murmur and such a discontent and disunion of hearts and hands from this labour and forwarding the means of redeeming us from hence, as each one wrought with his mate how to divorce him from the same.

In such circumstances mutiny was not an unexpected outcome, but it was in the handling of the crises that Gates showed his mettle, working an almost 'good cop, bad cop' routine with Somers to convince the malcontents of the foolishness of their ways and the logic and mercy of Gates's rule. Thus, even a murderer was pardoned, and mutinous men were granted just sufficient of their wishes, such as being left alone on an island, to realize that they preferred to remain part of the company. However, when the plotting got ugly, Gates seized and sentenced the ringleader to death, his sole concession being that he was shot at dusk not hanged at dawn. Then he turned to Somers to effect the reconciliation with the other would-be mutineers.

And therefore lovingly conjured Sir George, by the worthiness of his (heretofore) well-maintained reputation, and by the powers of his own judgement, and by the virtue of that ancient love and friendship which had these many years been settled between them, to do his best to give this revolted company (if he could send unto them) the consideration of these particulars, and so work with them (if he might) that by fair means (the mutiny reconciled) they would at length survey their own errors, which he would be as ready, upon their rendering and coming in, to pardon, as he did now pity them; assuring them in general and particular that whatsoever they had sinisterly committed or practised hitherto against the laws of duty and honesty should not in any sort be imputed against them.

In which good office Sir George Somers did so nobly work and heartily labour as he brought most of them in, and indeed all but Christopher Carter and Robert Waters, who by no means would any more come amongst Sir George's men, hearing that Sir George had commanded his men (since they would not be entreated by fair means) to surprise them if they could, by any device or force. From which time they grew so cautious and wary for their own ill, as at our coming away we were fain to leave them behind.

Thus, through excellent combined leadership, the great majority of those shipwrecked survived to reach Virginia. They left behind just two mutineers, five adult dead, of whom one had been murdered, and two neonatal fatalities. In the tragic history of the sea few marooned mariners have achieved so much in such desperate circumstances.

For Gates and Somers, their professional standards stood them and their men in good stead but, in the early invasion of America, professional military experience was not a guarantee of leadership success on strange shores and unfamiliar circumstances.

De La Warr, Gates, Dale and Argall

The lenient and understanding Gates of Bermuda was soon replaced, in the harsh conditions of Virginia, by the vengeful and violent Gates of Jamestown, who became part of a revolving triumvirate that would impose a rule of fear over both their own and their opponents. In support of these land commanders Samuel Argall, whose character has also been much criticized, acted as the sea commander. Between them they created the best joint operational team since the colony was founded.

Argall had begun his involvement with Virginia by pioneering in 1609 a new, more northern and faster route from England to the Chesapeake, which would limit the risk of meeting with the Spanish enemy at sea, a major priority for resupply convoys, although ironically it was the following of Argall's track that led the *Sea Venture* onto the coral reef of Bermuda. Having completed the first task of a naval force commander, Argall, in *Mary and John*, slipped seamlessly into the second when, on 14 July, the day after he anchored in the Chesapeake before moving up to Jamestown, a lookout reported another ship had anchored in the bay overnight. As so often in the history of Jamestown, the coincidence of timing worked to the advantage of the English, for this new arrival was *La Asunción de Cristo*, commanded by Captain Francisco Fernández de Écija, tasked with seeking out, spying on, and reporting back to his Spanish masters on the strength of the English settlements in Virginia. Indeed, had Écija not been prevented by Argall's presence and threatening behaviour from sailing up the James River, he might, seeing the weakness of the colony, have attempted to destroy it himself. Instead he found himself crowding on sail to escape from his much larger and determined opponent. Argall, satisfied that Écija had fled, turned upstream, where he was soon able to tell the surviving settlers that a great resupply would soon be heading their way.

Argall completed his round trip in time to be appointed to De La Warr's three-ship fleet that was ferrying the Governor and 150 settlers out to Jamestown, where they arrived just in time to turn back the fleet that was evacuating the beachhead. To overrule his deputy, and in such dire circumstances, took courage and self-confidence but De La Warr could not have saved the settlement without the support provided by Argall, who, although appointed as a mere captain of a company of fifty soldiers, would be, for a short time Admiral Somers's second-in-command, and soon the de facto naval commander when Somers failed to return from his vital resupply voyage to Bermuda in *Patience*, while Argall berthed at Jamestown with *Discovery*'s hold full of fish acquired off Maine.

No sooner had he completed this foraging mission than Argall was ordered to take the offensive against the Warraskoyack, who lived along the Pagan River downstream and on the opposite bank of the James from Jamestown. An earlier ploy to bargain the return of their captured chief in exchange for corn had gone wrong and De La Warr, lacking the patience of diplomacy and determined to enforce fear along both banks of his domain, considered Argall's naval units ideal for the task. Argall sailed with two companies of soldiers and, in a clinical raid, the inhabitants having fled, fired both their villages and their fields.

Such scorched-earth tactics were effective, but De La Warr soon realized that they denied sustenance to both sides so, once again, Argall was dispatched to find a community who lived further away and thus might be willing to trade with the English. Argall sailed up the Potomac and 'after many days acquaintance' became a firm friend, almost 'brother' to Iopassus, the local chief, aided by the fact that Henry Spelman, the youth John Smith had left with Powhatan, was living with him. After celebrating Christmas with Iopassus, Argall arrived back in Jamestown with a hold full, this time, of corn.

Argall returned triumphant, only to find his commander arriving back from the Falls having failed disastrously to establish a new settlement at Henricus. This setback floored the already-sick De La Warr, so that his next order to Argall was for him to take the weary Governor for some rest and recuperation ashore in England's first West Indian colony, Nevis, leaving the ineffective Percy in temporary command. Contrary winds put paid to this scheme and, much to his embarrassment, De La Warr found himself having to explain to the Virginia Company why he had made such a precipitous return to England, the Governor for life having spent less than nine months in Virginia.

Argall, however, rapidly resumed his colonial service, sailing on 23 July 1612 back to Virginia, in Sir Robert Rich's *Treasurer*, which was built for piratical purposes, the future Earl of Warwick having seen an opportunity to revive the earlier concept of a privateering haven being established in the Chesapeake. But this was not to be Argall's immediate mission, for once again the colony was short of food and Marshal Dale needed the naval man both to supervise the repair of the small local fishing fleet as well as to renew his friendship with the generous Iopassus. Twelve months, almost to the day, after his previous relief voyage, Argall unloaded over 1,000 bushels of corn at Jamestown, so much that a shallop had to be built to ferry back that which would not fit in *Treasurer*'s hold.

By mid-1613 Dale was confident enough in his control of the local environment to order Argall to combine a fishing trip with an investigation as to the presence of French settlers in northern Virginia. The competent Argall achieved both, returning with cod and some prisoners taken at Port Royal, to which he returned later to complete his work of destruction. The reason why Dale had felt able to deploy his admiral could be found upstream at Henricus, where Powhatan's favourite child, Pocahontas, was receiving an education, having been kidnapped in April 1613 by Argall after being lured onboard *Treasurer* by the admiral's 'brother' Iopassus while the ship was anchored in the Potomac. The original capture had been intended to put pressure on Powhatan to release eight captured Englishmen and to return some stolen arms, but her father's obduracy and John Rolfe's love complicated the matter, and in 1614 Argall, with Dale embarked, led a fleet of ships back up the Potomac to discuss terms. The fact that such a sizeable force could be transported so easily into the heart of enemy territory without encountering any hostility speaks volumes for the advantages of amphibious operations in the wide waters of the Chesapeake and its broad rivers.

The peace brought about by the kidnapping of Pocahontas was to last until 'skyfall' in 1622, in which massacre, ironically, John Rolfe – the last of the remaining major characters involved in the iconic episode – met his own death. Argall, as a reward for his exertions, was appointed Governor of Jamestown in April 1617, at which time, finding himself free of the restraint of working in harness, he turned to organizing piracy, earning such a reputation for selfish aggrandizement that De La Warr was dusted down and dispatched to investigate his old comrade's behaviour. Ill as ever, De La Warr died on the passage, meaning that Sir George Yeardley was dispatched to relieve Argall of his command. Forewarned, Argall fled, but defended his corner so well that he became a member of the Council of New England and, at last, received the recognition that his earlier actions deserved by being created Admiral of New England. He too died at sea, in 1626.

Brewster and Standish

The settlers who sailed to Virginia tended to be indentured, unskilled, young single males, often escaping from both poverty and the law. By contrast, those who sailed for New England were generally older adults travelling as a family unit whose head was either a yeoman farmer or a craftsman with a skill appropriate for an infant colony. Additionally, many who emigrated did so as small uprooted communities bonded by a desire to practise their religion without fear of persecution. Searching for, finding and exploiting new sources of wealth to make them exceedingly rich was not their aim; contentment for them would lie in survival, fellowship and freedom of worship, although it would not be long before that latter was stained with unpleasant caveats. Providence, not profit, was their watchword, and they departed England's shores normally after much discussion with their friends, family and co-religionists. If they sought precedent it was not the rapacious expeditions of contemporary Spain but the exodus of the children of Israel and the example of the Protestants who fled abroad during Catholic Mary's reign. And, with such religious exemplars, they were very aware that they had to live up to the calling that they professed. John Winthrop, the first Governor of Massachusetts, wrote:

> we shall be city upon a hill, the eyes of all people are upon us; so that if we shall deal falsely with our God in this work we have undertaken . . . we shall be made a story and a by-word through the world, we shall open the mouths of enemies to speak evil of the ways of God . . .

So, although superficially there is a resemblance between the appointment by election of Wingfield as the first President of Jamestown, and John Carver as the leader of the Pilgrims, on reflection it is most noticeable how they were not mirror images, and that, whereas the one was destined to fail, the other had all the ingredients for success. Wingfield was the Hobson's choice of seven pre-selected council members who were already factionalized and who had little faith in their elected leader's attributes. Carver, on the other hand, was not only well known to all the party with whom he had travelled but was respected enough to be elected to the leadership by a poll of all those present. Thus did democracy arrive in America centuries before a similar suffrage was permitted in England.

In addition, before they had even landed, the Pilgrims introduced a code of conduct under which they all agreed to serve – the Mayflower Compact. It was their own democracy. One of the features of the arrival of new governors in Jamestown was their assembling of survivors so that they could listen to the article of authorization by which the Virginia Company, safe and secure in London, directed how those risking and losing their lives on the Company's behalf should be ruled. The *Laws Divine, Moral and Martial* that controlled the lives of those in the south could scarcely be imposed on the northern colony once they had adopted the compact by which they agreed to live.

The northern group also benefited from a continuity that was not present in the south. When death not dissention led to Carver being replaced, having served in office for just five months, the unanimous choice of successor was William Bradford, who was made in much the same mould as his humble and wise predecessor and was to govern until his death in 1657.

In the one area in which Bradford lacked practical experience, warfare, he was well served by a most able lieutenant, Miles Standish, a man whose behaviour has not endeared him to future generations but whose ability to drill and instruct civilians in military matters may well have saved the nascent plantation. Standish bears comparison with John Smith, whose offer to accompany the Pilgrims had been turned down, much to his chagrin. But, whereas Smith, who of course wrote his own accounts, comes over as an effective and fearless negotiator full of roguish charm, the unlettered Standish is seen as a proud and bloodthirsty belligerent who fully deserves to lose out to the diffident younger John Alden in seeking the hand of the 'Puritan maid' Priscilla, as recounted in Longfellow's romantic poem 'The Courtship of Miles Standish'. Despite the evidence to the contrary, many still link Smith romantically with the Powhatan maid, Pocahontas. De la Warr may have his river, bay and state, Dale his county, but it is Smith whose statue stands in Jamestown Fort, looking proudly out across the river that he knew so well.

Both Smith and Standish were prepared to foray into the forests with few men to seek out and sort out the 'savages' who surrounded their settlements. Yet Smith prided himself on being a negotiator, never happier than when he returned with a hold full of grain or a verbal agreement by way of a truce. With Standish one feels that his proudest moment may well have been when he marched into Plymouth carrying the head of Wituwamat. Certainly Standish, short of both stature and fuse, seems to have been more a figure of fun behind his back than was Smith, although it was the latter that lost the confidence of his jealous peers. William Hubbard, a contemporary witness, spoke of Standish as 'a man of very little stature, yet of very hot and angry temper'. Yet, at no time did Standish, unlike Smith, employ either his anger or his military expertise to attempt a coup against his elected leader. He had no need so to do; in New England the governorship was both elected and enduring; it was not so in the south.

DISCIPLINE

In 1578 Francis Drake, ashore in South America and faced with gentlemen reluctant about his circumnavigation, had one executed and then, gathering together the company, which numbered roughly the same as those that landed at Jamestown in 1607, told them:

> We must have these mutinies and discords that are grown amongst us redressed, for by the love of God it doth even take my wits from me to think on it; here is such controversy between the sailors and the gentlemen, and such stomaching between the gentlemen and the sailors, that it doth make me mad to hear it. But, my masters, I must have it left, for I must have the gentlemen to haul and draw with the mariner, and the mariner with the gentlemen. What, let us show ourselves all to be of one company, and let us not give occasion to the enemy to rejoice at our decay and overthrow. I would know him that would refuse to set his hand at a rope, but I know

there is not any such here; and, as gentlemen are very necessary for government's sake in the voyage, so have I shipped them for that . . .

The government of Jamestown required far fewer gentlemen than had been shipped out on the first voyage but it lacked a Drake to make them haul and draw together. Indeed, it is not surprising that by far the most successful of the early settlements was the military one established by Lane in which the soldiers were 'all of one company'.

Many of the gentlemen that sailed to Virginia were idle wasters – why else were they venturing abroad? – who showed themselves most unwilling to strip off their shirts and sweat for the common good. The governing body seemed unable to impose its will and preferred to scheme against itself. Only Smith had any success in his short and resented rule, stating that, 'he who would not work will not eat', but his unpopularity can be gauged by the presumption that the agonizing explosion of his powder bag upon his chest while he lay sleeping, which 'tore the flesh from his body and thighs, nine or ten inches square in a most pitiful manner', was no accident.

Following Smith's medical evacuation, none succeeded in managing the men until the arrival of De La Warr, who immediately read out the commission which granted

Sir George Calvert's residence at Ferryland. Despite building this comfortable mansion house for himself here, Sir George Calvert, Lord Baltimore, found the Newfoundland climate not to his liking and sailed south to establish a colony in the milder meadows of Maryland. (Colony of Avalon).

him 'full and absolute power and authority to correct, punish, pardon, govern and rule, all such subjects of his majesty, his heirs and successors, in any voyage thither, or that should at any time inhabit . . . the said Colony'.

To add to his authority De La Warr imposed the harsh code of conduct based on the one issued by Gates entitled *Laws Divine, Moral and Martial* but with extra bite, which restored discipline and, probably, morale. The men were now divided into four fifty-man militias who were being trained in 'martial manner and warlike discipline', while, for their daily work they were formed into parties of ten or twenty, each under a competent supervisor.

The laws were harsh. Most crimes listed, such as murder, rape, adultery, treason, theft of Company profit or unauthorized trading with the Amerindians, were punishable by death; other lesser crimes were punished by flogging or even maiming. There seemed to be no leniency. This brought home to the settlers their true situation: they were a small group of disparate souls perched precariously on an unwelcoming shore and surrounded by people who wished to be rid of them.

The punishments were carried out without the mercy that Gates had shown to his mutineers on Bermuda, but occasionally with strange effect, as Strachey reported when there was discovered:

> a conspiracy plotting amongst some of our men which wrought in iron mines to run away with a barque. The same being discovered my Lord, for an example adjudged one of them by martial law to be executed. The execution proving strange and seldom heard of I thought not to omit, for the party being thrown off the ladder what with the swing and weight of his body the rope did break and he fell upon the ground. And in regard of the accident my Lord pardoned him although it nothing availed him having received his death with the gird of the rope and extremity of the fall.

De La Warr swept in, swept up and swept out, but in his forty-two weeks in command he had stopped the evacuation of the settlement and started the extermination of the 'savages'. There was some degree of failure: his attempt to re-establish a settlement at the Falls had to be abandoned and he was unable to alter significantly the appalling death rate among the settlers, a third of whom died during his tenure. What he did do was retain what had already been won and restore the morale of sufficient of the settlers so that they were prepared to move forward and not away.

The peace of Pocahontas brought with it a relaxing of both authority and alertness. Coupled with that came the arrogance of success, with many of the once-destitute indentured labourers making their fortune through growing tobacco, so that Jamestown gained a reputation for drunkenness and, when available, debauchery, so that the Company felt it had to issue instructions 'to suppress too much drunkenness, and that all kind of riot both in apparel and otherwise be eschewed'. At the mouth of the river an illicit exchange of rot-gut wine for tobacco was freely practised, the same blind eye being turned to this as was surveying the decaying fortifications, which people were too busy and too confident to repair so that 'our people by degrees fell again to their ordinary watch'.

The belief that the war was over was supported by the creation of the General Assembly for Virginia, which was designed to be 'a form of government . . . to the greatest benefit and comfort of the people, and whereby all injustice grievance and oppression may be prevented'. Given the reputation of the colony, it seems appropriate that its Speaker, when it met first on 30 July 1619, was the notorious soak, John Pory. Yet, without an ever-present professional and disciplined soldiery, democracy can be a danger on the front line, and so it proved in Virginia. Hell arrived on 22 March 1622 but, for the English, it lasted just one day; it was the Amerindians whom its flames consumed.

CHAPTER 14

Summary

In Memory of
John Pott MA
Learned Doctor
Of Medicine
Physician General
Member of the Council
Governor of the Colony
Resident of Jamestown
1621–1635
Plaque in the reconstructed chapel at Jamestown Fort.

Despite the above career description of the maverick medic John Pott, his memorial stone could have read:

Poisoner
Enslaver
Cattle Rustler
Rebel

It was Pott who poisoned the wine that disposed of some 200 Powhatans at the May 1623 conference, leaving another fifty so ill that they were readily shot. He gave a repeat prescription to a smaller group of Amerindians two years later with the same effect. He also held in bondage a widow of the 1622 massacre whose release from Amerindian captivity he had secured for two pounds of glass beads which, Pott considered, paid for her indenture. Later, he not only coveted his neighbour's livestock but reacted to the appointment of his admittedly unpopular successor as Governor, by staging an abortive *coup d'état*. His epitaph, as ever, is written to reflect what its writer wished to preserve. The American experience in the long sixteenth century is recorded in a similar way by the victors, with the added influence that, in a country devoted to tracing its colonial heritage, few wish to either discover or announce that they are descended from villains. This has led to a counter-current of criticism and yet, as with Pott, both descriptions are true; there is no such thing as a one-sided coin.

The English desire to invade, conquer and settle North America was an extraordinary ambition entrusted to infra-ordinary people who, initially, were not going to be the principal beneficiaries of their labours. Those who stood to gain the most understood the least about the land and were responsible for providing their travellers with objectives which were counter to and in conflict with the latter's simple aim of survival.

The English intelligentsia and merchants sent people across the Atlantic for two main reasons. The first was to discover a short route to Cathay, whose fabled wealth would then be theirs to bring home at great profit. It proved to be an evasive ambition: the first sailing vessel to complete a northwest passage in one season did so in 2007. The second reason was to find gold, the desire for which threaded its way through all the Charters while an elusive search for it was carried out from Baffin Island to Guiana. In both cases, the investors refused to believe the evidence that was presented before them in the form of maps or minerals. Had they concentrated on more realizable but less glamorous objectives America might have been settled the sooner.

A third published aim was that of conversion but, lacking the Catholic convictions of the *conquistadors*, the English committed just petty acts of irritating, defensively inspired violence against the natives rather than the gruesome genocides practised by the Jesuit-inspired Spanish. This meant that the Amerindians were able to both ignore the limited proselytizing and defy the attempts at intimidation. When the gold also failed to materialize the investors realized that they had been gulled by their own greed, at which point the invaders knew that they would need to rely on their own resources should they wish to remain in a land whose potential wealth they alone appreciated. The result was the development of the trade in tobacco and furs, both of which – but especially the former – required the invaders to move out from their beachheads to seize or negotiate for new tracts of land. For this reason John Rolfe, rather than Walter Ralegh, should be viewed as the true begetter of the lasting English presence in America. Had he succeeded in returning to the colony with his wife, Pocahontas, and son, the relationship between the English and the Amerindians might have proceeded in a more friendly way, more Ruth and Boaz than Israelite and Midianite. Ironically, Rolfe died at the time of the 1622 'massacre', a vicious proof of the failure of his attempt at fraternizing, while his marriage was fated to be a singular challenge to the mythical biblical mores that prevented the English from intermarriage.

The English failed to dominate the new world in its early years, not because they lacked the vital spark that burnt within the Spanish soul. Nor was the main cause of the failure to thrive due to a dampening of that spark during their long Atlantic deployments or depressing, deprived winters ashore. They failed because the sponsors had the wrong aim, or aims, associated with unrealizable, short-term ambitions, compounded by the fact that their enterprise was neither supported nor controlled from the top. Whatever fine words the Charters stated, whatever argument for colonization the propagandists published, for the Crown the new world was ever eccentric to their main interests, which were domestic and European, twin causes of their unease. The Americas might pour wealth into the coffers of the King of Spain, but for the English sovereign they were a potential drain. Thus the English monarchs were happy to grant lands which were not theirs to give, provided that they were not called upon to gift ships, soldiers or specie to underwrite the enterprises. With royal favour but without royal funding the invasions were both undermanned and under-resourced.

The undermanning was almost fatal. In September 1493 Columbus returned to the Americas in command of a fleet of seventeen ships packed with hundreds of settlers. Despite the fact that they established their township, Isabella, in a fever-ridden swamp on Santo Domingo, the settlers managed to extract gold from the Amerindians, hundreds of whom they either employed or shipped home as slaves. By 1495 some 300,000 of the indigenous population had been killed; a few years later there were no survivors to serve the well-established Spanish. However, it has been estimated that the Spanish Crown's original investment in Columbus's first voyage provided a return of 1,733,000 per cent. By contrast Grenville, leading the second English voyage to Virginia, landed just over 100 soldiers at Roanoke; a few years and one further voyage later, there were no survivors, and no reward for the original financial backers. Popham's colony ended likewise, as did several others along the northern littoral. The only place that the English could hope for returns similar to that being realized by the Spanish was at sea, plundering the richly laden Iberian fleets. Walter Ralegh, for all his declared interest in Virginia, sent far more ships a-pirating than he did a-planting, and got far greater returns from those enterprises than he managed from the sale of sassafras. There was one new world commodity that offered reasonable reward, and that was cod, but commercial fishing was not a trade that appealed to the English gentry, nor did it require new world settlements for it to thrive, yet it would go on to support far more English families, both in the newfound lands and at home, than ever would tobacco or fur.

Although England's first settlement in Virginia was a military one, Lane's men did not act with the belligerency of Columbus's soldiers. The English as a nation were, after all, seamen not soldiers, having no equivalent of the experienced professional Spanish troops. One just has to contrast the achievements and the derring-do of Drake, Howard, Hawkins, Grenville and many others with the failure of Tudor land forces led by an incapable aristocracy such as Suffolk, Norfolk, Essex, Leicester and Buckingham, from whose professional incompetence their countrymen were protected by the seamen in the Channel who kept their better-trained, more numerous enemies away. Nevertheless, this amateur army of invaders eventually succeeded not only in securing their hold in the new world but in encouraging a flood of their compatriots to pour upon the land which the warriors of Virginia and New England could resist but not dam. The reason can be found not in military prowess but in a simple census.

If the England cricket team played in a league in which every other member was a village team they would inevitably finish top even if occasionally an embarrassing defeat stuttered their progress. It was the same with America: England, a small kingdom by European standards, was a colossus compared with any Amerindian nation. Thus it was capable of replacing its losses with far greater ease than could the Amerindians; in a war of attrition there could only be one winner regardless of tactics, strategy, bravery, leadership or weapons.

The weapons that the English brought, along with the ships and boats which could transport them and their users to where they were needed, enabled them to achieve a local superiority. What they never achieved during the invasion period was a superiority of civilization. Kenneth Clark, a man whose very being epitomized culture, was unable in his classic 1969 television series, *Civilisation*, to define the essence of that title. Instead he tried to explain what elements were necessary both to develop and retain civilization; and what were the corrosive substances that could eat away at this frail amalgam. Confidence, vigour, vitality and a sense of permanence were some of his contributory building materials; while exhaustion, hopelessness, fear of famine or failed harvests and an implacable foe would eat away at the very base of the structure. These latter conditions held sway on the eastern seaboard among the original English settlements in their early years where, true to Clark's diagnosis, they either collapsed or held on like limpets on seawrack, just surviving the fierce onslaught of the many and various land-based storms that fell upon houses built on sand. Yet the balance slowly shifted. In due course, as reinforcements arrived along with better leadership, confidence grew and, when it did, it was the besieging forces that experienced the famine, the disease, the destruction of their villages and the killing of their children. When that impacted, and they were unable, even with alliances, to put sufficient troops in the field, the cracks in the dykes widened and the English flooded onto their lands, which were irretrievably lost. The wars of conquest that followed lie beyond the scope of this book but the inevitable result could have been forecast the day Jamestown was able to retaliate against the 1622 massacre, or when Standish appeared in Plymouth with Wituwamat's severed head in his hand. Nye and Morpurgo wrote a clear summary of the period:

> For close on four hundred years the white man had to fight for the control of the American continent against those who had owned it before he came. Often he suffered disaster at their hands, sometimes, particularly in the early days of settlements, his hold on the newly won lands seemed about to be broken, but always he had behind him the inventive and industrial genius of Europe and which provided him with weapons of destruction which the Indian could not equal. At least his peer in the skills of pitched battle, and, to the every end, his master in fieldcraft, the Amerindian soon learnt to use the white man's weapons – and soon learnt to steal them – but the manufacture of firearms, their invention, and their improvement, he never learnt. By the time the Indian had the muzzle-loader, the white man was already at work on a breech-loader, by the time the Indian had the breech-loader, the white man was rifling his weapon, when the Indian had caught up with this development, his enemies were preparing repeaters and machine-guns. The organization, both industrial and military, which is necessary for the use of artillery, the Indians never mastered.

During this whole period the English exercised a social and sexual apartheid between themselves and all native peoples with whom they came in contact. Mixed marriages led to ostracism and the spurning of their offspring; going native could be punished by banishment or even hanging. This most mongrel of European nations invaded the new world with Old Testament attitudes that precluded, except in rare cases such as Rolfe and Pocahontas, befriending as equals. This proved to be one of the lasting tragedies of the age.

The English invaders did not succeed because they represented a more civilized, better organized, braver or even more barbaric society for, in every one of these criteria, they delivered short. They won through because they commanded the seas and the waterways, by which means they could replenish and reinforce their pioneers in a way that was not available to their opponents. In the end, as was appropriate for a maritime nation, it was support from the sea that proved the single most powerful weapon in the invaders' armoury. Yet, paradoxically, it was not the armed forces of the Crown that provided the vital succour but the merchant marine. England's first overseas colony was created by civilian settlers and merchant seamen – the uniformed services did not provide a significant presence until the invasion was completed.

On 24 May 1624 the Virginia Company's Charter was revoked and responsibility for the colony was placed under the direct control of the Crown. Coincident with that decision, the age of coastal conflict ended and the age of continental conquest began. The English would now move out from their beachheads to horizon-stretching frontiers, from their forts to villages and towns, and from sea to shining sea. Much hatred and betrayal was yet to come, but from within their bailiwicks the invaders emerged with a vital locally grown idea – that of democracy. The nurturing of that frail plant alone would have made the long time spent on their limited littoral worthwhile.

In the end the invaders won the fair maid, but it had been a long and difficult courtship. It began with the faint-hearted approach of Cabot, continued with the failed flirting of Gilbert, Ralegh and Popham, after which a further forty-five years of rough wooing were to pass before the still-reluctant land could be considered their own. Even then, if the victors had looked down at their fingers, they would have seen they were still only grasping her hand.

APPENDIX I

Chronology

1492 Columbus reaches West Indies

1493 Columbus's second expedition to the West Indies, Cuba and Jamaica

1494 Treaty of Tordesillas

1497 John Cabot lands in Newfoundland

1498 Columbus's third expedition lands on mainland South America
      John Cabot lost at sea

1509 Henry VIII succeeds Henry VII

1512 Ponce de Leon explores Florida

1513 Balboa sights Pacific from Panama

1519–22 Magellan's circumnavigation

1521 Cortes conquers the Aztecs

1528 Narvaex expedition along north coast of Gulf of Mexico

1531 Pizarro conquers the Incas

1539 De Soto expedition across southern North America

1547 Edward VI succeeds Henry VIII

1553 Mary crowned Queen

1558 Elizabeth succeeds Mary

1564 French build Fort Caroline in Florida near Jacksonville

1565 Menendez destroys Fort Caroline

1570–80 Drake's circumnavigation

1583 Humphrey Gilbert arrives St John's, Newfoundland – reads Royal Charter to claim land. Lost at sea on homeward journey

1584 Walter Ralegh funds reconnaissance voyage to Pamlico Sound by Amadas and Barlowe

1585 Ralegh proposes new land be called Virginia to honour Queen Elizabeth
      Richard Grenville sails with Lane's colonists to establish settlement on Roanoke Island

1586 Francis Drake razes Spanish settlement of St Augustine, Florida, on his way to Roanoke, from where he evacuates Lane's group. Grenville resupply fleet arrives but finds colony abandoned

1587 John White's settlers disembark at Roanoke. White returns to seek support

1588 Thomas Harriot's *A Briefe and True Report* published
      The threat from the Spanish Armada leads to an embargo on all sailings to Americas. White, however, is able to depart in two ships but fails to reach Roanoke

1590 White reaches Roanoke but finds settlers gone
      Theodor de Bry publishes *America* with Harriot's account and John White's drawings

1595   Ralegh's first Guiana expedition – a failure
1600   Richard Hakluyt published third volume of *Principal Navigations*
1602   Bartholomew Gosnold explores Cape Cod and Martha's Vineyard
        Pirate Peter Easton establishes base in Newfoundland
1603   James I succeeds Elizabeth
        Ralegh tried for treason
        Martin Pring explores Maine to Cape Cod
1605   Samuel Champlain builds French settlement at Port Royal, Acadia, Nova Scotia
        George Waymouth explores Maine coast and kidnaps five natives, including
            Squanto, who will act as interpreter to Plymouth Pilgrims
1607   George Popham establishes settlement at Fort St George at mouth of
            Sagadahoc (Kennebec) River
        First settlers arrive in Chesapeake and establish settlement at Jamestown on
            James River. Newport explores upriver to The Falls
        John Smith captured by Powhatans; released after Pocahontas's intervention
1608   Samuel Champlain sites colony at Quebec
        Popham Colony of Fort St George evacuated
1609   Henry Hudson explores Hudson River
        John Smith badly injured and evacuated to England
        With onset of winter 'Starving Time' begins
1610   Gates and Somers land at Jamestown from Bermuda; decide to evacuate colony
            but De La Warr arrives and turns ships back
        Gates issues *Laws, Divine, Moral and Martial*
        John Guy sails with thirty-nine colonists for Cupid's Cove, Newfoundland,
            arrives August
1610–14 First Powhatan War
        English attack Paspahegh killing sixty-five, including the Queen and her
            children
1611   De La Warr departs, Percy resumes command
        Dale assumes command; seizes land at Appomattoc and palisades New
            Bermuda
        Gates returns and takes command
        Work begins on building Henricus
        John Rolfe plants new strain of tobacco
1613   Pocahontas captured
        John Rolfe makes first shipment of new tobacco from Virginia to England
1614   John Smith explores Norumbega and charts its coast. Proposes to name area
            New England
        Rolfe and Pocahontas marry
        Pirate Henry Mainwaring raids Newfoundland
1615   Pocahontas gives birth to son Thomas
1616   Newfoundland Company splits in two. Vaughan granted land in Avalon
        John Rolfe and Pocahontas leave for England
1617   Merchant Venturers granted Bristol Hope, Newfoundland. Welsh settlers arrive
        Start of Harbour Grace settlement

Whitbourne arrives as Governor of Vaughan's settlement

Pocahontas dies in London; Rolfe returns to Virginia

Ralegh's second Guiana expedition – a failure

1618 Welsh settlement at Renews, Newfoundland, abandoned

Chief Powhatan dies; his brother Opechancanough succeeds him

Sir Walter Ralegh executed

1619 Calvert sends settlers out to Ferryland, Newfoundland

1620 Mayflower arrives Cape Cod; Plymouth Colony established

1621 First Thanksgiving celebrated at Plymouth

1622 Wessagusset settlement established

John Mason and Ferdinando Gorges granted province of Maine

1622–32 Second Powhatan war begins with 'massacre' of English on James River, 22 March

1623 Lord Falkland's Colony established, Newfoundland

Two hundred Powhatans and allies poisoned at peace talks

Standish attacks Massachusetts encamped around Wessagusset; in response Wessagusset colony disperses

1625 Charles I succeeds James I

1624 Dutch purchase Manhattan; New Netherlands established along Hudson River

To create interest in Nova Scotia Sir William Alexander publishes *An Encouragement to Colonies*

Eight hundred Powhatans defeated by sixty English in battle

Dorchester Colony established Cape Ann.

1626 Falkland Colony abandoned

Salem settlement established

1627 Calvert, Lord Baltimore, arrives Newfoundland

Dorchester Colony, Cape Ann, abandoned

1628 Calvert seizes French pirates

Lord Ochiltree establishes fort on Cape Breton, Nova Scotia

Endecott establishes New England Puritan colony at Naumkeag

1629 After short peace, Powhatan conflict resumes until 1632

Calvert abandons Newfoundland for Maryland

Sir William Alexander (jr) establishes Fort Charles settlement at Annapolis Royal, Nova Scotia

Lord Ochiltree's settlement captured by French

Kirke brothers capture Quebec

John Mason establishes New Hampshire; Gorges creates New Somersetshire (later Maine) in north

1630 Winthrop fleet arrives in Massachusetts Bay: establishes Boston settlements

1632 Nova Scotia returned to French by Treaty of Saint Germain en Laye

APPENDIX 2

Principal Charters
of the Invasion Period

Date	Granted by	To whom	Area
3 Feb 1498	Henry VII	John Cabot	Lands unknown to all Christians
11 June 1578	Elizabeth I	Humphrey Gilbert	Lands not possessed by any Christians
25 March 1584	Elizabeth I	Walter Ralegh	Virginia
10 April 1606	James I	Virginia Company of London (First Charter)	First colony: 34–41°N Second colony: 38°–45°N
23 May 1609	James I	Virginia Company of London (Second Charter)	
2 May 1610	James I	London and Bristol Company	Newfoundland
12 March 1611	James I	Virginia Company of London (Third Charter)	Extended from sea to sea
3 Nov 1620	James I	Council of New England	New England: 40–48°N
10 Sept 1621	James I	Sir William Alexander	Nova Scotia
10 Aug 1622	James I	Sir Ferdinand Gorges John Mason	Maine: between Merrimack and Sagadahoc Rivers
7 April 1623	James I	Sir George Calvert	Newfoundland: province of Avalon
4 March 1629	Charles I	Massachusetts Bay Company	Merrimack to Charles River
1629	Earl of Warwick	William Bradford and associates, Colony of New Plymouth	Coahassett to Naraganset Rivers
7 Nov 1629	Charles I	John Mason	New Hampshire

APPENDIX 3

Significant English Voyages to the New World, 1497–1630

Ship(s)	Masters (admiral in bold)	From/to	Dates	Comments
One, unknown	John Cabot	Bristol/Westward	Summer 1496	Voyage abandoned
Matthew	John Cabot	Bristol/ Newfoundland	May 1497	
Four or five, unknown	John Cabot	Bristol	May 1498	Lost at sea
Ayde plus many other vessels	**Frobisher**	London/Baffin Island	1576, 1577, 1578	
Ten ships	Humphrey Gilbert	Dartmouth	26 Sept 1578	Voyage abandoned
Delight, Swallow, Golden Hind, Squirrel, Bark Ralegh	Humphrey Gilbert	Plymouth/ Newfoundland	June 1583	*Swallow* and *Golden Hind* return; rest lost
Dorothy, Bark Ralegh	Barlowe Amadas	Plymouth/Roanoke/ London	27 April /mid-July/ mid-Sept 1584	
Tyger, Elizabeth, Roebuck, Dorothy	**Grenville** Cavendish Amadas Barlowe Bernard Drake	Plymouth/Roanoke/ Plymouth	9 April/ Aug/18 Oct 1585	
Elizabeth Bonaventure, Ayde, Galleon Leicester, Primrose	**Francis Drake** Frobisher	Plymouth/West Indies/Roanoke/ Portsmouth	14 Sept/Dec 1585/ 9 June/28 July 1586	
100-ton bark		Plymouth/Roanoke	April /late June 1586	
Tyger, Roebuck Four others	**Grenville**	Bideford/Roanoke/ Plymouth	April/July 1586	

Ship(s)	Masters (admiral in bold)	From/to	Dates	Comments
Three ships	**Ferdinando**	Plymouth/Roanoke/ Plymouth	1587	
Flyboat then *Monkey*	White	Roanoke/ Southampton	27 Aug/8 Nov 1587	
Brave *Roe*	Facy (White)	Bideford/Bideford	22 April/23 May 1588	
Hopewell, Little John, John Evangelist, Moonlight, Conclude	**Cocke** (White) Newport Spicer	Plymouth/Roanoke/ England	March/15 Aug/Oct 1589	
Concord	**Gosnold**	Falmouth/New England/Exmouth	26 March 1602 /14 May/23 July	
Speedwell, Discoverer	Pring	Bristol/Maine/Bristol	20 March 1603/ 7 June/2 Oct	
	Waymouth	London/New England/ Dartmouth	5 March/17 May/18 July 1605	
Richard	Challons	Plymouth/Florida Channel	12 Aug/10 Nov 1606	Captured by Spanish
Susan Constant, Godspeed, Discovery	**Newport**	London/Jamestown	Dec 1606/14 May 1607	
Gifte of God, Phoenix	**Newport**	London/Jamestown	arrived Jan 1608	First supply
Mary and John, Gifte of God	**Raleigh Gilbert** George Popham	Plymouth/Saghadoc River	31 May/17 Aug 1607	
Mary Margaret, Falcon, Starr, Susan, Swallow	**Newport**	London/Jamestown	Oct 1608	Second supply
	Argall	Portsmouth/ Jamestown	5 May/13 July 1609	Short northern route – west from Azores

Ship(s)	Masters (admiral in bold)	From/to	Dates	Comments
Sea Venture, Diamond Falcon, Blessing, Unity, Lion, Swallow, Virginia	**Somers** John Ratcliffe John Martin	London/Bermuda (wrecked)	2 June/28 July 1609 2 June/11 August 1609	Third supply
Deliverance, Patience	**Somers**	Bermuda/Jamestown	10 May/23 May 1610	
Mary and John		Plymouth/ Sagadahoc/ Plymouth	9 July/Sept/Nov 1608	
Half Moon		Amsterdam/Albany/ Dartmouth	4 April/17 Sept/ 5 Nov 1609	
De La Warr, Blessing, Hercules	**De La Warr**	London/Jamestown	1 April/10 June 1610	
	Guy	Bristol/ Newfoundland	5 July/Aug 1610	Settled Cupid's Cove
Mayflower	Jones	Plymouth/New Plymouth	6 Sept/10 Nov (Provincetown)/ 16 Dec 1620	
Fortune		Plymouth, New England	1 Dec 1621	Taken in Channel
Arbella, Talbot, Ambrose, Jewel, Mayflower, Whale, Success, Charles, William and Francis, Hopewell, Trial	Winthrop	Yarmouth, Isle of Wight/Salem, Massachusetts	May/July 1630	700 Puritans onboard

Investment and Returns from the Virginia and East India Company Voyages and from Piracy

COMPANY VOYAGES

Year	1578	1585	1585	1595
Voyage	Frobisher's third	Lane's Virginia	Drake's West Indian raid	Drake's last voyage
Aim	Gold mining	Invasion	Plunder	Plunder
Ships (tonnage)	Ayde (250), Thomas Allen, Judith, Anne Francis, Hopewell, Beare, Thomas of Ipswich, Emmanuell of Exeter, Frances of Foy, Moone, Emmanuell of Bridgwater, Dennis, Gabrierll, Michael	Tyger(200),* Roebuck, Lyon, Elizabeth, Dorothy, 2 pinnaces	Elizabeth Bonaventure (600)*, Ayde (250),* Primrose (400), Tiger,† Sea Dragon,† White Lion, Talbot, Speedwell, Bark Bond, Hope, Bark Hawkins, Galiot Duck, Bark Bonner, Thomas Drake, Elizabeth Drake, Francis, Benjamin, 5 other ships, 18 pinnaces	Defiance,* Garland,* Hope,*Elizabeth Bonaventure,*Adventure,* Foresight,* Concord (330),† Susan Bonaventure (250),† Salomon,† Saker,† Desire (246),† Amity,† John Bonaventure (200),† Elizabeth,† Jewel,† Little John,† Pegasus,† Phoenix (80),† Help,† Richard,† Pulpit (150), Exchange (140), Delight, Elizabeth Constant, Francis, Nannycock, Blessing
Shore party	100 miners	107 soldiers	1,500 soldiers	1,000 soldiers
Investors	Company of Cathay Earl of Oxford: £1,000	Queen: £400 gunpowder Ralegh	Queen: £10,000 cash, £10,000 in ships Others: £40,000	Queen £33,266 13s 4d Others £16,666
Returns	A loss	From colony – nil £50,000 from seizure of Spanish vessel £60,000 from piracy by Bernard Drake's relief fleet	£60,000	Minimal

* Queen's ships † London Merchants

RETURNS FROM VOYAGES AND FROM PIRACY

Year	Piracy	Virginia and Virginia Company	East India Company
1580	Drake's circumnavigation: £200,000		
1585	*Santa Maria*: £10,000 Great West Indies raid: £60,000	Lane at Roanoke: return – nil	
1586		White at Roanoke: return – nil	
1587	*San Felipe*: £114,000		
1588	Cavendish voyage: £30,000		
1592	*Madre de Dios*: £140,000 Thomas White's prize: £100,000		
1594	*Cinque Llagas*: lost in fire Lancaster raid on Perambuca: fortune		
1596	Cadiz raid: £300,000		
1600			Incorporated 31 December
1601			First voyage
1602	*St Valentine*: £130,000		
1603	*Veniera*: £130,000		
1604			Second voyage
1606		Incorporated First Jamestown voyage: return – nil	
1607		Popham Colony: return – nil	Third voyage
1608		First resupply: return – nil Second resupply: timber	Fourth voyage: both ships lost
1609		Third resupply: return – nil	
1609			Combined sales of first two voyages realize profit of 95 per cent Fifth voyage returns with spices
1610			Sixth voyage
1611			Seventh voyage: textiles – profit 200 per cent
1613			Eighth voyage
1614			Tenth voyage
1615			English naval victory over Portuguese at Tapti River
1619			500 bales silk reach England
1620		*Mayflower* voyage: return – nil	
1626			First cargo of saltpeter delivered

APPENDIX 5

Governors of Jamestown and Plymouth Plantation

The long list of the early governors of Jamestown speaks volumes, more eloquent than written criticism.

Date	Jamestown	Plymouth
April 1607	Captain Edward Maria Wingfield, President of the Council	
10 Sept 1607	Captain John Ratcliffe, President of the Council	
7 Sept 1608	Captain John Smith, President of the Council	
23 May 1609	Thomas West, Lord De La Warr, appointed Governor and Captain General, but did not reach Virginia until 10 June 1610	
1609	Captain George Percy, President of the Council	
10 June 1610	Thomas West, Lord De La Warr, Governor	
1611, Mar. 28.	Captain George Percy, Deputy Governor.	
19 May 1611	Sir Thomas Dale, High Marshall, and Deputy Governor	
Aug 1611	Sir Thomas Gates, Acting Governor	
March 1612	Sir Thomas Dale, Acting Governor	
April 1616	Captain George Yeardley, Lieutenant or Deputy Governor.	
9 April 1617	Captain Samuel Argall, Lieutenant or Deputy Governor	
9 April 1619	Captain Nathaniel Powell, Senior Councillor, Acting Governor	
19 April 1619	Sir George Yeardley, who had been knighted and appointed Governor and Captain General, November 18, 1618, arrived in the Colony	
11 Nov 1620		John Carver
6 April 1621		William Bradford, until Jan 1633
8 Nov 1621	Sir Francis Wyatt, Governor	
1626	Sir George Yeardley, Lieutenant Governor	
19 April 1626	Sir George Yeardley, Governor (Commission dated 19 April)	
14 Nov 1627	Captain Francis West elected Governor by the Council	
5 March 1628	Dr John Pott	
1629–30	Sir John Harvey	

APPENDIX 6

Sites to Visit

ENGLAND

England does not celebrate the departure of the colonists with the dedication and joy with which North America commemorates their arrival. England instead offers a feel for the land which they left and an idea of the major people involved in sponsoring the plantations.

Houses and Towns

Buckland Abbey, Yelverton, Devon
The home of both Sir Richard Grenville and Sir Francis Drake, the Abbey clearly shows the wealth that was accrued by those involved in piracy and privateering. Owned by the National Trust.

Compton Castle, Paignton, Devon
The Gilbert family home and a magnificent example of a fortified house. Tributes to, and the story of, Sir Humphrey and Raleigh Gilbert are displayed. Owned by the National Trust.

Dartmouth Harbour, Devon
This cosy harbour, with its narrow entrance, can still evoke memories of the many voyages to the new world that began here.

Littlecote House, Ramsbury, Wiltshire
Now an hotel, this was the home of Sir John Popham, and its magnificence reflects his position in the Stuart hierarchy.

Sherborne Castle, Sherborne, Dorset
The home of Sir Walter Ralegh while he was the Queen's favourite; another demonstration of how wealth was accumulated by the privileged few.

Plymouth Barbican, Plymouth, Devon
Walk around the old heart of Plymouth and call at Island House, now the Tourist Information Centre, to see where the *Mayflower* Pilgrims spent their last night in England. Study their story at the Plymouth Mayflower.

Ships

Matthew, Bristol
This seagoing replica of Cabot's ship, which has crossed the Atlantic, is a most careful reconstruction which immediately imposes upon the visitor a feel for the diminutive size of this Tudor merchant ship and the cramped conditions onboard.

Golden Hind

There are two reproductions of Drake's *Golden Hind*, the ship in which he landed in California during his circumnavigation of the globe. Although not a settlers' ship, the two vessels are very similar in all respects to those in which the first invaders travelled. The two reproductions, both of which do extensive educational events, are located at Brixham in Devon and on the Thames near London Bridge at Southwark.

CANADA

Most of the major Canadian sites are run by the Canadian Parks organization, which provides detailed information about the sites, their facilities and opening times online. Newfoundland has numerous museums that display finds and features pertinent to the settlement of their immediate locality. But, above all, the rugged landscape and the exposed coast tells a tale worth a thousand artefacts.

Newfoundland

Colony of Avalon, Ferryland

An archaeological site featuring excavations of Lord Baltimore's colony dating to 1621, interpretation centre, conservation laboratory, a reconstruction of a seventeenth-century kitchen, heritage gardens and gift shop.

Cupid's, near St John's

A small but well laid-out museum which displays finds from the oldest surviving colony in Newfoundland.

The Rooms, St John's

A large modern museum tells the story of the first English explorers, fishermen and settlers and their relations with the native Beothucks.

Nova Scotia

Port Royal National Historic Site, Annapolis Royal

A reconstruction of the original Port Royal habitation (1605), a French fur-trading post built by the company of Sieur de Mons and Samuel Champlain. It was destroyed by Argall in 1613. Costumed interpreters bring Port Royal to life.

Charles Fort, Annapolis Royal

Located underneath the restored Fort Anne National Historic Site of Canada, there are no above-ground resources to show where Charles Fort once was. Nevertheless, from the site one can look out over the confluence of the Annapolis and Allain Rivers. A perimeter is officially recognized around the supposed location of the fort, which was built by Sir William Alexander and was occupied by Scottish colonists from 1629 to 1632, when the territory was restored to France.

UNITED STATES

Museums and Theme Parks

Fort Raleigh, Manteo, Roanoke Island, North Carolina
Has exhibits, artefacts and a video highlighting the cultural heritage of the early inhabitants of Roanoke Island. The seventeenth-century English village is a re-creation of the small farming and maritime community built by the Pilgrims along the shore of Plymouth Harbour.

Henricus Historical Park, near Richmond, Virginia
This reproduction of the short-lived capital of Virginia demonstrates most vividly how the early settlers lived. Included in the buildings is the first colonial hospital and several artisanal workshops.

Historic Jamestowne
The original site of the Jamestown colony. Located on Jamestown Island along the Colonial Parkway, this unique site is administered by the National Park Service and Preservation Virginia. Jamestown Settlement is a state-operated living-history museum adjacent to the original site.

Jamestown Settlement, Virginia
This is a large site with a full sized replica of the Jamestown fort as its major outdoor draw. Alongside this is a reconstruction of an Amerindian village and demonstrations of Amerindian boat-building techniques. Berthed close by are replicas of the first settlement ships, while the large museum hall tells the story of the colony in graphic and clear detail. A joy to visit.

Maine Maritime Museum, Bath, Maine
On the Kennebec River, this very active museum tells the story of Popham's Colony at the river mouth and the building of *Virginia*.

Roanoke Island Festival Park, Manteo, Roanoke Island, North Carolina
A most friendly small theme park which includes, along with the replica *Elizabeth II*, an Algonquin village similar to those visited by Ralph Lane and John White. Nearby, a busy encampment recreates what life was like in the early days of the English military settlement before any housing was erected.

Ships

Deliverance, St George's, Bermuda
The replica of the ship built from the timbers of the wrecked *Sea Venture* is docked close to where the original ship was built.

Elizabeth II, Manteo, Roanoke Island, North Carolina
The design of *Elizabeth II* was based on the first Roanoke vessels. It is a seagoing vessel manned by well-informed costumed interpreters.

Half Moon, Albany, New York State
Henry Hudson's voyage in *Half Moon* up the river that bears his name led directly to the founding of the Dutch settlement on Manhattan. Once aboard the ship, the visitor sees and feels the experience of life aboard ship four hundred years ago. The *Half Moon* is fully operational, and has sailed as far as Lake Michigan and south to North Carolina. Most of its time is spent operating in the historic waters of New Netherland, with extensive operations on the Hudson River and extending outward to the Delaware River and Bay and to the Connecticut River.

Mayflower II, Plymouth, Massachusetts
If the Jamestown ships best represent a part of the invasion fleet, then *Mayflower II* would qualify as the flagship of the period. This most loving and authentic reproduction was built in Devon and crossed the Atlantic in 1957.

Onrust, Hudson and Mohawk Rivers
Onrust was a Dutch ship built by Adriaen Block and the crew of the *Tyger*, after *Tyger* was destroyed by fire. It was the first decked vessel to be built entirely in America. The construction took one winter (January to April, 1614) on Manhattan Island. The ship was 42 feet long and capable of carrying 16 tons. This replica was launched in 2009 using traditional techniques

Susan Constant, Godspeed, Discovery, Jamestown, Virginia
Alongside in Jamestown, the first three ships dispatched by the Virginia Company to southern Virginia are a triumph of reconstruction and well worth several hours of exploration. Well-informed 'sailors' are on hand to answer any questions about seamanship, victuals and life onboard.

BERMUDA

Bermuda's Maritime Museum tells well the story of the discovery and founding of the colony.

References and Bibliography

Most of the original documentation referred to in this book has been drawn from two sources: the very accessible and visitor-friendly records at The National Archives in Kew (or online) and the magnificent publications of the Hakluyt Society, in which original manuscripts are presented and commented on with scholarship, erudition and an infectious enthusiasm which makes them a joy to read.

THE NATIONAL ARCHIVES

Acts of the Privy Council (PC 1-1)
Calendar of State Papers – Domestic, Henry VIII (SP 1)
    Domestic, Edward VI (SP 10), Foreign (SP68)
    Domestic, Mary and Philip and Mary (SP 11), Foreign (SP69)
    Domestic, Elizabeth (SP 12)
    Domestic, James VI (SP 14)
    Domestic, Charles I (SP16)
    Foreign, Edward VI and Mary
    Foreign, Elizabeth (SP70)
    Foreign, France (SP78) & Spain (SP 94)
    Colonial, America and West Indies

HAKLUYT SOCIETY

First Series, Part I

1. *The Observations of Sir Richard Hawkins, Knt., in his Voyage into the South Sea in the Year 1593*, ed. C. R. Drinkwater Bethune, 1847.
2. *Select Letters of Christopher Columbus, Relating to his Four Voyages to the New World*, ed. R. H. Major, 1847.
3. *The Discovery of the Large, Rich, and Beautiful Empire of Guiana, by Sir W. Ralegh*, ed. R. H. Schomburgk, 1849.
4. *Sir Francis Drake his Voyage, 1595, by Thomas Maynarde*, ed. W. D. Cooley, 1849.
5. *Narratives of Voyages towards the North-West, in Search of a Passage to Cathay and India. 1496 to 1631*, ed. Thomas Rundall, 1849.
6. *The Historie of Travaile into Virginia Britannia, by William Strachey*, ed. R. H. Major, 1849.
7. *Divers Voyages touching the Discovery of America and the Islands adjacent, collected and published by Richard Hakluyt, 1582*, ed. J. W. Jones, 1850.
9. *The Discovery and Conquest of Terra Florida, by Don Ferdinando de Soto*, ed. W. B. Rye , n.d..
16. *The World Encompassed*, by Sir Francis Drake, ed. W. S. Wright Vaux, 1854.

23. *Narrative of a Voyage to the West Indies and Mexico in the years 1599–1602, by Samuel Champlain*, ed. N. Shaw, 1859.

27. *Henry Hudson the Navigator*, ed. G. M. Asher, 1860.

38. *The Three Voyages of Martin Frobisher, in Search of a Passage to Cathay* , ed. R. Collinson, 1867.

43. *Select Letters of Christopher Columbus*, ed. R. H. Major, 1870.

47. *Reports on the Discovery of Peru*, ed. C. R. Markham, 1872.

First Series, Part II

54. *The Three Voyages of William Barents to the Arctic Regions*, 1853.

57. *The Hawkins' Voyages*, ed. C. R. Markham, 1878.

59a. *The Voyages and Works of John Davis the Navigator*, ed. A. H. Markham, 1880.

59b. *The Map of the World, A.D. 1600, called by Shakspere 'The New Map, with the Augmentation of the Indies'*, 1880.

65. *The History of the Bermudas or Summer Islands*, ed. J. H. Lefroy, 1882.

79b. *Sailing Directions for the Circumnavigation of England, and for a Voyage to the Straits of Gibraltar*, from a fifteenth-century MS, ed. J. Gairdner, 1888.

88. *The Voyages of Captain Luke Foxe of Hull, and Captain Thomas James of Bristol, in Search of a North-West Passage, in 1631–32*, ed. M. Christy, 1893.

Second Series, Part I

2/23, 24, 25, 30, 40. *The True History of the Conquest of New Spain. By Bernal Diaz del Castillo*, ed. A. P. Maudslay, 1908–16.

2/71. *Documents Concerning English Voyages to the Spanish Main, 1569–1580*, I. A. Wright, 1932.

2/83, 84. *The Voyages and Colonising Enterprises of Sir Humphrey Gilbert*, ed. D. B. Quinn, 1940.

Second Series, Part II

2/93. *Richard Hakluyt and his Successors*, ed. E. Lynam, 1945.

2/99. *Further English Voyages to Spanish America, 1583–1594* , ed. I. A. Wright, 1951.

2/103. *The Historie of Travell into Virginia Britania (1612), by William Strachey*, ed. L. B. Wright and V. Freund, 1953.

2/104, 105. *The Roanoke Voyages, 1584–1590* , ed. D. B. Quinn, 1954, 1955.

2/111. *English Privateering Voyages to the West Indies, 1588–1595*, ed. K. R. Andrews, 1956.

2/113. *The Troublesome Voyage of Captain Edward Fenton, 1582–158*, ed. E. G. R. Taylor, 1957.

2/120. *The Cabot Voyages and Bristol Discovery under Henry VII*, J. A. Williamson, 1962.

2/121. *A Regiment for the Sea / and other Writings on Navigation, by William Bourne*, ed. E. G. R. Taylor, 1963.

2/136, 137. *The Jamestown Voyages under the First Charter, 1606–1609*, ed. P. L. Barbour, 1969.

2/142. *The Last Voyage of Drake and Hawkins*, ed. K. R. Andrews, 1972.

2/144, 145. *The Hakluyt Handbook* , ed. D. B. Quinn, 1974.

2/147. *An Elizabethan in 1582, The Diary of Richard Madox*, ed. E. Story, 1974.

2/148. *Sir Francis Drake's West Indies Voyage*, ed. M. F. Keeler, 1981.

2/160. *Newfoundland Discovered, English Attempts at Colonisation, 1610–1630*, ed. G. T. Cell, 1982.

2/161. *The English New England Voyages, 1602–1608*, ed. D. B. and A. M. Quinn, 1983.

2/185, 2/186. *The Purchas Handbook: Studies of the Life, Times and Writings of Samuel Purchas 1577–1626*, ed. L. E. Pennington, 1997.

Third Series

6. *The Third Voyage of Martin Frobisher to Baffin Island, 1578*, ed. J. McDermott, 2001.

15. *Sir Walter Ralegh's Discovery of Guiana*, ed. J. Lorimer, 2006.

Extra Series

Extra [1–12] *The Principal Navigations Voyages Traffiques & Discoueries of the English Nation Made by Sea or Over-land to the Remote and Farthest Distant Quarters of the Earth at any Time within the Compasse of these 1600 Yeeres, by Richard Hakluyt*, 12 vols, 1903–7.

Extra [14–33] *Hakluytus Posthumus or Purchas His Pilgrimes Contayning a History of the World in Sea Voyages and Lande Travells by Englishmen and others, by Samuel Purchas*, 20 vols, 1905–7.

Extra 45. *A Particuler Discourse Concerning the Greate Necessitie and Manifolde Commodyties that Are Like to Growe to this Realm of Englande by the Westerne Discoueries Lately Attempted, Written in the Yere 1584, by Richarde Hakluyt of Oxford, known as, Discourse of Western Planting*, ed. D. B. and A. M. Quinn, 1993.

Occasional Booklets

OB 1. 'Richard Hakluyt: His Life and Work. With a Short Account of the Aims and Achievements of the Hakluyt Society. An Address Delivered by Sir Clements Markham, K.C.B., F.R.S. (President), on the Occasion of the Fiftieth Anniversary of the Foundation of the Society', 1896.

Talks in Annual Reports and Separately Published Annual Lectures

Quinn, D. B., 'Richard Hakluyt and his Followers', 1972, pp. 1–11.

de Beer, E. S., 'The Literature of Travel in the Seventeenth Century', 1975, pp. 1–6.

Scammell, G. V., 'The Great Age of Discovery, 1400–1650', 1981, pp. 1–9.

Porter, H. C., 'The Tudors and the North American Indians', 1983, pp. 1–13.

McDermott, J. *The Navigation of the Frobisher Voyages*, 1998.

Fernández-Armesto, F., *Philip II's Empire: A Decade at the Edge*, 1999.

Tyacke, S. *Before Empire: The English Cartographic View of the World in the Sixteenth and Seventeenth Centuries*, 2001.

Books

Andrews, K. R., *Drake's Voyages*, London: Weidenfeld & Nicolson, 1967.

Axtell, J., *The European and the Indian*, Oxford: Oxford University Press, 1982.

—— *Beyond 1492*, Oxford: Oxford University Press, 1992.

—— *The Rise and Fall of the Powhatan Empire*, Williamsburg, VA: Colonial Williamsburg Foundation, 1995.

Baker, W. A., *The Mayflower and other Colonial Vessels*, London, Conway, 1983.

Butler, N., *Boteler's Dialogues, 1630*, ed. W. G. Perrin, London: Navy Records Society, 1929.

Bradford, W., *Of Plymouth Plantation, 1620–1647*, ed. S. E. Morison, New York: Knopf, 1970.

Bunker, N., *Making Haste from Babylon*, Oxford: Bodley Head, 2010.

Burrage, H. S., *The Beginnings of Colonial Maine*, Portland, ME: Printed for the State, 1914.

Childs, D., *The Warship Mary Rose*, London: Chatham, 2007.

—— *Tudor Sea Power*, London: Seaforth, 2009.

Dee, J., *The Perfect Arte of Navigation*, 1577.

Doherty K., *Sea Venture*, New York: St Martin's Press, 2007.

Firstbrook, P., *The Voyage of the Matthew*, London: BBC Books, 1997.

Gerson, N. B., *Survival: Jamestown*, New York: Messner, 1967.

Hamor R., *A True Discourse on the Present State of Virginia*, London 1615.

Hibbert C., *Cavaliers and Roundheads*, London: HarperCollins, 1993.

Horn J., *A Land as God Made It*, London: Basic Books, 2005.

Hughes P. F. and J. L. Larkin (eds), *Tudor Royal Proclamations*, New Haven, CT: Yale University Press, 1964, 1969.

—— *Stuart Royal Proclamations*, Oxford: Clarendon Press, 1973, 1983.

Jennings, F., *Invading America*, Chapel Hill, NC: University of North Carolina Press, 1975.

Lavery, B., *The Colonial Merchantman, Susan Constant, 1605*, London: Conway, 1988.

Loades, D., *The Making of the Elizabethan Navy, 1540–1590*, Woodbridge: Boydell Press, 2009.

Lacey, R., *Sir Walter Ralegh*, London: Weidenfeld & Nicolson, 1973.

McDermott, J., *Martin Frobisher*, New Haven, CT: Yale University Press, 2001.

McGhee, R., *The Arctic Voyages of Martin Frobisher*, London: British Museum Press, 2002.

MacMillan, K., *Sovereignty and Possession in the English New World*, Cambridge: Cambridge University Press, 2006.

Manwaring, G. E. (ed.), *The Life and Work of Sir Henry Mainwaring*, 2 vols, London: Navy Records Society, 1920, 1921.

Milton, G., *Big Chief Elizabeth*, London: Hodder and Stoughton, 2000.

Monson, W., *The Naval Tracts of Sir William Monson*, ed. M. Oppenheim, 5 vols, London: Navy Records Society, 1902–14.

Moore, S. H., *Pilgrims, New World Settlers and the Call of Home*, New Haven, CT: Yale University Press, 2007.

Murdoch, B., *A History of Nova Scotia*, 3 vols (1866), BiblioBazar, 2008–9.

Nelson, A., *The Tudor Navy*, London: Conway, 2001.

Nickerson, W. S., *Land Ho! 1620*, 1931, republished East Lansing: Michigan State University Press, 1997.

Percy, G., *A True Relation of the Proceedings and Occurances of Moment which Have Happened in Virginia from the Time Sir Thomas Gates Shipwrecked upon the Bermudes Anno 1609 until my Departure out of the Country which was in Anno Domini 1612*, London, 1624.

Philbrick, N., *Mayflower, A Voyage to War*, London: Harper Press, 2006.

Price D. A., *Love and Hate in Jamestown*, London: Faber & Faber, 2004.

Pritchard, E. T., *Henry Hudson and the Algonquins*, Tulsa, OK: Council Oak Books, 2009.

Quinn, D. B., *England and the Discovery of America, 1481–1620*, London: Random House, 1974.

—— *European Approaches to North America, 1450–1640*, Aldershot: Ashgate, 1998.

—— *England and the Discovery of America*, London: Allen & Unwin, 1974.

—— *Ralegh and the British Empire*, London: Pelican, 1973.

Rodger, N. A. M., *The Safeguard of the Sea*, London: HarperCollins, 1997.

Rowse, A. L., *Sir Richard Grenville*, London: Jonathan Cape, 1937.

Smith, J., *The Complete Works*, ed. P. L. Barbour, East Lansing: University North Carolina, 1986.

Spectre, P. H. and D. Larkin, *A Goodly Ship*, New York: Houghton Mifflin, 1992.

Strachey, W., *A True Reportory of the Wreck and Redemption of Sir Thomas Gates, Knight, upon and from the Islands of the Bermudas: His Coming to Virginia and the Estate of that Colony Then and After, under the Government of the Lord La Warr*, London, 1610.

Symonds, W. (ed.), *The Proceedings of the English Colony in Virginia since their First Beginning from England in the Year of our Lord 1610, till this Present 1612, with all their Accidents that Befell them in their Journeys and Discoveries*, 1612.

Taylor, E. G. R., *Tudor Geography, 1485–1583*, London: Methuen, 1930.

—— *The Haven Finding Art*, London: Hollis and Carter, 1967.

Unwin, R., *A Winter Away from Home*, London: Seafarer, 1995.

Vaughan, A. T., *American Indians in Britain, 1500–1776*, Cambridge: Cambridge University Press, 2006.

Villiers, A, *The New Mayflower*, Leicester: Brockhampton, 1959.

Woolley, B., *Savage Kingdom*, London: Harper, 2007.

Articles

Barker, R., 'A Manuscript of Shipbuilding circa 1600, Copied by Newton', *Mariner's Mirror*, vol. 80, 1994.

Fraser, A., 'Nova Scotia, The Royal Charter of 1621', *Transactions of the Royal Canadian Institute*, vol. 14, 1922.

Mekens, A., 'Michael Coignet's, Nautical Instructions', *Mariner's Mirror*, vol. 78, 1992.

Morris, M., 'The Rise of the English Sailcloth Industry, 1565–1643', *Mariner's Mirror*, vol. 84, 1998.

Pipping, O., 'Whipstaff and Helmsman', *Mariner's Mirror*, vol. 86, 2000.

Ransome, D. R., 'An Instrument of Early Stuart Sea Power, the Armed Merchantman, *Abigail*, 1615–1639', *Mariner's Mirror*, vol. 85, 1999.

Rutman, D. B., 'The Pilgrims and their Harbour', *William & Mary Quarterly*, 3rd series, vol. 17, 1960.

Solver, C. V. and G. F. Marcus, 'Dead Reckoning and the Ocean Voyages of the Past', *Mariner's Mirror*, vol. 44, 1958.

Websites

www.Americanjourneys.org – an excellent library of digital texts covering those from the earliest times until the eighteenth century, compiled by the Wisconsin Historical Society.

www.Avalon.law.yale.edu – the Avalon Project includes all the relevant Charters.

www.british-history.ac.uk –gives access to the State Papers of the time.

www.Cupidscovechatter – gives details of the historic site.

http://mith.umd.edu//eada/ – Early Americas Digital Archive, a collection of contemporary documents, well worth browsing

www.Henricus.org – provides information about the Henricus settlement and visitor centre.

www.loc.org – Library of Congress, excellentm especially the Jefferson Collection, which includes the Virginia Company records.

http://pc.gc.ca – Parks Canada, lists all the Canadian historic sites.

www.gutenberg.org – Project Gutenberg, holds many of the early accounts.

www.roanokeisland.com

www.virtualjamestown.org – a broad selection of material about the early Virginia settlements.

Index

Page references in italics indicate ilustrations